THE REIGN OF
RICHARD II

THE REIGN OF
RICHARD II

ESSAYS IN HONOUR OF
MAY McKISACK

EDITED BY

F. R. H. DU BOULAY

AND

CAROLINE M. BARRON

UNIVERSITY OF LONDON
THE ATHLONE PRESS
1971

Published by
THE ATHLONE PRESS
UNIVERSITY OF LONDON
at 2 Gower Street London WC1

Distributed by Tiptree Book Services Ltd
Tiptree, Essex

U.S.A.
Oxford University Press Inc
New York

ISBN 0 485 11130 6

Printed in Great Britain by
W & J MACKAY & CO LTD, CHATHAM

Editorial Preface

This volume is offered to Professor May McKisack in token of admiration and friendship and as a small return for that mixture of scholarly interest and personal care which her pupils, colleagues and friends have received from her over the years. The collection of a book of essays is not altogether an easy task, because for many reasons it is necessary to shape it round a unitary theme, and not everyone who would have liked to contribute has been able to offer a study on the reign of Richard II. Behind the present work, therefore, are the good wishes of many other scholars whose names are not numbered in the list of contributors. For them, too, we sign this Preface. The recipient must know that gratitude cannot be measured but only expressed in symbolic ways.

Caroline Barron
Robin Du Boulay

Contributors

MARGARET ASTON
*formerly Research Fellow of
Newnham College, Cambridge*

CAROLINE M. BARRON
*Lecturer in History, Bedford College,
University of London*

PIERRE CHAPLAIS
*Reader in Diplomatic,
University of Oxford*

R. R. DAVIES
*Lecturer in History, University
College, University of London*

F. R. H. DU BOULAY
*Professor of Medieval History,
Bedford College,
University of London*

V. H. GALBRAITH
*formerly Regius Professor of Modern
History, University of Oxford*

BARBARA HARVEY
*Fellow of Somerville College,
Oxford*

JOHN H. HARVEY
*Consultant Architect to
Winchester College*

ROSALIND HILL
*Professor of History, Westfield
College, University of London*

J. N. L. MYRES
President of the Society of Antiquaries

J. J. N. PALMER
*Lecturer in History,
University of Hull*

R. L. STOREY
*Reader in History,
University of Nottingham*

J. A. TUCK
*Lecturer in History,
University of Lancaster*

ROGER VIRGOE
*Lecturer in History,
University of East Anglia*

BEATRICE WHITE
*Emeritus Professor of English,
University of London*

Contents

CONTENTS

Maps

Illustrations

Abbreviations

Annales	*Johannis de Trokelowe et Henrici de Blaneforde Chronica et Annales 1259–1296; 1307–1324; 1392–1406*, ed. H. T. Riley (Rolls Series, 1866) (For the *Annales Ricardi Secundi* by Thomas Walsingham)
B.I.H.R.	Bulletin of the Institute of Historical Research
B.M.	British Museum
C.Ch.R.	*Calendar of Charter Rolls* (H.M.S.O.)
C.Cl.R.	*Calendar of Close Rolls* (H.M.S.O.)
C.F.R.	*Calendar of Fine Rolls* (H.M.S.O.)
C.P.R.	*Calendar of Patent Rolls* (H.M.S.O.)
Correspondence	*Diplomatic Correspondence of Richard II*, ed. E. Perroy (Camden Third Series, 1933)
Emden, *Cambridge*	A. B. Emden, *A Biographical Register of the University of Cambridge to 1500* (Cambridge, 1963)
Emden, *Oxford*	A. B. Emden, *A Biographical Register of the University of Oxford to A.D. 1500*, 3 vols. (Oxford, 1957–9)
E.H.R.	*English Historical Review*
Eulogium	*Eulogium Historiarum sive Temporis Chronicon ab Orbe condito usque ad annum domini 1366; a monacho quodam Malmesburiensi exaratum*, ed. F. S. Haydon, 3 vols. (Rolls Series, 1858–63)
Knighton	*Chronicon Henrici Knighton*, ed. J. R. Lumby, 2 vols. (Rolls Series, 1889, 1895)
Monk of Westminster	*Polychronicon Ranulphi Higden*, ed. J. R. Lumby, ix (Rolls Series, 1886)
P.P.C.	*Proceedings and Ordinances of the Privy Council*, ed. N. H. Nicolas, 6 vols. (1834–7)

P.R.O.	Public Record Office
R.P.	*Rotuli Parliamentorum* etc., 6 vols. (1783–1832)
Tout, *Chapters*	T. F. Tout, *Chapters in the Administrative History of Medieval England*, 6 vols. (Manchester, 1920–34)
T.R.H.S.	*Transactions of the Royal Historical Society*
Walsingham	*Thomae Walsingham Historia Anglicana*, ed. H. T. Riley, 2 vols. (Rolls Series, 1863–4)

May McKisack

MAY McKISACK comes of Northern Irish stock on both sides. Her father and mother sprang from long-established and long-lived families with deep roots in Belfast. Her father, Audley John McKisack, was a solicitor there, and her mother, born Elizabeth McCullough, will be remembered by many much younger friends as a lady of great character and charm who gaily carried into extreme old age all the social graces and good looks that had made her the toast of Belfast society three-quarters of a century before. She had also a full measure of courage and good sense, for May's father died young, leaving his widow with two small children and very inadequate resources. Realizing that they would have to make their own way in the world, and would need the best education she could afford to give them, she migrated to Bedford, perhaps the best spot in the country at that time to provide first-class schooling for boys and girls at moderate cost. May's own career, and that of her brother Audley, who was knighted in 1958 after a lifetime in the colonial legal service which culminated with his appointment as chief justice of Uganda, showed how wise this choice was. It was indeed a source of very proper pride and delight to Mrs McKisack in her old age to find both her children adding lustre to the pages of *Who's Who*.

So from Bedford High School, where her interest in history had been stimulated by the teaching of Agnes Sandys, later fellow of St Hilda's College, Oxford, May went up as Mary Ewart Scholar to Somerville in 1919. There she fell immediately under the spell of her tutor Maude Clarke, who also came from Northern Ireland, and was in the 1920s the most distinguished of the women History dons in Oxford, and a brilliant and sympathetic exponent of the middle ages. Her teaching and example did much to direct May's natural inclination to study English constitutional questions in the fourteenth and fifteenth centuries. After taking her degree she stayed on at college as Mary Somerville Research Fellow and won a B.Litt. for her thesis on the parliamentary representation of the English boroughs in the middle ages. This work, subsequently revised and published under the same title in the Oxford Historical

Series, was not her first appearance in print. Her promise became apparent in 1926 when her edition of Thomas Favent's *Historia Mirabilis Parliamenti* was included in the *Camden Miscellany* xiv, and this led to her election as Fellow of the Royal Historical Society in 1928.

By this time she had left Oxford for Liverpool University, where she held a lectureship in medieval history from 1927 to 1935. While she was there her *Parliamentary Representation of the English Boroughs* was published in 1932 and confirmed her growing reputation as a student of English institutions in the later middle ages. It was therefore natural that, on the early and much-lamented death of Maude Clarke, who had become a very close personal friend, Somerville should call her back to Oxford in 1936 to maintain as fellow and tutor in medieval history the high reputation which the college had established for itself in historical studies under her predecessor.

For nearly twenty years May remained at Somerville teaching generations of students the medieval subjects in the syllabus for the honour school of modern history. Working in double harness for about half the time with her close friend Lucy Sutherland, who looked after the modern side of the syllabus, she was able to use her gifts to the full in developing those sympathetic personal relationships with her pupils which the Oxford tutorial system encouraged. It was indeed a system peculiarly suited to her talent for wide-ranging and intimate friendships with students from every sort of background and with every kind of taste. To many, whether their bent was toward her own period or not, she made the middle ages intelligible and congenial, and medieval people more like the human beings that they must have been. During this period, busy with college and faculty affairs and often preoccupied with the personal problems of her more wayward pupils, May published little: her paper on London and the succession to the crown in the Powicke *Festschrift* (1948) being a notable exception. But she took a full part in the work of the modern history school, held for some years a university lectureship at a time when these were coveted posts much less widely available to college tutors than they are now, and served on the Board of Faculty, and as an examiner in the final honour school, where her colleagues came to value greatly the steadiness and reliability of her judgement and the

sympathetic acuteness with which she assessed the merits and de-
merits of those awkward candidates whose performance suggested
some elements of alpha-bogus quality.

In 1955 May was translated to the professorship of history at
Westfield College, University of London, and remained there for
twelve years until her retirement in 1967. Any doubts she may
have had about undertaking this new task in the bracing air of the
metropolis were quickly dissipated, and she entered with enthusiasm and success into the complexities of university life in London
and the arduous business of running the history department at
Westfield, which was then entering a period of rapid change and
development. May's inexhaustible interest in people, whether
students or colleagues, served her well: she was a good listener who
welcomed confidences, and thus quickly came to grasp the essen-
tials of many ambitious projects then under discussion, and to form
her own view on their desirability and viability. Among the
changes she sponsored was a new special subject on the reign of
Richard II in the London honours school of history, the success of
which is reflected not only in the number of able pupils it attracted,
but in some measure by the contents of this book. She also served
for a spell as acting principal and steered the college safely through
the difficulties arising from an unexpected vacancy.

Nor did she cut her links with Oxford. Somerville had made
her an honorary fellow in 1956 and she delivered the James Bryce
Lecture there in 1959. With her mother still living in her house in
Oxford she spent most weekends and part of most vacations there,
thus maintaining contacts with her wide circle of Oxford friends
and continuing to use the Bodleian Library extensively for her
research. Thus she was able to carry to publication in 1959 her
great work on *The Fourteenth Century* volume of the Oxford History of England, which she had undertaken some years earlier on
the withdrawal of its previously intended author. This book, the
culmination of her historical writing on the period of her primary
interest in English history, was in a special sense a work of *pietas* to
May, for, when the series was first planned, Maude Clarke was to
have written it, and was only prevented from doing so by her untimely death. May thus always thought of *The Fourteenth Century*
as in some way an offering to Maude's memory, and it owes much
to her continuing inspiration.

May's reputation as a teacher led to her appointment in 1961 as a member of the committee on teaching methods set up by the University Grants Committee. It led also to her being invited to spend the year following her retirement from Westfield as visiting professor at Vassar College, Poughkeepsie. This too was an outstandingly successful venture. May had never visited America before, but she responded at once to the open-minded and open-handed attitudes of American academic life, and returned with a fund of delicious stories illustrating the strange effects her efforts to inculcate the elements of English medieval history sometimes had on virtually untutored, if far from unsophisticated, minds.

May has always had a taste for academic adventure and has never been reluctant to enter lions' dens. Thus an invitation to address the history specialists at Winchester College was eagerly seized as an occasion for a realistic excursion into the backstairs corridors of fourteenth-century power which had provided William of Wykeham with the wherewithal to become the archetype of all pious founders. Needless to say, this exercise in the debunking of traditional respectability was received with enthusiastic applause by the latter-day beneficiaries of the bishop's generosity, and a good time was had by all. May's genius for friendship has indeed never been limited to the circles, however wide, of academic colleagues and official pupils. To the children of her friends, in particular, she has been the best sort of universal aunt, and she must have as large a quiverful of unofficial godchildren as any professor in the country. Nor have they been unresponsive to her forthright interest in their affairs: one at least, now a professor in Canada, is known to have spent a great part of several school vacations in the laborious task of binding for her several dozen volumes of her set of the *English Historical Review*.

So it is not only as a tribute to a distinguished scholar, from whom many have learnt much, that this book is offered. It comes also as a token of friendship and affection from some of those whose lives have been enriched by the warmth of May's personality. We hope that it will both promote those studies which she has made specially her own and also in some measure express the esteem in which she is held and our gratitude for what she has done for us.

J. N. L. MYRES

I

Richard II's System of Patronage

J. A. TUCK

IN RECENT work on English medieval history, political conflicts have been depicted as conflicts between the 'ins' and the 'outs' for royal favour and for the material benefits which flowed from royal favour: in effect, as struggles over the control and direction of patronage. Professor Southern has shown how Henry I 'first directed the whole range of government patronage with which we are later familiar', and how he used it as 'a means of government ... an instrument of social change, and ... a means of consolidating the position of that class of society later known as the gentry'.[1] The recipients of Henry's favour, those 'new men' whom, in Orderic's famous phrase, he raised from the dust and placed over earls and castellans in power and wealth,[2] formed the nucleus of the opposition to Stephen and rallied to the Empress in the hope of recovering the positions of power and influence from which they had been dislodged after Henry I's death.[3] Professor Holt has looked at the baronial opposition to King John from a similar standpoint: 'By its very nature,' he argues, 'medieval government always left the door ajar so that those "out" could see those "in" enjoying the warmth and pleasures of royal favour. One of the features of the situation in 1215 was that those "out" considered the chances of being invited in so small that they combined and organized to burst wide the door, ransack the house, and eject the occupants, including the owner.'[4] In other words, the barons rebelled not merely because they were 'out', but because they had been driven so far into the wilderness that only by armed rebellion could they regain access to power and influence.

---

[1] R. W. Southern, 'The Place of the Reign of Henry I in English History', *Proceedings of the British Academy*, xlviii (1962), p. 132.
[2] Ibid., p. 133.   [3] Ibid., p. 142.
[4] J. C. Holt, *The Northerners* (Oxford, 1961), p. 218.

One of the consequences of this manner of interpretation has been to blur the distinction between 'medieval' and 'modern' history, and to suggest instead that there is much in common between the methods of medieval and early modern government: that if a break occurs, it comes some time between 1760 and 1860 rather than in the sixteenth or seventeenth century. Professor Neale has made Elizabethan government sound, in Professor Southern's phrase, 'surprisingly medieval': 'There were hundreds of offices in (the Queen's) gift . . . There were . . . royal lands to be leased or sold, or to be granted as reward for services; a source of great wealth, and most eagerly solicited. Finally, there were all those grants by letters patent, whether charters, licences, monopolies, or whatever they were, which conferred some benefit upon the recipient.' In Elizabeth's reign, 'the place of party was taken by faction, and the rivalry of factions centred on what mattered supremely to everyone: influence over the Queen, and, through that influence, control of patronage with its accompanying benefits'.[5] In a famous essay, Professor Trevor-Roper has emphasized the importance of access to patronage and in particular profits from office, in determining the fortunes of the gentry under James I and Charles I,[6] and Professor Kenyon has argued that from 1685 onwards James II 'conducted an all-out assault on the privileges and influence of the nobility',[7] placing his own friends in positions of power, and thus alienating precisely that group on which he depended for support. After the Revolution, as Dr Mingay has pointed out, the centre of patronage tended to shift from crown to parliament: 'Once the Hanoverian regime was well established it was no longer possible to hope, as in the sixteenth and seventeenth centuries, that the personal favour of the crown might lead to gifts of offices, monopolies, and lands . . . In the eighteenth century the monarch could neither make nor unmake as hitherto, and the road to advancement lay rather through government office and ministerial patronage.'[8] And in addition the abolition of feudal military

---

[5] Southern, op. cit., p. 129; J. E. Neale, 'The Elizabethan Political Scene', *Proceedings of the British Academy*, xxxiv (1948), pp. 4–5, 12.

[6] H. R. Trevor-Roper, *The Gentry 1540–1640*, Supplement to the *Economic History Review* No. 1, passim.

[7] *The Nobility in the Revolution of 1688* (Hull, 1963), p. 7.

[8] G. E. Mingay, *English Landed Society in the Eighteenth Century* (London, 1963), p. 27.

tenure and all its incidents in 1660 removed from the crown a most important source of patronage: in the late seventeenth and in the eighteenth centuries support was purchased primarily by office and pension. But patronage was still the main instrument of government, and through the work of Sir Lewis Namier we have long been familiar with the intricacies of the system 'at the moment of its greatest articulation, before the rise of parties and principles destroyed it for ever'.[9] The process of destruction was gradual: between 1780 and 1830 legislation and administrative reform inexorably broke up the old system of patronage,[10] but its epitaph was not pronounced until 1834, when a select committee appointed to investigate sinecures wrote: 'Anything in the nature of a sinecure office, with emoluments attached to it at the public charge, is alike indefensible in principle, pernicious as a means of influence, and grievous as an undue addition to the general burthen of the nation'.[11]

The exercise of patronage in medieval and early modern England was therefore a powerful means of building up support, and exclusion from patronage was a powerful incentive to political action; but none the less it is possible to exaggerate its political importance. Men did not quarrel in the middle ages merely over the distribution of lands, offices, wardships, and marriages, and not every political crisis was provoked by 'outs' trying to get 'in'. Not every grant had political implications, and not every wardship, office, or custody was bestowed in order to solicit support or reward service. Patronage was as much a financial as a political instrument and in many cases the king's main interest in granting an office or in selling an incident of feudal tenure was merely to get a job done or to secure a satisfactory financial return from the windfalls of feudalism.[12] The patronage over which men quarrelled was merely a small part of a colossal system: only when a group of men felt systematically excluded from patronage, when important offices or lands fell to the crown, when there was a conflict over

[9] Southern, op. cit., p. 130.
[10] A. S. Foord, 'The Waning of the "Influence of the Crown"', E.H.R., lxii (1947), pp. 484–507.
[11] Quoted in Foord, art. cit., p. 500.
[12] For a discussion of this general point, see The English Government at Work, 1327–36, iii, ed. J. F. Willard, W. A. Morris, and W. H. Dunham jr. (Cambridge, Mass., 1950), pp. 3–34.

the contol of the central administration itself, or when the king seemed to be rewarding his too numerous followers in too liberal a manner, did the control and direction of patronage become a political issue. At other times it was an ordinary, uncontentious, and regularly functioning part of the administrative and financial system.

By the end of the fourteenth century the working of the system of patronage had become highly bureaucratic. Of course, the king still authorized many grants himself, and he was still the goal of petitioners seeking favours of all kinds, but it would be inaccurate to suppose that he was personally responsible for every appointment to every office, every provision to a benefice, or every wardship and custody. Control over the bulk of routine patronage, in which the crown's interest was mainly financial, was in the hands of the great officers of state, and above all the treasurer: in other words, it had become part of the province of the bureaucratic machinery of government, and the whole process of obtaining a grant, from the submission of a petition to the issue of letters patent under the great seal, worked as a settled, regular, and well-established system. The exercise of influence on behalf of petitioners might be held to detract from the bureaucratic nature of the system; but influence was brought to bear in most departments of state to obtain preferential treatment for individuals and it did not generally affect the routine by which a department conducted its business.[13]

The first stage in obtaining a wardship, marriage, office, or other grant was to petition for it. The importance of the petition in medieval government can hardly be over-emphasized: patronage as much as justice was founded upon it. It was the subject's means of gaining access to government, to bringing local and particular grievances and requests to the notice of a government which was bound otherwise to remain ignorant or indifferent, and of obtaining all kinds of acts of grace from the crown or those to whom the crown's powers of patronage were delegated.[14] A parallel procedure was used in the later middle ages to obtain a

[13] See, for example, G. L. Harriss, 'Preference at the Medieval Exchequer', *B.I.H.R.*, xxx (1957), pp. 17–40, esp. pp. 27–30.

[14] For another discussion of the importance of the petition, see A. L. Brown, 'The Authorization of Letters Patent under the Great Seal', *B.I.H.R.*, xxxvii (1964), pp. 148–9.

benefice from the pope: it was the duty of the pope—as it was of the king—'to listen to the pleas of petitioners, to provide remedies for their grievances and to satisfy their demands',[15] and papal control over the disposal of benefices grew up not for financial or political reasons, but because petitioners sought to make use of the papal right of intervention: it was from them that the initiative came.

The king and the great officers of state to whom petitions of this kind were addressed therefore had little room for the arbitrary exercise of their powers of patronage: they had to balance the conflicting interests of ordinary petitioners, of officials supplicating on behalf of their dependants and friends, of their own clerks and servants who expected to be rewarded for their diligence, and of members of the royal household, favourites, and officials, who expected some recognition of their service and loyalty. Members of the household in particular expected an office, custody, or wardship to reward their services and supplement their meagre fees; and the growth in the size of the household under Richard II must have severely strained the resources of royal patronage.[16]

In the early years of Richard's reign the king was, of course, too young personally to reply to the petitions addressed to him, and the chamberlain seems to have been responsible for dealing with them and transmitting them to the chancellor or the council for formal ratification. In normal times the chamberlain's signed bill probably represented a decision taken personally by the king, but during the minority it is more likely that the chamberlain took decisions himself, perhaps in consultation with other household officials. Aubrey de Vere, who was acting chamberlain from early 1377, and Simon Burley, under chamberlain from the beginning of the reign, were responsible for signing successful petitions and transmitting them either to the council for approval or to the chancellor for direct action.[17] By virtue of their positions within

---

[15] G. Barraclough, *Papal Provisions* (Oxford, 1935), p. 157.

[16] A comparison of the wardrobe books for 1376–7 and 1384–5 (P.R.O. Exchequer Accounts Various, E.101/398/9 and E.101/400/26) suggests that Richard's household was at least 20 per cent larger than that of Edward III. The number of chamber knights in particular rose from three in 1377 to eleven in 1385 and seventeen in 1388. For commons' complaints about the size and extravagance of the household in 1381, see *R.P.*, iii, p. 101.

[17] For petitions signed by Simon Burley, see P.R.O. Ancient Petitions,

the household these two men thus wielded considerable power and from very early in the reign were able to influence the direction of royal patronage. The ending in 1380 of the system of continual councils widened the scope of royal activity in patronage by removing a rival goal of petitioners. The reaction which this extension of royal activity provoked in some circles is evident from the growing insistence by the commons in parliament on some measure of supervision of the royal household.[18] But the really striking increase in governmental activity by the court does not occur until the Peasants' Revolt. The administrative chaos caused by the murder of the chancellor and the treasurer encouraged suitors to go straight to the king; and those round the king, taking advantage of an unforeseen situation, moved into the vacuum created by the sudden removal of the officials and, temporarily at least, took over the reins of government. There is a notable upsurge in the number of grants warranted *per ipsum regem* and a significant number of these were grants to members of the royal household.[19] The king had now become a power in his own right, the goal of suitors and petitioners, and once again parliament's reaction to this increase in royal actitivy was to press for the appointment of Arundel and Pole as guardians of the king.[20] It is not clear when the two guardians' term of office came to an end but by autumn 1382 the king was once again taking a more active part in government. Grants to his favourites and household officials become frequent and the signet letter comes to be used more frequently as a warrant to the chancellor.[21] Royal authority over patronage was not now to be checked until the Wonderful Parliament of 1386.

From early in the reign, therefore, the king and those round him exercised some measure of control over patronage and received requests for grants and favours of all kinds. But the king

S.C.8/236/11787A, 11788, 11791; for Aubrey de Vere's authorization of business, see ibid., S.C.8/185/9204, 5; S.C.8/236/11793.

[18] *R.P.*, iii, pp. 73-4, 101.

[19] For a full discussion of the significance of notes of warranty in this period, see pp. 139-49 of my unpublished thesis, 'The Baronial Opposition to Richard II, 1377-89', in Cambridge University Library. More generally, see A. L. Brown, 'The Authorization of Letters Patent under the Great Seal', *B.I.H.R.*, xxxvii (1964), pp. 125-55.

[20] *R.P.*, iii, p. 104.   [21] J. A. Tuck, 'Baronial Opposition', pp. 162-4.

himself did not always reach a decision on every petition submitted to him: he was content sometimes merely to pass a petition on to the treasurer.[22] Many petitions which were of no personal or political concern to the king were dealt with in this way;[23] but if the petitioner was an important member of the royal household, or otherwise influential at court, the king himself generally took a decision. For instance, in 1385 Geoffrey Chaucer petitioned the king to allow him to appoint a deputy in his office of controller of the London customs,[24] and above the petition is written 'Le Roy lad grante'. Even clearer evidence of personal action by the king is given on a petition from John Beauchamp of Holt, asking to be appointed keeper of Conway Castle for life: it is noted above the petition that it was granted by the king at Eltham on 1 November 1382, 'et tradita domino Cancellario per ipsum regem execucionem demandanda'.[25] The petition with the superscription formed the warrant for the issue of letters under the great seal and in such instances, when the king sent a direct warrant to the chancellor, he also sent a separate letter to the treasurer, if a fee or farm were to be collected from the grantee, informing him of the grant.

The mass of routine petitions, however, was dealt with not by the king but by the treasurer. Most of them consist simply of a request for the custody, wardship, or office in question; some name the sum the petitioner is prepared to offer; others give details of its value, often by quoting from the pipe roll[26] or an extent,[27] while others give reasons why the petitioner should be preferred to others. If the petition was accepted the petitioner was required to find two mainpernors who would go surety for the sum to be paid and the treasurer then sent a warrant to the chancellor for the issue of letters under the great seal, which constituted the petitioner's title to his prize. In the Michaelmas term of 1386, for instance,

[22] See, for instance, a request from the king to the Treasurer to deal with a petition from John Brandon, customar of Lynn: B.M. Royal Mss 10 B IX fo. 3.
[23] The presence amongst the Exchequer Bille (P.R.O. class E.207) of several petitions addressed to the king suggests that this was so.
[24] P.R.O. Chancery Warrants, C.81/1394/87. The warrant was signed by the Earl of Oxford, chamberlain.
[25] C.81/1394/86.
[26] E.g. P.R.O. Exchequer Bille, E.207/6/18: petition from William Reve of Waxcombe for grant of assarts in Savernake Forest.
[27] E.g. E.207/7/7: petition from John Mornyle for the lands of William Capell and lands in Modford escheated to the king and worth 13s 4d p.a.

David Pouman petitioned the treasurer to grant him the custody of the lands and marriage of John, son and heir of John Elyot, and if he should die within age the wardship and marriage of Isabelle his sister and next heir.[28] The petition was accepted; the sum agreed upon was 100 shillings and James de Billyngford of Norfolk and Walter Lambard of Gloucestershire mainperned for its payment.[29] The treasurer then sent a bill to the chancellor,[30] who issued the letters patent on 1 November, in the same terms as Pouman had originally proposed.[31] This same formal procedure must have been repeated over and over again in the routine administration of the feudal incidents which fell to the crown.

In some cases the granting of lands and offices was done locally. The farming of the ancient demesne of the crown proceeded in each shire according to an old and settled routine,[32] but the administration sometimes preferred to delegate to local officials the minor details of farming an inheritance which fell temporarily to the crown. In 1381, for instance, the March inheritance came to the crown when the earl died leaving his son under age, Henry Englissh was appointed steward of the Honour of Clare during the minority of the earl's heir,[33] and amongst other duties he was required to 'lesser e ordeigner touz les terres e tenementz e touz autres choses appurtenantz a nostre Seigneur le Roy e al dit office'. But he complained to the council that he could not find anyone willing to take the farm lands or other appurtenances, 'sinoun qil poet avoir estat tanqe al pleyne age du dit heir'.[34] This reluctance may well have been one consequence of the political dispute which arose in 1382 over the disposal of the inheritance and which led to the dismissal of the chancellor, Sir Richard Lescrope.[35]

The petitions which the king and treasurer most frequently received were for wardships, marriages, and custodies, those incidents of feudal tenure which had now all but lost their original meaning and were used mainly to increase the royal revenue and to reward favourites and dependants. Wardships and marriages were much sought after: they provided a means of temporary enrichment and, if the heir or heiress were wealthy, to permanent

[28] E.207/7/7.   [29] Ibid.   [30] Which in this case has not survived.
[31] C.P.R., 1385–9, p. 231. Warranted By Bill of Treasurer.
[32] R. S. Hoyt, The Royal Demesne in English Constitutional History (New York, 1950), pp. 156 ff.
[33] C.P.R., 1381–5, p. 104.   [34] E.207/6/14.   [35] Walsingham, ii, pp. 69–70.

social advancement, while the guardian of a young but politically important heir might permanently influence his political allegiance. Professor Hurstfield has shown how, in Elizabethan times, the system of wardship and marriage was institutionalized in the court of wards, and was a highly organized business, an essential part of the machinery of patronage.[36] The court of wards did not of course exist in Richard II's reign but the king was no less anxious than Elizabeth to exploit and capitalize his feudal rights. And although the institutional framework was different, the procedure for obtaining a wardship changed little between the fourteenth and sixteenth centuries. The essential first stage was the discovery of the wardship. Officially, this was the work of the escheator who, when a tenant-in-chief died, received the writ of *diem clausit extremum* and held the inquisition at which the deceased tenant's lands were extended and the name and age of the heir ascertained. He then certified this information back to the crown.[37] But the escheator, in Richard's reign as in Elizabeth's, was an unpaid administrator, a member of the local gentry, and quite capable of concealing a wardship or persuading the jury to return an evasive answer, such as 'of whom the land is held, and by what tenure, they say they do not know'. In such circumstances the discovery of a wardship was left to private enterprise, to informers, upon whom Richard's government as much as Elizabeth's depended for knowledge of concealments. For instance, the only difference between the two following petitions is one of language:

Plese a tresreverent piere en Dieu et tresgracious seigneur levesque de Seint David et Tresorer Dengleterre a remembrer touchant un Johan fitz et heir de Johan Borrard qui est gard a nostre seigneur le Roy et est dedeins age et ore est ensi que le Sire le Roos ad seise le dit heir en sez mayns torceuousement sanz ascun title de droit et concellement dicelle de nostre seigneur le Roy . . . Et autre ceo vous plese de vostres pluis habundante grace grauntier que le dit Johan Borrard pier du dit heir puisse avoir son dit fitz en sa garde ensemblement ove les terres et tenementz appurtenantz al dit fitz et heir."[38]

May it please your Lordship, there is one Francis Jennye, in the county

[36] J. Hurstfield, *The Queen's Wards: Wardship and Marriage under Elizabeth I* (London, 1958).
[37] *The English Government at Work*, ii, ed. W. R. Morris and J. R. Strayer, (Cambridge, Mass., 1947), pp. 120–40.
[38] S.C.8/254/12662.

of Suffolk, gent., who died above a year sithence, and [it] is thought that his heir, being within age, ought to be Her Majesty's ward, which they intend to conceal. If it would please your Lordship to grant the wardship of him to your servant, Gilbert Wakering . . .[39]

Borrard perhaps had a better case than Wakering: though a minor, he was the father of the heir in question; but being a kinsman was not necessarily a reason for the grant of a wardship, and in the three main points, concealment of the wardship, informing of the concealment, and petitioning for the wardship, the two petitions are essentially the same. The crown may sometimes have turned a blind eye to devices designed to deprive it of its feudal rights,[40] but where no such devices existed it sought out and enforced its rights. The chancery regularly issued commissions to enquire into concealed wardships and marriages,[41] and in administering these incidents the exchequer in Richard's reign occupied very much the same position, and exercised the same powers, as the Tudor court of wards.[42]

Once a wardship had been brought to the crown's notice, there were many ways by which a suitor might press his claim to it: by influence at court, by soliciting the aid of a great magnate, or by downright bribery; but no suitor could omit the essential second step in obtaining a wardship, the presentation of a petition. Most petitions were short and formal and, again, the only substantial change between the fourteenth and the sixteenth century seems to have been one of language:

Pleise au Tresorer nostre Seigneur le Roi graunter a Johan de Bryggeford la garde et mariage de William fitz et heir Johane qe fuist la femme Thomas Bulneys deinz age et en la garde nostre Seigneur le Roi esteant, paiant atant come apertient pur la mariage avauntdit.[43]

The request of Sir John Perrot. He humbly desireth that John Vowell, Alderman of Haverfordwest, may have the wardship of William Warren, who is son-in-law to the said Vowell, he paying therfor as

---

[39] Hurstfield, op. cit., p. 61.
[40] J. M. W. Bean, *The Decline of English Feudalism* (Manchester, 1968), pp. 212 ff.
[41] *Calendar of Inquisitions Miscellaneous, 1392–9*, pp. 116, 184, 192.
[42] Exchequer administration of wardships was, of course, well established long before Richard II's reign: *English Government at Work*, iii, pp. 17–19.
[43] E.207/6/5. The date of the petition is probably 1378.

much as any other will do. The lands of the said Warren, which is descended unto him, is about ten pounds a year.[44]

Some petitioners stressed that they had special claims, nearness of blood being an obvious example. Thus Margery, wife of Hugh Venables of Kinderston, petitioned for the wardship and marriage of her son and heir and the keeping of his lands during his minority,[45] and Thomas Gech petitioned for the wardship of the lands of Thomas de Halughton on the grounds that he was 'prochien amy a lenfaunt, cestassavoir uncle depart sa miere'.[46] Both these petitions were granted, Gech procuring an additional concession that if 'any other person shall be willing to render an additional five marks or more for the keeping', then Gech shall continue to have it provided he pays as much as the rival bidder was prepared to offer.[47]

Along with the petition it was customary to deposit with the exchequer evidence, such as writs of *de etate probanda*, livery of seisin, *diem clausit extremum*, charters, fines, and records of debts, so that the treasurer's clerks could establish whether the wardship was genuine and how much it should be sold for. Thus in 1390, Richard Bulkley, son of William Bulkley of Cheadle, died: on November 18 the writ of *diem clausit extremum* was issued and the wardship and marriage of the heir were eventually granted to Ranulph le Maynwaring and his wife for the sum of £230, to be paid at the rate of £46 a year.[48] To substantiate his claim, Maynwaring deposited at the exchequer the writs *de etate probanda* and *diem clausit extremum* of Bulkley, together with his writ of livery of seisin and a whole series of charters and fines going back to the early fourteenth century proving Bulkley's title to his lands and property.[49] This must have been part of the regular procedure for obtaining a wardship,[50] though only the accident of survival and the carelessness of the petitioner in failing to recover his documents enable the process to be followed in detail in this instance. There is no reason to believe that this volume of evidence was required because the wardship was disputed or the title in doubt: the ex-

[44] Hurstfield, op. cit., p. 60.   [45] E.207/6/16. Date: 1381.
[46] E.207/7/9. Date: 1387.   [47] Ibid.; *C.F.R., 1383–91*, p. 204.
[48] *C.P.R., 1391–6*, p. 507.
[49] P.R.O. Records of the Court of Wards, Wards/2/14/53D 20–39.
[50] Wards/2/14 passim: evidence deposited by other petitioners temp. Richard II.

chequer clerks would naturally require a substantial amount of material to satisfy themselves of the genuineness of the title and the extent and value of the ward's lands. The sum for which the wardship was granted was usually based on the value of the ward's lands as shown in the inquisition and there is sufficiently close correspondence in a sufficiently large number of instances between the value given in the extent and the sum asked by the exchequer for the wardship and custody to establish that this was the usual procedure. But the value in the extent could be grossly inaccurate, for many individuals had an interest in concealing the true value of the lands, and here was another opportunity for informers interested in obtaining the transfer of a wardship to themselves.

In most negotiations for a wardship the exchequer disposed of three separate items, the custody of the heir's lands, the custody of his person, and his marriage. These last two frequently went together and in many routine and unimportant grants all three were often granted to the same person at the same time. But they did not always stay together. There was a brisk market in wardships and marriages and guardians often sold their rights at a profit. John Blake, for instance, who forfeited in the Merciless Parliament of 1388, bought the wardship of John son of Richard Deneys from Sir John de la Pomeray, the original exchequer grantee, but, according to the inquisition held after Blake's forfeiture, he 'sold the marriage of the heir for cash down about a year ago'.[51] This example is by no means untypical and in such circumstances the exchequer must have found it difficult to keep track of the actual guardians of an heir or his property. Occasionally, too, the custody of the heir and of his lands might be separated for political reasons. For instance, when Edmund, earl of March, died in December 1381, leaving his son Roger as his heir aged nine, the custody of the inheritance was eventually granted to a group of magnates, including the earls of Arundel and Northumberland, but the marriage of the heir was sold for 6000 marks to Thomas Holland, earl of Kent, Richard's half-brother,[52] and this divided control made for political complications when the heir came of age.[53] But in other instances the crown retained the marriage of the ward and

[51] Cal. of Inq. Misc., 1377–88, pp. 218–19.   [52] C.P.R., 1381–5, p. 452.
[53] J. A. Tuck, 'Anglo-Irish Relations 1382–1393', Proceedings of the Royal Irish Academy, lxix (C 2, 1970), pp. 29–31.

when he approached full age there was more petitioning and informing. In the spring of 1378, for example, an unknown petitioner requested the treasurer 'penser del mariage leir de Fyenes qappertient a Roi et qe demoert ovesque monsieur Estephne de Valoyns, et quel heir est bien pres son plein age a ceo qest dist'.[54] Suitors pressed their own claims or the claims of close relations: there was no question of an heir or heiress having any freedom of choice, for the marriage of an heiress in particular was too valuable a commodity for that. When an aspiring husband presented himself and the king or treasurer had satisfied himself of his suitability and solvency, the heiress was presented with instructions to marry, in a document which was both a proposal and a threat:[55]

Treschere et bien amee. Porce que nostre cher et foial chivaler de nostre chambre Thomas Trevet a cause de lentiere affeccioun quele il porte envers vostre persone desire de tout son cuer de vous avoir en sa espouse et compaigne a ce qil nous ad bien dit. Nous considerantz la pruesce du dit chivaler et le bon service qil nous ad fait molt vaillantment en noz guerrez depardela sicome nous est faite par plusours vraie relacioun et desirantz par tant daccompler son desire en ceo cas, vous prions cherement que au dit Thomas veullez porter bone affeccioun et lui prendre en vraie marite pur amour de nous et pur consideracioun des choses susditz. Pur la quele chose nous vous volons savoir molt especialement bon gree et monstrer a vous ambideux sibone seigneurie en temps avenir que vous ent tiendrez tresbien pur content si dieu plest. Entendant que vous estez nostre veve est nostre volunte que vous preignez le dit Thomas en vostre mariz et de prendre aucun autre nous ne sumes en volente de vous doner congie.

The guardian had certain obligations towards his ward. He was required to maintain his land and property, to do no waste, to provide proper sustenance for him, and to marry him or her without disparagement. But these obligations were frequently dishonoured. There are numerous instances of guardians wasting wards' lands and of bringing pressure to bear on them: in 1388, for instance, an inquiry was held into whether 'Enora, now deceased, daughter of John brother of James Cruclewe, being aged fourteen years and in the ward of Robert Tresilian, knight, deceased, was by force compelled by the said Robert to execute a writing enfeoffing him of a messuage and an acre of land in Cruclewe,

[54] E.207/6/1.   [55] Cambridge University Library Ms Dd. 3 53 fo. 81v.

though seisin was not delivered thereof, whereof she was seised in her demesne as of fee'.[56] The accusation was found to be true but it is unlikely that it would have come to light had Tresilian not been executed and his property forfeited in the Merciless Parliament. There must have been many similar cases which never reached the ears of the government.

The majority of surviving petitions to the treasurer are for wardships and custodies but the exchequer was also responsible for granting numerous offices that were connected with the financial administration. Petitions for office are much rarer than petitions for lands or wardships. Perhaps this is merely the accident of survival; perhaps it is because they were less lucrative and therefore less eagerly sought after; or perhaps, because their availability was more predictable than wardships or marriages, there was a more regular routine for filling them, comparable with the selling or granting of reversions characteristic of later periods. Only a few petitions to the treasurer for office survive from Richard's reign. They are short and formal and reveal little about the working of the system. It is even difficult to say why some petitions were accepted and others rejected. Unsuccessful petitioners may merely have been outbidden, or there may have been some political or personal objection to granting the petitioner the office he sought.[57]

Wardships, marriages, custodies and offices were hotly competed for and the system resembled a continuous auction. Few holders of grants had much security and any farmer or office holder might find himself dispossessed unless his grant specifically gave him protection. It was routine to dispossess a farmer if a higher offer were made and Hoccleve's Book of Precedents includes a formula 'pur ouster un tiel de tiele garde et graunter icelle a un autre parce qil voet plus doner pur mesme la garde'.[58] The exchequer dealt ruthlessly with defaulters. In 1384 John Peytevyn owed £11 6s 8d on his farm of two manors of the March inheritance and the debt was immediately levied on Peytevyn's property in London. His chaplain and attorney Thomas

---

[56] Cal. of Inq. Misc., 1377–88, pp. 126–7.

[57] For petitions to the Treasurer for office, see e.g. E.207/7/2, unsuccessful petition from John Thame for the office of steward of the courts of Berkhamsted 1385; E.207/7/7, petition from Geoffrey Blakethorne for the office of ulnager in Cambridgeshire and Huntingdonshire 1386.

[58] B.M. Add. Mss. 24,062 fos. 19v–20.

Corenger had to petition to the treasurer to respite the debt until the following Michaelmas.[59] Not even a yeoman of the king's chamber was secure: John Horewode failed to pay for the keeping of half the manor of Shrewley in Warwickshire and a laconic note at the bottom of the memorandum referring to his case says: 'Fiant letters patentes Egidio Fillilode . . . de custodia predicta.'[60]

One of the surest ways of having a petition accepted and of securing concessions which mitigated the rigours of the system was to have influential friends at court or in the administration; and the exercise of influence by lords who had access to the king was one of the principal reasons why the system of patronage was liable to become politically contentious. A good lord was expected to obtain favours at court for his clients and dependants, to sponsor petitions, and to provide 'connections (hence the Spanish *enchufe*— plug-in) with the institutional order'.[61] He had to act as a link between the client and the central institutions which could provide what the client wanted; and to fulfil such a function it was vitally important for the lord to have personal access to the king or influence with the great officers of state. The possibility that disappointed clients might look to another lord provided a strong incentive for a magnate to oppose men who appeared to be monopolising the king too completely. He had to safeguard not only his own interests but also the interests of all those who looked to him to provide good lordship.

For his own part, however, a magnate might prefer to reward his followers with gifts and grants obtained for him from the king and the central administration rather than with fees provided out of his own financial resources. Such patronage had more than financial advantages. For if a lord solicited a gift at court for his follower, he had a claim on his follower's loyalty without at the same time having any responsibility for what the follower did with what he received and without having any formal connection which might imply responsibility. The gifts created dependence and the threat of their cessation might be a useful means of discipline. And in a political climate such as developed after 1388,

[59] E.207/6/20.
[60] E.207/7/9; C.F.R., 1377–83, p. 355; ibid., 1383–91, p. 203.
[61] E. R. Wolf, 'Kingship, Friendship, and Patron-Client Relations in Complex Societies', in *The Social Anthropology of Complex Societies*, ed. M. Banton (London, 1966), p. 18.

when lords were coming under increasing pressure to take responsibility for the lawless acts of those who wore their liveries, the creation of informal connections was all the more valuable.[62] Access to royal patronage was a most important means of maintaining and extending a lord's informal connections.

Numerous instances of the sponsorship of petitions by the magnates survive from Richard's reign. In 1380 Thomas Percy, at this time merely one of the king's bachelors, asked his brother the earl of Northumberland to use his influence with the treasurer to obtain for him the custody of the lands of Thomas de Maulay. Northumberland put the matter in the hands of his council, who conducted the negotiations and obtained the wardship.[63] And in 1397 John Spenser wrote to the treasurer:

Treshonore et reverent Seigneur ie moy recommande a vous en taunt come ie sai ou pluis puisse. Et pur ceo que mon treshonore Seigneur le Count de Kent vous ad certifiez par son lettre de mon demaunde a le Roy pur la garde de les terres et tenementz queux feurent a William Marche chivaler esteantz en les mains du Roy par meindre age de Thomas son fitz et heir la quele garde ovesque la mariage ieo voudra avoir si vous plerroit paiauntz resonablement pur ycelles. Issint vous plese treshonore seigneur monstrer vostre bon seigneurie a Thomas Chipstede portour dycestes qui vous certifiera pleinement et ferra ovesque vous fin depar moi en cest matire toutdys vous supplianz que ieo les puisse avoir devant ascun autre paiantz resonablement pur ycelles solonc vostre sage et honurable discrecioun. Escrit a Northampton le xxii iour de Juyll. Vostre clerc si vous plest Johan S.[64]

Kent used his influence successfully, and Spenser was granted the wardship on 6 April 1398.[65] And in 1386 Kent's father, Thomas Holland, the king's half brother, used his influence to procure the transfer of a custody to one of his clients. The keeping of the lands of William B., an outlaw, had been entrusted to Richard B. the elder, but the king wrote to the chancellor that 'Nientmoins nous vuellions par consideracion de ce que nous est reportee que nostre chier et bien amee Rauf Ryce Excuier est cousin et prochain heir au dit William es terres et tenementz avantditz', and has offered as

---

[62] See for example, the Monk of Westminster's account of the debate on livery and maintenance in the Cambridge parliament of 1388: Monk of Westminster, pp. 189–90.

[63] E.207/6/8; *C.F.R., 1377–83*, p. 372. [64] B.M. Royal Ms 10 B IX fo. 6v.

[65] *C.F.R., 1391–9*, p. 254.

much as B. used to render. Therefore 'nous de nostre grace especiale et a la priere de nostre treschier frere le Conte de Kent avons grantee au dit Rauf la garde des ditz terres et tenementz'.[66] In ecclesiastical matters magnates intervened just as actively with the chancellor. In 1393 Henry, earl of Derby, asked him to issue letters of denizenship under the great seal, recently granted by the king to the prior and chapter of Pontefract.[67] Occasionally the favour of a magnate was actively solicited by the clergy: in 1381 the prior of Bermondsey wrote to Gaunt asking him to use his influence to procure letters of denizenship for the priory:

A tresgracious et tresexcellent Seigneur le Roy de Castel et de Leoun Duc de Lancastre supplie humblement son pover Chapellayn le Priour de Bermundeseye qest del fundacioun de progenitours nostre Seigneur le Roy que vous pleise de vostre tresecellent seigneurie eider qe nostre Seigneur le Roy voile graunter par sa patente al dit Priour que il et ses successours puissent estra acceptez et affermez perpetuelment denizens . . .[68]

The petition was granted and letters of denizenship duly issued.[69] Sometimes a magnate brought pressure to bear on the subordinate clerks in a department, as happened in 1395 when the earl of Arundel wrote to one of the chancery clerks asking for David Carpenter to be presented to the vicarage of St Michael's in his lordship of Abergavenny, if this could be done without the know-ledge of his brother the chancellor! It evidently could, for Carpenter was presented to the benefice on 15 November 1395.[70]

One of the charges in the Appeal of Treason in 1388 was that the king's favourites had used their influence to procure 'diverses Manoirs, Terres, Tenementz, Rentes, Offices, et Bailiffs' for 'diverses . . . persones de lour affinite'. [71] The charges against the favourites in 1388 are the clearest evidence that royal patronage had become a politically contentious issue; and the charge, if taken at its face value, implies that the use of influence to obtain gifts was regarded as theoretically objectionable. But the charge should not be considered out of context. The whole purpose of the appeal was to condemn the king's conduct of government by attacking

[66] B.M. Harleian Ms 3988 fo. 37.
[67] M. D. Legge, *Anglo-Norman Letters and Petitions* (Oxford, 1941), p. 408.
[68] S.C.8/93/4628.   [69] *C.P.R., 1381–5*, p. 18.
[70] Legge, op. cit., p. 327; *C.P.R., 1391–5*, p. 638.   [71] *R.P.*, iii, p. 230.

his favourites and ministers who, it was argued, had taken advantage of the king's youth to infringe his 'liberty' and control the government. The Appellants objected not so much to the use of influence in itself, as to its successful use by a group of courtiers with a king who paid little attention to his traditional and natural advisers. But even though the Appellants were as ready to use their influence with the king after they came to power on behalf of their clients and dependants,[72] there were nonetheless certain limitations on the king's freedom to grant what he wished to whom he wished, and these, if infringed, might justify criticism of the administration of the patronage system. For more than a century it had been assumed that the ancient demesne of the crown should not be alienated[73] and although this assumption was not always honoured in practice such a restriction on the king's freedom to dispose of his own lands made him dependent for much of his resources of patronage on the windfalls produced by the working of the feudal system. However, the development of the trust in the second half of the fourteenth century reduced this source of patronage considerably.[74] It is not clear how far down the social scale the trust had penetrated by the end of the fourteenth century but it was certainly found in a fully developed form amongst landowners of the second rank[75] and in some sections of the knightly class, as well as amongst the titled nobility.[76] Although Dr Bean has shown that the crown made some effort to safeguard its feudal rights, such efforts were generally spasmodic and half-hearted,[77] and in all probability Richard II disposed of fewer feudal incidents than his grandfather or great-grandfather. Lords may therefore have competed more hotly because less was available.

Furthermore, the crown's financial difficulties in the last thirty

---

[72] Tuck, 'Baronial Opposition', pp. 407–10.

[73] Hoyt, op. cit., pp. 146–8, 164–6.

[74] Bean, loc. cit.; G. A. Holmes, *The Estates of the Higher Nobility in Fourteenth Century England* (Cambridge, 1957), pp. 45–57.

[75] For a good example of enfeoffment to uses and instructions to feoffees at this level of society, see Northumberland Record Office, Ravensworth Deeds No. 41, indenture between Sir Ralph de Lumley, and John Fuller, chaplain, and John de Sadberge.

[76] Holmes, op. cit., p. 55.

[77] Bean, loc. cit.; see also in this connection K. B. McFarlane, 'The English Nobility in the Middle Ages', *12th International Congress of Historical Sciences* (1965), pp. 337–45.

years of the fourteenth century led to pressure from the commons in parliament to retain in the king's own hands or farm for the greatest possible amount property that came to the crown from various incidental sources: not only feudal escheats and wardships but also such windfalls as the alien priories, lands held by tenants with a life interest only, or the lands of outlaws, felons, and lunatics.[78] The commons wanted financial rather than political or personal criteria to determine the king's policy towards property and offices that fell to him. The Appellants of 1388 clearly hoped to enlist the commons' sympathy by attacking the king's generosity towards his favourites, though their subsequent conduct shows their lack of real interest in financial retrenchment. In the 1390s, however, Richard accepted some measure of conciliar supervision of his government and this supervision extended to his patronage. The motive appears to have been primarily financial rather than political: a committee consisting of Gaunt, York, Gloucester, and the chancellor was set up to ratify all grants that 'purra tournir a disencrees du profit du Roi',[79] and there is some evidence that Gaunt at least took his supervisory role seriously.[80] The council in the 1390s clearly intended that the king's resources should be safeguarded and not frittered away satisfying insistent petitioners.

The continuing financial difficulties of the reign, as well as the recurrent political upheavals, explain the complex and sometimes contradictory attitudes towards patronage that are discernible within the political community. The interest of the commons as a collective body was to safeguard the financial resources of the crown (though their interests as individuals might be very different); the interest of the exchequer was to produce a satisfactory financial return from the sale of offices and the incidents of feudal tenure. The interest of petitioners and men of influence was to increase their personal wealth and to reward their clients and friends: to do so required access to the king. The king for his part was concerned to create and retain loyalty, to give favour, reward service, and maintain what balance he thought correct amongst the various interests seeking what he had to give. The interaction of these various interests produced a network of petitions, bribes and

[78] *R.P.*, iii, p. 115.   [79] *P.P.C.*, i, pp. 18–19.
[80] P.R.O. Ancient Correspondence, S.C.1/40/190: letter from Gaunt to the chancellor in 1390 concerning the office of sheriff of Shropshire.

douceurs, of pressure and influence, given shape by a bureaucratic routine for the administration of patronage; and it produced too an undercurrent of criticism on financial and political grounds. Much of the routine work of patronage administration went on uninterrupted by political upheavals and uninfluenced by political considerations. But if one group were systematically excluded from patronage and another rewarded in too lavish a manner, the whole question of the direction and control of patronage became a contentious political issue with important financial implications. This is what happened between 1382 and 1386. The king's favourites monopolized access to him and the exclusion of the great magnates from influence and patronage is a most powerful reason for their opposition to the king and the court party in the 1380s.

II

English Diplomatic Documents
1377-99

PIERRE CHAPLAIS

THE EVIDENCE suggests that by 1200 at the latest, and probably much earlier, a uniform technique of diplomatic relations was already prevailing throughout the western world. Whichever countries were involved, the diplomatic practice was substantially the same. Neither was this uniformity purely accidental nor had it been brought about by a formal agreement of some kind between the western rulers: universal common-sense, more than any other factor, had been responsible for it. Not only did diplomatic technique continue to be impervious to national differences until the end of the middle ages, but also, once it had been settled, by the early part of the thirteenth century, it remained practically unaffected by the passage of time. A diplomatic envoy of Henry III's reign would have had little difficulty in adapting himself to the conditions of Richard II's time.

The 'foreign business' of any medieval ruler consisted either of sending communications to the leaders of other countries or of negotiating and concluding agreements with them, each of those two types of business requiring a different technique. Short communications of a more or less routine character generally took the form of letters close carried to their destination by ordinary couriers. On the other hand, messages which were either too lengthy or too confidential to be sent abroad in writing were conveyed by word of mouth through trusted envoys. Even in the case of an oral message, recourse to writing could not be altogether avoided. To safeguard the interests of the sender, who had to be sure that his envoy would carry out his mission faithfully, it was not uncommon for the message to be committed to writing before the envoy's departure. In England, in Henry III's reign, this

21

writing, often known as the envoy's 'credence', was drawn up in the form of a bipartite indenture, one half of which was retained by the king and the other was delivered to the envoy. The recipient of the message also had to be satisfied that he could have complete confidence in the envoy. For this reason, before the envoy set out on his journey, he was supplied with 'letters of credence'. These were letters close, addressed by the author of the message to its intended recipient and asking that full credence be given to what the bearer, mentioned by name, would say on his behalf. Once the envoy had reached the foreign court, he first presented his letters of credence and then delivered his message orally: sometimes he was required to recite *verbatim* the actual words of his credence, sometimes he was allowed to adapt it in his own words.

The procedure which led to the conclusion of treaties—truces, treaties of peace, military and matrimonial alliances or trade agreements—was more complex, and entailed the drawing-up of a large variety of documents. Preliminary soundings had first to be made in order to ascertain whether the proposed negotiations were likely to reach a satisfactory conclusion. For truces and peace treaties between countries at war with one another, this preliminary work was normally undertaken by a third party, often the pope, sometimes a ruler on friendly relations with the leaders of the two countries concerned. For other types of treaties, the interested parties themselves tested one another's reactions by direct exchanges of oral and written messages. Once a favourable climate had been created, the time had come for the actual negotiations to begin. Arrangements were made—again by means of oral and written messages—for representatives of both sides to meet at an agreed place and date. Both delegations normally consisted of high-ranking ecclesiastics and laymen, for example bishops and earls, often accompanied by clerks learned in law. The formal appointment of those representatives was made by letters patent of procuration, sometimes described as their 'full powers' or 'commission', which defined in very general terms the tasks assigned to them, for example the negotiation and conclusion of a truce, and contained a promise that their principal would ratify the agreement which they were to make on his behalf. The procuration of each delegation was designed to safeguard the interests of the opposite side. For his own protection, each of the two principals also gave his proctors written 'instructions', in which were set out, sometimes in great detail, the concessions which they were authorized to make to the other side in order to reach agreement. In many respects, including their physical make-up, instructions resembled the credences given to the bearers of oral messages.

At their first meeting the two delegations exchanged their respective procurations, but each side was generally warned by its principal to keep its own instructions secret. If the negotiations were successful, the final task of the two delegations consisted of preparing a joint text, the 'articles of agreement': either each delegation issued a document drawn up in the names of its members and sealed with their seals, for delivery to the other side; or exact duplicates of the same document were issued in the joint names of the two delegations and sealed with all their seals. Their mission thus completed, the proctors returned home, leaving it to each of the two principals to confirm the agreement by issuing a formal 'ratification' in his own name.[1]

*   *   *

The diplomatic methods which have been outlined above had been followed by the kings of England from the early thirteenth century and possibly even earlier. They were still current in Richard II's reign. Then, as before, the king was constantly sending information and addressing requests to the pope and to secular rulers by means of letters and oral messages, the latter method being used for communications of a delicate and confidential nature. The subject-matter of the king's foreign correspondence remained much the same as it had always been. As could be expected, Richard often wrote to the pope on behalf of his clerks, so that they might be promoted to a bishopric, provided to vacant benefices or shown favours in cases pending in the papal curia. Thus in 1379 or 1380 Urban VI was asked to provide John Fordham, keeper of the privy seal, William Pakington and Reginald Hilton, respectively treasurer and controller of the household, to

[1] For more details on medieval diplomatic practice as illustrated in English records of the thirteenth and fourteenth centuries, see P. Chaplais, 'English Diplomatic Documents to the end of Edward III's Reign', *The Study of Medieval Records: Essays in Honour of Professor Kathleen Major*, ed. D. A. Bullough and R. L. Storey (Oxford, 1971).

some of the English benefices seized from the Clementine cardinals.[2] A few years later Richard wrote to the pope to recommend a chancery clerk for the archdeaconry of Richmond[3] and Richard Medford, king's secretary, for a bishopric.[4] Other letters of recommendation were sent to Boniface IX on behalf of John Waltham, bishop of Salisbury and treasurer of England, in connection with a case pending in the curia between the bishop and his chapter.[5] In another letter to the pope—apparently Urban VI—Richard expressed his impatience at the slowness of the proceedings concerning the proposed canonization of Edward II.[6]

Royal letters to secular rulers were as varied in their contents as those sent to the pope. A letter to Sigismund, king of Hungary, simply gives news of the good health and successful rule of Richard and formulates the hope that similar information will be received in return.[7] In two letters written in 1393 to King João I of Portugal, Richard's ally, the question of the well-being of both sender and addressee is only the first of two subjects mentioned, the other being the progress of the Anglo-French peace talks held at Leulingham.[8] Some letters to foreign rulers are requests for safe-conducts on behalf of various people about to visit or pass through the addressee's country.[9] Others are strongly-worded notes demanding speedy redress for losses suffered by the king's subjects and friends at the hands of the addressee's own subjects.[10] Sometimes the news given in writing was to be supplemented by an oral message, in which case the letter contained a clause of credence asking the addressee to believe what the bearer would tell him on Richard's behalf.[11] Examples of similar letters could be quoted for the reigns of Edward I, Edward II and Edward III. In those reigns, however, a substantial number of royal letters close to foreign rulers—as opposed to formal treaty-documents sent patent—were still sealed with the great seal. By Richard's reign the king's foreign correspondence was generally closed up by the privy seal

---

[2] *Correspondence*, no. 8.   [3] Ibid., no. 86.   [4] Ibid., no. 118.
[5] Ibid., nos. 182A–C.   [6] Ibid., no. 95.
[7] Ibid., no. 71. These letters were called *littere de statu*.
[8] Ibid., nos. 196–7.   [9] Ibid., nos. 5, 27.
[10] Ibid., nos. 119, 144, 149, 160, 180, 198, 209–10. These letters were known as *requisiciones* or *littere requisitorie*.
[11] Ibid., nos. 63, 151. Michel de Boüard, *La France et l'Italie au temps du grand schisme d'Occident* (Paris, 1936), p. 407.

or the signet. Letters of request demanding the restoration of English goods seized abroad were still occasionally sealed with the great seal,[12] but even for them the use of the privy seal was frequent.[13]

Even Richard II's foreign correspondence under the signet contains very little information of a secret nature. For confidential communications Richard, like his predecessors, used oral messages, credences and letters of credence. The letters of credence issued during his reign[14] were, like the rest of his foreign correspondence, sent close under the privy seal or under the signet, and resembled in most respects those issued at the end of Edward III's reign. In so far as credences were concerned, they were still drawn up in the form of bipartite indentures in 1366 and 1367.[15] Whether the indenture system was retained in the first few years of Richard's reign is uncertain. At any rate, it had been discontinued by 1390 at the latest, to be replaced by the issue of one single non-indented document, sealed with the great seal, the privy seal and the signet, and sometimes further authenticated by the royal sign manual ('Le roy R S').[16] This new type of credence remained in use until the end of the middle ages. There are exceptions, but they mostly concern credences given to foreign envoys returning home: in such cases, before and after 1390, the credence was simply sealed with the privy seal applied on its face and, unlike the credences of

[12] E.g. T. Rymer, *Foedera*, etc. (Record Comm. edn. 1816–1869), iv, p. 103.

[13] Above, note 10. In Edward III's reign diplomatic letters close under the privy seal were closed up in the same way as administrative writs close under the same seal. From 1345 to 1377 the method consisted of applying the seal on the dorse of the letter over a tongue and slit; the outside address was written on the loose end of the tongue (see P. Chaplais, *English Royal Documents, King John–Henry VI* (Oxford, 1971), p. 31). After 1377 administrative writs close continued to be sealed in this fashion, but diplomatic letters close were now normally sealed in the same way as signet letters: the seal was applied on the dorse over the two ends of a thong, and the outside address was written on the dorse of the letter itself. The cross of red wax, however, at the centre of which the signet was applied, was dispensed with in the case of the privy seal (see Chaplais, op. cit., pp. 37–8). For the reign of Richard II, see the originals cited in *Correspondence*, nos. 16, 32, 206; for the reigns of Henry V and Henry VI, see Brit. Mus., Add. MS. 14820 A; Barcelona, Archivo de la Corona de Aragón, Pergaminos extra inventario, no. 1409; Copenhagen, Rigsarkivet, E. England, no. 1 bb.

[14] *Correspondence*, nos. 4, 26.

[15] *The Ancient Kalendars and Inventories* . . ., ed. F. Palgrave, 3 vols. (Record Comm., 1836), i, pp. 209, 213.

[16] See Appendix no. 2 and compare *P.P.C.*, i, pp. 19, 22: instructions and credences seem always to have been drawn up in the same form.

English envoys, was delivered by the foreign envoy to his master.[17] Normally the written credence was not shown to the recipient of the oral message. Therefore it is generally impossible to know whether or not the envoy delivered his message faithfully. In one case, however, that of William Lescrope's mission to France in June 1396, the envoy's original credence has survived as well as a French official account of the actual message which Lescrope delivered orally to Charles VI.[18] The original credence, dated 15 June 1396, mentions three main requests to be made to the king of France. Firstly Charles was to be asked to swear that he would observe the Anglo-French truce and to obtain similar oaths from his uncles, his brother and other members of the French royal house. Secondly Lescrope was to arrange for Richard II's bride, Isabella, Charles VI's daughter, to join her husband in Calais on 1 August or within the next fifteen days at the latest. If the French objected that in such a short time neither could Isabella's dowry be raised nor her jewels be got ready, Richard would be satisfied if Isabella brought with her two-thirds of her dowry and jewels, as long as he was given an undertaking that he would receive the balance at Michaelmas. Should that offer be turned down by the French, Richard was prepared to cut his demands further: one half only of the dowry and jewels was to be brought with Isabella, the balance to be settled at Michaelmas. Thirdly Lescrope was to investigate the possibility of a meeting between Richard and the dukes of Berry and Burgundy in Calais, where they might discuss together the question of the union of the Church and other matters of common interest to both kingdoms.

According to the French account, Lescrope gave his message to Charles VI on 1 July 1396. The message consisted of four points: the first concerned the French oaths to observe the truce, the second the delivery of Isabella to her husband, the third the question of a meeting between Richard and the dukes of Berry and Burgundy; the fourth dealt with the matter of the union of the Church, referring in particular to two letters written on this subject, one from the university of Paris and the other from the university of

[17] Rymer, *Foedera* (Record Comm. edn.), iv, pp. 86-7 (23 May 1380); Staatsarchiv Düsseldorf, Urkunde Kurköln, no. 1944 (21 May 1439).

[18] Appendix no. 2; T. Rymer, *Foedera etc.* (original edn. 1727-1735), vii, p. 834. See E. Perroy, *L'Angleterre et le grand schisme d'Occident* (Paris, 1933), pp. 376-7 and notes.

Oxford. On the first three points the French account is very close indeed to the text of Lescrope's original credence, except on the question of the delays within which Isabella was to join Richard II in Calais. Apparently the envoy told Charles VI that Richard wanted his bride with him either on 1 August or within the next week at the latest, that is to say one week earlier than suggested in the original credence. The fourth point of the French version of Lescrope's message hardly appears at all in the original credence. These discrepancies show beyond doubt that the original credence was not shown to the French; they also suggest that it never left England. But it is difficult to imagine how Lescrope could have forgotten that it was *two* weeks' grace after the first of August—not *one*—that he was to give Charles VI for taking Isabella to Calais. Since it meant that Charles was given five weeks at the most, instead of six, to make preparations for Isabella's departure, this could hardly be described as a trivial alteration. Lescrope, Richard's chamberlain and obviously very close to him, would have done his best not to misrepresent Richard's wishes to the French. There is every reason to believe that it was at his master's secret bidding that the envoy took liberties with his written credence, which may have expressed the views of the king's council rather than the king's own wishes. Perhaps we should also attribute to Richard's intervention the addition of the fourth point regarding the union of the Church.[19] Whether this interpretation is correct or not, the discrepancies between the written credence and the oral message are most disturbing.

In negotiating and concluding treaties Richard II also followed the same procedure as his predecessors had done for about two hundred years. The same types of document were issued, letters of procuration, instructions, articles of agreement and ratifications, whose form varied only in small details from that used by Edward III. The most conspicuous change concerns the form of instructions, for which, as for credences, the indenture system was replaced in or before 1390 by the issue of a single document sealed with the great seal, the privy seal and the signet, to which was sometimes added the royal sign manual.[20]

[19] See J. J. N. Palmer, 'England and the Great Western Schism, 1388–1399', *E.H.R.*, lxxxiii (1968), pp. 516–22.
[20] P.R.O., Exch. T.R. Dipl. Doc. (E. 30), nos. 317, 319, 326, 327, 342 etc.

In Richard's reign diplomatic proctors were appointed by letters patent, which were normally sealed with the great seal in natural wax appended on a tongue. Exceptionally, on 25 June 1382, John Harleston, knight, John Appleby, dean of St Paul's, London, and Masters John Barnet and John Blanchard, doctors of laws, sent to Brittany to conclude a truce and a trade agreement with Duke John IV, received their commission under the privy seal.[21] This departure from normal English practice may have been due to the fact that the duke of Brittany had in the past occasionally used his privy seal for sealing similar procurations.[22] The document is in any case unusual in other ways: for example, it is difficult to imagine what sort of truce ('treves, soeffrances et abstinences') the proctors could conclude between two rulers, who, as stated in the letters, neither were, nor intended to be, at war with each other.

Some of the procurations under Richard's great seal are written in Latin, others in French.[23] Some have a general address ('Omnibus ad quos presentes littere pervenerint', 'Universis presentes litteras inspecturis', etc. or their French equivalent);[24] others are addressed to the proctors themselves.[25] Some have no address or greeting, but simply begin 'Nos Ricardus Dei gracia rex Anglie et Francie et dominus Hibernie tenore presencium notum facimus universis quod nos . . .',[26] a form which suggests that the draftsman may have been a bishop's clerk. The main part of the document consists of a number of clauses, which vary considerably from one procuration to the next. One defines the type of business which the proctors were empowered to conclude. It might be a truce,[27] a matrimonial[28] or military alliance,[29] or any other type of agreement. It might simply consist of receiving a sum of money on the king's behalf: for example, on 7 November 1397, Thomas Merks,

[21] Nantes, Arch. Dép. Loire-Atlantique, E. 120, no. 15. I owe this reference to kindness of Dr Michael Jones, of the University of Nottingham.
[22] e.g. Rymer, *Foedera* (Record Comm. edn.), iv, pp. 74–5.
[23] For examples of procurations in French, see Rymer, *Foedera* (Record Comm. edn.), iv, pp. 27, 46, 70, 83, 137.
[24] Ibid., iv, pp. 28, 34, 45, 46, 51 etc.   [25] Ibid., iv, pp. 27, 67, 70, 83, 117 etc.
[26] Ibid., iv, pp. 114, 115, 116.
[27] Ibid., iv, pp. 27, 137; (original edn.), vii, p. 412.
[28] Rymer, *Foedera* (Record Comm. edn.), iv, pp. 105, 118; (original edn.) vii, pp. 815–17.
[29] Rymer, *Foedera* (Record Comm. edn.), iv, pp. 117, 119, 151, 153, 163 etc.

bishop of Carlisle, was appointed as Richard's proctor to request and receive 100,000 gold francs owed by Charles VI as part of Queen Isabella's dowry.[30] Normally, the proctors were authorized to negotiate and conclude, but in the case of an embassy sent to Bernabo Visconti of Milan in March 1379 Richard's proctors were only empowered to discuss the possibility of a marriage treaty between the king and Bernabo's daughter, Catherine, and report the result of their discussions to the king.[31] This document shares with a procuration of June 1380, also connected with Richard's search for a bride, this time in Germany, the unusual feature of having a time-limit: both procurations were to be valid for half-a-year only.[32] Two other clauses appear to have been essential in all procurations: one, the 'quorum' clause, gave the minimum number of proctors required to be present; the other, the clause 'de rato', promised that the king would ratify the agreements entered into by his proctors.

As a rule, diplomatic procurations are not particularly conspicuous for their literary merits. The proem, which gave the draftsman of medieval documents some scope for Latin and French composition, is generally absent from procurations; instead, their main text often begins with routine phrases which express the king's full trust in his proctors' faithfulness and wisdom.[33] Early in Richard's reign, however, proems begin to appear in some of the most important letters of procuration. The following example comes from a procuration of 26 December 1380 for an alliance with Wenceslas, king of the Romans:

Inter gloriosas rei publice curas et regalium solicitudinum fructus uberes estimamus precipuum aliorum principum et regum sublimium sibi copulare presidia ac cum talibus ligarum, affinitatum et amiciciarum specialium inire federa, per quos principatus hincinde amoris ind¹ssolubilis nexu conjuncti insurgentibus ex adverso resistere et ab omni oppressionis clade, coadunatis viribus, poterunt mutuo se tueri.[34]

The next proem occurs in a procuration, also dated 26 December 1380, for the proposed marriage of Richard II to Anne of Bohemia:

Inter cetera que regnorum aliorumque principatuum jure successorio

---

[30] Appendix no. 3.   [31] Rymer, *Foedera* (Record Comm. edn.), iv, p. 60.
[32] Ibid., iv, p. 90.   [33] Ibid., iv, pp. 153, 166, 167.   [34] Ibid., iv, p. 104.

sanguinis delatorum felicius firmant regimina est principancium hujusmodi prolis fecunditas ex matrimonio legitimo derivata, per quam,
exclusis nedum extraneis set collateralibus suis et legitimis heredibus,
successiones hujusmodi directa linea deferuntur.[35]

The first of these two proems was used time and time again,
throughout Richard's reign, for full powers to negotiate and conclude military alliances.[36] The second, fitting only for procurations
concerning proposed marriage agreements, became obsolete when
Richard married Anne of Bohemia in 1382.[37] After the death of
Anne, in 1394, Richard's search for a second bride might have been
an occasion for reviving it. Since, however, the main argument of
the proem was based on the need for kings to have direct heirs in
order to exclude collaterals from the succession to the throne, its
use would have been hardly appropriate in procurations designed
to bring about Richard's marriage to Isabella, daughter of a Valois
king. A more innocuous proem was therefore substituted:

Plasmator hominum ipse Deus, matrimonii bona pia consideracione
prospiciens, primo dominancium legem dedit qua et ejus frueretur bonis
et speciem continuaret in posteris, adjutorii sibi dati legitima gaudens
conjunccione sub sincere dileccionis ac anime et corporis unitate, ex cujus
legalis conjunccionis federe plerumque provenit Deo grata sobolis pro-
creacio, linealis successio, consanguineorum hinc et inde laudabilis
alligancia, amoris soliditas in dilectis et discordantibus via pacis.[38]

The articles of agreement of Richard's reign again resemble
those of earlier reigns: they were normally in the form of letters
patent issued either separately by each delegation or jointly in the
names of the proctors of both sides. Those of the marriage treaty
between Richard and Anne of Bohemia, dated in London, 2 May
1381, belong to the second type and have a proem which has much
in common with that used in the procurations of 26 December
1380:

Illa consuetudo recte regnancium, ille mos juste principancium semper
fuit bonum commune subditorum quibuscumque privatis preferre
commodis talibusque rem publicam munire presidiis, per que posset

---

35 Ibid., iv, p. 105.
36 Ibid., iv, pp. 108, 117, 119, 151; (original edn.), vii, p. 659.
37 Rymer, *Foedera* (Record Comm. edn.), iv, p. 118.
38 Rymer, *Foedera* (original edn.), vii, pp. 802, 816.

continue, exclusis cecis inquietacionum turbinibus, quieta persistere et sub optate pacis votiva felicitate letari, quod tunc satis utiliter creditur promoveri, cum principes cristiani et potentes, in unam fidei catholice unitatem et veram amiciciam conjuncti, in unam mentis consonanciam affectuose conveniunt et insimul indissolubilis amoris federe copulantur.[39]

There is little doubt that this proem was composed by an English clerk, although the view expressed in it that it was the duty of a king to place the common good of his subjects before his own private interests was not new at the time; it occurs in William of Ockham's *Octo Quaestiones* as well as in the *Songe du Verger*.[40] A very similar proem is found in the Portuguese articles of agreement of the Anglo-Portuguese alliance of 1386:

Illud pium propositum recte regnancium illaque finalis intencio juste principancium esse debet bonum commune subditorum privatis preferre commodis talibusque subjectam eis rem publicam munire presidiis, per que, exclusis cecis inquietacionum turbinibus exterminatisque adversancium incursibus, plebs fidelis, que talibus gubernatur auctoribus nedum augeatur prosperis set sub optate quietis et pacis amenitate conservetur continue in adversis, quod re vera tunc apcius procurari speratur, cum cristianissimi reges et principes, in vera unitate et obediencia sacrosancte Romane ecclesie persistentes, in unam mentis consonanciam conveniunt et invicem indissolubilis amoris federe copulantur.[41]

These Portuguese articles of agreement, dated at Windsor, 9 May 1386, are notarially attested by one of Richard II's chancery clerks, John Bouland, clerk of the diocese of Carlisle and notary public by apostolic authority. In the case of the alliance between John of Gaunt (as king of Castile) and Richard II, the articles of agreement drawn up in the names of Gaunt's proctors (Westminster, 28 April 1386) are also notarially attested by Bouland and have virtually the same proem as the procuration of 26 December 1380 for Richard's alliance with Wenceslas ('Cum inter gloriosas rei publice curas . . . poterunt uberius se tueri').[42]

---

[39] Rymer, *Foedera* (Record Comm. edn.), iv, p. 111.

[40] *Guillelmi de Ockham Opera Politica*, ed. J. G. Sikes, i (Manchester, 1940), p. 75; *Le Songe du Vergier*, Book I, Chapter 34 (*Revue du Moyen Age Latin*, xiii (1957), reprint of J.-L. Brunet's edition).

[41] Rymer, *Foedera* (original edn.), vii, p. 515.   [42] Ibid., vii, p. 510.

The articles of agreement of Anglo-Scottish treaties were often indented and written in English.[43]

Richard II's ratifications of treaties were little more than letters patent of 'inspeximus', which recited the English articles of agreement and ended with a ratification clause. As in previous reigns, they were sealed with the great seal, and the seal attachment as well as the colour of the wax varied from one type of treaty to another: truces, which were to last only for a limited period, were sealed in natural wax and the seal was appended on a tag, whereas treaties of peace and matrimonial and military alliances, which ranked as perpetuities, were sealed in green wax and the seal was appended on silk cords.[44]

Every type of 'international business' which required letters of procuration seems to have also required a ratification of some kind. For example, in the case of Charles VI's payment of 100,000 gold francs to Richard II as part of Queen Isabella's dowry, at the end of 1397, three original documents have survived in the French archives: (1) Richard's letters patent, dated 7 November 1397 and empowering Thomas Merks, bishop of Carlisle, to request and receive the money from the king of France; (2) a quittance drawn up in the name of the bishop and dated in Paris, 19 December 1397, the actual date of payment; (3) Richard II's own quittance under the great seal, dated 7 November 1397. The document mentioned last, which amounted to a backdated royal ratification of the bishop's quittance, was in fact drawn up and sealed in advance and given to the bishop at the same time as his letters of procuration. As on 7 November the name of the French official who was to deliver the money on Charles VI's behalf was not known in England, a blank was left in Richard's quittance for the name to be inserted at the time of payment by the bishop or one of his clerks, which was duly done on 19 December 1397.[45]

Foreign ratifications, like foreign articles of agreement, were sometimes drafted and even written by English clerks. This applies, for example, to the Portuguese ratification of the Anglo-Portuguese alliance of 1386. The extant original, dated at Coimbra, 12 August 1387, is written in three different hands: (1) the first hand, that of an English clerk, wrote the major

---

[43] E.g. ibid., vii, pp. 468, 526.   [44] See Paris, Arch. Nat., J. 643, nos. 5 and 7.
[45] Appendix nos. 3–5.

part of the document:

Johannes Dei gracia rex Portugal' et Algarbii, omnibus ad quos presentes littere pervenerint, salutem. Inspeximus tractatum pacis, concordie et perpetue amicicie inter . . . inviolabiliter observare;

(2) the second hand, also probably English, wrote the last sentence of the text and the first four words of the corroboration clause:

Que omnia et singula prout superius tractata sunt et concordata inviolabiliter observare et observari facere per hec sancta Dei ewangelia per nos inspecta et corporaliter tacta promittimus et juramus. In cujus rei testimonium;

(3) the third hand is that of the Portuguese notary public by royal authority, *Johannes Alfonsi* of Coimbra, who completed the corroboration clause, and added the dating clause and his notarial mark and subscription. The document is sealed with João I's leaden seal appended on silk cords. The presence of a number of slits in the parchment and of the endorsement 'Nobilibus et strenuis viris Fernando magistro [ordi]nis sancti Jacobi in regnis Portugalie et Algarbii et Laurencio Johannis Fogaca cancellario Portugalie, militibus, amicis nostris dilectis', written in an English hand, suggests that the document in its unfinished state was sent close from England to Portugal, where is was completed and sealed before being returned to England.[46] It is likely that the unfinished document was taken to Portugal by William Elmham and William Faryngdon in January 1387.[47]

Sometimes the articles of agreement stipulated that other documents should be issued besides the ratifications. For example, in the marriage treaty between Richard and Isabella, sealed by the English proctors in Paris on 9 March 1395/6, it was agreed that Richard's close relations would send to Charles VI letters in which they promised that Isabella, if she wished, would be allowed to return to France in the event of Richard's death.[48] The original letter which was accordingly drawn up on 1 May 1396 in the names of the three dukes of Lancaster, York and Gloucester and of the earls of Derby, Rutland, Kent, Huntingdon and Nottingham

[46] P.R.O., Exch. T.R. Dipl. Doc. (E. 30), no. 311.
[47] See P. E. Russell, *The English Intervention in Spain and Portugal in the time of Edward III and Richard II* (Oxford, 1955), p. 443 and n. 3.
[48] Paris, Arch. Nat., J. 643, no. 6.

and sealed with their seals is still extant in the Archives Nationales. Much of its text consists of a recital of the relevant article of the treaty. The clerk who wrote it seems to have used as his model a copy of the English articles of agreement, which ended as follows:

... En tesmoign' de ce nous contes de Ruthland et de Notingham et chambellan dessuisdiz avoms fait mettre noz seaulx a ces lettres. Donnees et faites a Paris le ix^e jour de mars lan de grace mill ccc iiij^{xx} et xv^e.[49]

While adapting these final clauses to his document, the clerk omitted to alter the year of grace and wrote 'le primer jour de may, lan de grace mille troiscentz quatrevyntz et quinze'. The error was spotted when the letter came before the king and council, and the word 'quinze' was erased to be replaced by 'sesze'. The correction was then authenticated by the following note: 'We have caused the date of this letter to be corrected and "iiij^{xx} et sesze" to be written instead of "iiij^{xx} et quinze". Signed by our command in the presence of our chancellor and others of our council: E W (written in monogrammatic form)'.[50] The monogram E W stands for E(dmund) W(arham), clerk of the diocese of Norwich and notary public by apostolic and imperial authority.[51]

Subsidiary agreements in the king's name were sometimes issued in the form of letters patent or bills sealed with the privy seal: four documents of this kind were delivered to Charles VI in 1396, one in May,[52] and three at the end of October while Richard was in France;[53] all four were written by Robert Fry, clerk of the privy seal, and three of them were also signed by him.[54]

★   ★   ★

Between 1355 and 1375 Master John de Branketre, clerk of the

---

[49] Ibid.   [50] Appendix no. 1.

[51] The E W monogram, obviously Warham's short signature, also occurs in both left and right margins of the original Anglo-French truce agreement made in the names of the earls of Rutland and Nottingham and of William Lescrope and dated in Paris, 9 March 1395/6 (Paris, Arch. Nat., J. 643, no. 15): in this document the name *Warham* is written below the monogram. On Warham's career, see Emden, *Oxford*, iii, p. 1988.

[52] *Correspondence*, no. 228.

[53] Paris, Arch. Nat., J. 644, no. 19; J. 655, nos. 23 and 23 bis.

[54] See *English Royal Documents, King John—Henry VI*, ed. P. Chaplais, plate 19 and p. 72.

diocese of Norwich, notary public by apostolic and imperial authority, by the end of his life chancery clerk of the first bench and from 1355 holder of the office of 'notary in chancery', had supervised the work involved in drafting and writing diplomatic documents issued under the great seal.[55] Not only did he draw up many public instruments of a diplomatic nature, but his name occurs at the bottom of countless letters patent and other documents relating to Edward III's dealings with foreign rulers. When he died, in September 1375, his seat on the first bench of chancery and presumably the office of notary in chancery were granted to Master John Bouland, clerk of the diocese of Carlisle and notary public by apostolic authority, but a year later, in October 1376, Bouland was apparently removed from Branketre's former position in chancery and replaced by Master Walter Skirlaw, clerk of the diocese of York and also notary public by apostolic authority.[56] When Skirlaw was appointed keeper of the privy seal, his chancery seat was given by the king to Master Richard Ronhale (8 October 1382), former warden of the King's Hall, Cambridge.[57] Ronhale, a graduate in law, who may or may not have been a notary public, died between 27 February and 5 March 1401.[58] Skirlaw and Ronhale may have been the titular holders of the office of notary in chancery, but they do not appear to have been actively engaged in the supervision of the diplomatic work of the chancery, although they took part in many foreign missions. Bouland, on the other hand, after his alleged removal from Branketre's place drew up several diplomatic documents in notarial form, for example in 1386, when he added his notarial mark and attestation to the 'foreign' articles of agreement of Richard II's alliances with João I of Portugal and John of Gaunt.[59] Like Branketre, he also drew up a number of notarial documents recording episcopal renunciations

[55] See P. Chaplais, 'Master John de Branketre and the Office of Notary in Chancery, 1355-1375', *Journal of the Society of Archivists*, April 1971, pp. 169-99.

[56] See Emden, *Oxford*, iii, pp. 1708-10, for Skirlaw. His notarial sign is reproduced in J. S. Purvis, *Notarial Signs from the York Archiepiscopal Records* (London and York, 1957), plate 21. For Bouland, see B. Wilkinson, *The Chancery under Edward III* (Manchester, 1929), pp. 70, 148, 177, 180, 205, 226.

[57] See Emden, *Cambridge*, pp. 487-8.

[58] John Le Neve, *Fasti Ecclesiae Anglicanae, 1300-1541*, vi, Northern Province, ed. B. Jones (London, 1963), p. 45.

[59] P.R.O., Exch. T.R. Dipl. Doc. (E. 30), nos. 1087 and 310; Rymer, *Foedera* (original edn.), vii, pp. 510-23.

of the words prejudicial to the king contained in papal provisions.[60] He does not appear, however, to have at any time acted as supervisor of the chancery diplomatic work as a whole. Indeed there were other notaries who may have worked for the king as frequently as Bouland, in and outside the chancery. Master Denis Lopham, clerk of the diocese of Norwich and notary public by apostolic and imperial authority, was one of them.[61] Another was Master John Prophete, clerk of the diocese of St David's and notary public by apostolic authority, who held in Richard's reign the office of clerk of the privy seal and, from about 1389 until about 1395, that of clerk of the council.[62]

It seems that during the whole of Richard's reign it was the keeper of the chancery rolls who controlled the issue of diplomatic documents, in the same way as he was supposed to supervise the rest of the chancery work. It is his name which generally appears in the bottom right-hand corner of chancery diplomatic documents, much more frequently than the names of other chancery clerks and much more consistently than on chancery documents of domestic interest. For example, the name *Waltham* occurs on two diplomatic documents dated respectively 4 November 1383 and 26 December 1385;[63] *Burton'* on two documents of 10 August 1389 and 5 June 1394;[64] *Scarle* on five documents, the earliest of which is dated 5 July 1395 and the latest 7 July 1397;[65] *Stanley* on six documents whose dates cover the period from 7 November 1397 to the end of the reign.[66] The name *Billyngford'* occurs on three diplomatic documents, one of 7 November 1396 and two of 5 April 1399.[67] James Billingford was clerk of the crown in chan-

[60] E.g. P.R.O., Chanc. Misc. (C. 47), 15/1/8, 10, 14, 15, 17, 18.

[61] See Rymer, *Foedera* (original edn.), vii, p. 462; P.R.O., Exch. T.R. Dipl. Doc. (E. 30), nos. 303, 303A, 305, 306, 307A.

[62] For a notarial instrument drawn up by Prophete, see P.R.O., Chanc. Misc. (C. 47), 15/1/23 (30 June 1395). See Alfred L. Brown, *The Early History of the Clerkship of the Council* (Glasgow, 1969), pp. 8–16.

[63] P.R.O., Chanc. Misc. 28/6/24, 25.

[64] Paris, Arch. Nat., J. 642, no. 23, which also bears the note 'Examinatur per Johannem de Burton' et magistrum Ricardum Ronhale, clericos', J. 643, no. 5, which also bears the note 'Examinatur per Burton'.

[65] P.R.O., Exch. T.R. Dipl. Doc. (E. 30), no. 320; Paris, Arch. Nat. J. 643, nos. 7 and 15; Staatsarchiv Düsseldorf, Urkunde Kurköln, nos. 1299, 1300.

[66] Paris, Arch. Nat., J. 644, no. 22; J. 655, nos. 16 and 16 ter; P.R.O., Exch. T.R. Scottish Doc. (E. 39), 5/27; Staatsarchiv Düsseldorf, Urkunde Berg, no. 923.

[67] Paris, Arch. Nat., J. 643, no. 13; P.R.O., Exch. T.R. Scottish Doc. (E. 39), 96/9 and 16.

cery.[68] All the other names are those of successive keepers of the chancery rolls: John Waltham, keeper from 1381 to 1386, John Burton (1386–94), John Scarle (1394–7) and Thomas Stanley (1397 to the end of the reign and beyond).

It is doubtful, however, whether the keeper of the rolls wrote many chancery diplomatic documents in person. This work was left to less important clerks. On 20 July 1380 the treasurer and chamberlains of the exchequer were ordered to pay Thomas Stanley—the future keeper of the rolls—100 shillings of the king's gift:

pur lescripture des alliances nadgaires faites entre nous et nostre frere de Bretaigne et pur parchemyn, laces et autres coustages par le dit Thomas faitz a cause de mesmes les alliances.[69]

On Saturday 12 August 1391 the same Thomas Stanley received forty marks from the exchequer, of the king's gift:

pro custubus et labore per ipsum habitis et factis circa scrutinium diversorum rotulorum et recordorum tangencium tractatus pacis inter dominum regem et adversarium suum Francie factos.[70]

On Monday 7 July 1393 he received a further sum of 13s 4d from the exchequer:

pro labore et diligencia per ipsum et clericos suos habitis circa scripturam diversorum bullarum et instrumentorum treugas apud Cales' nuper captas tangencium missorum ad duces Acquitann', Glouc' et alios ambassiatores regis ibidem existentes pro plenaria noticia eorundem habenda.[71]

On 22 June 1386 John Kirkeby, John Scardeburgh and Simon Gaunstede, clerks (of the chancery), acknowledged that they had received from the keeper of the hanaper the sum of nine marks:

pro labore nostro quem circa scripturam diversarum ligarum inter prefatum dominum nostrum regem et Johannem regem Castelle et Legionis, ducem Lancastrie, ac regem Portugalie nuper factarum.[72]

---

[68] Wilkinson, op. cit., p. 85.
[69] P.R.O., Exch. of Receipt, Writs and Warrants for Issues (E. 404), parcel 12, file 77.
[70] P.R.O., Exch. of Receipt, Issue Rolls (E. 403), no. 533, m. 14.
[71] Ibid., no. 543, m. 15.
[72] P.R.O., Exch. K.R. Accounts Various (E. 101), 213/8/15.

The alliances in question are the articles of agreement drawn up in the name of the proctors of João I of Portugal (9 May 1386)[73] and the articles of agreement issued in the names of John of Gaunt's proctors (28 April 1386).[74] It has already been stated that the two documents were authenticated by the notarial sign and subscription of John Bouland, who, however, did not write the documents themselves. It is interesting to note that John Scarburgh and Simon Gaunstede are the last-mentioned witnesses in John of Gaunt's alliance with Richard II,[75] and that the name of John Kirkeby is also the last one in the list of witnesses of the Portuguese alliance.[76]

The chancery clerks and the keeper of the rolls were, of course, only responsible for the documents which were issued under the great seal and occasionally for some foreign articles of agreement. Instructions and credences seem to have been drafted in council and written in the privy seal office: a council memorandum of 22 December 1391 states that the sub-chamberlain sent a roll to the keeper of the privy seal, 'to have the instructions made according to the king's emendation as written within, in the margin';[77] the hand of original instructions to proctors sent to France in July 1395 has also been identified as that of Robert Fry, clerk of the privy seal.[78]

---

[73] P.R.O., Exch. T.R. Dipl. Doc. (E. 30), no. 310; see also no. 309.
[74] Ibid., no. 1087.   [75] Rymer, *Foedera* (original edn.), vii, p. 515.
[76] Ibid., vii, p. 520.   [77] *P.P.C.*, i, p. 40.
[78] P.R.O., Exch. T.R. Dipl. Doc. (E. 30), no. 317 (8 July 1395), written in the same hand as Paris, Arch. Nat., J. 643, no. 8, J. 644, no. 19, and J. 655, nos. 23 and 23 bis.

Appendix

1. Letter, originally misdated, in which John of Gaunt and others promise the return of Queen Isabella to France in the event of Richard II's death. Windsor, 1 May 1396 (Paris, Arch. Nat., J. 643, no. 11: original, sealed with eight seals appended on tags).

Nous Johan filz au roy, duc de Guyene et de Lancastre, conte de Derby, de Nicole et de Leycestre, seneschal Dengleterre, Esmon filz au roy, duc Deverwyk et conte de Cantebrugg, Thomas filz au roy, duc de Gloucestre et conte Dessex et de Bukyngham, conestable Dengleterre, Henry de Lancastre, conte de Derby, de Herford et de Norh't', seignur de Behennok, Edward Deverwyk, conte de Rutteland et de Cork, Tomas de Holand, conte de Kent et seignur de Wake, Johan de Holand, conte de Huntyngdon', chamberlain Dengleterre, Thomas Moubray, conte de Notyngham, mareschal Dengleterre, uncles, freres et cousins a nostre soveraigne seignur le roy. Faisons savoir a toutz que, come par vertue de traitee faite entre nous Edward Deverwyk', conte de Rutteland et de Cork, Thomas Moubray, conte mareschal et de Notyngham susditz, et William Lescrop', chamberlain du roy nostre dit seignur, dune part, et les nobles et puissantz princes les ducs de Berry, de Burgoigne, Dorlians et de Burboun, uncles et frere de son cousin de France, dautre part, de et sur la mariage de nostre dit seignur le roy et de la tresnoble dame, dame Isabelle de France, eit este accordez, enconvenancie et promys que nostre dit seignur le roy et les prochains seignurs de sa corone et de son linage serroient tenuz, promettroient et sobligeroient expressement et bailleroient leurs lettres en forme covenable et suffisante que, si nostre dit seignur le roy trespassoit avant la consummacioun du dit mariage, la dite dame Isabelle franche et desliee de toutz liens et empeschementz de mariage et autres obligacions queconqes serroit et serra ensemble toutz ses joiaulx, moebles et biens rendue et restituee a son cousin de France, piere de la dite dame Isabelle, ou a son heriter et successours. Et semblablement, sil avenoit que le roy nostre dit seignur morust apres la consummacioun de la dite mariage, ycelle dame Isabelle, si lui plesoit, sen purroit aler et retournir en France franchement et emporter toutz ses joiaux, moebles et biens sanz ce que ele fust ou peust estre detenue, liee ne obligee ne que aucun empeschement lui feut mys en sa persone ne en ses ditz biens. Nous desusditz uncles, freres et cousins de nostre dit seignur le roy, considerantz les tresgrandes biens et profitz que sont disposez davenir a leide de Dieu par le moien du dit mariage non soulment as ditz roy nostre seignur et a son cousin de France, les roiaumes, terres, seignuries et subgiz, mais aussi a toute crestientee, a lunioun de seinte eglise et a la confusioun des mescreantz, avons nous toutz ensemble et chescun de nous par soy et particulerement pour nous, noz heirs, successours et aians cause enconvenancie et promys, enconvenanceons et promettons par la teneure de ses lettres de certeine science et plein voloir que, si nostre dit seignur le roi aloit de vie a trespassement paravant la consummacioun de dit mariage, la dite dame Isabelle franche et desliee de toutz liens et empechementz de mariage et autres obligacions queconqes serroit et serra ensemble toutz ses joiaux, moebles et biens rendue et restituee pleinement a son dit piere ou a son heriter et successour. Et semblablement, sil avenoit que le roy nostre seignur morust apres la consummacion du dit mariage, la dite dame Isabelle, si lui plesoit, sen purroit aler et retournir en France franchement et emporter ses ditz joiaulx, moebles et biens sanz estre ne povoir estre detenue, liee ne obligee ne que aucun empeschement lui feust mys en sa personne ne en ses ditz biens. Et ainsi nous et chescun de nous, pour nous, noz ditz heirs et successours et aians cause, le voulons, enconvenancons et promettons en bone foie et par noz seremens et loiautees fere et fere faire, enteriner et accomplir entierement a noz loiaux poairs et empescher de fait en tant qil nous serroit possible, si aucuns ou aucun voloient ou voloit faire et entreprendre au contraire, en obligeant et ypothecant expressement nous, noz ditz hoirs et successours et aians cause et noz et leurs biens queconqes moebles et inmoebles presentz et avenir pour ses choses et chescune dycelles estre tenuz, gardez, faitz, enterinez et accompliz au plein selon le forme et teneur de ces presentes et du traitie desusdit et sanz estre purposez, alleggez, dit ou fait taisiblement, expressement ne autrement conment qil soit au contraire. En tesmoignance de ce nous ducs et contes desusditz avons fait mettre noz sealx a ces lettres. Donees et faites a Wyndesore le primer jour de may, lan de grace mille troiscentz quatrevyntz et *sesze*.[79] *Nous avons fait corrige la date de ceste lettre et mettre iiij^{xx} et seze en lieu de iiij^{xx} et quinze. Signe par nostre commandement en presence de nostre chaunceller et autres de nostre conseil. E W.*[80]

2. Original credence of William Lescrope, envoy to Charles VI of France (15 June 1396), and French account of the oral message actually delivered by him to Charles VI on 1 July 1396 (The original credence (P.R.O., Exch. T.R. Dipl. Doc. (E. 30) 326) was formerly sealed with the great seal, privy seal and signet appended

[79] The word *sesze* is written over an erasure.
[80] *Nous avons . . . W.* in a different hand.

on tags; the great seal is now missing. The sign manual, 'Le roy R S', is in Richard II's own hand. The French account of the oral message (Paris, Arch. Nat., J. 644, no. 21) is in a contemporary hand).

[A]

Cest linstruccioun et charge donne depar le roy nostre soverain seigneur a William Lescrop', soun chamberlayn, alantz en Fraunce.

Primerement que touchant la confirmacioun du traictie de mariage pour quoi le viscount de Meleun est venu, il est tout delivre come fuist acorde au dit traictie.

Item que soun pere et cousin de Fraunce soit requis de jurer les treves et faire fere as autres semblablement come le roy nostre seignour ad fait et fra fere pour sa part.

Item que touchant la venue de la royne, que le roy nostre seignour desire grandement sa venue et que ele soit briefment ovec lui et ce pour beaucoup des diverses choses queles purront estre declarez.

Item que, si soit allegge que les sommes queles deussent estre paiez a sa venue et les joiaulx ne purront estre si briefment prest, soit acorde davoir a sa venue les deux partz de les sommes et de les joiaulx et davoir seure obligacioun davoir la surplus a le fest de seint Michel prochein venant.

Item en cas que ce ne puet estre acorde, que soit apporte ovec elle la moite de les sommes et de les joiaulx, davoir bon et seur obligacioun de la surplus a la fest de seint Michel prochein venant, come desus est dit.

Item que sa venue soit pour estre a Caleys le plus tost que bonnement se purra et par especial a plus tarde le primer jour daust ou dedeins quinze jours apres prochein ensuantz.

Item coment le roy nostre seignour est en voluntee et entent daler a Caleys pour veoir ses lieux et marches depar dela et pour lui esbatre pour un certain temps tiel come a lui plerra.

Item que en cas que les ducs de Berry et de Burgoigne y feussent sur celles marches a celle foys ou qils purront bonnement estre, le roy nostre seignour parleroit volunters ovec eulx et principalment pour nourrir lamour et laffeccioun entre eulx et pour lunioun de lesglise et le bien de lui et de son pere et cousin, leurs roiaumes et subgitz, et serroit expedient et ne purroit venir que bien qils aient sufficeant poair pour les choses desuisdites et toutz autres que purront estre pour le bien de lour roiaumes et subgitz avantditz.

Item si soit demande de lour part queux seignours deussent venir ove le roy nostre seigneur, que lour soit pleinement demonstre tiels et tiels. En tesmoignance de quele chose a ceste presente instruccioun nostre dit seignour le roy ad fait mettre ses grand et prive sealx et son signet. Donne a le manoir de mesme nostre seignour de Haveryng le quinzisme jour de juyng, lan du regne de nostre seignour le roy suisdit dys et noefisme.

Le roy R S.

[B]

La creance que a dicte au roy messire Guillaume Scrop, chevalier et chambellan du roy Dengleterre, son filz, le premier jour de juillet, lan de grace mil ccc iiij^{xx} et xvj contient quatre poins.

Le premier que le visconte de Meleun, quant il ala derrain depar le roy par devers le dit roy Dengleterre, son filz, porta les lettres tant de lacort du mariage du dit roy Dengleterre avecques madame Ysabel de France a present royne Dengleterre, sa femme, comme des treves prinses entre les seigneurs dessusdiz a fin que le dit roy Dengleterre les jurast et les feist jurer par ses oncles et ceulx de son lignage, la quele chose le dit roy Dengleterre fist et fist fere par les seigneurs de son lignage dessusdiz. Et aussi le dit chevalier a requis le roy depar le dit roy Dengleterre, son filz, quil voulsist jurer les dictes treves et les faire jurer par nossires ses oncles et frere et les autres de son sang.

Le second que le dit roy Dengleterre desire moult et aussi font les seigneurs et le peuple de son royaume veoir briefment la dicte royne Dengleterre, sa femme, et lui prie moult affectueusement que il la lui vuille fere ordener pour estre menee a Calaiz, si que elle y soit le premier jour daoust ou dedens le viij^e jour du dit mois au plus tart.

Le tiers est que le dit roy Dengleterre entent soy venir esbatre au dit lieu de Calaiz et es marches denviron et que il vouldroit moult que, quant il y sera, nossires de Berry et de Bourgogne ou lun deulx se traisissent par dela, car il prendroit grant plesir que ilz se esbatissent avecques lui, et aussi pourront parler ensemble sur le fait de lunion de leglise et de moult dautres choses touchant le bien et honneur de lui et du roy et de leurs royaumes.

Le quart est que, quant le patriarche Dalexandrie, le dit visconte et autres du conseil du roy furent ensemble devers le dit roy Dengleterre, son filz, ilz lui parlerent du fait de lunion de leglise et fu bailliee au dit roy Dengleterre une espitre faicte en luniversite de lestude de Paris touchant le dit fait de la dicte union, la quele le dit roy Dengleterre a envoiee a son estude de Oxennford' et a eu sur ce son conseil. Et que certains clercs du conseil du roy Dengleterre et de la dicte estude estans lors en la compagnie du dit chambellan diorient au roy ce que par dela a este advise sur ce, les quelz apportoient au roy une espitre faicte et composee par les clercs dicelle estude Doxennford', sicomme ilz lui diront plus pleinement.

Sur les quelz quatre poins le roy a fait response . . .

3. Letters of procuration giving Thomas, bishop of Carlisle, power to receive 100,000 gold francs from Charles VI as part of Queen Isabella's dowry. Westminster Palace, 7 November 1397 (Paris, Arch. Nat., J. 655, no. 16 ter: original, formerly sealed with the great seal (now lost) appended on a tongue).

Ricardus Dei gracia rex Anglie et Francie et dominus Hibernie, omnibus ad quos presentes littere pervenerint, salutem. Sciatis quod nos, de fidelitate et circumspeccione provida venerabilis patris Thome episcopi Karliolensis plenissime confidentes, eidem episcopo ad exigendum, petendum et recipiendum pro nobis et nomine nostro cum omni diligencia qua decet de carissimo patre nostro Francie aut ejus commissariis vel deputatis centum milia francorum auri et nobis in regno nostro Anglie usque presenciam nostram deferend' et prefato patri nostro litteras nostras acquietancie de predicta summa centum milium francorum inde confectas deliberandas et ad omnia alia que circa premissa necessaria fuerint et oportuna facienda et exequenda, prout ejus discrecioni videbitur convenire, plenam tenore presencium conferimus et committimus potestatem. Promittentes nos ratum, gratum et firmum habituros quicquid per prefatum episcopum actum vel gestum fuerit in premissis. In cujus rei testimonium has litteras nostras fieri fecimus patentes. Dat' in palacio nostro Westm' sub magni sigilli nostri testimonio vij die novembris, anno regni nostri vicesimo primo. Per ipsum regem. Stanley.

4. Royal letters of quittance for the same 100,000 gold francs, prepared in advance and sealed with the great seal, a blank being left for insertion of the name of Charles VI's official who was to give the money to the bishop of Carlisle. Westminster, 7 November 1397 (Paris, Arch. Nat., J. 655, no. 16: original, sealed with the great seal appended on a tongue; a step represents a lost wrapping-tie).

Richard par la grace de Dieu roi Dengleterre et de France et seignur Dirlande, a toutz ceux que cestes lettres verront ou orront, salutz. Come nostre trescher et tresame piere de Fraunce fuist tenuz de paier et bailler a nous a nostre certein mandement pur contemplacion del mariage fait entre nous et Isabelle, leisne file de nostre dit piere, oet centz mil francs dor, cestassavoir trois centz mil francs a lanel et solempnisacioun du dit mariage et cent mil francs a la fyn del an apres ycelle solempnisacioun et ainsi des lors en avant cent mil francs de an en an jesques au plein paiement dicelles oet centz mil francs, la quelle somme de trois centz mil francs nous furent baillez et paiez depar nostre dit pier par lez mayns de Raoul Danquetomul, soun esquier, le quart jour de novembre, lan de nostre regne vintisme. Savoir faisons que nous avons rescieu diccelluy nostre piere par les mayns de *Mychiel du Sablon*[81] a ceo commys depar luy la somme de cent mil francs, quelle nous devoit estre paiez a la fyn del primer an apres la solempnisacioun du dit mariage, de la quelle somme de cent mil francs nous tenons a bien contentz, paiez et agreez, et dycelle somme de cent mil francs pur le paiement del primer an suisdit et de toutes les accions et demandes que pur occasioun de mesme la somme de cent mil francs pur le paiement de le primer an suisdit purrons faire a nostre dit piere nous quitoms mesme nostre piere, ses heirs et successours perpetuelment et a toutz jours sanz ce que jammes en temps avenir nous, nostre dite compaigne ne les heirs et successours de nous et de ele en puissons ascune chose demander, requirer ne fair accion ou demande envers nostre dit pier, ses heirs et successours en quele manere que ce soit touchant les cent mil francs a nous ensi paiez pur le primer an suisdit. Et promettons en bone foye et en parole du roy avoir et tenir a toutz jours ferme et agreable ceste nostre presente quitance et contre la teneure dicelle noun venir ne fair venir en quelque manere que ceo soit en temps avenir. En tesmoignance de quele chose[82] nous avons fait faire cestes noz lettres patentes. Don' souz nostre grand seal a Westm' le vij jour de novembre, lan de nostre regne vynt et primer. Per ipsum regem. Stanley.

5. Letters of quittance issued in the name of the bishop of Carlisle and acknowledging receipt of the 100,000 gold francs. Paris, 19 December 1397 (Paris, Arch. Nat., J. 655, no. 16 bis: original, sealed with the bishop's seal appended on a tongue; a step represents a lost wrapping-tie).

Pateat universis per presentes quod nos Thomas permissione divina episcopus Karleon' de mandato excellentissimi principis et domini nostri metuendissimi domini Ricardi Dei gracia regis Anglie et Francie et virtute litterarum suarum, quarum tenor sequitur in hec verba: Ricardus . . . (*as above, no. 3*) . . . vicesimo primo. Predictam summam centum milium francorum dicto domino nostro regi debitam contemplacione et per tractatum matrimonii inter predictum dominum nostrum regem et Isabellam, primogenitam illustrissimi principis Karoli

---

[81] The last three words are in a different hand.
[82] *Chose* corrected from *choses*.

regis Francorum, contracti a dicto rege Francorum per manus Michaelis de Sabulone, receptoris generalis predicti regis Francorum, hodie numeravimus et recepimus et eidem regi Francorum litteras acquietancie dicti domini nostri regis suo magno sigillo sigillatas de dicta summa centum milium francorum tradidimus oportunas, et nos nomine domini nostri regis predicti in quantum nos tangit predictum regem Francorum et prefatum Michaelem de dicta summa centum milium francorum tenore presencium quietamus. In cujus rei testimonium sigillum nostrum fecimus hiis apponi. Dat' Parisius decimo nono die mensis decembris, anno prefati domini nostri regis vicesimo primo.

III

Thoughts about the Peasants' Revolt

V. H. GALBRAITH

FOR ALL practical purposes research upon the Peasants' Revolt begins with Bishop Stubbs's *Constitutional History*. This 'rising of the Commons' as with his usual precision he called it, clearly puzzled, even bewildered him,[1] as well it might for some of the sources we use today had not then been discovered! And in the ten closely packed pages he devoted to it, his footnotes show him struggling with the as yet unsorted materials at his disposal. Whatever we think of the results, Stubbs certainly did not underrate its importance. For him, in its 'indirect permanent results', it was 'one of the most portentous phenomena to be found in the whole of our history', a verdict with which I find myself in complete agreement. Between the *Constitutional History* and the first world war wider horizons of research opened out as the chancery enrolments were made available in calendars, and the poll tax records, the wardrobe books and much else were examined. In this advance the French joined, more especially Charles Petit Dutaillis and André Réville, whose *Soulèvement des travailleurs d'Angleterre en 1381* was of special importance. Interest in the Revolt was further stimulated by the discovery of various new literary sources of which the most important was the Anonimalle Chronicle of St Mary's, York,[2] with which I am here largely concerned.

---

[1] How bewildered is apparent from his long discussion of serfdom and manumission in vol iii, pp. 620 ff., where he leaves the problem to a time 'when we have a much more thorough investigation of the manorial records' (p. 624). This has now been done and more recent writers seek a solution in purely economic terms.
[2] *The Anonimalle Chronicle, 1333–1381*, edited by V. H. Galbraith (Manchester, 1927). I would here like to thank Dr Richard Hunt and Mr Clive Sneddon for valuable advice and help with this paper.

As a result of this expanding revelation, after the 1914–18 war the time seemed ripe for a new assessment of the enigmatic Richard II, the study of whose reign is still for me interwoven with memories of Maude Clarke. As early as 1926 she was engaged upon a 'Life', and a few years later she undertook the 1307–99 volume of the Oxford History of England, a task abruptly halted by her death in 1935; though not before she had published several 'trenchant' studies, which have inspired most later writers. The combination of a ruthlessly efficient scholarship, a lively imagination and an Irish sense of humour had already made her *primus inter pares*, and it was only after an interval of years that the Oxford History was undertaken by her friend and pupil, May McKisack. Miss McKisack's more than worthy fulfilment in 1959 of this heavy assignment is one of the reasons why her friends have written this book.

The Anonimalle Chronicle was published more than forty years ago, and its chief value to historians rests upon two passages, which it seemed to me then, had been 'lifted' entire by its monastic author from another (or possibly two other) narratives written in London. The first passage deals with the parliament of 1376 (pp. 79–94); the second, even more demonstrably borrowed, begins at the bottom of p. 133 with a brief preface and ends on p. 151 as follows:

et au darrein, come Dieu voilloit, le roy aperceivaunt qe trop des ses liges gentz serrount defaitz et moult saunk espandu, prist pitee en soun coer et conseilla ovesqe soun conseil, et fuist ordene par asseut qils deveroient avoir grace et pardoune de lour mesfaites, issint qils ne leverount iames apres sur payne de vie et membre et qe chescune des eux averoit une chartre de pardoune et paier al roy pur le fee del seal xxs. pur luy fair riche; et issint finist cest malveys guerre.

I am here concerned only to add, as it were, a long footnote to what I wrote forty years ago about this Peasants' Revolt insertion.

The view that these eighteen pages were 'the most valuable of surviving contemporary accounts' of 1381, was first advanced by George Kriehn in America[3] who decided that it was the work of 'someone who was in the following of the King—perhaps a courtier, clerk or lay'. Kriehn, who wrote *before* the discovery of

[3] *American Historical Review*, vii (1901), pp. 266–8.

the original manuscript from which the Chronicle was printed, further said that the admixture of English words and the idiom of the language all showed it to be the work of an Englishman. This struck me as a just conclusion and I merely went on to endorse it by quoting instances of the writer's remarkable acquaintance with the details of the royal administration, ending with the remark that 'perhaps Mr Kriehn's conclusions should be modified to the extent of assuming some clerk in the administration to be the author of the passage—possibly Thomas Hoccleve, the poet, who was all his life a clerk of the Privy Seal'.[4] Looking back, I regret Hoccleve—though he was only a suggestion—the more so as I want here to suggest a wholly new *possible* author. This is William Pakington, whom I think I would have preferred to Hoccleve in 1927 if the later volumes of Tout's *Chapters in the Administrative History of Mediaeval England* had then been in print.

It is rather a long story, which begins with a well-known passage from Leland's *Collectanea*, vol. i, part ii, p. 455:

Wylliam de Pakington, Clerk and Tresorer of Prince Edwardes, Sunne to Edwarde the 3. Household yn Gascoyne, did write a Cronique yn Frenche from the IX Yere of King John of Englande on to his tyme, and dedicated it to his Lord Prince Edwarde. Owte of an Epitome in French of this afore sayde Cronique I translatid carptim thes thinges that folow yn to Englische.

Eight pages of these extracts in English follow ending with the events of the year 1346. The next two pages of Leland's book are blank, and on p. 471 he begins further extracts from another manuscript.

F. W. D. Brie, a German, who edited the English *Brut Chronicle* (E.E.T.S.) claimed to have found this epitome, but Tout's insatiable curiosity seems to have shown that his discovery was just another mare's nest, and since Pakington's official career runs from the early sixties to 1390 he concluded wisely that the 'connection of Pakington with chronicle-making must therefore remain doubtful in the present state of our knowledge'.[5]

At this point it is relevant to summarize Pakington's career as

---

[4] *Anonimalle Chronicle*, p. xlii.

[5] Tout, *Chapters*, iv, pp. 194–5. For the later references see the admirable index in vol. vi.

Tout sets it out. He is first heard of in 1364 when he received protection as about to join the Black Prince's following in Aquitaine; and may have served him even earlier, though his name is not found among Tout's list of the Black Prince's household staff. After the prince's death in 1376 he became general receiver of his widow, the Princess Joan, until in the summer of 1377 he was made keeper of the king's wardrobe, an office he held continuously until his death in 1390, Reginald Hilton, a priest from the diocese of Lichfield becoming his controller. He received other preferments in this period—a house forfeited by John of Northampton in 1385, the deanery of the king's free chapel of Stafford, and the deanery of St Martin's-le-Grand, 'still a special preserve of wardrobe clerks'. His most interesting appointment was to the chancellorship of the exchequer in 1381, to which office he was posted for life, thus combining a 'household' with a 'state' department. It is difficult, as Tout says, to form any idea of Pakington's personality from these bald details. Yet they prove that though the new king's intimates are to be sought in the chamber, rather than the wardrobe, Pakington was a most trusted official, whose whole life was spent in the service successively of the prince, his widow and her son. It is also significant that his greatest promotion—the chancellorship of the exchequer for life—occurred immediately after the Peasants' Revolt. In the light of these facts is there ground for associating him with the account of the Revolt preserved in the Anonimalle Chronicle? To answer this question we must first speculate regarding the 'make-up' of the Anonimalle Chronicle as we have it: and secondly examine its evidence regarding the Black Prince, the Princess Joan and Richard II himself.

The Anonimalle Chronicle, though written by a monk of St Mary's Abbey, York, is the continuation of a French Brute whose author, one presumes, was not a monk, but a secular priest. As such it is different in kind from monastic chronicles. The Brute was intended for a wide public; while the appeal of monastic authors was—primarily at any rate—to their fellow monks, and those of neighbouring houses. The Anonimalle Chronicle repeatedly reflects the writer's borrowings from other sources, some of monastic provenance, others of the more popular Brute type. Of these borrowings the two most important, viz., the parliament of 1376 and the Peasants' Revolt, were not translations from a Latin

49

original, but extracts from a vivid, contemporary French narrative. All this suggests that the faithful William Pakington may well
have written a lost French chronicle, either as a memorial to his
dead master, the Black Prince, or in continuation of a narrative
begun before his death. Leland, who saw only an epitome of this
work, is at least good evidence that William Pakington wrote
some such work.

This, of course, is no more than an hypothesis, but there are two
things to be said in its favour.

(1) The account of the Peasants' Revolt in the Anonimalle
Chronicle has never received the attention it deserves from historians owing to the fact that from 1898 when G. M. Trevelyan
found Thynne's sixteenth-century transcript until 1927 when its
immediate source was printed in full scholars were somewhat loth
to prefer this late, inaccurate copy of a French MS to the more
detailed, Latin narratives of Thomas Walsingham and Henry
Knighton. By 1927 our historians had already made up their minds
about the Revolt, excusably suspicious of a narrative about London
written in Yorkshire. This latest-to-appear of all narratives has
thus had to make its way in the world of scholarship since 1927.
And this, in fact, it has done beginning with Tout's elaborate narrative, followed by Mr Anthony Steel's *Richard II* and some later
books. But long before the original MS turned up, the late Professor
James Tait—whose life of Richard II in the *Dictionary of National
Biography* is still valuable—showed that the Westminster Chronicle
(1381–94) in volume nine of the *Polychronicon* was firmly based on
our French text. To this I would now add a still more important
debtor, that is Thomas Walsingham himself, the greater part of
whose factual information is confined to St Albans and Bury St
Edmunds and neighbourhood. A close collation[6] would prove his
indebtedness to the Anonimalle author for events in London. The
same would be true of Henry Knighton who is also weak on what

[6] E.g. Walsingham, like the Anonimalle author, states that Richard II allowed
the commons to enter the Tower and seize Sudbury and Hales (i, p. 458). His
account, too, of the killing of John Legge, William Appleton, and the Flemings
(ibid., i, p. 462) groups these diverse happenings in the same way as the Anonimalle writer (p. 145). Walsingham was also intrigued by the mention of the 'dagger'
(p. 148) which he twice refers to (ibid., i, 464) 'cultello quem "daggere" vulgo
dicimus', repeated on p. 15 of vol. ii. So too Knighton mentions the *'cultellum
evaginatum* quem "dagger" vulgus vocant' (p. 137).

was the main revolt, that is events in London. All this strongly suggests that an authoritative French narrative, written very close to events, was widely known and used by monastic writers soon after the rising.

(II) The Anonimalle version itself supports such a conclusion. It gives valuable information about the last illnesses and death of both the Black Prince and Edward III, as well as intimate touches about Princess Joan not elsewhere found. To all this must be added the personal manner in which events in London are grouped around Richard II, standing 'pensive et triste' in a 'turret del graunde Toure de Loundres', surrounded by fifteen[7] frightened councillors, including Archbishop Sudbury, whose failure in the crisis is vividly brought out. And when, after Smithfield, it was all over 'le roy prist sa vay devers Loundres a sa garderope pur luy esere de sa graunde travaille'. William Pakington was keeper of the wardrobe at that moment. Nor do I need to repeat[8] the author's close acquaintance with the names and offices of so many minor officials in the royal service who perished in the revolt. Commentators have noted inaccuracies in regard to the Christian names of some of these, and also in his chronology. But this is no more than we should expect in the turmoil of those hectic days.[9] William Pakington's dates suggest that Leland was not wrong in attributing just such a work to him, of which fragments survive in the Anonimalle Chronicle for the parliament of 1376 and the Peasants' Revolt in 1381.

The literary sources for the fourteenth century pose a new problem for the medieval historian. They are trilingual—French, Latin and English—and each language has its own experts. The Latin sources are still the best for political history, since their authors were the most highly educated and in close social touch with the ruling class. But for the same reason they are at their worst when dealing with popular discontent, which, whether municipal or

[7] I seize the opportunity to correct an error on p. 139, l.17 of the *Anonimalle Chronicle* where the imaginary bishops—evesqes—are the scribe's mistake for 'ovesqe'=avec, with. This misled me in the Note on p. 195.

[8] *Anonimalle Chronicle*, p. xlii.

[9] Tout, *Chapters*, iii, p. 368, n. 4 is incorrect in stating that the Anonimalle Chronicle 'is seldom accurate with official titles'. His knowledge of the 'small fry' is astonishing, as is also his obvious familiarity with the topography of the Tower of London. He may well have been there as events happened.

rural, seemed to them equally and wholly abominable. For the Peasants' Revolt they actually mislead the historian by their uniform attitude of contempt, tempered by fear of the 'lower classes'. In Thomas Walsingham's eyes the rioters are not merely *bondi, villeins* but villains (*ganeones*), and those who led, sympathized with or helped them 'ministers of Satan'. So when he assesses the causes of 1381, he tells us that some people attributed the rising to the laxity of the bishops, especially as regards that 'mirror of hypocrites, sower of schism and plain liar', John Wycliffe. Others, he says, blamed the infidelity of the nobles; and a third group the criminality of the general public; while, for his part, he blames the friars, though, perhaps, he concludes we are all of us somewhat to blame.[10] Such is his 'last word' on the most elaborate and well documented account of the revolt that has come down to us. He has nothing to hide, but his narrative is 'like the ox and the ass, without understanding', for his raving hostility is impartially directed against both the rural serfs and the 'free' townsmen of St Albans, who—and it is a most significant fact—acted in partnership against the Abbey of St Albans. Elizabeth Levett devoted many years to the study of St Albans in the fourteenth century. She was a pioneer of economic history but the only clear moral that emerges from her book is that at St Albans agrarian policy was not consciously governed by economic arguments; for she found an unchanging adherence to the *status quo* before 1381 and, after the revolt, to the *status quo ante*. The barely intelligible economic analysis of high farming, the Black Death, the Statute of Labourers, etc. with which recent writers seek to explain the revolt takes little account of the living social attitudes and aspirations which really matter most, and for these we must turn to the vernacular sources, French and English.

These tell a different story, and outstandingly among them the Anonimalle Chronicler who though sharing the normal upper class prejudices of his time writes on a higher because a more realistic plane. He is no monk but a man of the world, concerned to tell a story to a general audience in very much the same way as a newspaper correspondent today. He is not writing for the Establishment, to whom the revolting peasants were a collection of

[10] Walsingham, ii, p. 15.

scoundrels, *capables de tout*. Contrariwise, he is trying simply to convey the thoughts and aspirations of the rioters. And so he pinpoints the actual occasion of the troubles, as the measures taken to enforce the poll tax of 1380, and tells us—with unique detail—exactly how and where it began, viz., in Fobbing and Corringham in Essex. Then, objectively, he traces the sequence of events to the final climax, setting out without comment the rebels' demands, and vividly conveying both their hopes and their fears. And so to its tragic end, quoted above. The king took pity on them at last, and arranged for charters of pardon 'at the usual rate'. For the chronicler, the core and meaning of the revolt are to be found in the march on London, under the leadership of Wat Tyler. To events elsewhere—what we should call today the 'sympathetic strikes' connected with the true rising—he devotes no more than two short paragraphs. The whole narrative is in a different key from the wild gossip of Walsingham and Knighton (whose narratives still colour and distort our books), and is therefore our best guide to the ideals and aims from which it sprang. What were these?

In the Anonimalle author's view the supreme and overriding purpose of the revolt was the abolition of villeinage and all that went with it. This was the heart of the matter: and he nowhere confounds this basic issue with the other, accidental elements, such as the town revolts, with which the monastic writers so persistently confuse it. Whether or no this demand for personal freedom before the common law was 'revolutionary' it most certainly was not 'new' or the product of such recent events as the Black Death, etc., which with the poll tax were its 'occasion'. The christian middle ages had taken over slavery from classical Rome and slowly transformed it into serfdom. We can already trace the dumb resentment of the unfree before the Norman Conquest in the death bed 'manumissions'.[11] or in the sorrows of Aelfric's ploughman, whose lot was almost unbearable 'because I am not free' (*quia non sum liber*).[12] By the late eleventh century the future of serfdom itself was in the balance as intellectual horizons widened. The church, Professor Southern tells us, was still ready to allow its rustics—with an eye towards Heaven—to incur willingly and for ever the taint of serf-

[11] *Diplomatarium Anglicum*, ed. B. Thorpe (1865), pp. 621–51.
[12] Aelfric's *Colloquy*, ed. G. N. Garmonsway (London, 1939), p. 21.

dom. But, *more suo*, he is careful to add: 'but there was another, less elevated view of the matter which was shared by the majority of men free and unfree alike . . . To nearly all men serfdom was without qualification, a degrading thing.'[13] And he quotes Gerald of Wales, who contrasted the light-heartedness of liberty (*hilaritas libertatis*) with the oppression of servitude. Some would question how and why the love of liberty is less 'exalted' than the view of the church; but however that may be, it is as old as political society itself.

In the twelfth century, as our sources multiply, we become aware of two new powerful forces at work. On the one hand, villeinage is formally embodied in the legal theory of English feudalism. 'The Dialogus de Scaccario' gives it in a few words: the lords are owners not only of the chattels but of the bodies of their *ascripticii*, they may transfer them wherever they please, and sell or otherwise alienate them if they like. Glanville and Bracton, Fleta and Britton follow in substance the same doctrine, although they use different terms.'[14] But simultaneously with the hardening of legal theory, we can trace a process of rapid *social* integration among the free and unfree peasants in village life. This is not brought about by the church, but by the state, which was revolutionizing English political society at every level. The unfree who as late as 1181 were not included in the Assize of Arms, by 1225 are found *iurati ad arma*, a crucial advance. Still more impressive is the evidence of the *Curia Regis Rolls*, edited by C. T. Flower, some of which were never seen by Vinogradoff and Maitland. From many of the cases there recorded we can actually reconstruct villein pedigrees. No unfree person could *de iure* plead in the king's court; but some in fact did so, and it is beyond question that many of these, owing to intermarriage, were themselves uncertain which side of the line they fell. The test, which a century later would have turned upon their services and dues, here repeatedly turns on birth —was the man's father free or unfree? Helen Cam, who examined these pedigrees commented that 'The sociological interest of these cases lies in the evidence they afford that in the life of a village where intermarriage went on so freely between freemen and villeins there can have been no class barriers along the line of legal

13 *The Making of the Middle Ages* (London, 1953), p. 106.
14 P. Vinogradoff, *Villainage in England* (Oxford, 1892), p. 44.

freedom and legal serfdom.'[15] The concentration in my lifetime upon legal and economic history has diverted recent attention from this and much other evidence. Both tend to argue in centuries, and their theories and abstractions[16] take no account of the unceasing social change which in every generation—then as now—alters the way in which the agricultural classes feel about their life and their condition. The thirteenth century is as full of the *communitas villae* as of the *communitas communitatum*, parliament. Before its close we meet with bondmen—unfree serfs—on juries, possessing their own seals and with them sealing their own charters. By the year 1300 the vast bulk of the population enjoyed, if that is the right word, a common village life, and serfdom had become an outrage, because it was now an anachronism. That it survived was due to the precocious growth of the common law in the same period, which remained to the end of the middle ages the deadly weapon of the 'possessioners', lay and clerical, against all aspirations towards a single, common citizenship. The anachronistic line it drew between bond and free was the real cause of 1381.

All this and just this can be safely inferred from the Anonimalle writer's succinct, objective and factual narrative; and the most astonishing fact about the Peasants' Revolt is not that it happened but that it had not happened long before. All that was best in the middle ages was long since on the way out: that they somehow rotted on for more than another century was due to a decadent aristocracy, a conservative Church Universal and the common law. I can find no justification for speaking of the 'oriental passivity' of the inferior classes at any time in the middle ages.[17] From start to finish they were full of ferment and violence, and their criminal records, preserved in the plea rolls, are far in excess, having regard to population, of those of later times; and the motive of most royal justice (*justitia*) was either money (*emolumentum*) or repression. Nor can we, with Powicke,[18] dismiss the Peasants'

[15] *Liberties and Communities in Medieval England* (Cambridge, 1944), p. 134.

[16] No historian—as opposed to a lawyer—could today accept Maitland's conclusion that Bracton by simplifying the contradictions inherent in serfdom 'greatly improved the legal position of the serf'. (See *History of English Law*, i, p. 430). The serf had by 1300 changed much more than the law.

[17] H. W. C. Davis, *England under the Normans and Angevins, 1066–1272*, (10th edn., London, 1930), p. 516.

[18] *Medieval England, 1066–1485*, p. 214.

Revolt as merely an 'incident' of no enduring importance in a world that stood for law, and 'hated all breaches of the peace'. What Stubbs called its 'indirect results' were decisive, and compared with continental Europe, rapid. What the state denied was silently achieved, though not till villeinage became economically unprofitable by the land-owning class. Villeinage was not abolished: it just faded away. This achievement again is as astonishing as it is significant, and the complicated process by which this happened owed much, perhaps everything, to the Revolt. *Some* incident!

This too may be safely inferred from the Anonimalle Chronicle, whose precise narrative differentiates sharply the Peasants' Revolt from the French Jacquerie. We are left in no doubt about the passionate loyalty to King Richard of the 'rebels' as we too lightly call them, who sought only to live under his full and Christian sovereignty, untrammelled by the 'traitors' surrounding him. Of these the two chief—the archbishop of Canterbury[19] and the treasurer, Hales—were deliberately sought out and put to death, and no doubt John of Gaunt would have shared their fate had he been at the Savoy. The rest of the council were not even names to the rustics who vented their hatred upon various humble government minions whose names are punctiliously recorded by the writer. So, though there was much 'communism' of the Christian variety, as for centuries before and centuries afterwards, the notion of the 'sovereignty of the proletariat' was wholly absent, and indeed inconceivable for centuries to come. There were, of course, many incidental victims, particularly lawyers, but much of the worst trouble arose around monastic boroughs, whose citizens joined in a movement purely rustic in origin. The sincerity, the restraint and the reasonableness of the rioters make them the poorest 'rebels' in English history, and they even left some of their number to guard the south-east coast from the French. Their single aim of legal enfranchisement seems to have enlisted some sympathy among their social superiors even during the troubles; and modern books still exaggerate events by over dependence upon the bitterly hostile chronicles of Walsingham and Knighton. In the

---

[19] George Holmes in *The Later Middle Ages* (London, 1962), p. 170, speaks of a 'crisis of anti-clerical feeling' at this time, citing Wycliffe, Chaucer and Langland. He might justly have added the rural commons in 1381, who firmly supported 'disendowment' of the Church. And none of it was new.

long run the studied moderation of the original rioters paid off and is beyond question the reason for their ultimate, if deferred, victory. But the middle ages, like Charles II, spent an 'unconscionable time a-dying', and with them vanished serfdom which had long since become an anachronism in England.

IV

Poet and Peasant

BEATRICE WHITE

'Petrus id est Christus'[1] are the words used by the poet Langland to mark the culmination of the process by means of which Piers Plowman, through progressive idealizations, is identified with Christ. But what appears on the first impact to be a startling, daring, even extravagant climax is, in fact, a mystical commonplace which admits the existence and growth of a divine element in *humanum genus* by the action of grace. Langland and Julian of Norwich were contemporaries. In her *Revelations of Divine Love* ('Revelation' 14, Chapter 51) Julian described and explained a remarkable 'shewing'. With minute particularity and vivid pictorial force she told how, in a vision, she saw God as a master, sitting in a wilderness, and standing by him, to his left, one clad as a labourer in toil-stained garments:

I saw the Lord sit stately, and the Servant standing reverently afore his Lord. In which Servant there is double understanding, one without, another within. Outwardly he was clad as a labourer which were got ready for his toil; and he stood full near the Lord, not evenly in front of him, but in part to one side, on the left. His clothing was a white kirtle, single, old, and all defaced, dyed with the sweat of his body, strait-fitting to him, and short, as it were a handful beneath the knee, thread-bare, seeming as it should soon be worn out, ready to be ragged and rent. . . . And inwardly in him was shewed a ground of love. . . . And then I understood that he should do the greatest labour and hardest travail: that is, he should be a gardener, delve and dyke, toil and sweat, and turn the earth upside-down, and seek the deepness and water the plants in time. . . . In the Servant is comprehended the Second Person

[1] *Piers Plowman*, B text, XV. 206. A similar identification was suggested with poignant dramatic relevance by Hartmann von Aue, years earlier, in his *Der arme Heinrich* (1199). The little maiden, who yearned to sacrifice her life to save her lord, saw Paradise in terms of her daily environment and Jesus as a free peasant. The so-called 'Christ of the Trades' mural is, perhaps, best interpreted as a warning to wantons against swearing.

58

in the Trinity, and in the Servant is comprehended Adam, that is to say, All-man. And therefore when I say the Son it meaneth the Godhead which is even with the Father; and when I say the Servant, it meaneth Christ's Manhood, which is rightful Adam.[2]

The double significance of this allegory with its wealth of realistic imagery admits, as Langland's poem does, full realization of the central role played in medieval life by the labourer both practically and symbolically.

Poet and mystic could have found authority for this emphasis in the Scriptures, both Old and New Testaments, and in classical literature, too, had either possessed the equipment of learning. The Jews were a pastoral and nomadic people and their language was rich in allusions to the vital work of shepherds and husbandmen. Was not Abel a shepherd and Cain a tiller of the soil? 'The Lord is my Shepherd', said the psalmist (*Ps.* 23) and found an echo in the New Testament's 'I am the good shepherd' (*John* x. 11 and 14), and 'My Father is the husbandman' (*John* xv. 1). Roman literature had an honourable place for the farmer, and a keen appreciation of his toil. Horace loved his Sabine farm and had a special affection for his country mouse (*Sat.* II. 6), and the *Georgics* bear witness to a great poet's practical knowledge of rural crafts and praise of those who could make plants grow. Cicero summed up the Roman attitude in his *De Officiis*: 'omnium rerum quibus aliquid acquiritur, nihil est agricultura melius, nihil uberius, nihil dulcius, nihil homine libero dignius'. A similar recognition of the worth and dignity of the work of the agricultural labourer gave the impetus to both poet and mystic, Langland and Julian, to develop and exploit a symbol of universal significance.

It has been pertinently observed that in medieval times the views and doings of the middle and lower classes were seldom reported except by prejudiced, hostile witnesses.[3] Monk and cleric were violently biased against the peasant though they occasionally paid grudging tribute to the men whose life of labour provided their food. Aelfric's *Colloquy*, in Latin with an interlinear English gloss, is in the form of a dialogue between master and pupils, who, for

---

[2] *Revelations of Divine Love*, ed. Grace Warrack. (6th edn., London, 1917), p. 107.

[3] *Historical Poems of the Fourteenth and Fifteenth Centuries*, ed. R. H. Robbins (New York, 1959), p. xli.

the purpose of enlarging the vocabulary of those learning Latin, profess many occupations including husbandry in its various branches—hard labour for the workman, 'because I am not free' (*quia non sum liber*). This Anglo-Saxon summary of rural duties with its reference to the hard lot of the un-free anticipates the detailed manuals of the thirteenth century and is vastly different in tone from the typical monkish censures of Bernard of Cluny, who, in his *De Contemptu Mundi*, considered the tiller of the fields to be wickedly perfidious, unscrupulously acquisitive, and litigious, for 'Hora novissima, tempora pessima sunt, vigilemus'. Few peasants were credited with the brains to batter their way into Paradise. Their place was below.

There are exceptions to the prevailing hostility, and sometimes a clerk will allow a rustic to score in a match of wits and have the last word. In his *Documentum de arte versificandi* Geoffrey of Vinsauf inserted the dialogue *De clericis et rustico*, based on a tale in the *Disciplina clericalis* of Petrus Alphonsi, which recognizes the shrewdness and quick wit of a *rusticus* on pilgrimage in the company of two clerks. In general, though, the peasant was regarded far more often with contempt than understanding. The author of *The Owl and the Nightingale* had no doubts about the rustic:

> A-sumere chorles awedeþ
> & uorcrempeþ & uorbredeþ;
> hit nis for luue noþeles,
> ac is þe chorles wode res;
> vor wane he haueþ ido his dede,
> ifallen is al his boldhede,
> habbe he istunge under gore
> ne last his luue no leng more.

The *De Arte honeste amandi* (c. 1185) of Andreas Capellanus, written at the behest of Countess Marie of Champagne, discusses, in the twelfth chapter of the first book, the role peasants, male and female, might be expected to play in the entrancing game of love:

It rarely happens that we find farmers serving in Love's court, but naturally, like a horse or a mule, they give themselves up to the work of Venus, as nature's urging teaches them to do. For a farmer hard labor and the uninterrupted solaces of plough and mattock are sufficient. . . . And if you should, by some chance, fall in love with some of their women, be careful to puff them up with lots of praise and then, when you find a convenient place, do not hesitate to take what you seek and to embrace them by force. For you can hardly soften their outward inflexibility so far that they will grant you one of their embraces quietly or permit you the solaces you desire unless first you use a little compulsion as a convenient cure for their shyness.[4]

The whole document, with its final retraction (cf. Chaucer's *Parson's Tale*) is better interpreted as a *jeu d'esprit* rather than as a serious practical guide to 'virtuous loving' (*honeste amandi*).

The sober chapter on serfs in the *De Proprietatibus Rerum* of Bartholomew Anglicus (*c.* 1250) was, as far as it concerned England, largely outdated when Trevisa translated it in 1397. But it conveys an attitude and a warning: 'A bondservant suffereth many wrongs, and is beat with rods, and constrained and held low with divers and contrary charges and travails among wretchedness and woe. Unneth he is suffered to rest or to take breath.' This is bad enough but hark what follows: 'When they be not held low with dread, their hearts swell, and wax stout and proud, against the commandments of their sovereigns. Dread maketh bond men and women meek and low, and goodly love maketh them proud and stout and despiteful.'[5]

The writer of the following lines knew what he was talking about:

> He that aye has lived free
> May not know well the property,
> The anger, nor the wretched doom
> That is coupled to foul thraldom.
> But, if he had assayed it,
> Then all *par coeur* he should it wit,
> And should think freedom more to prize
> Than all the gold in world that is.

He was John Barbour (1316?–95), archdeacon of Aberdeen, a serf-owner and dealer, who had the opportunity to observe the sufferings and frustrations of the un-free at first-hand, and the detachment to comment on them.

---

[4] Andreas Capellanus, *The Art of Courtly Love*, with Introduction, translation and notes by John Jay Parry (New York, 1941), p. 149. Cf. the opening lines of the *Wife of Bath's Tale*.
[5] Lib. VI, cap. 12.

In thirteenth-century Germany the knightly philanderer Neidhart von Reuenthal represented himself as an irresistible magnet to the village maidens but was wary of the village youths and resentful of their pretensions in aping the dress and manners of their social superiors. In his view the male peasants were brutal and aggressive, 'poor, clumsy louts', and he wondered how the girls could endure them. His contemporary, Wernher der Gartenaere, had a very keen appreciation of the vital importance of the farmer to the community and in his *Meier Helmbrecht* (*c.* 1250) he put into the mouth of the old father of a wilful son a strong conviction of the value of peasant labour:

> Lieber sun, daz waerest dû,
> ob dû mir woldest volgen nû,
> sô bûwe mit dem phluoge;
> sô geniezent dîn genuoge:
> dîn geniuzet sicherlîche,
> der arme und der rîche,
> dîn geniuzet wolf und ar
> und alliu crêatiure gar,
> und swaz got ûf der erden
> hiez ie lebendic werden.
> lieber sun, nû bouwe
> jâ wirt vil manec frouwe
> von dem bûwe geschoenet:
> manec künec wint gekroenet
> von des bûwes stiuwer.
> wan niemen wart sô tiuwer,
> sîn hôchvart waere kleine,
> wan durch daz bû aleine.[6]

This sympathy, dramatically relevant in the poem, is exceptional. The prevailing clerkly prejudice finds expression in the songs of the Goliards and in such Latin poems as the *Altercatio rusticorum et clericorum* which ends with the clerks victorious.[7]

Town and country encroached on each other in the fourteenth

[6] Ed. C. E. Gough (Oxford, 1942), ll. 543–60. 'Till with the plough and many people, poor and rich, will undoubtedly profit from your way of life. So too, you will even profit wolf and eagle and every creature living on earth. Through the farmer's toil many a woman will be made more lovely, and because of the farm's produce many a king will be crowned. In fact there is no one so high in rank that his pride would not be humbled were it not for the farmer.'

[7] F. J. E. Raby, *Secular Latin Poetry* (Oxford, 1934), ii, p. 305.

century. Townsmen were familiar with rural sights and occupations, especially if, like Langland, they had drifted to London
from provincial communities. This century of disturbances, war,
pestilence, revolts, famines, and civil convulsions leading to great
economic changes, saw, as society grew more complex, the rise of
a class of prosperous peasants, the yeomanry. Three major poets
emerged in England in this time of social upheaval. Langland,
Chaucer, and Gower were each aware, in varying degrees, of the
important contribution made by the husbandman to the development of his country's economy. From the first sudden, compelling
appearance of Piers Plowman in the poem that bears his name we
are aware of his dynamic magnetism, and the poet's purposeful
manipulation of a symbol of such potency:

'Peter!' quod a plowman, and put forth his hed,
'I knowe hym [Truth] as kyndely as clerke doþ his bokes.'[8]

Perhaps the close juxtaposition here of ploughman and clerk is not
altogether fortuitous.

Langland was well acquainted with poverty, its griefs and pains,
and could write convincingly of the sad lot of the poor shared by
Piers:

'I have no peny' quod Peres 'poletes forto bigge,
Ne neyther gees ne grys but two grene cheses,
A few cruddes and creem and an hauer cake,
And two loues of benes and bran ybake for my fauntis.'[9]

The poet's inspiration, like that of the mystics, is strongly pictorial and makes a massive breach in the emotional defences of the
hearer or reader:

poure folke in Cotes,
Charged with childrene, and chef lordes rente,
That thei with spynnynge may spare spenen hit in houshyre,
Bothe in mylke and in mele to make with papelotes,
To a-glotye with here gurles that greden after fode.'[10]

The hunger, the cold, the waking in the night to rock the
cradle, the carding and combing of wool, the patching and washing
of clothes, the relentless round of work made it hard to describe

[8] B Text, v. 544. C VIII. 183.   [9] B Text, VI. 282.   [10] C Text, X. 72 ff.

the painful lot of women 'that wonyeth in Cotes'. But there were
others who suffered from hunger and thirst, who tried to keep up
appearances and were too proud to beg from neighbours:

> Ther is payn and peny-ale as for a pytaunce y-take,
> Colde flessh and cold fyssh for veneson ybake,
> Frydayes and fastyng-dayes a ferthyng worth of muscles
> Were a feste for suche folke other so fele Cockes.

The poor man had few comforts:

> For smoke & smolder smyteth in his eyen,
> Til he be blere-nyed, or blynde, and hors in the throte,
> Cougheth, and curseth that Cryst gyf hem sorwe
> That sholde brynge in better wode, or blowe it til it brende.[11]

But in times of plenty the labourers became demanding—bluster-
ing forth, like beasts, to their desperate amusements:

> Laboreres þat haue no lande to lyue on but her handes,
> Deyned nouȝt to dyne a-day nyȝt-olde wortes.
> May no peny-ale hem paye, ne no pece of bakoun,
> But if it be fresch flesch other fische fryed other bake,
> And þat *chaude* or *plus chaud* for chillyng of here mawe.
> And but if he be heighlich huyred ellis wil he chyde,
> And þat he was werkman wrouȝt waille þe tyme.[12]

Then the taverns rang to their laughter and horseplay as a violent
reaction to their normal lives of monotonous drudgery:

> þer was laughyng and louryng, and "Let go þe cuppe!"
> And seten so til euensonge, and songen vmwhile.[13]

When Piers addressed the Knight he cautioned him:

> And mysbede nouȝte þi bonde-men þe better may þow spede,
> þowgh he be þyn vnderlynge here, wel may happe in heuene,
> þat he worth worthier sette and with more blisse,
> þan þow, bot þou do bette, and lyue as þow shulde;
> *Amice, ascende superius.*

[11] B Text, XVII. 323.   [12] B Text, VI. 309.
[13] B Text, V. 345. cf. *Jacob and Josep* (13th century):
> While men loueden meri song, gamen and feire tale,
> Now hem is wel leuere gon to þe nale
> Vcchen out þe gurdel and rume þe wombe,
> Comen erliche þider and sitte þer ful longe.

For in charnel atte chirche cherles ben yuel to knowe,
Or a kniȝte fram a knaue þere.[14]

The forceful but obvious commonplace had a wide currency in the
Middle Ages, deriving from Seneca and such texts as *Job* III.19 and
Colossians IV.I, and had already been memorably expressed by
Walter von der Vogelweide in the preceding century.[15]

The theoretical liberal and practical conservative John Gower,
moralist and landowner, looked at the peasant with distrust and
suspicion, if not positive dislike. In his French work, *Mirour de
l'Omme* (*Speculum Meditantis*), a discursive allegorical poem on
current abuses, in which all ranks of society were weighed in the
balance and found wanting, Gower discovered evil rampant everywhere in a world all of whose inhabitants were equally bad.
Impressive as the cumulative weight of this is, it is really the rhetorical amplification through hundreds of lines of a common
axiom of medieval morality. Gower was certainly aware of
trouble brewing, which, in the Latin *Vox Clamantis* he described
erupting. Written probably between 1376 and 1379 the *Mirour de
l'Omme* testified to the prevailing discontent:

> Trop vait le mond du mal en pis.
> Qant cil qui garde les berbis
> Ou ly boviers en son endroit
> Demande a estre remeriz
> Pour son labour plus que jadys
> Le mestre baillif ne soloit . . .

The upper classes seemed disastrously unaware of mounting
danger:

[14] B Text, VI. 46.
[15] Seneca, *Epistulae Morales*, 47: 'Reflect that the man you call your slave was
born of the same seed, has the same good sky above him, breathes as you do, lives
as you do, dies as you do. . . . Whenever the thought of the powers you wield
over your slave comes into your head, let it come into your head also that your
master wields the same powers over you.' Compare *Job*, III, 19: 'The small and
great are there, and the servant is free from his master,' and *Colossians* IV. I: 'Masters, give unto your servants that which is just and equal: knowing that ye also
have a Master in heaven.' The poor had, through Christianity, acquired a status
denied to them earlier. See W. de Burgh, *Legacy of the Ancient World*, p. 225, n. I:
'Prior to Christianity the Greek word for "poor" (ptóchos) was used in a deprecia-
tory sense to mean one who cringes and begs.'

Me semble que la litargie
Ad endormi la seignourie,
Si qu'ils de la commune gent
Ne pernont garde a la folie,
Ainz souffront croistre celle urtie
Quelle est du soy trop violent.

The world was upside-down. Labourers, once simply clad, were decked out in unsuitable finery and their masters behaved like churls:

La povre gent voi plus haltein
Qe celly q'est leur soverein.
Chascuns a son travers se tire;
Car ly seignour sont plus vilein
Et plus ribald que n'est vilein,
Et pour mal faire et pour mal dire.

But all had a common ancestry in Adam and Eve:

Tous suismes d'un Adam issuz,
Combien que l'un soit au dessus
En halt estat, et l'autre en bass;
Et tous au mond naquismes nudz.

Three things were equally calamitous, flood, fire, and the common people when they gained control and proved immune to reason or discipline:

Trois choses sont d'une covyne,
Qui sanz mercy font la ravine
En cas q'ils soient au dessus:
L'un est de l'eaue la cretine.
L'autre est du flamme la ravine,
Et la tierce est des gens menuz
La multitude q'est commuz:
Car ja ne serront arrestuz
Par resoun ne par discipline,
Et pour cela sanz dire plus,
Ainz que le siecle en soit confus,
Bon est a mettre medicine.[16]

In the Latin *Vox Clamantis* the peasantry appeared brutal and

[16] *Mirour de l'Omme*, ed. G. C. Macaulay (Oxford, 1901), ll. 26438 ff., 23389 ff., 26497 ff.

raging, and in the English *Confessio Amantis* there was no room for them in an allegory completely courtly in style and content.

Gower had sounded the tocsin. But his friend, Chaucer, seemed deaf to it and did not allow his awareness of the disturbed times he lived in to ruffle the serene mood of his poetry or agitate the smooth surface of his verse. To this great poet the violent revolt of 1381 was a small affair like the farmyard hubbub when a cock is stolen by a fox. His *saeva indignatio* worked subtly through irony and cut more keenly because of the concealment. Chaucer had not, like Langland, plumbed the depths of poverty in a cot on Cornhill; he had not, like Gower, recoiled before the reckless rabble in action. The fringes of poverty he saw, and he understood the ways and speech of such 'churls' as came within his orbit. His attitude to the poor was the conventional one of pity, with recognition of the commonplace concerning equality resorted to both by Langland and by Gower.

If we compare Chaucer's Plowman with Langland's Piers, we are comparing a correct rhetorical exercise with a perception of something 'far more deeply interfused'—a spiritual experience. Chaucer's Plowman, like his brother, the Parson, is altogether too good to be true. The lines describing him are like a panegyric or a saint's legend. He is the essence of perfection. Maybe the poet, remembering the conventions of classical satire with its belief in a Golden Age providing an ideal standard as a yardstick by which to measure contemporary vice and condemn it, used a refinement of actuality to describe his 'good' characters, in order to delineate his rascals and ruffians more clearly by contrast, and bring them into sharper focus. Or perhaps he was saying, 'This is how the *rusticus*, the *villanus*, *ought* to behave. But just take a look round and you'll see for yourselves how it is', and by a double irony he was presenting the best so that the worst should be the more conspicuous. Notice that his paragon was properly attired and mounted according to his station:

> A trewe swynkere and a good was he,
> Lyvynge in pees and parfit charitee.
> God loved he best with al his hoole herte
> At alle tymes, thogh him gamed or smerte,
> And thanne his neighebor right as hymselve.
> He wolde thresshe, and therto dyke and delve,

For Christes sake, for every povre wight,
Withouten hire, if it lay in his myght.
His tithes payde he ful faire and wel,
Bothe of his propre swynk and his catel.
In a tabard he rood upon a mere.[17]

Langland had tasted poverty; Gower dreaded its effects.
Chaucer, the detached observer, recorded its disciplined virtues
rather than its vices. The poor widow 'somdeel stape in age',
whose barnyard saw the rape of the learned and vain Chauntecleer,
'in pacience ladde a ful symple lyf, For litel was hir catel and hir
rente'. Three large sows she had, three cows and a sheep called
'Malle'. Her 'narwe cotage, Biside a grove, stondynge in a dale',
had two sooty rooms—a bower where she slept, and a hall where
she ate: 'Repleccioun ne made her nevere sik; Attempre diete was
al her phisik'. The 'old rebekke', Mabely, in the *Friar's Tale* did
not possess twelve pence but was a successful curser. Griselda grew
to maturity in 'a throop, of site delitable' on a 'lusty playn
habundant of vitaille', 'povreliche yfostered up', and knowing
'wel labour, but noon ydel ese'. While she watched her few sheep
she span, and brought home 'wortes or othere herbes', 'The
whiche she shredde and seeth for hir lyvynge, And made hir bed
ful hard and nothyng softe'. We all know what happened to her,
but peihaps are not familiar with Boccaccio's comment on her
story: 'even into the cots of the poor the heavens let fall at times
spirits divine, as into the palaces of kings souls that are fitter to
tend hogs than to exercise lordship over men'.

The Prologue to the *Man of Law's Tale* was deeply indebted to
Pope Innocent's *De Contemptu Mundi* and gave a searing picture of
'impatient' poverty:

If thou be povre, farwel thy reverence!
Yet of the wise man take this sentence:
'Alle the dayes of povre men been wikke.'

If thou be povre, thy brother hateth thee,
And alle thy freendes fleen from thee, allas!

These lines had a muted echo in the description of Poverty in the
translation of the *Roman de la Rose* generally attributed to Chaucer:

[17] *Canterbury Tales*, ed. F. N. Robinson (Cambridge, Mass. 2nd edn., 1957),
p. 25. *Prologue*, l. 531.

Pover thing, wherso it be,
Is shamefast and dispised ay.
Acursed may wel be that day
That povere man conceyved is;
For, God wot, al to selde, iwys,
Is ony povere man wel yfed,
Or wel araied or wel clad,
Or wel biloved, in sich wise
In honour that he may arise.

The attitude to poverty of the old woman in the *Wife of Bath's Tale*
was dictated by Boethius and Dante:

Al were it that myne auncestres were rude
Yet may the hye God, and so hope I,
Grante me grace to lyven vertuously.
Thanne am I gentil, whan that I bigynne
To lyven vertuously and weyve synne.

We can hardly avoid the conclusion that Chaucer's view of
poverty was a bookish one. The majority of his peasants belonged
not to the oppressed, but to the more affluent members of their
class, on their way up the social ladder, people more likely than
their unfortunate brothers to come to the personal notice of a
government official.

These three men—Langland, Gower, Chaucer—were the outstanding English poets of the fourteenth century. We can now ask,
'Did the rank and file of versifiers, the anonymous poets and
scribblers, the minstrels, the ballad-writers, ever stop to consider
the lot of the peasantry?' Most certainly they did, and some give
the impression of being sincerely concerned about, if not intimately
involved in, the hard lot of the farm-worker. About 1300 someone wrote the *Song of the Husbandman* preserved in Harley manuscript 2253. It enumerated the specific grievances that farmers had
against grasping officials, the hayward, the woodward and the
bailiff. In able alliterative verse and linking stanzas the poet complained bitterly of the exploitation of the poor by heavy taxation
and extortion:

Luþer is to leosen þer-ase lutel ys,
& haueþ monie hynen þat hopieþ þer-to:
þe hayward heteþ vs harm to habben of his;

þe bailif bockneþ vs bale & weneþ wel do;
þe wodeward waiteþ vs wo, þat lokeþ vnder rys;
ne mai vs ryse no rest, rycheis ne ro.
þus me pileþ þe pore, þat is of lute pris.
nede in swot & in swynk swynde mot swo.
Nede he mot swynde, þah he hade swore,
þat haþ nout en hod his hed forte hude.
þus wil walkeþ in lond, & lawe is forlore,
& al is piked of þe pore, þe prikyares prude.[18]

This was pretty plain speaking, but it was surpassed by the author
of *Pierce the Plowman's Crede* who was deeply resentful of the
bitter misery endured by the poor:

And as I wente be the weie wepynge for sorowe,
I seigh a sely man me by opon the plow hongen . . . .
His wiif walked him with, with a long gode,
In a cutted cote cutted full heyghe,
Wrapped in a wynwe-schete to weren hire fro weders,
Barfote on the bare iis that the blod folwede.
And at the londes ende lay a litell crom-bolle,
And theron lay a litell childe lapped in cloutes,
And tweyne of tweie yeres olde opon a-nother syde.
And alle they songen o songe that sorwe was to heren;
They crieden all o cry—a carefull note.
The sely man sighede sore and seide: 'Children, beth stille!'[19]

Such lines enshrine a moment of truth caught with vivid intensity
and in the cruel details—the ragged ploughman guiding his
exhausted, half-starved oxen, the patient, bare-foot wife marking
the snow with her blood-stained footprints, the little child weep-
ing in its 'crumb-bowl' at the end of a furrow—we are spared
nothing of the hopeless distress suffered by a tiller of the soil.

The *Plowman's Tale*,[20] dated by Skeat *c.* 1395 and attributed to
the author of the *Crede* (*c.* 1394) is a religious allegory with a pro-

[18] *Historical Poems of the Fourteenth and Fifteenth Centuries*, ed. R. H. Robbins
(New York, 1959), p. 7. Compare the poem *Money, money* (Robbins, p. 134):
The plowman hym-selfe dothe dyge & delue
In storme, snowe, frost, and rayne,
money to get with laboure and swete—
yet small geynes and muche peyne.'

[19] *Pierce the Plowman's Crede*, ed. W. W. Skeat (Early English Text Society,
1906), ll. 420 ff.

[20] *Chaucerian and Other Pieces*, ed. W. W. Skeat (Oxford, 1897), p. 148.

logue describing a ploughman's forthright reaction to current injustices. He is represented as tired-out, sweaty, ragged and sunburnt:

> Our host him axed, 'What man art thou?'
> 'Sir,' quod he, 'I am an hyne;
> For I am wont to go to the plow,
> And erne my mete yer that I dyne.
> To swete and swink I make a vow,
> My wyf and children therwith to fynd,
> And serve God, and I wist how,
> But we lewd men ben fully blynd.'

The tyranny which condemned him to harsh toil he attributed to the practices of 'clerks', the traditional enemies of the *rusticus*:

> For clerkes saye, we shullen be fayn
> For hir lyvelod [to] swete and swinke,
> And they right nought us give agayn,
> Neyther to ete ne yet to drinke.
> They mowe by lawe, as they sayn,
> Us curse and dampne to helle brinke;
> Thus they putten us to payn,
> With candles queynt and belles clinke.
>
> They make us thralles at hir lust,
> And sayn, we mowe nat els be saved;
> They have the corn and we the dust,
> Who speketh ther-agayn, they say he raved.[21]

How the Ploughman learned his Paternoster strikes a different note. This ploughman was highly skilled in all branches of husbandry and his application had brought him wealth:

> His hall rofe was ful of bakon flytches,
> The chambre charged was with wyches
> Full of eggs, butter, and chese,
> Men that were hungry for to ease;
> To make good ale, malte had he plentye.

[21] The prose tract *Jack Upland*, ed. P. L. Heyworth (Oxford, 1968), some years later, noticed with strong disapproval that labourers were leaving the land for the towns: 'To þe comoun peple haþ Anticrist gouun leue to leue her trewe laboure and bicome idil men ful of disceitis to bigile eche oþere, as summe bicome men of crafte & marchauntis professid to falsnes.'

> And Martylmas befe to hym was not deyntye;
> Onyons and garlyke had he inowe,
> And good creme, and mylke of the cowe.
> Thus by his labour ryche was he in dede.[22]

In geniality of atmosphere this poem, a good-natured moral fable, suggests the jolly shepherd of Balliol manuscript 354:

> His name was called Joly Joly Wat,
> For he was a gud herdes boy,
>   Ut hoy!
> For in his pipe he made so much joy,

and the poem *Speed the Plough* which praised the work of the farmer and begged a blessing on those who cherished him:

> Gode lete hem wel to spede,
> & longe gode lyfe to lede,
> All þat for plowe-men pray.

Moreover the poet recognized the important basic fact that:

> The merthe of alle þis londe
> Maketh þe gode husbonde,
> With erynge of his plowe.[23]

The Robin Hood cycle of ballads is pure yeomanry material and it is worth noticing that Robin demanded special protection for the farmer:

> Loke ye do no husbande harm
> That tylleth with his plough.[24]

Both tillers of the soil and shepherds appeared in the Miracle Cycles and were developed as grotesques (e.g. Cain) and used as vehicles for criticism of contemporary abuses (e.g. *Prima and Secunda Pastorum*, Wakefield cycle). It is through the shepherds in the Nativity scenes of this cosmic drama that contemporaneity envelops the Gospel narrative most successfully, for the life of the shepherd, like that of the farmer, is a basic existence and universal.

---

[22] *Reliquiae Antiquae*, ed. T. Wright and J. O. Halliwell (1841), i, p. 43.
[23] *Early English Lyrics*, ed. E. K. Chambers and F. Sidgwick (London, 1926), pp. 127, 241; *Historical Poems*, ed. R. H. Robbins, p. 97.
[24] *Little Geste of Robin Hood*, stanza XIII.

Pastoral poetry, with its opportunities for escapism, allegory, and satire, is beyond the scope of this essay.

We should notice that already in the thirteenth century the words *rusticus* and *villanus* were terms of abuse, reflecting the general inimical attitude to the medieval peasant. But the Anglo-Saxon word *ceorl* had an honourable connotation. Dunnere, the 'unorne ceorl' of Maldon, was a 'plain, blunt man'. The word suffered a steady deterioration in sense until in *Havelok* (*c.* 1300) churls are reckoned to be of 'Cain's kin' (l. 2045) and lumped together with the 'eotenas, ylfe ond orcneas' of *Beowulf*, monsters all, like Grendel, deformed and degenerate descendants of the first murderer.[25] Churls were held to be surly oafs and as such they were traditionally described in the 'class-ridden' romances, where they appear as creatures shockingly brutalized by toil whose preposterously horrible features were transferred to those elemental, fearsome beings of chaotic force—the giants of venerable antiquity who are stock characters in these poems. Both churl and giant provided a violent contrast to courtly heroes invented for the entertainment of a leisured class. The Fabliaux, another product for the leisured class, if we are to trust the evidence of the expensive manuscripts in which they are preserved, see the peasant as shrewd, calculating, full of low cunning, as well as envy, greed, malice and the rest of the seven deadly sins.

The traditional churlish giants of the fourteenth-century romances were completely evil. A projection, perhaps, of primitive fears into tales intended to admonish as well as to amuse and entertain, they never deviated from wrong-doing. They were the embodiment of terrors like those aroused by the revolt of 1381 when the peasants made a bid for freedom and were seen in nightmares of hideous and frightening ugliness by the poet Gower. In fact medieval poets, as might be expected, were often prejudiced and unreliable witnesses to the hard lot of the peasant, tending to present him as humble saint, surly, embittered serf, carousing bumpkin, patient toiler, or menacing figure of evil. The mirror they held up to nature distorted the reflections in one direction or

[25] According to Rabbinical legend Cain, conceived after the disobedience and before the true repentance of Adam and Eve, was the ancestor of all monsters. Cf. *Beowulf*, l. 111. There may be some connection here with the apocryphal *Book of Enoch* which equates giants with evil spirits. See *Old English Newsletter*, iii, (Ohio) R. E. Kaske, '*Beowulf* and the *Book of Enoch*'.

another and it is seldom that a wholly recognizable portrait in clear perspective and balanced proportions emerges from the conflicting patterns. Balance, perhaps, is the keyword here. Between poets and chroniclers lies a thorny barrier of intention, and all the difference between literal, factual truth, and imaginative, emotional truth. We should be unwise to use poets or chroniclers in isolation as guides along the 'wikked' way to truth which, in all its cochleary windings, is sufficiently daunting and tortuous to defeat the capacity of any one individual to negotiate it. Poetry and chronicle supplement each other as memorials of the past and must be studied in conjunction if we are to arrive at a fuller comprehension of life in previous ages.

V

English Foreign Policy 1388-99

J. J. N. PALMER

NO FEATURE of Richard II's personal rule has been more severely or more unanimously criticized than his foreign policy. In his alleged anxiety to obtain assistance from France against his domestic enemies, he is believed to have sought peace with her 'whatever the cost', sacrificing English interests abroad to the extent of becoming virtually a French puppet, 'an upholder of French policy in Europe'. He surrendered Cherbourg, then Brest; married a French princess; tamely followed the French lead during the Schism; offered to assist Charles VI to conquer north Italy; and, in general, desisted from any action which might annoy the French court. 'He promised everything he was asked by Charles VI and his uncles, and in so doing lost the respect and ultimately the support of his own subjects.' But even this was not the full extent of his foolhardiness. For having alienated most Englishmen by his craven attitude to France over the better part of a decade, he then proceeded to antagonize the French by making a fantastic bid for the imperial crown in 1397. As a result, when Henry of Lancaster invaded England in the summer of 1399 he did so with French backing, yet was everywhere received as a champion of English interests vis-à-vis France.[1]

If any one of these charges were warranted, then there could be no two views as to the merits of Richard's foreign policy. Yet there are grounds for believing that the entire indictment is a travesty of the facts. In the long list of his 'crimes and failings' compiled in 1399, there is only one reference to Richard's relations with

I would like to express my gratitude to my colleague, Dr H. A. Lloyd, for his most helpful criticisms of the final draft of this essay.
[1] E. Perroy, *The Hundred Years' War* (London, 1951), pp. 197, 199; D.M. Bueno de Mesquita, 'The Foreign Policy of Richard II in 1397: Some Italian Letters', *E.H.R.*, lvi (1941), pp. 631, 634, 636.

foreign powers, and that might very reasonably be taken as a tribute in disguise.[2] When his avowed enemies found so little to criticize, his record in foreign affairs could scarcely have been as disastrous as it has been painted. The uncharacteristic reticence of the Lancastrians entitles him to another hearing.

At the outset, the motives which shaped his policies require brief comment. It has often been said that he disliked war as such, and that this dislike was reinforced by his need for French assistance against his domestic enemies, which impelled him to court the favour of Charles VI. But there is little or no evidence for either belief. On the contrary, Richard's career shows that he was neither a coward, nor a pacifist, nor even indifferent to the chivalrous and martial tastes of his class and age. He turned a constitutional crisis into civil war in 1387 rather than bow to opposition, and in 1399 he ignored the advice of his counsellors to flee to Aquitaine, choosing instead to confront his enemies in the field despite the odds against him. His reaction to the execution of his friends and advisers and the loss of his own power in 1388 was to purge his emotions in an orgy of hunting. He was an enthusiast for tournaments, on at least one occasion carrying off the prize of honour himself. Not only did he lead three major military campaigns, but he planned half a dozen others. Twice when confronted by the threat of foreign invasion he impetuously put himself at the head of the English armies sent against the invaders. In short, the pale poetic aesthete of Shakespeare's drama bears little or no resemblance to his historical model, despite the powerful influence which this fictional creation has exercised over the minds of generations of historians. As for the belief that Richard's foreign policy was designed to buttress a domestic tyranny, this has even less foundation. It is based on a single insignificant financial transaction arising out of the negotiations for his marriage to Isabel of France, a transaction which has been consistently misinterpreted, and one which will not bear the construction normally placed upon it.[3] Foreign policy was of course affected by domestic considerations, but not of this kind. The two most important limiting factors were the need to reduce taxation at home and to free resources for use in

---

[2] R.P., iii, p. 420, accusing him of duplicity.
[3] For this and what follows see my forthcoming book, *England, France and Christendom, 1377–99.*

Ireland. Both inclined the king to seek peace abroad, but neither impelled him to buy it 'whatever the cost'.

★　　★　　★

For Richard II—as for every other English king in the three centuries or so between the disintegration of the Angevin empire and the consolidation of that of the Habsburgs—France dominated the international scene, relations with other powers being very largely conditioned by their potential value as allies against her. Except for brief moments of crisis, peace or truce negotiations with the French government dwarfed all other English diplomatic activity during the 1390s. The manner in which these negotiations were handled therefore provides the acid test of the general tendencies of English foreign policy.[4]

When Richard resumed the reins of government in May 1389, the war with France had already been brought to a close and a truce was imminent. Initially concluded for three years on 18 June 1389, the truce of Leulingham was never allowed to expire and was eventually extended in 1396 to last until 1426. In the long run this continuing state of truce entailed one unavoidable sacrifice. By virtue of obligations contracted by a baronial government at the beginning of his reign, the king was obliged to return Cherbourg and Brest to their rightful owners, the king of Navarre and the duke of Brittany. He could only have avoided this sacrifice at the cost of renewing the war, an exorbitant price which he was not prepared to pay, and rightly so. Cherbourg was handed over in 1393, Brest in 1397.

Though this surrender undoubtedly benefited Charles VI— who acquired Cherbourg from the king of Navarre—it was not a unilateral concession to him. The return of both towns was tied to the progress of the peace negotiations, from which England stood

---

[4] The next five paragraphs very briefly summarize some of the materials presented in my book (n. 3) and in the following articles: 'Anglo-French Peace Negotiations, 1390-1396', *T.R.H.S.*, 5th series, xvi (1966), pp. 81-94; 'Articles for a Final Peace between England and France, 16 June 1393', *B.I.H.R.*, xxxix (1966), pp. 180-5; 'England and the Great Western Schism, 1388-1399', *E.H.R.*, lxxxiii (1968), pp. 516-22; 'The Background to Richard II's Marriage to Isabel of France (1396)', *B.I.H.R.*, xliv (1971) pp., 1-17; and 'The War Aims of the Protagonists and the Negotiations for Peace', *The Hundred Years' War*, ed. K. A. Fowler, pp. 51-75.

to gain considerably. Richard's terms for peace were no less stiff than those of his predecessors: a very greatly enlarged Aquitaine; a substantial war indemnity (or the arrears of King John's ransom); and his retention of certain key ports, notably Calais. In return he offered—like Edward III and the baronial governments of his minority—to separate England and Aquitaine and confer the duchy on a Lancastrian dynasty which would be subject to the sovereignty of the French crown in certain limited and clearly defined respects. These terms were accepted as a basis for negotiation. At each stage of the ensuing discussions the French were induced to increase their offers step by step. Eventually, by a draft treaty concluded on 16 June 1393, Charles VI agreed to cede Calais and perhaps La Rochelle; to pay an indemnity of 1,200,000 francs; and to settle the whole of Aquitaine south of the Charente on the duke of Lancaster. This practically doubled the extent of any previous offer, and it was not to be exceeded until after Henry V's victorious Norman campaigns. In itself this belies the suggestion that Richard was unduly soft in his dealings with France.

Unfortunately, the foundations of this agreement were undermined by events in Aquitaine beyond the control of either king. Despite this setback, Richard continued to press for a final peace, though he now agreed to conclude an interim settlement on the basis of a marriage alliance and a long truce. This has been generally held to mark the point at which his 'softness' degenerated into subservience, leaving him a willing tool in the hands of the French monarchy. In fact, however, his attitude remained as hard-headed as ever. It can best be seen in the two sets of instructions issued to his ambassadors on 8 July 1395, at the outset of the negotiations. By the first, they were required to demand a dowry of 2,000,000 francs, though they were empowered to settle for half this sum; but by the second,[5] they were to ask for no less than the entire Angevin empire. For himself Richard wanted all the territories granted by the treaty of Brétigny, plus the arrears of King John's ransom; and for the children borne to him by Isabel of France, he demanded Normandy, Anjou, Maine, and French assistance to conquer Scotland. Even as a bargaining position, this was somewhat extreme, and very far indeed from being subservient. His demands—the stiffest of the reign—were of course rejected; but in

[5] Published as appendix to my book.

their anxiety to conclude a settlement the French felt obliged to make quite considerable concessions. The marriage contract of 9 March 1396 set Isabel's dowry at £133,333, a substantial sum; and the terms of the twenty-eight year truce concluded on the same day were equally advantageous. It allowed Richard to retain a *de facto* sovereignty in Aquitaine without requiring him to make a comparable concession by ceasing to use his title to the French throne. Despite these gains, the king continued to press for the additional advantages he could expect from a final peace. And just as he had exploited Charles VI's eagerness for the marriage alliance to secure advantageous terms in 1396, so after that date he played upon his father-in-law's need of English support for his efforts to end the Schism to compel him to continue the peace negotiations. Before this pressure could bring results, however, Richard had lost his throne.

Throughout these negotiations, Richard was consistently hard-headed and far tougher than he has ever been given credit for. At no point can it be said that English interests were disregarded, let alone sacrificed. The concessions made by Charles VI balanced, if they did not outweigh, those made by his rival. To understand why this was so, it is necessary to examine the nature of English relations with the neighbours of Valois France.

★　　★　　★

Outside France itself, there were four major areas of English diplomatic activity: Brittany, Spain, Italy and the Low Countries. Of these, the latter pair were undoubtedly the most important after 1389. The sting had been taken out of Anglo-French rivalry in Spain by John of Gaunt's renunciation of his claim to the Castilian throne in 1388, while tension in Brittany had been greatly alleviated by Charles VI's recognition of John de Montfort as duke of Brittany and by the release of de Montfort's rival, John de Blois, from an English prison at the end of 1387. Though it could not be claimed that the Spanish and Breton problems had been solved, their importance had certainly been greatly reduced.During the post-war period, attention was increasingly focused on Italy and the Low Countries.

The Low Countries had always been (and would remain)

The Low Countries in 1397

Legend:
- Anglo–Guelders bloc
- Burgundian bloc
- Uncommitted or ambivalent
- Bdys. of major principalities
- Bdy. between France & Empire
- River

NORTH SEA

GERMANY

FRANCE

HOLLAND
UTRECHT
GUELDERS
ZEELAND
C. CLEVES
BERG
COLOGNE
JÜLIERS
HEINSBURG
FLANDERS
BRABANT
LUXEMBURG
PALATINATE
HAINAULT
NAMUR
OSTRE-VANT
ARTOIS
CALAIS
BOULOGNE
ST. POL
PONTHIEU
CAMBRAI

0   100 kms
0   100 miles

crucially important to English statesmen, by reason of their close proximity, their strategic position, and the strength of the economic ties which bound them to England. At no time were they more important than in the last decade of the fourteenth century, when economic ties were at their strongest and the political situation at its most dangerous. During the previous few years, a series of deaths and marriages had transformed the political map of the region.[6] Following the death of Count Louis of Flanders in January 1384, the succession had devolved upon his son-in-law, Philip of Burgundy, while the almost simultaneous death of the duke of Brabant had made it highly probable that Philip would very shortly add Brabant to his Flemish inheritance. Joanna, duchess of Brabant, was chronically ill, a sexagenarian, and childless. She had three possible heirs: her niece Margaret, Philip's wife; her youngest sister Marie, widow of the duke of Guelders; and Wenzel, king of the Romans, who claimed the duchy both as heir to his uncle—the deceased duke of Brabant—and as an imperial fief which (he claimed) could not be transmitted to a woman. Given Marie's junior status and Wenzel's remoteness and indolence, a Burgundian succession appeared inevitable; and given Joanna's age and ill health, its occurrence could not, it seemed, be long delayed. Moreover, Philip lost no time in further strengthening his already strong position. Within a year of acquiring Flanders he had secured Joanna's support for his succession to Brabant. Following this, in January 1385, Joanna was instrumental in arranging the double marriage of Philip's heir, John of Nevers, to Margaret, daughter of Albert of Bavaria, ruler of Holland, Zealand and Hainault, and of Albert's heir, William of Ostrevant, to Philip's daughter Margaret. One of the clauses of the marriage contracts stipulated that John of Nevers would inherit Brabant as well as Flanders. Thus in a little over a year the French prince who was effective ruler of France at this date had established his dynasty in Flanders, virtually guaranteed its succession to Brabant, and bound the ruler and heir of Holland, Zealand and Hainault to his house by the strongest of all possible chains. The richest, most

[6] For what follows, F. Quicke, *Les Pays-Bas à la veille de la période bourguignonne, 1356–1384* (Brussels, 1947), and H. Laurent and F. Quicke, *Les Origines de l'état bourguignonne: l'accession de la maison de Bourgogne aux duchés de Brabant et Limbourg, 1383–1396* (Brussels, 1939), are indispensable.

powerful and most centralized provinces of the Low Countries had thereby come under French control or French influence.

This rapid expansion of French power completely transformed the course of the Anglo-French war, underlining the crucial importance of the Low Countries. France immediately took the offensive. In three successive years from 1385 to 1387 England was faced by invasion from massive armadas concentrated at Sluys. They were backed by an economic blockade imposed by Philip which severed English trade with Flanders and threatened to disrupt commercial relations with Spain and the Baltic. The desperate efforts of the baronial council to break this military and economic stranglehold were only partially successful. During the last year of the war, the duke of Gloucester and his colleagues were compelled to acknowledge their impotence when the French launched a full-scale attack on the duke of Guelders, their one ally in the Low Countries. He was left to face the French onslaught single-handed, and so forced to submit to their terms. Though these were not onerous, the Guelders campaign humiliated England, seriously discouraged her potential allies, and seemingly put French ascendancy beyond challenge. So great was the prestige of Philip of Burgundy by this date that it was believed that the German princes of the Low Countries would offer him the imperial crown.[7]

This was the situation inherited by Richard II in 1389. Blinded by hindsight, historians have tended to overlook the very real dangers to which it appeared to expose England. But in 1389 no one could have foreseen that the Flemish inheritance would be a source of internal weakness to France, and no English government could have viewed the consolidation of Burgundian power with anything but dismay. To check its further expansion was a task which had to be accorded first priority, and this was the task which Richard set himself. In this he was so successful that before the end of his reign the German princes were prepared to offer him the imperial crown which they had apparently intended to offer to Philip only nine years previously.

His first opportunity arose within a few months of his resump-

[7] J. Vielliard and L. Mirot, 'Inventaire des lettres des rois d'Aragon à Charles VI . . conservées. . á Barcelone', *Bibliothèque de l'École des Chartes*, ciii (1942), no. 109 (hereafter referred to as *B.E.C.*).

tion of power. One of the few chinks in Philip's armour was the fact that his Flemish subjects were Urbanists when he himself adhered to the 'French' pope, Clement VII. Naturally enough, Philip wished to remedy this situation, and seized the opportunity afforded by the death of Urban VI in October 1389 to do so. At the beginning of 1390 the Flemish Estates were summoned before his chancellor and required to reconsider their religious allegiance. Shortly afterwards, the Flemings were subjected to the hectoring of Clementist legates, while Urbanist legates who were rash enough to venture into the county were arrested by the authorities.[8] All this provoked considerable unrest which Richard was quick to exploit. He let it be known in Ghent—the inevitable focus of opposition to the duke—that 'if the king of France or the duke of Burgundy should harm you on account of your faith', England would 'sustain you in all possible ways'. In the event, the king was not called upon to honour this pledge. Philip renounced the use of force and his subjects maintained their allegiance to the 'English' pope. Just how far this was due to the threat of English intervention, it is impossible to judge, but to all outward appearances, the English government had won its first diplomatic victory in the Low Countries.

This was not an isolated episode. A few months later Richard again intervened in the internal affairs of the Burgundian bloc, this time to exploit a quarrel between Albert of Bavaria and his heir, William of Ostrevant. The quarrel had been provoked by William's scandalous liaison with one Adeline de Poelgeest,[9] so Philip—William's father-in-law—was inescapably involved. The opportunity to embarrass him was too good to be missed. In the autumn of 1390 William was invited to England and invested with the Order of the Garter. Despite the outcry this provoked in France, Richard did not draw back. In the following January, William was granted an annual retainer of five hundred marks in return for his homage and the promise of military service. All this seriously embarrassed Philip and the French government at a

---

[8] O. Cartellieri, *Philip der Kühne* (Leipzig, 1910), pp. 55-7 and documents 5-7; for what follows, Archives départementales du Nord, B.1337/14601bis, letter dated 16 April [1390].

[9] Laurent and Quicke, pp. 389-93; for what follows, Monk of Westminster, p. 241; Rymer, *Foedera etc.* (original edn. 1727-1735), vii, pp. 695-6; and below, p. 96.

particularly critical moment in their relations with England, when they could ill afford the luxury of internal dissensions. It was some time before this family dispute was settled.

Relations between Philip, his family, and their subjects never again became sufficiently strained to permit England to intervene. Henceforth, Richard concentrated his attentions on building up an anti-Burgundian coalition among the neighbouring rulers outside the Burgundian bloc. From the start, the duke of Guelders was destined to be the centre of this coalition. The choice was almost inevitable, for—it has been aptly observed—Duke William 'seems to have conceived himself as the bastion of the Germanic Low Countries against Franco-Burgundian influences and infiltration'.[10] Everywhere he turned, William was confronted by opposing Burgundian claims: in Brabant, Limbourg and Outre-Meuse by Philip and his aunt Joanna; in the duchy of Juliers by Burgundian enclaves; and in the duchy of Luxembourg by Philip's ally and close relative, Waleran of Luxembourg. He was therefore a natural ally of any power determined to check further Burgundian expansion and was treated accordingly by the English government. On 10 June 1387 he was granted an annual retainer of £1000 in return for his homage and his promise to supply 500 men-at-arms in any war against the king of France and the duke of Burgundy. This agreement remained the basis of Anglo-Guelders relations for the rest of the century. The retainer was paid regularly and periodically supplemented by generous bonuses. Gifts were heaped on William himself and pensions on his followers. He was created Knight of the Garter in 1390; he visited England in 1390, 1392 and 1396; and in the intervals there was a steady stream of embassies between Westminster and Nimwegen. It was a very long time since any foreign prince had been accorded so much attention and treated with such generosity.

In 1393 William succeeded his father as duke of Juliers, thereby doubling his power and sensibly heightening the tension between himself, the duchess of Brabant and Philip of Burgundy. It was no coincidence that his succession in Juliers was followed by the revolt of a large number of Burgundian vassals and allies, a revolt which

[10] R. Vaughan, *Philip the Bold* (London, 1962), p. 97; for what follows, Rymer, vii, pp. 535–7; *Correspondence*, nos. 123, 161, 163, 178, 203, 204, 216, 217; Laurent and Quicke, Chap. 11.

was to continue spasmodically over the next few years.[11] Once again, the English government exploited the situation, drawing most of the rebels from the Burgundian into the English camp. The lords of Heinsberg and Löwenberg, the archbishop and archdeacon of Cologne, the counts of Mors and Saarwerden, and the duke of Berg and count of Ravensberg, and the heir to Guelders and Juliers, were all granted pensions at the English exchequer in return for their homage and the promise of military service. At the same time these agreements were supplemented by others of a like nature with the eastern neighbours of Burgundy and France, of whom the count palatine of the Rhine was by far the most important. Initiated in 1393, negotiations with Count Rupert II were brought to a successful conclusion in September 1396, when he was granted a pension of £1000. In the following May he rendered homage and promised military aid, as did his son Rupert III—the future emperor—who also received a pension. These negotiations were to have been crowned by a marriage alliance. Richard himself appears to have sought a bride from the palatinate in 1394;[12] and later discussions for a match between the future Emperor Rupert and the (?daughter) of the duke of Norfolk had reached an advanced stage before they were wrecked by the domestic crisis of 1397. Despite this setback, Richard had by this date created a network of alliances which comprised virtually every important ruler between the Rhine and the North Sea outside the Burgundian bloc (see map p. 80).

This network stabilized the political situation in the Low Countries, erected a bulwark against further Burgundian expansion, and greatly enhanced English prestige abroad. In offering him the imperial crown in 1397 the German princes were paying a tribute to the success of the policies he had pursued during the previous decade. It is symptomatic of the nature of his achievement that their offer was conveyed to him by the archdeacon of

[11] Loc. cit; and *Documents pour servir à l'histoire de la maison de Bourgogne en Brabant et en Limbourg*, ed. H. Laurent and F. Quicke in *Bulletin de la Commission royale d'histoire*, xcvii (Brussels, 1933), pp. 39–188. For what follows, see Rymer, vii, pp. 854–6, 858–9; ibid., viii, pp. 1–6, 21–4, 36–8, 66, 80–2; P.R.O., Exchequer Diplomatic Documents (E.30), nos. 329–38, 1088, 1228–38, 1358, 1508, 1514; *Correspondence*, nos. 230–1; *C.P.R., 1396–9*, p. 25.

[12] Palmer, *B.I.H.R.* xliv, p. 3, n. 2; for what follows, P.R.O., Chancery Warrants (C.81), no. 1355/30 (damaged).

Cologne, once a Burgundian vassal, now an English ally and head of a Rhenish coalition which had recently done considerable damage to Burgundian interests in that area.[13] Richard had effected a minor diplomatic revolution in the Low Countries, a revolution which had gone some way towards restoring the balance of forces between England and France.

★   ★   ★

Because of the fortunate and unexpected longevity of the aged duchess of Brabant—who outlived both Richard and Philip—a major confrontation between England and France in the Low Countries was averted during Richard's lifetime. In Italy, however, French aggression brought him face to face with a crisis of European dimensions during the first eighteen months of his personal rule. The manner in which he handled this critical situation provides the best possible case-study of the aims and methods of his foreign policy.

French ambitions in Italy were no new phenomena in the 1380s, but on the eve of that period they had been given renewed stimulus and much greater scope by the outbreak of the Great Schism. Until 1388, however, the French princes had been unable to take anything like full advantage of these new opportunities because of the war with England, which absorbed virtually all of their energies and resources. Once the war had ended the pent-up ambitions of a decade immediately sought their release. From the very outset of the post-war period, therefore, Italy threatened to become the main focus of Anglo-French rivalries, and consequently the danger spot of European politics.

Even before the truce of Leulingham had been finally sealed, the French had begun their preparations to intervene in Italy. In May 1389 Charles VI knighted his young cousin, Louis II of Anjou, and promised to support his bid to conquer the kingdom of Naples, which he claimed by papal grant and as heir to the murdered queen, Joanna. Louis was crowned king of Sicily in the presence of Charles VI by Pope Clement in November, and in the following

[13] E. Perroy, *L'Angleterre et le grand Schisme d'Occident* (Paris, 1933), pp. 342–3; *Documents pour servir . . . Limbourg*, nos. 37, 43.

July set sail for Naples accompanied by a papal legate and with an army financed by royal and papal taxation.

This was only the first and least important part of the French plans. Throughout the summer, autumn and winter of 1390 military and diplomatic preparations for a massive invasion of north Italy in the following spring were pursued with ever increasing vigour. Treaties were negotiated with the empire, Scotland, Castile and Milan; an effort was made to secure the neutrality of England and Florence; troops were recruited in Scotland and France; and armour, supplies and equipment were purchased in Milan, Avignon, Flanders and Paris and stockpiled in France. At the end of the year the French army was ordered to rendezvous at Lyons on 15 March 1391. It was expected to number 60,000 combatants. Charles VI himself was to command, assisted by his brother Louis of Orleans,[14] his uncles Philip of Burgundy, John of Berry and Louis of Bourbon, the constable and admiral of France, and most of the greater peers, including the count of Savoy, lord Coucy, Waleran of St Pol and Bureau de la Rivière. In addition, Clement VII and Giangaleazzo Visconti of Milan were to supply between them a further 7500 troops under their personal command. In all, the expedition promised to be the most ambitious undertaking of the reign, if not of the entire century.[15]

The motives which prompted this vast enterprise deserve close scrutiny, for they were to inspire French policy for some time to come. According to Boniface IX,[16] Charles VI had six separate but related objectives in view: to expel him from Rome and instal Clement VII in his place; to drive Ladislas of Durazzo from

---

[14] I use this title throughout the essay, though Louis was only duke of Touraine until 1392, when he was created duke of Orleans.

[15] There is a huge bibliography on this subject, but the following works are particularly important for their documentation: A. L. Champollion-Figeac, *Louis et Charles, ducs d'Orléans* (Paris, 1844); P. Durrieu, *Les Gascons en Italie* (Auch, 1885); A. de Circourt, 'Le duc Louis d'Orléans, frère de Charles VI', *Revue des Questions Historiques*, xlii (1887), pp. 5–67; ibid., xlv (1889), pp. 70–127; E. Jarry, *La vie politique de Louis de France, duc d'Orléans, 1372–1407* (Paris, 1889); E. Jarry, 'La *voie de fait* et l'alliance Franco-Milanese', *B.E.C.*, liii (1892), pp. 213–53, 505–70; N. Valois, *La France et le grand Schisme d'Occident*, ii (Paris, 1898); G. Romano, *Niccolo Spinelli di Giovinezza* (Naples, 1902); L. Mirot, *La politique française en Italie de 1380 à 1422, i: les préliminaires de l'alliance Florentine* (Paris, 1934); M. de Bouard, *Les origines des guerres d'Italie: la France et l'Italie au temps du grand Schisme d'Occident* (Paris, 1936).

[16] Monk of Westminster, pp. 251–3, clearly derived from an official document.

Naples and so secure the kingdom for Louis of Anjou; to conquer the States of the Church for Louis of Orleans; to win 'great advantages' for the duke of Burgundy; to obtain the imperial crown for Charles VI himself; and, finally, to create a kingdom in Lombardy and Tuscany for 'a certain other lord', who could have been no other than Giangaleazzo of Milan, the father-in-law of Louis of Orleans and ally of France. In short, if we are to believe Boniface IX the expedition was designed to partition Italy among the French princes, to perpetuate the 'Babylonish captivity' of the papacy on Italian soil, and to transfer the empire from Germany to France. Such extravagant ambitions have inspired universal disbelief: how far can Boniface be trusted?

There can be absolutely no doubt as to the accuracy of the first of his allegations, for Charles VI's determination to lead Clement VII to Rome was the one publicized feature of his expedition. It was the sole motive attributed to him by the chroniclers and their accounts are substantiated by financial, diplomatic and administrative documents in the French and Burgundian archives[17] and by the *ex parte* statements of Charles VI and Clement. On the very eve of the expedition, Clement announced that he was to accompany the French armies to Italy and began levying subsidies and collecting supplies for 'the expedition to Rome' (*pro viagio Rome*); while shortly after it was cancelled, Charles reminded the pope that 'he had recently undertaken to lead the Holy Father to Rome and would have done so' but for other problems which had demanded his attention. This evidence does not admit of much doubt, and any that remains should be dispelled by the testimony of three strictly contemporary letters written from Avignon early in 1391.[18] Two of them affirm—on the authority of the pope himself—that Clement was to go to Rome that spring in the company

[17] Documented by Jarry, *Louis de France*, pp. 56–73; Jarry, *B.E.C.*, liii, pp. 231–41; and Mirot, *Politique française*, p. 51. For what follows, see documents in Champollion-Figeac, *Louis et Charles*, p. 8; and Valois, ii, pp. 175–7.

[18] R. Brun, 'Annales avignonnaises de 1382 à 1410 extraites des archives de Datini', *Mémoires de l'Institut Historique de Provence*, xii (1935), pp. 126–7; S. Steinherz, *Dokumente zur Geschichte des grossen abendländischen Schismas, 1385–1395* (Prague, 1932). Neither of these works has previously been utilized, though they are perhaps the two most valuable sources. On the dating of the documents published by Steinherz, see H. Stein, 'Zu den Verhandlungen Erzbischof Pilgrims II von Salzburg um die Beilegung des grossen abendländischen Schismas', *Mitteilungen des Instituts für österreichische Geschichtsforschung*, xlviii (1934), pp. 434–9.

of a French army; while the third, written at Clement's behest by an ecclesiastic high in his confidence, corroborates this central point and provides important additional information on the preparation of the expedition:

To the lord of Lichtenstein. Dear Sir, . . we have certain information that the king of France will personally escort Clement VII to Rome and instal him there . . . The king is to be here in Avignon by Easter next, and he and the pope will set out with their entire might just as soon as their preparation are complete. They will be accompanied by the dukes of Berry and Burgundy, by the king's brother [Orleans], and by all the powerful lords of their lands. The duke of Burgundy and the king's brother are already on their way to Milan to conclude an agreement with the lord Giangaleazzo which will clear the way for the French forces. I send you this news because I well know that you would like to see a happy end to this crisis in Christendom [i.e. the Schism], and hope to God that this campaign will bring a simple and just solution. It should do so, for the king is young and innocent; he has great power and might; he has many friends, allies and contacts in Italy and other lands; and he is accompanied by lords who are clear-headed and wise in the ways of this world.

The sheer weight of this testimony has had an hypnotic effect on modern historians, causing them to ignore the remaining points of Boniface's indictment or to reject it out of hand as a piece of blatant and scurrilous propaganda. Boniface was, of course, a hostile witness who cannot be taken on trust. Yet the French sources are equally biased in their own way, being clearly designed to emphasize the altruism of the French court to the exclusion of any more mundane interests it may have had. Moreover, a moment's reflection will show that there must be some element of truth in Boniface's charges; for however large a part the march on Rome may have had in the plans of the French princes, it can scarcely have been their sole objective. Quite apart from the manifest improbability of their embarking on so vast an enterprise for the exclusive benefit of a third party, they were well aware that it would be a waste of their time, money and effort to conduct Clement VII to Rome unless they also made provision to maintain him there. To do this, they would have to retain a strong French 'presence' in Italy. As they explained to Clement in the following year, his security in Rome could only be guaranteed by expelling the allies of Boniface IX from the States of the Church and the kingdom of Naples and replacing them by French princes with a vested interest in the new regime.[19] The retention of Rome demanded the conquest and partition of half of Italy.

The Angevin conquest of Naples was therefore an essential and integral element in the political and strategic objectives of the French court, not an isolated and accidental manifestation of the ambitions of one princely house. Plans for the attack on Naples and for the invasion of north Italy were formulated simultaneously, during the meetings between Charles VI and Clement VII at Avignon in the winter of 1389–90, when Louis was crowned king of Sicily and Charles first promised to lead Clement to Rome.[20] So closely were the two projects related that as late as March 1391 there was still a possibility that the French would transfer the forces allocated to north Italy to the south, in order to assure their position in Naples before marching on Rome.[21] In the end, however, they decided to pursue the two objectives simultaneously, dividing their forces in order to divide their enemies. On the eve of his own invasion of north Italy, Charles VI again emphasized the interdependence of French activities in northern and southern Italy when he urged the Genoese to favour Louis of Anjou, 'whose enterprise—which we regard as our own—is for the glorification of the crown and royal house of France as well as for the status, honour and advantage of our brother, the duke of Touraine (Orleans), and of all our other friends and well-wishers'.[22]

The 'status, honour and advantage' of Louis of Orleans brings us to the third of Boniface IX's allegations, and to perhaps the most immediate objective of the projected invasion of north Italy: the conquest of the States of the Church. There is abundant proof that Louis of Orleans aspired to carve himself an Italian kingdom—to be called the kingdom of 'Adria'—from the territories of the Roman Church *after* 1391,[23] but no unequivocal evidence that he

[19] Published in Romano, *Spinelli*, pp. 611–23.

[20] This last point—often disputed—is substantiated by a letter in Brun, *Mémoires . . Provence*, xii (1935), p. 119.

[21] Document in Mirot, *Politique française*, p. 53.

[22] Archives départementales du Nord, B.18822/23154 (cf. the Genoese reply, no. 23242), [c. January 1391].

[23] P. Durrieu, 'Le royaume d'Adria: Épisode de la politique française en Italie, 1393–1394', *Revue des Questions Historiques*, xxviii (1880), pp. 43–78; published separately with documentary appendices, Paris, 1880.

sought to do so before that date apart from the partisan statement of Boniface IX. Despite the absence of direct corroborative evidence, however, it is difficult to believe that Orleans was innocent of the designs which the Roman pope attributed to him. His entire previous history, as well as his subsequent career, militates against this belief.

Almost from the moment of his birth, the younger of Charles V's two sons was marked out for a political career in Italy, partly no doubt to further French interests in the peninsular but largely (one suspects) to remove him from France, where he might otherwise provide a dangerous focus of opposition to his elder brother.[24] As a mere child, he was betrothed to Katherine, one of the three heiresses of Louis the Great of Hungary, whose dowry was to have been the Hungarian claims on Naples and Provence. This project collapsed when Orleans's uncle, Louis I of Anjou, persuaded the ruling queen of Naples, Joanna, to adopt him as her heir in 1380, thereby excluding his nephew Orleans. After the death of Louis of Anjou in 1384, the project was briefly revived, only to be frustrated a second time by Sigismund of Luxembourg, who seized and married Orleans's intended bride, Marie of Hungary, sister of the now deceased Katherine. With the Hungarian claims to Naples and Provence in the hands of a German prince, the house of Valois closed its ranks. Henceforth, Louis II of Anjou was left to acquire Naples without the distraction of having to fend off his own first cousin and namesake, Louis of Orleans.

But Orleans did not abandon his Italian ambitions at this point. He simply transferred them from the kingdom of Naples to north Italy and the States of the Church, territories which had previously been earmarked as the Angevin sphere of interest. Before being adopted by Joanna of Naples, Louis I of Anjou had been promised the kingdom of Adria by Clement VII in return for his assistance in driving Urban VI from Italy. In acquiring Naples, Anjou had to forgo Adria, to which Orleans promptly staked a claim. The negotiations for his marriage to Marie of Hungary collapsed in the autumn of 1385; by 1386 he was negotiating for the hand of the daughter and heiress of Giangaleazzo Visconti of Milan, whose alliance was to be the cornerstone of his efforts to acquire a kingdom in north Italy. For his wife's dowry, Orleans received the

[24] Jarry, *Louis de France*, pp. 1–43 for what follows.

county of Asti, the 'Calais of Italy'. The marriage was approved by Clement VII who, in May 1387, sanctioned the transfer of Asti to Orleans, at the same time promising to grant him 'at a favourable moment' the towns and territories of Rimini, Pesaro and Fossumbrone in fee and a papal vicariate over Faenza, Imola, Bertinoro and Forli.[25] Though these territories comprised only a part of the Adrian kingdom previously offered to Louis of Anjou, Clement's promise clearly mapped out the future direction of Orleans's ambitions. The 'favourable moment' to realize them would arrive when he appeared in Italy at the head of an army.

In view of this background, there can be little doubt as to the motives which inspired Louis's enthusiastic participation in the projected expedition of 1391, nor much doubt that the expedition was intended to further his interests—'his status, honour and advantage'—by conquering all or part of the States of the Church. Despite the publicity they gave to their intention to march on Rome, the French gave priority in their preparations to an attack on Lombardy and the Romagna, the northern territories of the papal state. This emerges from a number of their administrative measures,[26] but most clearly of all from the terms of a secret treaty negotiated by Orleans himself with Giangaleazzo in March 1391, at the very moment when the expedition was due to set out for Italy.[27] Though it made passing reference to the plan to march on Rome, this treaty was primarily concerned with diplomatic and military arrangements for a concerted attack on Bologna, the key to the Romagna. If the attack were successful, Bologna was to fall to Clement, Charles VI, or Orleans himself. Bologna was a papal city which Orleans could only legitimately acquire by papal grant. This provision therefore implied that his ambitions were by no means confined to the territories promised to him by Clement in 1387. Other clauses in this treaty point to a similar conclusion. They envisaged French conquests in Tuscany and the March of Ancona, as well as Lombardy and the Romagna; and although the direct beneficiary of such conquests was not specified, they would

[25] Ibid., document 8.

[26] Paris, Bibliothèque Nationale: Pièces Originales, Tanques, nos. 24–5; ibid., Bourcher, no. 14; Collection Clairambault, Sceaux, vol. 113, no. 8821.

[27] Published by Mirot, *Politique française*, pp. 49–54. It is astonishing that the contents of the treaty have not prompted a reconsideration of the objectives of the expedition of 1391.

clearly have placed Orleans in a very powerful negotiating position vis-à-vis Clement VII, a position which he would scarcely have failed to exploit.

All this indicates that the allegation of Boniface IX, though tinged with exaggeration, was substantially accurate. It should perhaps be added that the pope's own actions at this time show that he himself believed his charge to be true. He granted Bologna privileges which virtually made the city independent of his authority for a quarter of a century, and he legitimised the rule of the Malatesta tyrants over Rimini, Pesaro, Fano and Fossumbrone —the territories promised to Orleans by Clement—and over their other possessions in the Romagna and the March of Ancona by conferring on them a papal vicariate for two generations.[28] Both concessions can only have been made to stiffen resistance to Orleans, and their extreme generosity must be taken as a measure of the seriousness with which Boniface viewed the French threat to the papal state.

The remaining charges which he levelled against the French contained a similar measure of truth. The Franco-Milanese treaty of March 1391 provided that Giangaleazzo be created lord of Lombardy and of the March of Treviso—not Tuscany, as Boniface had stated—'with such title...as he should require,...if Pope Clement should happen to crown anyone emperor'. As far as Giangaleazzo's ambitions were concerned, therefore, Boniface was very close to the mark; and as far as the imperial title was concerned, he may well have scored a bull. In subsequent elaborations of the Franco-Milanese treaty negotiated in 1392, 1393 and 1394, the 'anyone' designated as future emperor in the agreement of 1391 was identified as Charles VI or one of his immediate family.[29] It is difficult to see who else could have been intended in 1391. Belief in the imperial destiny of the house of Valois was widely diffused at this time, not least among the royal circle itself. The merits of Louis of Orleans had been advertised in 1385, those of Philip of Burgundy in 1388, and those of Charles VI himself in 1386, 1389 and 1391. Whether Clement VII ever seriously

[28] Valois, ii, pp. 160–2; P. J. Jones, 'The Vicariate of the Malatesta of Rimini', E.H.R., lxvii (1952), pp. 329–30.
[29] Published by Jarry, Louis de France, pp. 421, 427; and Jarry, B.E.C., liii (1892), pp. 556–7, 564–5.

intended to satisfy these ambitions is another matter; but he had only himself to blame for the widespread belief that he would do so. Quite apart from his promises to Orleans, his support for Anjou, and his intimate connection with the projected invasion of 1391, he had on at least two recent occasions shown himself ready to set aside the imperial rights of Wenzel of Bohemia for the benefit of his French patrons. In 1387 he had invested Orleans with Asti on the grounds that the empire was 'vacant', and in 1390 he had extended the imperial vicariate over the kingdom of Arles previously granted to Charles VI by the Emperor Charles IV, presumably on similar grounds. He was so far identified with the house of Valois on the imperial question that when he offered to crown Wenzel emperor in 1390, he found it necessary to protest that 'he was not in any way obliged to the king of France'. Wenzel reacted by publicly reaffirming his commitment to Boniface IX and by preparing his own expedition to Italy to secure his imperial coronation, both clear manifestations of his profound distrust of Clement VII.[30]

Despite universal scepticism as to the validity of Boniface IX's allegations, therefore, they were in all probability substantially accurate. The expedition of 1391 presented a far more formidable threat to the Italian states and to the balance of power in Europe than has hitherto been appreciated. What made it really dangerous, however, was not so much the scope of French ambitions as the unusual degree of harmony and cohesion with which the French princes pursued their various objectives. Before 1390 they had had no coherent policy towards Italy. There had been an Angevin policy, an Orleanist policy, a royal policy, a Savoyard policy, and an Avignonese policy; and as often as not, these policies were at war with each other. For reasons which will be examined below, there was a reversion to this state of affairs in the later 1390s. But at the beginning of that decade, the princes sank their differences and combined their interests, to the mutual advantage of all concerned. The king, his 'Marmouset' government, his brother, all three of his uncles, the count of Savoy, and the constable and admiral of France, as well as many lesser figures, threw themselves wholeheartedly into the preparations for the Italian expedition. Backed

---

[30] Steinherz, *Dokumente*, pp. 52, 62; *Deutsche Reichstagakten unter König Wenzel* ed. J. Weizsäcker, ii (repr. Göttingen, 1956), pp. 369–75.

by Clement VII, by Giangaleazzo of Milan, and by Angevin partisans in Naples, they appeared to be irresistible. Why, then, was this great enterprise abruptly cancelled a matter of days before it was scheduled to set out for Italy?

A multitude of explanations has been suggested: sabotage by the duke of Brittany; the activities of the count of Armagnac; rivalry between Burgundy and Orleans; antagonism between Giangaleazzo and Clement VII; the duplicity of the king of England; and finally, sheer inertia. When weighed against the full seriousness of the French threat, none of these answers carries much conviction, and most of them have at one time or another been refuted in detail.[31] The true (yet unsuspected) explanation is at once more simple and more serious: the English government threatened to invade France if she invaded Italy and took steps to convince the French that it meant business.

Richard II's attitude in this crisis was succinctly outlined in his reply to the embassy sent by Boniface IX to warn him of the alarming scope of the French plans. After delivering this dire warning, Boniface asked for English support. He requested that no separate peace be concluded with Charles VI unless he first promised not to invade Italy; that England contribute a subsidy towards the defence of the church in Italy in the event of a French invasion; and that an attempt should be made to enlist the support and co-operation of the emperor, Wenzel. On all three points he was given the assurances he desired. Richard promised not to conclude peace with France without sufficient guarantees of the pope's position, and added that in the meantime 'other measures' would be taken to dissuade the French from their plans. He also agreed to give Boniface financial assistance unless he himself went to war with the French, in which case they would have their hands too full to attack Italy. Finally, he informed the papal nuncio that an embassy had already been sent to Wenzel for the purpose advocated by the pope.[32]

In addition to soliciting the support of the emperor, the 'other measures' taken by the government were fully commensurate with the seriousness of the situation. The three months between November 1390 and January 1391—the period when the French preparations reached their climax—were crammed with political,

[31] See the works listed in n. 15.   [32] Monk of Westminster, pp. 253-8 (cf n. 16).

diplomatic and military preparations for war. At the outset, an effort was made to secure the neutrality or even the assistance of potential allies of France in the Low Countries, Spain and Scotland. Scotland was subjected to intensive diplomatic pressure by increasingly vociferous complaints about alleged infractions of the truce of Leulingham;[33] Navarre was courted by dangling the prospect of the return of Cherbourg before her king; and Aragon was wooed by releasing the son of the count of Denia. After having languished in an English prison for twenty-three years, Alphonse of Denia was suddenly released in November 1390, given 1000 marks for his expenses, and granted an annual pension of 500 marks in return for his homage and his promise to serve Richard 'in peace and in war'. Two months later, in January 1391, an embassy was sent to negotiate an alliance with the king of Castile 'against all men in the world' or—failing that—a unilateral peace or a truce for thirty years or more.[34] Finally, as we have already seen, between October 1390 and January 1391 an attempt was made to embarrass the duke of Burgundy in the Low Countries by courting the friendship and alliance of his son-in-law, William of Ostrevant, the heir to Holland, Zealand and Hainault.

In his efforts to bully, beguile or bemuse potential enemies, Richard did not neglect his natural allies. In January 1391 the duke of Guelders was encouraged by an advance of £2000 from the exchequer, while a month previously the king of Portugal had been firmly reminded of his military and diplomatic obligations under the treaty of Windsor (1386). The latter episode was particularly revealing. Earlier in the year, King John of Portugal had informed the government that he had concluded a three-year truce with the king of Castile, a truce he hoped to extend or even convert into a final peace. He had included England as his ally and asked that this be approved. Approval was readily given; but Richard took this opportunity to remind King John that England would only be bound by the truce while she was at peace with France, and to insist that any future agreement between Castile and Portugal must

---

[33] P.R.O., Memoranda Rolls (E.159), no. 168, *Brevia*, Michaelmas term, m. 26; for remainder of sentence, Rymer, vii, pp. 692-3; *C.Cl.R., 1388-92*, p. 307; P.R.O., Issue Rolls (E.403), no. 532, m. 26.

[34] Rymer, *Foedera* (orig. edn. 1727-35), vii, pp. 680-2 (misplaced); cf. p. 83 above.

leave John free to fulfil his military obligations to England 'if war should break out between England and France'.[35]

John of Portugal must have been dismayed at the possibility of the renewal of the Anglo-French war, which could have done him nothing but harm. The remaining English allies, however, all had a vested interest of their own in opposing Charles VI and Giangaleazzo of Milan, and every reason to welcome English intervention. Apart from Wenzel and Boniface IX—both of whom had been approached—there were four other allies who fell into this category: Florence, Brittany, Armagnac, and the disinherited sons of Bernabo Visconti, who had been deposed and murdered by Giangaleazzo in 1385. During the autumn and winter, these four parties had drawn together in common opposition to France and Milan. Carlo Visconti and his brothers enrolled in the Florentine armies sent against Milan in 1390. In October of that year the count of Armagnac—whose sister was married to Carlo Visconti—undertook to lead an army to the assistance of the republic as soon as possible.[36] While preparing to do so, Armagnac busied himself with negotiating a double marriage alliance and pact of mutual military assistance with the duke of Brittany,[37] whose subsequent efforts on behalf of the Florentine-Armagnac coalition were sufficiently important to earn him the ecstatic thanks of the republic.

Each of the allies in this tightly knit group was encouraged and supported by the English government, with whom they had evidently reached a common understanding. While Carlo Visconti fought in the Florentine army, his younger brother Mastino appears to have made the long journey to England, for which he was substantially rewarded at the exchequer.[38] In September, and again in November 1390, the duke of Brittany sent embassies to England, both in all probability for the purpose of negotiating a

[35] Issue Rolls, no. 532, mm. 17, 20; *Correspondence*, no. 109 (9 December [1390], misdated by the editor).

[36] G. Romano, 'Gian Galeazzo Visconti e gli eredi di Bernabo', *Archivio Storico Lombardo*, xviii (1891), pp. 29–43; Durrieu, *Gascons en Italie*, pp. 49–50, 234–44; D. M. Bueno de Mesquita, *Giangaleazzo Visconti, Duke of Milan, 1351–1402* (Cambridge, 1941), pp. 117–26.

[37] Archives de la Loire-Atlantique, E.8, E.181 (kindly supplied by Dr M. C. E. Jones); for remainder of sentence, letter published by Durrieu, *Gascons en Italie*, pp. 260–1.

[38] Issue Rolls, no. 530, m. 16.

diplomatic and military alliance.[39] Shortly afterwards, in January 1391, an English embassy was sent to the count of Armagnac to entice him into the 'faith and obedience' of the English crown.[40] Finally, at about the same time the government appears to have made overtures to the republic of Florence; for in a rather extravagant letter written to Richard on 8 February 1391, the republic declared that 'more than all the other peoples of Italy, we honour the English . . . regarding them as our own citizens, on which account we have incurred the anger of many men'. Given the political situation at this date, the 'many men' must have included Giangaleazzo, if not Orleans and Anjou. If they had been angered by the relations between Florence and England, these had presumably involved more than an exchange of flowery compliments.

These extensive diplomatic preparations were backed by serious military measures. Parliament met in November 1390, granting a subsidy 'for the defence and salvation of the kingdom', £6000 of which was paid over to the duke of Lancaster in the following January for the defence of Aquitaine 'because of the war moved (sic) between us and the French'.[41] Even before this date, John of Gaunt had begun to whip up support in the duchy, where his retainers had been busy spreading the news that war was imminent and that the duke himself would shortly take the field with a large army. Their efforts were supplemented by those of the English commissioners for the preservation of the truces in Aquitaine. While publicly warning the Gascons and 'English' routier captains to observe the truce of Leulingham, these commissioners privately urged them to prepare for war. Some were incautious enough to jump the gun, including the infamous Merigot Marchès, at whose trial in the following July all these facts came to light.[42] It is worth remarking that these truce commissioners were the very men empowered to negotiate an alliance with the count of Armagnac, whose army was very largely recruited from the 'English'

[39] P.R.O., Treaty Rolls (C.76), no. 75, mm. 10, 8. There survive several draft treaties from the early 1390s which may belong to this period: Exchequer Diplomatic Documents (E.30), no. 289ᵃ; *P.P.C.*, i, pp. 41–4, 89–93.

[40] Rymer, vii, p. 693; for what follows, letter in Edinburgh University Ms 183, fos. 68v–69.

[41] *R.P.*, iii, p. 279; Issue Rolls, no. 532, m. 27 (cf Memoranda Rolls, no. 169, *Brevia*, Trinity term, m. 17).

[42] *Registre criminel du Châtelet de Paris*, ed. Duplès-Agier, ii (Paris, 1864), pp. 177–213.

captains of southern France. Finally, in addition to its preparations in Aquitaine, it appears that the English government drew up contingency plans to send an army to Lombardy should Charles VI persist in his threatened invasion of north Italy.[43]

In February 1391, when his preparations were complete and the French army was just about due to mobilize, Richard sent an embassy to Paris to warn Charles VI—in the words of one French chronicler—'that if he attacked the pope of Rome, he would be breaking the truce'. In view of the recent activities of the English government, the implications of this warning could not possibly be misconstrued. Charles took the hint. Rather than face war with England, he immediately cancelled his Italian expedition. As he later reminded Clement VII, he had been forced to do so 'because of the problem of peace' with England. Two strictly contemporary letters confirm that his memory had not deceived him.[44] One, written from Avignon on 13 April 1391, explained that peace negotiations between England and France had caused the postponement of the enterprise; while the second, written from the papal court on 5 March, was even more explicit:

You will have heard that the pope of Avignon was to have left here for Lyons after Easter in order to join the king of France, with whom it is said he was going to Lombardy and Rome. He and his men had begun their preparations, buying horses and other necessities. But it is now said that yesterday the pope received a letter from the king of France saying that he will be unable to come as he is to meet the king of England in conference on 24 June. So it seems that the expedition will not take place this year.

The agreement for an interview between the two kings had in fact been sealed in Paris nine days previously, on 24 February,[45] and had evidently been accompanied by an assurance that the invasion of Italy would be called off. The royal interview was almost certainly arranged in order to save the face of the French king. Since Charles could not be both at Calais and in Italy in the coming

---

[43] B. M. Cotton Ms, Nero B.VII, fo. 6, outlines this project but is undated: 1391 seems preferable to 1397, the only likely alternative.

[44] *Chronique des quatres premiers Valois*, ed. S. Luce (Paris, 1862), pp. 316–17; and documents published by Champollion–Figeac, *Louis et Charles*, p. 8; Steinherz, *Dokumente*, p. 67; Brun, *Mémoires . . . Provence*, xii (1935), p. 127.

[45] Published by H. Moranvillé, 'Conférences entre la France et l'Angleterre, 1388–1393', *B.E.C.*, 1 (1889), pp. 369–70.

summer, his meeting with Richard provided a plausible public pretext for cancelling his Italian enterprise. But it was only a pretext, not a matter of choice on his part. By threatening to go to war, the English government had forced him to abandon his Italian ambitions.

The Anglo-French confrontation over Italy in the winter of 1390-1 was the most important event in international politics in the immediate post-war period. Though it was to be some time before this became fully apparent, its outcome dealt a fatal blow to the ambitions of the French princes, with dire consequences for the internal unity of France. The French were forced to reconsider almost the whole of their foreign policy, and ultimately to abandon or greatly modify their designs on Italy and the empire and reverse their attitude towards the Schism. A diplomatic victory of this magnitude would be hard to parallel. Yet the achievement of the English government has hitherto gone unrecognized.

It is unnecessary to trace in detail the later evolution of English policy towards Italy, since in general it followed the pattern established at the beginning of the 1390s. In the immediate aftermath of the crisis of 1391, Richard was called upon to define his future policy in answer to the appeal of Boniface IX. As we have already seen, he then assured the pope that Rome and Italy would not be sacrificed in the interests of peace with France. There is abundant proof that this promise was more than adequately fulfilled. Towards the end of 1392, Giangaleazzo informed the French government that Boniface IX intended to conclude a league with Richard II and a number of Italian states in order to protect the States of the Church, safeguard imperial rights, and ensure the independence of the smaller Italian powers in the face of French aggression. Boniface had even tried to inveigle Giangaleazzo himself into this alliance, assuring him that he need not fear French retaliation since 'The king of England would promise and solemnly oblige himself to invade France in person . . . with such power that the king of France would be compelled to recall any forces he had sent to Italy.' There is no means of telling whether or not this assurance was well founded, but Charles VI took it seriously enough. The Franco-Milanese treaty of 1391 was immediately modified so as to provide for Milanese aid to France if she were attacked by England as a consequence of her intervention in Italy. This modification was incorporated in all subsequent agreements between France and Milan.[46]

As it happened, Italian affairs never again brought France and England to the brink of war, and this clause remained a dead letter. Nevertheless, there were several minor confrontations in the later 1390s, all of which were firmly handled by the English government. The first arose in the early summer of 1393, when the duke of Orleans planned to invade the States of the Church from the north in alliance with Giangaleazzo, while his uncle, the duke of Bourbon, gathered a large army in Provence to reinforce the Angevin forces in Naples. After five months spent in preparing these expeditions, both were abruptly cancelled in May 'because'— in the words of our most reliable source—'it is said that there will be war in France, the English and French being unable to reach agreement' on the terms of peace. It can scarcely be a coincidence that the two sides did subsequently reach an agreement, immediately after the French forces had been cashiered.[47]

A little over a year later a similar crisis arose, largely as a result of the activities of the duke of Orleans in north Italy. While continuing to negotiate with Clement VII for the Adrian kingdom on which he had set his sights, Orleans made a vigorous military and diplomatic effort during the autumn and winter of 1394 to extend his Italian base at Asti by the acquisition of Genoa and Savona and their territories.[48] His activities—which met with a fair measure of success—provoked considerable alarm throughout northern and central Italy, where they were seen as the first step towards a large-scale French invasion. Early in 1395, the Genoese government appealed to England for help, an appeal which was immediately echoed by Boniface IX. Alarmed by French activity on his own back doorstep, even Giangaleazzo turned towards England, offering a marriage alliance between his sister-in-law, Lucia Visconti, and Richard II's favourite, the earl of Rutland. It is generally believed that these appeals were ignored. After all, 'what did it matter to Richard II if the duke of Orleans carved himself out a

[46] Jarry, *Louis de France*, p. 420 (quotation); Jarry, *B.E.C.*, liii (1892), pp. 552–4, 560–1 (treaties).

[47] Brun, *Mémoires . . Provence*, xiii (1936), pp. 63, 66.

[48] E. Jarry, *Les origines de la domination française à Gênes, 1392–1402* (Paris, 1896), is the standard work; for what follows, *Correspondence*, nos. 218 (Genoa), 226 (Milan); Perroy, *L'Angleterre et le grand Schisme*, document 12 (Boniface).

kingdom beyond the Alps?'[49] But in fact Richard took a far less phlegmatic view of French aggression in Italy and did his best to ensure that Orleans would not extend his conquests beyond the borders of Piedmont. Negotiations were opened with Milan on the basis of Giangaleazzo's marriage offer. Lest this should fail to deter Orleans, direct pressure was put on the French court to order his withdrawal. In July 1395, at the outset of the negotiations for his marriage to Isabel of France, Richard made it one of his conditions for a final settlement that Boniface IX be included as his ally.[50] Had this been accepted, the States of the Church, Rome, and the kingdom of Naples would all have been guaranteed against future French aggression. As it happened, however, all three objectives were to be achieved by other means, making it unnecessary for Richard to press his demand.

For reasons which will be examined below, the year 1395 witnessed a revolution in French policy towards Italy, a revolution which manifested itself in the rejection of the understanding with Milan in favour of an alliance with Florence, and which entailed the renunciation of the use of force against Boniface IX, the States of the Church and—to an extent—the kingdom of Naples. Though this *volte-face* greatly diminished the French threat to Italy, the English government did not drop its guard. The immediate consequence of the French *rapprochement* with Florence was an English understanding with Milan. Before 1395, English relations with Milan had been decidedly cool,[51] the inevitable result of Giangaleazzo's close association with France; but after the initial cracks had appeared in the Franco-Milanese *entente*, relations grew steadily warmer. The marriage alliance proposed by Giangaleazzo in 1395 was still under consideration on the eve of the Lancastrian revolution, providing in the interval tangible evidence of English diplomatic support for Milan. The efficacy of this support was revealed during the winter of 1397–8, the one occasion on which Giangaleazzo was seriously threatened by French pressure. Then, at his behest, Richard twice intervened on his behalf at the French court, first requesting Charles VI to work for peace in north Italy,

[49] Ibid., pp. 361–3; F. Lehoux, *Jean de France, duc de Berri*, ii (Paris, 1966), p. 341 (quotation).
[50] Published as appendix to my book (see n. 3).
[51] *Correspondence*, nos. 119, 148, 174. For what follows, ibid., no. 226; *C.Cl.R., 1396–9*, p. 8; D. M. Bueno de Mesquita, *E.H.R.*, lvi (1941), pp. 631, 634, 637.

then subsequently reminding him in rather stronger terms that

he had concluded a marriage alliance with him in order to bring peace to (Italy and France) and in order to terminate the Schism and put an end to the troubles of Christendom. He therefore disapproved of his being involved in this war (against Milan) in Italy, which was contrary to these good resolutions; and he would be pleased if the Armagnacs and all other French subjects who intended to enter the war were forbidden to do so.[52]

The reminder was effective; once again, the French forces failed to cross the Alps.

One final episode in Richard's relations with Italy requires attention, since it is the only one which invariably features in accounts on his reign, and has been so misconstrued as to give a totally distorted impression of the general tendencies of his policy. At his meeting with Charles VI outside Calais in October 1396, Richard agreed to collaborate with France in an expedition to north Italy in the spring of 1397. It has been generally assumed that the purpose of this expedition was to have been the conquest of Lombardy—or, more specifically, the destruction of Milan—for the exclusive benefit of France, a purpose which has not unnaturally called forth strong criticism of the abject servility of English foreign policy. Yet the assumption on which this criticism is based is not only improbable in itself but is directly refuted by three important sources which have somehow been overlooked. These sources[53] agree that the purpose of the Anglo-French expedition was to facilitate a compromise solution to the Schism. Writing in 1396, Philippe de Mézières—a man high in the confidence of Charles VI —prophesied that the two kings would employ armed intervention in Italy 'to seek and find some good treaty, without the spilling of Christian blood, whereby the Church of God, bride of Jesus Christ, divided and troubled as it was, might by the mercy of God be reunited under a single and true pope at the behest of the kings of England and France'. According to the normally reliable Italian

[52] Ibid., p. 637.
[53] A. H. Hamdy, 'Philippe de Mézières and the New Order of the Passion', *Bulletin of the Faculty of Arts* (Alexandria), xviii (1964), pp. 48–9, 61–2; A. H. Hamdy *Philippe de Mézières*, *'De la Chevalerie de la Passion de Jesu Christ'* (typescript, 1964)— both works kindly lent to me by Professor G. W. Coupland; Brun, *Mémoires . . Provence*, xiv (1937), p. 35; *Cal. of Papal Registers: Letters, 1362–1404*, pp. 294, 300 (cf *Annales*, pp. 200–1).

correspondent at Avignon, this prophecy was to have been fulfilled by the expedition of 1397. In December 1396 he reported
that 'it is believed that the king of France, or even the king of
England, will come here next April to enforce union on the
Church, and will go to Lombardy for this purpose'. Boniface IX
himself corroborates this report. In two bulls dated 1 March 1397,
he 'commended the purpose of John Holand, earl of Huntingdon
(one of the English commanders) to come shortly to Italy and
other parts for the extermination of schismatics, rebels, and usur-
pers of cities and lands of the pope and the Roman Church'; and
appointed him 'gonfalonier of the Holy Roman Church, vicar in
temporals in all provinces, cities, lands, castles and other places in
Italy and elsewhere belonging to the pope and the said Church,
and captain-general of all men-at-arms fighting in their service'.

The testimony of these sources must be seen against the background of Anglo-French policy towards the Schism at this date.
At their meeting outside Calais, the two kings had not only agreed
to lead a joint expedition to Italy in the following spring, but also
to send a joint delegation to the two popes demanding their resignation. The Anglo-French *démarche* at Rome and Avignon and the
Anglo-French expedition to Italy were evidently two halves of a
single plan, a plan designed to secure the unanimous election of a
new pope endowed with sufficient power in Italy to guarantee his
position.

In the event, this ambitious project collapsed, largely as a result
of the Nicopolis disaster and the subsequent ill health of the French
king. Later, when its original purpose had been perverted to forward the dynastic ambitions of the count of Armagnac, Richard
withdrew his support, threw his weight behind Giangaleazzo, and
reminded Charles VI that their original object had been to end the
Schism and bring peace to Christendom.[54]

★   ★   ★

The consequences of English intervention between France and
Italy were far-reaching. In the first place, the French were gradu-
ally forced to abandon their Italian ambitions and with them their
hopes of perpetuating a French papacy and of securing the imperial

[54] Above, pp. 102–3.

crown. The process was a slow one, but its outcome was already implicit in the French defeat in 1391. By the beginning of 1393, Charles VI had expressly disowned his own ambitions in the peninsula;[55] and although he made no immediate effort to restrain those of his brother or of his Angevin cousins, neither did he again lend them any very substantial support. After the fiascos of 1391 and 1393 Louis II of Anjou was starved of further reinforcements; and after French renunciation of the *voie de fait* in 1395 he was even denied the assistance of the Avignonese papacy. Deprived of military support and diplomatically isolated, he quickly succumbed to the forces of Ladislas of Durazzo, who derived steady political, financial and diplomatic backing from Boniface IX, Florence and Sicily. By the summer of 1399, Louis had lost his capital and his kingdom and was forced to return to France, where he promptly joined the Orleanist opposition to 'Burgundian' foreign policy.

Orleans's own ambitions suffered a somewhat similar fate. After 1391 he continued to negotiate with Clement VII for the creation of a kingdom for his benefit from the States of the Church; but his inability to secure French resources on a scale which would have enabled him to undertake the conquest of this kingdom effectively deterred Clement from alienating his patrimony. Clement, indeed, made most of the running in these negotiations, all of which eventually foundered on Orleans's refusal—or inability—to fix a date for his campaign or to specify the forces he would employ. Finally, in 1394 Orleans was forced to acknowledge his impotence by demanding that the entire project be postponed for four years.

Long before this period had elapsed, Orleans's ambitions had received their death blow. At the beginning of 1395, the French government renounced any further unilateral attempt to terminate the Schism by force as being 'too perilous'.[56] This decision implied the end of serious French intervention in Italy. The logical consequence of the renunciation of the *voie de fait* was the Franco-Florentine alliance of 29 September 1396.[57] By this alliance,

[55] Champollion-Figeac, *Louis et Charles*, p. 10; for next paragraph, Durrieu, *Revue des Questions Historiques*, xxviii (1880), pp. 43-78.
[56] *Veterum scriptorum . . amplissima collectio*, ed. E. Martène and U. Durand, vii (Paris, 1732), p. 439.
[57] Published in J. C. Lunig, *Codex Italiae Diplomaticus*, i (Frankfurt and Leipzig, 1725), cols. 1093-1104.

France abandoned her Milanese ally, on whose co-operation all previous plans of conquest had been founded. Her new ally was, always had been, and was to continue to be the hub of anti-French forces in Italy. Florence had consistently backed Boniface IX, whom Charles VI had threatened to unseat; she had contributed moral and financial support to Ladislas of Durazzo against Louis of Anjou; and she was allied to the lords of the Romagna, whom Louis of Orleans had hoped to dispossess. Her alliance with France did not oblige her to modify any of her earlier commitments. The treaty in fact guaranteed the security of Bologna and the Mala-testa, thus dealing the death blow to the pretensions of Louis of Orleans; excused Florence from assisting the Angevins in Naples; and while committing her to work with France for the peaceful reunion of the church, expressly absolved her from participating in any activities which might harm Boniface or the papal state. Thus, by denouncing the *voie de fait* and concluding this alliance, France forsook most of the Italian, imperial and ecclesiastical ambitions which had moulded her policy since the outbreak of the Great Schism.

This revolution in French policy had been brought about by the steady diplomatic pressure exerted by the English government. England, with nothing to gain from the Schism, had declared in favour of a compromise solution as soon as the war with France was over;[58] France, with everything to gain, could only be induced to agree to a peaceful compromise by *force majeure*. This force was applied by England. There is no foundation for the belief that Richard II was 'an upholder of French policy in Europe'. If any-thing, Charles VI upheld English policy.

A succession of grave diplomatic defeats in Italy and elsewhere produced a fundamental and increasingly bitter division among the French princes. At the beginning of the 1390s they had combined their resources in a vast enterprise from which all hoped to gain and in which their various ambitions seemed to complement and reinforce each other. Under the stress of continual English pres-sure, this unity had been shattered, to be replaced by the emergence of two mutually hostile blocs: one, headed by the duke of Bur-gundy, whose concern for peaceful relations with England in the

[58] Palmer, 'England and the Great Western Schism', *E.H.R.*, lxxxiii (1968), pp. 516–22.

interests of his Flemish subjects forced him, though reluctantly, to oppose an adventurous Italian policy; the other, headed by Orleans (later joined by Anjou, Bourbon and others), whose Italian ambitions were sufficiently important to predispose them to risk conflict with England. In due course, this division was to gather a momentum of its own, and ultimately to degenerate into civil war. But in its origin, it had been the product of political conditions, rooted in the frustrated ambitions of Louis of Orleans. It is scarcely surprising to find that Orleans gave his backing to the Lancastrian revolution.

★　　★　　★

To argue that English policy was successful abroad is not to say that it was popular at home. Much, if not all of Richard's achievement in this field would have been invisible to the majority of his subjects, for he could not advertise his successes without jeopardising his principal objective, a firm but soundly based peace. After the spectacular successes of his father and grandfather, it is not really surprising that he was popularly thought to be too soft towards the French. But it is difficult to see how he could have acted other than he did, or how he could have achieved more. His policy was responsible, consistent and hard-headed. His supplanter paid him the compliment of imitating it down to the smallest details.

VI

The Monks of Westminster and the University of Oxford

BARBARA F. HARVEY

RICHARD II was the only king between the time of John and that of Henry VIII who pressed the monks of Westminster to elect as their abbot a candidate whom there is any reason to believe they were reluctant to receive. This he did in 1386, when he urged the claims of John Lakyngheth in succession to Nicholas Litlington, against those of William Colchester, and, although he was finally unsuccessful, his action in withholding his assent to Colchester's election for a month supports the Monk of Westminster's belief that freedom of choice was endangered; as a rule the royal assent to an election at Westminster was now given in half this time.[1] Eight years later it was in a settlement made under royal auspices that the monks finally abated their claim to jurisdiction within the precincts of the royal free chapel of St Stephen in the Palace of Westminster despite a papal ruling in their favour; and shortly afterwards it cost them nearly £300 to have their privileges confirmed by the king.[2]

I beg to thank the dean and chapter of Westminster and Mr N. MacMichael, keeper of the muniments, for permission to use the muniments of Westminster Abbey, and Mr T. H. Aston, keeper of the archives of the university of Oxford, for permission to use the early registers of Congregation. I wish also to thank Dr A. B. Emden, Mr H. Farmer, Mr G. F. Lytle and Dr W. A. Pantin; to Dr Pantin, who read a draft of this essay and suggested many improvements, I owe a particular debt.

[1] Monk of Westminster, pp. 89–90, where the date of Colchester's election is said to have been 21 December 1386. The royal assent was given on 21 January 1387 (*C.P.R., 1385–9.* p. 270). The entry in Westminster Abbey Muniments (hereafter referred to as W.A.M.), Liber Quaternus Niger, fo. 86 under the date 10 December 1386—*factum est instrumentum de electione Willelmi Colchestr' archidiaconi in abbatem*—refers to the licence to elect; but see also *C.P.R., 1385–9*, p. 245 where the licence is dated 12 December.

[2] W.A.M. 19879; Victoria County History, *London*, i (London, 1909), p. 568.

This was the level of rights and of the action that maintains rights. At a deeper level, Richard II's relations with the Abbey were altogether different. He venerated its principal shrine, that of Edward the Confessor, where he worshipped a few hours before the meeting at Smithfield in 1381;[3] he took a personal interest in the rebuilding of the nave, chose Westminster as the burial place of Anne of Bohemia, and was himself commemorated there in his lifetime by a notable portrait and by a representation, larger than life-size, of the white hart, his badge. Since Henry III there had not been so devout a patron, and the monks were not to see his like again for another century.

In the history of the religious observance at Westminster, however, these years do not form a distinct period. The monks' life there now differed in several respects from what it had been in the stormy days of Abbot Wenlok and his immediate successors, but the changes which brought this about are to be placed earlier in the century, nearer the beginning of Edward III's reign than that of his grandson. One of these affected particularly the formative years which came after clothing and profession; it was the practice of sending able monks to the university, which the community followed intermittently from the 1330s and then steadily, as soon as men could be spared after the mortality of the Black Death. From the beginning of the abbacy of Nicholas Litlington in 1362 until the dissolution of the monastery in 1540, the community at Westminster included a handful of university-educated men. How these monks were chosen, what they studied at the university, and their employment on their return to Westminster are the topics that will be considered in this essay. The chronological range of the essay is thus much wider than the years 1377 to 1399—in common with May McKisack's own interests it does indeed stray as far as the sixteenth century—but it is to the later fourteenth century and to the intellectual activity of these years at Westminster that it will finally return.

★   ★   ★

The Black Monks had the highest hopes of the benefits to be gained from educating their ablest members at the university. To

[3] Monk of Westminster, p. 4.

advance there beyond the primitive sciences which a monk might study in his own house was to be one of the means of restoring the former excellence of the order, and already, in 1290 or 1291, the president of the English general chapter could boast how it was generally known that the order was beginning to flourish again through the work at Oxford.[4] More particularly, it was hoped that every community, except those too poor to participate in the scheme at all, would find in its university-trained men a succession of well-equiped preachers. Accordingly, the chapter exempted monks who had been sent to the university with the special purpose of learning to preach from the obligation of graduating, either as bachelors or as masters.[5]

In the course of the fourteenth century two Black Monk communities acquired houses of studies at Oxford that were to become famous. These were Durham Cathedral Priory, for whom principally Bishop Hatfield founded Durham College, and Christ Church, Canterbury, whose monks eventually won control of Canterbury Hall, Archbishop Islip's foundation; and both the Durham and the Canterbury monks had a foothold in Oxford before the time of these foundations. Students from other houses occasionally lodged with the Durham or Canterbury monks, but Gloucester College remained the principal foothold in Oxford for monasteries of the southern English province; the experience underlying the code of conduct for monk-students which the provincial chapter enacted in 1343 had been gained for the most part here, or at home, in the houses which sent men to the university and had to absorb them into the common life at the end of their scholastic training there.[6] Although we do not know which chamber the monks of Westminster occupied before 1371, when they took over that in the north range belonging to Christ Church, it is certain that they were invariably members of Gloucester College from their first appearance at Oxford.

Despite the fact that the president who esteemed university studies so highly forty or fifty years earlier had been the abbot of

[4] *Documents Illustrating the Activities of the General and Provincial Chapters of the English Black Monks, 1215–1540*, ed. W. A. Pantin, Camden, third series, xlv, xlvii, liv (hereafter referred to as *Chapters*), i, p. 132. The abbot of Westminster was president of the chapter; see also ibid., pp. 126–7.

[5] Ibid., ii, p. 75.

[6] For the legislation of 1343 see ibid., pp. 55–8; cf. pp. 74–82.

Westminster himself, no one went from the abbey to Oxford until the 1330s. The first to go were Brothers Robert de Hamslape and Robert de Lake, and we know of their presence at Oxford from a payment of £2 10s which they received from the reeve of Islip, a neighbouring manor belonging to the abbot's portion of lands, in 1338–9.[7] Two years earlier, the abbot himself, Thomas de Henle, who was an unlettered man at the time of his election, had received licence to go overseas to study.[8] Thus Hamslape and Lake were probably not the first professed monks of the house to frequent a university, but they were the first to go to Oxford. So late a beginning, on the morrow of the publication of Benedict XII's Constitutions, betrays the indifference of the monks of Westminster to the legislation of the general and provincial chapters; papal commands, by contrast, were to be obeyed.

The choice of Hamslape and Lake was understandable, given the novelty of the enterprise and the absence, as yet, of any legislative guidance as to the age at which monks were to go to the university. Lake, who had been ordained only in 1338 and professed two or three years before,[9] was of the standing of an appreciable number of the monks destined to go to Oxford and Cambridge from Westminster in the future. Hamslape, by contrast, had been in the monastery nearly twenty years and had already held the offices of treasurer, sacrist and chamberlain; clearly he was to be in charge of his much younger companion. That he had also been precentor suggests that he was a bookish man and perhaps a willing, if elderly, choice, for the care of the monastic library had been one of the precentor's duties at Westminster since the twelfth century.[10]

In the year of the payment to Hamslape and Lake the community at Westminster numbered forty-six monks.[11] Sending two to Oxford thus fulfilled the letter of Benedict XII's requirement,

[7] W.A.M. 14792.

[8] C.P.R., *1334–8*, p. 238; see also ibid., p. 16, and *Cal. of Papal Registers: Letters, 1305–42*, p. 410.

[9] E. H. Pearce, *Monks of Westminster* (Cambridge, 1916) (hereafter cited as *Monks*), p. 89.

[10] J. Armitage Robinson and M. R. James, *The Manuscripts of Westminster Abbey* (Cambridge, 1909), pp. 1 ff. See also D. Knowles, *Monastic Order in England* (Cambridge, 1949), pp. 428–9, and *Monks*, pp. 80–1.

[11] W. A. M. 18721. The chamberlain bought cloth for forty-eight habits this year, but he and the prior were each allowed two.

to be reiterated in the legislation of the provincial chapter, that for every twenty monks, one should go. In the years immediately following the Black Death, when a sadly depleted community struggled to serve the abbey's altars and manage its elaborate economy, Westminster sent no monks at all. First to go after the disaster was probably Brother Thomas de Norton, who received money from the treasurer for his expenses at Oxford in 1356–7 and again in the following year.[12] By 1362–3 two monks were in residence, although there were still fewer than forty in the house.[13] Thereafter, and until the end of the fifteenth century, the abbey usually, though not quite invariably, fulfilled its obligation: a community normally of forty or fifty monks, it faithfully set apart two of its members for the university, and not infrequently during the fifteenth century three were in residence—a change possibly connected with the reduction of the monk-student's annual allowance from £10 to ten marks towards the middle of the century.[14] In 1423, when the abbot was reprimanded by the provincial chapter for having failed to allow any of his monks to go to a *studium* for the space of a year, Brothers William Bonnok and Edmund Kyrton were both in fact studying at Oxford, and the succession of monks of Westminster in residence there seems to have been unbroken since the beginning of the century.[15]

By the end of the fifteenth century the figures suggest, not merely obedience to a rule in this matter, but a real enthusiasm for higher education at Westminster. Despite the foundation of a Benedictine house of studies at Cambridge earlier in the century, the abbey still preferred Oxford for nearly all its students. It now became the invariable practice, however, to have three in residence there at a time, and occasionally the number was as high as five or six, and this in a period when there was no proportionate increase in the size of the monastic community, but, on the contrary, a decline. Nearly half the total number of monks that went from

---

[12] W.A.M. 19852–3. The small size of the payments (2 marks per annum), compared to the allowance of £10 per annum that soon became usual, is explained first by the help which the abbot gave the students from his own funds in the early days of the enterprise, and secondly by the fact that every obedientiary contributed ½d. in the mark towards their expenses in this period; for an example of such a contribution, see W.A.M. 19326.

[13] W.A.M. 19858.   [14] *Monks*, p. 26.

[15] W.A.M. 19918, 19920; see also W.A.M. 19883 ff., and *Chapters*, ii, p. 151.

Westminster to the university between the 1330s and the dissolution—c. 30 out of c. 70—went up after 1490.[16]

The practice of having two monks at the university, but not more, which the abbey followed for the greater part of the four-teenth and fifteenth centuries, entailed some variety in the standing of the monks who were chosen. For one the vacancy might occur as soon as he had completed his years as a junior, learning the liturgy and customs of the house; for another it might be delayed much longer. The great majority of those chosen went up within six or seven years of entering the house, and as many as a third within three or four years of doing so, but a few were of quite different standing. The pioneer Hamslape has already been mentioned. Later, in 1405, William Amondesham went to Gloucester College seventeen or eighteen years after entering the monastery; John Savery had been twenty years a monk when he went up in 1415, and Richard Teddyngton had been in the house nearly as long when he did so in 1447.[17] But the choice usually lighted on a monk in his early or mid-twenties. It was not considered essential at Westminster that a monk should have been ordained before going to the university, and seventeen or eighteen said their first mass after entering Oxford. In 1498 Thomas Gardyner and William Fenne, who were then studying at Gloucester College, received the order of sub-deacon at Oseney Abbey,[18] and from time to time others may have received the minor orders in or near Oxford. Yet, since it seems to have been the practice of the house by the second half of the fourteenth century to have its monks ordained as soon as they reached the canonical age, however short the time elapsing after profession, most of those who went to Oxford from Westminster within three or four years of their clothing were, even so, already priests.

★   ★   ★

Differences in the ages and standing of the monks who went to

[16] For the monks who went to the university, see *Monks*, passim, but add the following: Robert de Charleton, for whom see Emden, *Oxford*, ii, p. xiv; John Islip (below, p. 127 n.); Simon Langham (Emden, *Oxford*, ii, p. 1095); William Mane (below, p. 127 n.); Thomas de Norton (above, p. 112).

[17] *Monks*, pp. 122, 125, 143; Emden, *Oxford*, i, p. 31, iii, pp. 1647, 1853. For Savery see also below, p. 118.

[18] Emden, *Oxford*, ii, pp. 677, 743.

the university make it certain that there was no uniform pattern in the studies pursued there or in the preparatory education in the cloister. Our knowledge of these matters is derived mainly from the careers of the minority, numbering between twenty and twenty-five, who are known to have graduated; all except two of these monks were theologians, not canonists, and about half the number did not aspire to the master's chair but were content with the bachelorship.[19]

Like the friars, and largely as the result of struggles which engaged the friars at Oxford well before the regulars had a common house of studies there, the Black Monks were allowed to incept in theology without first incepting in the arts. Until 1448 this privilege depended on the granting of graces, and the vote of a single regent master would serve to delay or deny it in the individual case. Uncertain in its particular application, it was nevertheless secure in principle, and regulations about the opponency in theology for those who had not incepted in the arts found their way into the university statutes long before this date.[20] According to the statutes the opponency for such a student lasted a year, and no one was admitted to it without a year's study of theology in Oxford itself. This, however, was merely the residence requirement: a monk availing himself of the privilege of admission to the opponency without doing a regency in the arts had to swear that

[19] The following are known to have graduated or to have supplicated for the degree in question: *1350–1400*: William Colchester (B.Th.); Thomas Merks (D.Th.); William Sudbury (B.Th.) *1400–50*: John Amondesham (B.Th.); William Amondesham (D.Cn.L.); Edmund Kyrton (D.Th.); Robert Whateley (D.Th.) *1450–1500*: William Borow (B.Th. or D.Th.); John Islip (B.Th. or D.Th.); William Mane (B.Th. or D.Th.); Thomas Millyng (D.Th.) *1500–40*: Thomas Barton (D.Th.); Robert Benet (B.Th.); William Brent (B.Th.); Humphrey Charyte (D.Th.); John Clerke (D.Th.); Denys Dalians (B.Th.); Antony Dunston (D.Th.); Thomas Essex (B.Th.); Richard Gorton (D.Th.); Thomas Jaye (B.Th.); John Laurence (B.Cn.L.); Nicholas Lindsey (D.Th.); William Southwell (B.Th.).
  The likelihood of our knowing whether or not a student graduated is much greater in the periods for which the register of Congregation survives (1448–63, and, with a short break in 1517–18, from 1505). For Borow, Islip and Mane, see below, p. 127 n.

[20] Strickland Gibson, *Statuta Antiqua Universitatis Oxoniensis* (1931), pp. 157, 178, 273; see also ibid., pp. cxiii ff. The definitive account of the friars' privileges is A. G. Little, 'The Franciscan School at Oxford in the Thirteenth Century', in *Archivum Franciscanum Historicum*, xix (1926), pp. 823 ff.; see also H. Rashdall, *Universities of Europe in the Middle Ages*, 3 vols., revised F. M. Powicke and A. B. Emden (1936), iii, pp. 158–9.

he had studied theology under a master for six or seven years and logic and philosophy before that. At the end of the opponency he might be admitted to lecture on the Sentences, and it was to those who reached this stage that the order accorded the privileges of a bachelor. The doctorate took longer, and a monk who chose to do all his theology at Oxford had to spend at least nine years there before he could incept.[21]

Despite the impression so vividly conveyed by the long struggle over these privileges that the medieval university was beset by possessioners and mendicants eager to graduate as swiftly as a vigilant Congregation would allow, it must not be assumed that monks always pursued a single-minded course from the moment of their arrival in Oxford and covered their chosen ground in the shortest possible time, as a student today normally does. Many of them were conscripts to the academic life, sent to the university solely in order to fulfil the obligation of their monastery to maintain men there, and the Westminster evidence suggests that even among the ablest, who graduated, were some who may have resided so desultorily as to jeopardize their academic standing and multiply the number of years that necessarily elapsed before inception. A long interval between a monk's entry upon his studies at Oxford and opponency or inception tells us nothing certain, therefore, about the extent of his learning when he arrived, although often, no doubt, it does denote meagre preparation in the cloister. However, until the fifteenth century, when the university may have relaxed its earlier vigilance in the granting of graces, a very short period of residence has none of this ambiguity: a monk who achieved the bachelorship in theology after residing for not much more than the minimum number of years allowed by the statutes must be credited with teachers at home capable of taking him, not only through logic and philosophy, but over the threshold of theology itself.

As a rule, the residence of monks of Westminster at the university is recorded in the accounts of the abbey treasurers, who, from the 1360s, paid each student £10 or ten marks yearly and made special, additional payments to cover the expenses of opponency and inception. Predictably, this evidence suggests that monks of this house normally did the whole of their theology at the

[21] Gibson, op. cit., pp. 48, 179.

university. Thus William Sudbury resided seven years before he was admitted to oppose in 1382; the first reference to John Amondesham as a bachelor occurs not less than seven and possibly as many as nine years after his entering Gloucester College in 1432, and in the early sixteenth century Denys Dalians studied at Oxford for eight years before he was admitted to the opponency.[22]

Equally, such periods of residence point to the main study of logic and philosophy and the preliminaries elsewhere, and it seems clear also that in the fourteenth and fifteenth centuries a few of the abbey's graduates did begin or complete their theology at home. Too little is known about the early years of Thomas Merks for us to build conclusions on his career; it is, however, noteworthy that nothing in the abbey muniments, excellent though these are for the period in question, connects him with Oxford until 1388 or 1389, only some four years before he was admitted to lecture on the Sentences and six or seven before he incepted as a doctor.[23] William Colchester's career is better documented, and we can be confident that he achieved the bachelorship in theology despite the fact that he did not enter Gloucester College before 1365 or 1366 or stay there after 1370.[24] Thomas Ruston had been three years back at Westminster when he supplicated for the bachelorship in 1459; however, his tenure of the precentorship in the meantime makes it seem likely that he had persisted in more than desultory reading, and a generation later Ralph Langley became enough of a theologian to preach to his fellow monks at Westminster on the great occasions of Palm Sunday and Good Friday, although this was the particular task of the Oxford monks and Langley never, to our knowledge, frequented the university at all.[25] It is thus a possibility that the publication of Benedict XII's Constitutions

[22] For Sudbury see *Monks*, p. 113; for Amondesham, ibid., p. 144 and *Chapters*, iii, p. 106; and for Dalians, University of Oxford Archives, Reg. H 7, fo. 29ᵛ, and *Monks*, p. 183.

[23] W.A.M. 24540; *Monks*, p. 116.

[24] W.A.M. 19859–65; cf. *C.P.R., 1385–9*, p. 270, and *Monks* p. 103. Colchester was ordained priest in 1361–2, the year of the first reference to him at Westminster, and he may have been a relatively mature recruit.

[25] Ruston supplicated for admission to oppose on the ground of eight years in philosophy, nine in theology and many long vacations in both (University of Oxford, Reg. Aa 5, fo. 117). He resided at Oxford from 1448–56 (*Monks*, p. 145). For Langley, see ibid., p. 160. Since Langley was not ordained until five or six years after entering the monastery, it is clear that he was not a late recruit, who had studied theology before his profession.

provoked the abbey, not only to send its quota of monks to the university, but also to provide claustral lectures in theology.[26]

If some of those who proceeded to degrees did a little of their theology at home, it is natural to ask why all were not required to do so in the interests of monastic stability. The answer is partly, no doubt, that the community did not always include a master capable of teaching the subject, or command the services of one near at hand; but principally such inconsistencies betray the external source of the stimulus which drove the monks of Westminster to the university. Despite the monastery's long years of obedience to the papal rule that for every twenty monks one should go, residence at the university never became part of an ordered system of education, in which the abler monks of the house advanced from stage to stage in predictable sequence; it remained an externally imposed obligation which could be fulfilled by setting aside two monks yearly, and, on the whole, the individual monk was entered at Gloucester College and withdrawn from it to suit the monastery's need for a succession of students and not his own formation as a monk. Hence, among the élite represented by the graduates, who so regularly completed nearly all the preliminaries to theology before they went to Oxford, is one who nevertheless began near the beginning and did, so it appears, not only his logic and philosophy but virtually the whole of the arts course there. This is Robert Whateley. Whateley was professed in or about the year 1386–7 and said his first mass two years later; he was thus about 25 or 26 years old when he entered Gloucester College in 1390. He resided seventeen years in all and thirteen or fourteen before he was admitted to oppose, in 1403–4.[27] Clearly, unless he was negligent in keeping his terms or exceptionally slow at his books, Whateley was chosen for Oxford before he had even completed his study of grammar.

Whateley eventually incepted in theology. At the other end of the scale of academic distinction, and rather more obviously men on whom the lot had chanced to fall, are the monks who were sent to Gloucester College for the briefest of periods, as stopgaps

---

[26] Cf. W. A. Pantin, 'Abbot Kidderminster and Monastic Studies', in *Downside Review*, xlvii (1929), pp. 198 ff. For Benedict XII's Constitutions, see D. Wilkins, *Concilia Magnae Britanniae et Hiberniae*, ii (London, 1737), pp. 588 ff.

[27] *Monks*, p. 121; Emden, *Oxford*, iii, p. 2030.

to fill an unexpected vacancy and provide others already in residence in the abbey's chamber there with their necessary companions. Such were John Savery, who was chosen in place of William Norreys, when the latter died at Oxford in 1415, although he had been Norreys's senior by ten years and more in the community at Westminster, and William Surreys, who stood in for Edmund Kyrton for the one brief year that broke Kyrton's twenty-year residence at Oxford, first as student and then as *prior studentium*.[28] This happened the year after Norreys's death, and so in 1416–17 the abbey was represented at Oxford by two middle-aged freshmen, Surreys being probably 39 or 40 years old and Savery rather older.

Surreys and Savery were two of the large number of monks of Westminster—forty or fifty in all—who spent some time at the university but, as far as we know, never achieved a degree. Some of these stayed long enough to raise the suspicion that they, too, may in fact have become at least bachelors. Thomas Colchester, for example, was at Oxford from 1380 to 1390, and Richard Teddyngton was there for nine years in the mid-fifteenth century, although neither has left any record of proceeding to a degree.[29] Most members of this group, however, stayed for much shorter periods, and some for only two or three years. Not a few may have been failures, who unexpectedly disappointed the hopes placed in them when they were chosen for Gloucester College, but the only thing that is certain about the monks who returned to Westminster without a degree is that some of them had employed their time in learning to preach.

To secure a succession of duly qualified preachers was one of the main purposes of the Black Monk order in encouraging university studies for its members; and at the university the monks no doubt learnt the modern form of sermon-construction, which had developed in association with the Aristotelian revival of the earlier middle ages and was distinguished by the elaborate arrangement of its material. The chapter required preachers to be trained in the vernacular as well as Latin—a rule which does not necessarily imply a lay audience, for by the fourteenth century even the provincial chapter was occasionally regaled by its chosen preachers in

[28] W.A.M., 19907–19910; see also *Monks*, pp. 129–31.
[29] Ibid., pp. 115, 143; Emden, *Oxford*, i, p. 459; iii, p. 1853.

English.[30] It is clear, however, that the monks who studied at Gloucester College were prepared for public as well as private preaching.[31] As a passage in Jocelin of Brakelond's Chronicle shows, it had long been assumed by some in monastic circles that those who preached to the people should be well-educated,[32] and from the thirteenth century onwards the training of monks at the university specifically for this purpose was part of the work of rehabilitating the order in the face of mendicant rivalry, which the chapter had constantly in mind.

Such public sermons have been traced more often in the cathedral monasteries than elsewhere. At Westminster we hear little or nothing of the institution between the time of Osbert of Clare, who boasted of expounding the scriptures to a crowded audience in the church and chapter house, and Henry VII's provision for sermons—by graduates—at the foundation of his chantry.[33] But even before Henry made his benefaction, the abbey's tenant at Steventon, in Berkshire, was obliged to entertain the monks from Oxford if they came to preach publicly,[34] and this not only makes it certain that monks of Westminster were trained at Gloucester College in this kind of preaching but raises the presumption that some public preaching was done in the abbey itself. It was no doubt heard by the concourse of people who were brought to the abbey by its long accumulation of indulgences.

The monastic community itself heard sermons on Palm Sunday and Good Friday. One preacher was chosen each year and he seems usually, though not invariably, to have been a university-trained monk. Not surprisingly, since preaching was one of the scholastic acts required of them at the university, some of the abbey's bachelors and doctors were numbered among the chosen preachers. But other monks also came from Oxford for this purpose—John Moore did so after only one year at Oxford, in 1491[35]—

[30] *Chapters*, ii, p. 15. The public were admitted (ibid., pp. 60–1, 155).

[31] Ibid., ii, pp. 11–12; cf, iii, p. 28.

[32] *Chronicle of Jocelin of Brakelond*, ed. H. E. Butler (London, 1949), p. 12.

[33] *Letters of Osbert of Clare, Prior of Westminster*, ed. E. W. Williamson (Oxford, 1929), p. 56. For Henry VII's foundation, see below, pp. 126–7.

[34] W.A.M. Register Book, i, fos. 136ᵛ–137ᵛ. Cf. *Cal. of Papal Registers: Letters, 1471–1484*, p. 581. The provincial chapter required students to preach at least four times a year (*Chapters*, ii, p. 214).

[35] *Monks*, p. 169. The fact that Richard Excestre possessed a text of Bromyard at his death suggests that he, too, had been a preacher; see below, p. 125 n.

and even those destined to proceed to a degree might be far away from inception when they first preached. Robert Whateley probably did so in 1400, when he was four years away from the opponency, and Thomas Barton's supplication for the opponency in 1509 enumerates a sermon in the monastery among his qualifications.[36]

★   ★   ★

Many of the student-monks of Westminster thus resided at Oxford for periods which are comparable to those for which the university may claim members of the religious orders today: about a third of all whose names are known to us spent less than five years away from the monastery. But what, more precisely, did residence mean in the fourteenth and fifteenth centuries, and what contacts with the monastery were preserved while it lasted?

The academic year ran, in this period, from the second week in October to the end of the first week in July, and full term, during which lectures were given, comprised approximately thirty weeks.[37] Full term, however, did not monopolize all the acts and periods of study that counted for a degree. The provincial chapter had little to say about the period for which a monk should reside during the academic year, but it is clear that the monks of Gloucester College sometimes continued their private disputations in vacation; on the other hand, long absences occurred often enough to provoke legislation about monks who were absent from Oxford for whole terms.[38] Quite probably the practice varied according to the wealth of the monastery in question and its distance from Oxford.

Westminster Abbey was exceedingly rich among Black Monk houses; and two of its monks, unencumbered by a retinue, could easily cover the distance from Oxford in three days. Its students returned home relatively often, and by some the obligations of residence were taken very lightly indeed. Students normally returned for Christmas and for Palm Sunday and Easter, whether or not they were to preach, and they returned for any unusual event in the life of the community, at whatever point in the

[36] *Monks*, p. 121; University of Oxford Archives, Reg. G 6, fo. 67.
[37] Gibson, op. cit., pp. 51, 133, 236; see also pp. lxxx–lxxxi.
[38] *Chapters*, ii, p. 77.

academic year it occurred. Thus in 1386 William Sudbury and Thomas Colchester returned to Westminster in December for the election of a successor to Abbot Litlington, and Colchester returned, now with William Pulburgh as his fellow student, for the burial of Cardinal Langham in 1387 or 1388.[39] Sudbury's and Colchester's combined periods of residence at Oxford amounted to only thirty weeks in 1383–4, and in 1386–7 to no more than eighteen;[40] in 1387–8, when separate figures are recorded for each monk, Colchester was away from Westminster for thirty-three weeks and William Pulburgh for forty-two.[41]

We owe this information to the parsimony of the abbey treasurer, who refused to pay the kitchener an allowance for the students during their weeks of absence. The treasurer entered the periods in question in his account, although, as the figures which have been cited show, he was apt to regard the two monks at Oxford as a single unit for accounting purposes and convert two concurrent periods of residence into one consecutive term. Unhappily, he did not continue thrifty for long, and in any case his accounts do not survive in unbroken sequence. But it is clear, even in less well-documented years, that the regular vacations at Christmas and Easter might be long drawn out, and that a monk who was nominally in residence at Oxford by no means always pernoctated there. In 1491, for example, the four monks then at Oxford all returned to Westminster Abbey in February and stayed until May, although Palm Sunday and Easter, which were the real occasion of their visit, fell at the very end of March and beginning of April.[42] If the late fourteenth-century evidence shows us a

[39] W.A.M. 19874–5. [40] W.A.M. 19870, 19874.

[41] W.A.M. 19875. The other known periods of residence were: William Zepeswych and John Stowe, 58 weeks in 1362–3 and 74 in 1363–4; Richard Circestre and John Stowe, 74 weeks in 1364–5; William Colchester and John Farnyngho 72 weeks in 1368–9; William Colchester and Peter Combe 72 weeks in 1369–70; John Farnyngho 37 weeks and Peter Combe the whole year in 1371–2; William Sudbury 38 weeks and Richard Excestre the whole year in 1372–3; John Farnyngho and William Sudbury 82 weeks in 1378–9; William Sudbury and Thomas Colchester 84 weeks in 1380–1, 40 weeks in 1384–5 and 47 in 1385–6 (W.A.M. 19858 ff). As in the text, a single figure for two monks represents their combined periods of residence during the year in question. The phrase used to describe residence for a whole year—*quasi pro toto anno*—suggests that the period was not in fact 52 weeks but as near as made no difference to the internal accounting year of the Abbey.

[42] W.A.M. 19987; see *Monks*, p. 169.

typical state of affairs, it was an unusual student who did not spend three months in the year at Westminster, and some were there for still longer periods than this.

*   *   *

Even so, residence at the university gave relief for relatively long periods of time from the insistent, inescapable demands of the common life, and many students became for several years not much more than visitors at the abbey. The election of Robert Whateley as prior when he was in his seventeenth year as a student at Oxford may be described as a compliment to a well-tried guest, and the same is to be said of Thomas Millyng's election to this office nearly sixty years later, for Millyng was in his tenth year of residence.[43] For a monk who returned to be prior the difficulties of adjustment need not have been great, since the prior of Westminster had followed the abbot out of the common life into the enjoyment of private lodgings and tacit exemption from the round of duties in cloister and choir. At lower levels they may well have been acute, even for monks who had savoured the freedom of university life for no more than two or three years. If they were, the fact has left no trace in the sources of this period at Westminster; what these record is the equality with which the monks who had been to the university were usually treated on their return.

Not surprisingly, since the abbot was the monastery's representative in an increasingly well-educated world, such monks were frequently chosen for the highest office of all. Indeed, Thomas de Henle's case suggests that by the mid-fourteenth century an abbot of Westminster who had not been to the university quickly felt himself to be at a disadvantage that must be remedied. Yet one in two of the abbots who ruled Westminster between the mid-fourteenth century and the dissolution had not been to the university, and of the priors of this period, eight had spent some time there and eleven had not.[44] At the other end of the scale of impor-

---

[43] Ibid., pp. 121, 152–3.
[44] Of the abbots, Simon Langham, William Colchester, Edmund Kyrton, Thomas Millyng, John Islip and William Boston had been to the university, and, of the priors, Langham, Richard Excestre, Robert Whateley, Millyng, Islip,

tance were offices that were rarely, if ever, given to the university monks. Few were ever kitcheners, for example, and only one was ever infirmarer.[45] But in general those who had been to Oxford were accorded no special claim to office and none to exemption from it; the possibility of treating them in this way was one domestic advantage in permitting so few to graduate. Only the archdeacon's duties seem to have required their special gifts and skills; William Zepeswych, William and John Amondesham and William Borow were all appointed archdeacon within a year or two of their return, and nearly half the monks who are known to have held this office at Westminster during the whole course of the middle ages had spent some time at the university.[46]

What then happened to these monks, and what was the special occupation of those who were not assigned to preach, or of the preachers out of the homiletical season?

Several eventually passed, as Millyng did, into public life— Langham, for example, as bishop of Ely and later archbishop of Canterbury, and Merks to become bishop of Carlisle and fall into honourable disgrace as spokesman for Richard II at his deposition. At a humbler level, no fewer than five became in their turn prior of the abbey's dependent cell at Hurley;[47] two or three of these, however, spent long, uneventful years as ordinary choir-monks before their departure. In 1475, as an old man—he had entered Westminster nearly fifty years before—and many years after graduating in theology at Oxford, John Amondesham became rector of Aller, in Somerset.[48] Anthony Dunston in the sixteenth century ended his monastic life as abbot of Eynsham.[49]

A few evidently became men of letters. Perhaps many responded to their Oxford experiences in this way, but at this distance of time it is only a few who can be detected in the art of composition,

William Mane, Thomas Jaye and Denys Dalians. Boston was not by origin a monk of Westminster; see *Monks*, pp. 189–90.

[45] John Clerke, the exception, was infirmarer in 1536–7.
[46] *Monks*, pp. 98, 122, 144, 169, 212. The other archdeacons who had been to the university were William Colchester, Peter Combe, John Stowe, William Lambard and Robert Benet.
[47] William Pulburgh, Thomas Ruston, John Savery, William Southwell, William Zepeswych, for whom see *Monks*, pp. 118–19, 145–6, 125, 174, 98–9.
[48] Emden, *Oxford*, i, p. 31.
[49] *Monks*, p. 184. He became bishop of Llandaff in 1545.

the possession of books, or the enjoyment of the leisure for study afforded by the precentorship. By far the most interesting figure in the list of the university-educated precentors is Richard Southbrooke, who had incepted in the arts as a fellow of New College before he was professed at Westminster about 1412 or 1413. Southbrooke went to Gloucester College for three further years of study in 1417 and became precentor on his return. He held the office for eighteen years or more, possibly relinquishing it only in 1445, when he became a recluse.[50] As a graduate recruit to the Black Monks in the later middle ages he was a rarity.

From Southbrooke's pen nothing survives, but Richard Circestre, one of his predecessors at Oxford and in the precentorship, compiled a history of England down to the Norman Conquest, the *Speculum Historiale de Gestis Regum Angliae* and, with others to assist him, an inventory of the abbey vestry.[51] He has been identified by some as the Monk of Westminster, whose chonicle is a major source for the middle years of Richard II's reign, and there is this to be said for the suggestion, that Richard Circestre, like the Monk, was a man little touched by the learning of the schools.[52] To one of Southbrooke's successors, Thomas Ruston, the office gave the leisure that he needed to complete his studies for the bachelorship in theology after his return from Oxford in 1456.[53] Circestre had entered Westminster when Simon Langham was abbot, and of Langham's library, which returned to Westminster at his death, we can say that, if it does not exactly prove that this most famous son of the abbey continued in serious study when he left Oxford, it suggests at least that he valued books and wished to be known as one who possessed them; the collection, which is one of the largest private libraries in monastic hands of which we have any knowledge, went far beyond the necessary works of reference that a bishop had to possess.[54] It was one Oxford monk, Richard Excestre, who as prior received Langham's books when they

[50] Ibid., p. 132; Emden, op. cit., iii, pp. 1733–4.

[51] *Speculum Historiale de Gestis Regum Angliae*, ed. J. E. B. Mayor, 2 vols., (Rolls Series, 1863–9); for the inventory, see *Archaeologia*, lii, pp. 195 ff.

[52] J. Armitage Robinson, 'An Unrecognized Westminster Chronicler, 1381–1394', in *Proceedings of the British Academy*, iii (1907–8), pp. 61 ff.; cf. J. Taylor, *The Universal Chronicle of Ranulf Higden* (Oxford, 1966), p. 128.

[53] *Monks*, pp. 145–6; see above, p. 116.

[54] Robinson and James, *Manuscripts of Westminster Abbey*, pp. 4–7; and see also below, p. 129.

reached Westminster from Avignon in 1378,[55] and another, William Sudbury, who doubtless handled the scholastic items in the collections as he compiled his *tabule* of Thomist writings. Sudbury tells his readers that he began this work when he was opposing in the schools at Oxford in 1382 but completed it over a period of sixteen years in the cloister.[56] A century and a half later Leland noticed this book at Westminster.[57]

The list of the monks in whom Oxford kindled or fanned the spark of scholarship could be lengthened, but it would remain decent rather than impressive. Of seventy who went from Westminster to Oxford, only Sudbury, as far as we know, made any contribution to theology on his return, and he did not leave the lower slopes of achievement; he was less important to his age than Gilbert Crispin had been to his, a less interesting figure than Osbert of Clare.[58] Thomas Merks, although he made a name for himself as a bachelor lecturing on the Sentences and returned to the academic life after his disgrace, in 1401, wrote on the practical subject of the *dictamen*.[59] Some others, who spent only short periods at Oxford, were apparently quite unaffected in their mode of thought by their experiences there—an indication of the extent to which the more transient among the students at Gloucester College, who did not undertake the necessarily public acts that preceded inception, were shielded from the life of the secular schools. In Circestre's *Speculum Historiale* it is only the pages on the regalia that betray the learning of the schools or the authorship of

[55] *Monks*, p. 102. The following inventory was made of Excestre's own books when he died *c.* 1397: Hostiensis in summa; Prima pars Hostiensis in lectura; Rationale divinorum; Polycronicon cum libro Marci Pauli; Apparatus Pauli super Clementinas; Bromyerd, bonus; Bellum Troianum cum multis tractatibus; Scolastica historia; Dignus de regulis juris; Excerpta de viciis et virtutibus; Mappa Anglie; Mappa maris; Mappa Scotie (W.A.M. 6603)—a list in which light reading is easily distinguished from works of reference.

[56] B. M. Royal Ms, 9, F. iv, fo. 174.

[57] John Leland, *Collectanea*, ed. T. Hearne (London, 1774), iv, p. 49.

[58] For Sudbury's works, see Emden, *Oxford*, iii, p. 1813. They included a treatise on the Precious Blood of Christ.

[59] N. Denholm-Young, 'The Cursus in England', in *Oxford Essays in Medieval History presented to H. E. Salter* (Oxford, 1934), pp. 81, 100; *Formularies which bear on the History of Oxford, c. 1204–1420*, ed. H. E. Salter, W. A. Pantin and H. G. Richardson, vol. i (Oxford Historical Society, n.s., iv), pp. 18 ff. For a replication to a *quaestio* of Merks on the Sentences see S. L. Forte, *A Study of Some Oxford Schoolmen of the Middle of the Fourteenth Century, with Special Reference to Worcester Cathedral MS. F. 65* (unpublished Oxford B. Litt. thesis, 1947), ii, p. 256.

a mind which they had helped to form, and these were written, not by Circestre himself, but by Sudbury.[60] Much later Thomas Gardyner, who had been at least briefly in both Oxford and Cambridge during the 1490s, returned with a love both of history and of genealogy. He beguiled his declining years in writing a chronicle, now of little intrinsic interest, and in tracing the ancestry of Henry VIII to William the Conqueror, Alfred and Cadwaller.[61]

$$\star \qquad \star \qquad \star$$

It is the more surprising that so many monks went to the university in the very period which Gardyner's career at Westminster spanned. The number began to mount soon after 1490, and we know from Dr Pantin's study of Robert Joseph that a similar trend showed itself at Evesham Abbey at this time.[62] Despite their mediocre attainments as scholars, the monks of Westminster were at least capable of this response to the intellectual ambition of the world around them. The same influence, breaking the long monopoly of Gloucester College, attracted the first monks of Westminster to Cambridge, and a number now divided their university years, with a bewildering changefulness, between Oxford and Cambridge. Gardyner himself was at Gloucester College between 1497 and 1499 and in Cambridge for part of the next year; and a generation later Robert Cheseman also had two years at Oxford and one in Cambridge.[63]

Westminster Abbey's academic policy was also much influenced in these years by its patron, Henry VII. Henry was critical of the religious and of Westminster Abbey in particular, where he was

[60] *Speculum Historiale*, ed. Mayor, ii, pp. 26–39. These are the three tractates on the regalia which Tanner attributed to Sudbury; see Emden, *Oxford*, iii, p. 1813.

[61] Bodleian Library, Oxford, Rawlinson Mss D. 1020, fos. 1–33; ibid., Eng. Hist. e. 193. These manuscripts were identified as Gardyner's work by Dr J. J. G. Alexander and Professor McKisack, to whom I am indebted for my knowledge of their existence.

The pedigree is dated 1542, and the chronicle also extends to the reign of Henry VIII.

[62] *Letter Book of Robert Joseph*, ed. H. Aveling and W. A. Pantin (Oxford Historical Society, n.s. xix, 1967), p. xix. Cf. Cardinal Morton's legacy for the maintenance of at least 30 poor students at the two universities, 2 of whom were to be monks of Christ Church, Canterbury. W. A. Pantin, *Canterbury College, Oxford*, iii (Oxford Historical Society, n.s., viii, 1950), p. 227.

[63] *Monks*, pp. 175, 188.

dissatisfied to find only three monks who had achieved the bachelorship or doctorate in theology—the abbot, the prior and the monk-bailiff.[64] Since he intended that the monks who served his chantry at Westminster and preached there should be doctors, or at least bachelors, his disapproval coloured many of the splendid provisions of the agreement with the monastery which established his foundation there in 1504;[65] and it appears also that he had heard of the ample vacations enjoyed by the monks who studied at the university.

For the service of Henry's chantry, where prayers were to be offered during his lifetime for his prosperity and after his death for the safety of his soul, the monastery was to recruit three additional monks of the order, who were each to receive, beside the allowance of a monk of Westminster, a yearly stipend of 100s. Such a provision recognized the fact that the community at Westminster could not spare three of its number for the full-time duties that were to be the lot of the priests who staffed the royal chantry, but Henry envisaged that the first chantry priests would in fact be monks already in the house: three of these were to equip themselves for the task by graduating in theology as soon as possible. The king also directed that in future three other monks should be maintained annually at Oxford, on exhibitions of £10 each, until they had become bachelors and performed all the exercises for the doctorate. These monks were not to return to Westminster for more than fifteen days a year, if they came to preach, or for a month at a visitation or an election, and only a call to be abbot or one of the chantry priests might interrupt their studies.

Besides importing into the abbey the novelty of three salaried monks who held a perpetual office, Henry VII's foundation gave distinctive features to the careers of the monks while they were at the university. A higher proportion, about one in four, of those who were chosen now went up before ordination—some of them, after all, had been recruited with a view to their aptitude for study—and nearly half the total number who went stayed at the

[64] *Close Rolls, Henry VII*, ii (1500–9), p. 139. The abbot was John Islip, the prior William Mane, and the monk-bailiff William Borow. This is our only evidence that Islip and Mane went to the university or that Borow graduated.

[65] Ibid., no. 389. At one point in this document it is envisaged that the priests of Henry's chantry might have graduated elsewhere than in Oxford; see ibid., p. 141.

university long enough to graduate.[66] Of the graduates of this period, Humphrey Charyte, Denys Dalians, Thomas Essex, John Laurence and Richard Gorton were alive and still at Westminster in 1540. Charyte, Dalians and Essex became prebendaries of the new cathedral church, and the first-named survived to hold the same office in Elizabeth I's foundation at Westminster. Laurence perhaps found the new order less congenial; at any rate, he secured preferment as archdeacon of Wiltshire under Mary but was deprived by her sister. Not one of the four entered the Marian foundation.[67]

★　　★　　★

On a superficial view Westminster Abbey's fidelity over a long period of time to the rule that for every twenty monks one should go to the university brought the community little benefit except a succession of duly qualified preachers. This conclusion, however, falls somewhat short of the truth. A university education did not turn the monks of Westminster into schoolmen, and it did not give their house, what it had never possessed, a distinguished cultural tradition. But this sustained and expensive obedience to the papal ruling fostered in the monks a sense of identification with the life of the order as a whole that was stronger than anything experienced by Abbot Berking's or Abbot Ware's monks in the thirteenth century, and it cannot be doubted that the university connection affected the monastery's place in the ecclesiastical world at large. This is evident from the fact that, contrary to the custom of the twelfth and thirteenth centuries, the abbey now occasionally provided members of the episcopate. From the Conquest until the middle of the fourteenth century no monk of Westminster was promoted to the episcopate, but four were thereafter—Simon Langham to Ely in 1362, Thomas Merks to Carlisle in 1397, Nicholas Ashby to Llandaff in 1441 and Thomas Millyng to Hereford in 1464—and three of the four had been to the university. Langham was by far the most distinguished of the three, and the one who exercised the greatest influence on the

[66] For the graduates of this period, see above, p. 114 n. For information about them I am indebted to Dr Emden.

[67] Ex inf. Dr Emden; see also *Monks*, pp. 183, 185, 214–17, and J. McCann and C. Cary-Elwes, *Ampleforth and its Origins* (London, 1952), pp. 53 ff.

monastery itself. It is with him that this essay will end, and not altogether inappropriately, in view of his posthumous importance, although he died the year before Richard II came to the throne.

Langham is first mentioned at Westminster in 1339–40, but virtually nothing is known of him for the next ten years, except the fact that he went to Oxford;[68] the office of prior, to which he was elected in 1349, was probably the first that he held in the monastery. Very likely most of these early years were spent at the university, and it is not impossible that Langham proceeded to a degree there. How many books he already possessed and took with him when he departed for the see of Ely we do not know, but by the time of his death he had accumulated nearly one hundred titles.[69] On the scholastic side the library comprised standard works—the major theological works of St Thomas, his commentaries on the Physics and Metaphysics of Aristotle, Richard of Middleton—but also other, more topical items, such as the *quaestiones* and sermons of Fitz Ralph, that do in fact point to a continued, lively interest in theology and philosophy on Langham's part.

Despite his love of books, Langham made no direct contribution to the intellectual life of his times, but it was he who forged the permanent link between the abbey and Gloucester College. He did this, moreover, at a time when every counsel of prudence must have been against it, since the community's numbers had recently been halved, by the plague, in the space of weeks. In thus connecting the monastery regularly with the schools, he widened its field of recruitment at a truly critical moment in its history, and to his foresight in this matter is owing perhaps a little of the credit for the remarkable fact that numbers at Westminster were, not lower, but a little higher at the end of the fourteenth century than they had been a century earlier. There were fifty professed monks, beside the abbot, in the monastery in 1307 and fifty-seven in 1399, and these figures are typical of the periods in question.[70]

---

[68] Emden, *Oxford*, ii, p. 1095; see also Liber Quaternus Niger, fo. 150; John Flete, *History of Westminster Abbey*, ed. J. Armitage Robinson (Cambridge, 1909), pp. 130–2; D. Knowles, *Religious Orders in England*, ii (Cambridge, 1955), pp. 54–6; and J. A. Robinson, 'Simon Langham, Abbot of Westminster', in *Church Quarterly Review*, lxvi (1908), pp. 339 ff.

[69] Robinson and James, *Manuscripts of Westminster Abbey*, pp. 4–7.

[70] W.A.M. 24260, 19883; see also *Monks*, p. x. Langham gave the abbey 1000

Southbrooke was the only graduate whom the monks landed in their cloister, but the advantages of the university connection for Westminster consisted less in the possibility of recruiting in the university itself than in the ability to remain attractive to young men who, but for its new intellectual exertions, might never have looked in the abbey's direction at all. It was a compliment to the monastery, of a kind that would not have been deserved fifty years earlier, that in 1376 Adam Easton thought it sufficiently up to date to implore the abbot's assistance in obtaining copies of certain of Wyclif's works.[71]

marks to support four additional monks, who were to staff his and his parents' chantry (Flete, op. cit., p. 133).

[71] *Chapters*, iii, pp. 76–7.

VII

Liveries and Commissions of the Peace 1388-90

R. L. STOREY

THE 'Statute against livery and maintenance' of 1390 has been printed in three recent collections of historical documents[1] and it has been given significance in modern work on bastard feudalism. It provides the earliest statutory definition of types of retainer. 'The statute of 1390 was the first major attempt to regulate and control retaining'; it restricted to dukes, earls, barons and bannerets the right to give 'livery of company' and only to their domestics and to knights and esquires retained for life by indenture. This measure therefore gave 'a monopoly on retaining companies of knights and esquires to the lords temporal'.[2] By following this argument, one may claim that the enactment gave legislative approval to those baronial armies which engaged in private and eventually civil warfare from the middle years of the fifteenth century,[3] and, more immediately, brought about Richard's own downfall in 1399. It therefore seems extraordinary that Richard sanctioned this 'aristocratic monopoly over force and arms'[4] within a year of recovering the exercise of his prerogative to rule. In 1387 the superior retinues of the Lords Appellant had scattered

[1] It is given this or a similar title in B. Wilkinson, *The Constitutional History of Medieval England* (London, 1948–58), iii, pp. 231–2; *Select Documents of English Constitutional History 1307–1485*, ed. S. B. Chrimes and A. L. Brown (London, 1961), pp. 157–8; and *English Historical Documents 1327–1485*, ed. A. R. Myers (London, 1969), p. 1116.

[2] N. B. Lewis, 'The Organisation of Indentured Retinues in Fourteenth-Century England', *T.R.H.S.*, 4th series, xxvii (1945), pp. 29–30; W. D. Dunham, *Lord Hastings' Indentured Retainers 1461–1483* (New Haven, Conn., 1955), pp. 12, 69–70. The same term, 'monopoly', is applied in G. M. Trevelyan, *England in the Age of Wycliffe*, first published in 1899 (reprint of 1948), p. 64.

[3] R. L. Storey, *The End of the House of Lancaster* (London, 1966), p. 10, and *The Reign of Henry VII* (London, 1968), p. 38.

[4] Dunham, op. cit., p. 70.

his own supporters at Radcot Bridge. A statute so congenial to baronial interests would not seem inappropriate in the legislation of, say, the Merciless Parliament, but that one should pass when the king had so recently freed himself from magnate-tutelage is less easy to understand.

The measure against liveries was the consequence of pressure by the parliamentary commons. Complaints against the perversion of legal process by maintenance, and the involvement of liveried companies in these offences, were certainly no novelty. A statute of 1377 forbade the livery of caps or any other uniform for the maintenance of quarrels or other confederacies. Thus far, complaint and remedy had been confined to liveries given by 'gentz de petit garison'.[5] In 1384, the commons turned to the liveried retainers of lords and claimed that the law was rendered powerless by their schemes and the favour of their lords. On this occasion the commons were easily persuaded to abandon their call for remedy. The issue was resurrected by the commons in the Cambridge parliament of September 1388. Again according to the Monk of Westminster, they made grievous complaint that men who wore the badges of lords were so swollen with pride on account of their patrons' power that no fear could deter them from committing extortions in their shires (*patrias*), and in consequence people of few resources were prevented from obtaining justice.[6]

The boldness of the commons in criticizing the lords is the more remarkable when the date of this parliament is recalled. The Lords Appellant were in full control of the government after their destruction of Richard's entourage in the Merciless Parliament of the spring of that year. The same sheriffs were holding office at the times of the elections to both these parliaments, and it is thus not surprising that an unusually high proportion, a fifth, of the 248 elected members at Cambridge had sat in the Merciless Parliament. The shire-knights of the latter had exceeded the ferocity of the lords in their pursuit of Richard's servants.[7] No doubt a fair proportion of them were retainers or connections of the appellant

<hr />

[5] *R.P.*, iii, p. 23; *Statutes of the Realm*, ed. A. Luders and others (Record Commission, 1810–28), ii, p. 3.

[6] Monk of Westminster, pp. 40–1, 189.

[7] J. A. Tuck, 'The Cambridge Parliament, 1388' *E.H.R.*, lxxxiv (1969), p. 227; cf. N. B. Lewis, 'Re-election to Parliament in the Reign of Richard II', *E.H.R.*, xlviii (1933), p. 366.

magnates. Yet the second parliamentary commons of 1388 plainly exhibited its opposition to baronial leadership. This revulsion may in part be explained by the barren record of the Appellant regime, and by the humiliation of defeat by the Scots at Otterburn on 5 August. The petition against liveries, however, indicates that what most disturbed the commons, to the extent of open discord with the lords, was public order inside the country. This had presumably deteriorated since the appointment of the baronial commission of government in 1386. As will be shown, this commission paid little attention to the machinery for peace-keeping. Richard's attempt to recruit support in 1387, the movements of baronial armies, and the destruction of the judiciary by the Merciless Parliament would all have damaged the administration of justice. Unruly persons had less reason than ever to fear lawful retribution, particularly if they enjoyed powerful patronage. Whether there was a quantitative increase in crime at this time cannot be established, but a number of incidents in Leicestershire is suggestive. Their significance is that they involved men of substance, of the class customarily charged with peace-keeping duties. Moreover, this is a midland shire, not one of the northern counties where violence was endemic.[8]

The Leicestershire evidence also reveals serious shortcomings in the operations of legal and administrative processes. In 1386 Master Henry Birmingham and in 1387 Sir John Beaumont procured commissions of oyer and terminer on account of alleged trespasses against them by Sir Thomas Erdington. Birmingham was clearly frustrated in his quest for redress, for he required a similar commission for the same matter over two years later. Another suggestive detail is that Beaumont was appointed to head both of Birmingham's commissions. The case of Sir John Walcote is more sinister. On 30 March 1387 he failed in an attempt to kill William Lodbroke but injured and robbed him. In the following year, on 21 May, he again lay in wait for Lodbroke at Leicester during quarter sessions and this time slew his quarry. Not only did Walcote escape immediate prosecution; on 19 August 1388 he

---

[8] On 20 March 1388, a troop of Westmorland men seeking an enemy rode into Kendal *modo guerre et modo Scottorum*, so that the inhabitants fled to the hills and woods (P.R.O., King's Bench, Coram Rege Rolls (K.B.27), no. 518, Rex rot. 17). For Northumberland, see *C.P.R., 1385-9*, pp. 321, 325.

actually obtained the king's pardon for the assault of 1387. The council eventually received information of the murder and took action, ordering Walcote's committal to the Tower of London on 11 February 1389. On the 16th, the council appointed a commission to enquire into all unlawful assemblies, false alliances, maintenances and the like in Leicestershire. Obviously Walcote had influence or powerful friends in the shire and the processes of justice had thus far been frustrated on his behalf. In fact, it was only after the council's intervention that the county's justices of the peace, on 18 February 1389, received an indictment of Walcote for the murder.[9]

This clearly was the kind of unpunished crime that the commons of Cambridge had in mind; Walcote was still at large while they were in session. They would certainly have known about another recent outrage, for this took place within four miles of Cambridge itself. At midnight on 28 September 1387, a gang besieged the manor-house of Sir John Shardelowe at Fulbourn and stormed it with ladders, removing Sir John's widowed sister-in-law and a considerable quantity of valuables. The leader in this operation was John Pelham, who married the lady and so gained enjoyment of her estates, for she was an heiress in her own right. Judicial proceedings were soon put in motion and at least one of the smaller fry was hanged for his part; he was sentenced before justices of gaol delivery in Cambridge on 10 July 1388. Another received a pardon dated at Cambridge on 9 October, while parliament was still sitting.[10] Not only, therefore, was the siege of Fulbourn common knowledge to the shire-knights at Cambridge, it was clearly one of the incidents, probably the foremost, which inspired their petition against liveried retainers.[11] Pelham was a retainer of

[9] Ibid., pp. 171, 390, 500, 543; *1388-92*, p. 55; C.Cl.R., *1385-9*, p. 571; K.B. 27/515, Rex 28.

[10] L. F. Salzman, 'The Early Heraldry of Pelham', *Sussex Archaeological Collections*, lxix (1928), p. 58; P.R.O., Gaol Delivery Rolls (J.I.3), no. 175, rot. 3, 4; C.P.R., *1385-9*, pp. 390, 393, 517; *1388-92*, p. 150.

[11] It may even have been a reason why the parliament was called to Cambridge. There had been other disturbances in the county (C.P.R., *1385-9*, p. 392; *1388-92*, pp. 55, 140) and the council may have believed that the presence of the country's rulers and judges might help to restore order and morale. Some explanation is needed for the choice of Cambridge; no other parliament met there, understandably because the fens made access difficult from the west. And when there, parliament thought poorly of the town's amenities (Tuck, op. cit., p. 240).

Henry, earl of Derby, and he was obviously not in regular attendance on his lord. As the sequel shows, moreover, he was justifiably emboldened in his lawless resolution by the comforting assurance of the 'good lordship' of so great a magnate; in 1389 he was pardoned 'at the instance of the earl of Derby'.[12] Such pardons provide further evidence that certain, at least, of the nobility had some ruffianly followers. In 1388 alone Derby obtained pardons for seven men accused of homicide.[13] The commons were certainly not ignorant of this aspect of retaining.[14]

The parliamentary debate about liveried retainers occasioned Richard's first public intervention since the Merciless Parliament. The lords responded to the commons' charge by promising not to give liveries to malefactors and to punish offending retainers. This did not satisfy the commons: they demanded the abolition of all badges if the realm were to enjoy peace. Richard then offered to provide an example for the sake of good order by removing all his badges. This proposal, it was said, greatly pleased the commons. The lords remained obdurate and there were hard words between them and the commons. The king then mediated to produce concord, and the issue was shelved until the following parliament with an expression of hope that in the interval the king and lords of his council would devise some reform. This solution hardly merits description as 'a compromise'.[15] The commons' plea had been rejected and the king's council did not, so far as is known, propose any reform before the next parliament.

The debate on liveries had an important sequel when Richard re-established himself as the head of government in May 1389. In his proclamation announcing his resumption, Richard declared that his purpose was to provide greater tranquillity to the realm and a more ample provision of justice than it had hitherto enjoyed, and he banned all unlawful assemblies, maintenances and other violations of the peace.[16] In the following months Richard clearly

---

[12] *C.P.R., 1388–92*, p. 150. Gaunt appointed Pelham constable of Pevensey in 1393. He accompanied Henry into exile, returned with him in 1399 and eventually became treasurer of England (*The Register of Henry Chichele*, ii, ed. E. F. Jacob and H. C. Johnson (Canterbury and York Society, 42, 1937), p. 669).

[13] *C.P.R., 1385–9*, pp. 406, 409, 439, 452, 461, 510, 531; see also ibid., pp. 233, 241, 243, 354, 376–7, 408, 413, 431, 434, 518, 521, 524, 540; *1388–92*, p. 3.

[14] Below, pp. 143–4.   [15] Monk of Westminster, p. 190; Tuck, op. cit., p. 235.

[16] Rymer, vii, pp. 618–19; *R.P.*, iii, p. 404.

attempted to honour this undertaking. Between 10 May and 1 June three judicial commissions were sent to enquire into various offences in Gloucestershire, Norfolk, and Kendal, Westmorland. This number equalled the total of general commissions of enquiry issued since the appointment of the commission of government in November 1386. Other general commissions for Dorset and Somerset, Shropshire, Surrey and Kent, were issued between July 1389 and June 1390.[17] This unwonted policy of royal vigilance is well illustrated by another murder in Leicestershire. Richard Vilers, esquire, was killed on 20 June 1389. On 5 July a commission was appointed to identify his killers and those who sheltered them, and the commissioners were receiving this information in Leicester on 24 July.[18]

Richard had made notable changes among the leading personnel of the central administration and judiciary. In Tout's view, the king thus aimed to impress public opinion with the reality of his resumption of power, and so far succeeded that chroniclers tended to exaggerate the amount of change; thus one wrote that Richard removed all officers, 'greater as well as less'.[19] Such comment, indeed, was by no means unjustified. The extent of Richard's reorganization was felt in every shire when new commissions of the peace were appointed on 15 July 1389. The previous general review of these commissions had been made on 20 December 1382, when the justices were deprived of their powers to determine felonies and trespasses, although they continued to receive indictments of felonies, armed gatherings, ambush, livery and maintenance, and trespasses; they also remained responsible for enforcing the 'peace statutes' of Winchester, Northampton and Westminster (1361), they had powers to arrest suspects and those indicted before them and to take sureties for good behaviour, and they supervised wages, weights and measures, and other economic regulations.[20] Since

---

[17] *C.P.R., 1385-9*, p. 322; *1388-92*, pp. 53, 55, 59–61, 135, 142, 273. All other *ad hoc* commissions since 1386 related to specific incidents, most being purchased by complainants, and often seem to relate to disputes like those heard in the 'equitable' side of chancery from the fifteenth century.

[18] *C.P.R., 1388-92*, p. 132; K.B.27/515, Rex 20. Thomas Frysby and Thomas Neville of Reresby were said to have ordered the murder.

[19] Tout, *Chapters*, iii, pp. 456-7, citing Monk of Westminster, p. 211.

[20] *Proceedings before Justices of the Peace in the Fourteenth and Fifteenth Centuries*, ed. B. H. Putnam (London, 1938), pp. xxii–iv.

1382 most of these commissions had been superseded by others which made changes of personnel. Before the parliamentary commission deprived him of authority, Richard had replaced thirty-one of the forty commissions of the peace of 1382. The parliamentary commission contented itself with appointing commissions of the peace for six shires in 1387. The work of the Merciless Parliament made a complete review necessary, for the justices of king's bench and common pleas whom it had banished had been members of most of the county commissions. The Appellant regime, however, appointed new commissions for only five shires in July 1388.[21]

The lists of justices of the peace were consequently in urgent need of revision well before Richard's re-formed administration undertook the task. Not only had the dismissed judges to be replaced in the shire commissions by their successors in the central courts; death also would have thinned the ranks of the J.P.s chosen from the lords, knights and squires of their shires: six county benches were still operating under the commissions of 1382.[22] Richard's policy, however, was more far reaching than the mere replacement of departed J.P.s. The commissions of July 1389 were given the same powers as those of 1382, but their membership was drastically changed. In the first place, their size was much reduced. The average number of justices in commissions issued at all dates between 1382 and 1388 was 12·5; only four had under ten members, while seven had sixteen or more. There was far less variation in the sizes of the commissions of July 1389: six had six members, seven had ten and twenty-one had eight, with only Kent and Hampshire having nine J.P.s.[23] In the majority of commissions,

[21] The crown appointed commissions of the peace for every shire except the palatine counties of Chester, Durham and Lancaster; the three Yorkshire ridings and the three parts of Lincolnshire had separate commissions. The total number was forty. (Urban commissions are not included in this survey.) Details of the membership of commissions, though not of their powers, appear in *C.P.R.*, *1381-5*, pp. 251-4 (20 Dec. 1382), 346-8 (1383-4), 501-3 (1384-5); *1385-9*, pp. 80-3 (1385-6), 253-4 (June and July 1386), 385 (July and Dec. 1387), 545 (July 1388); *1388-92*, pp. 135-7 (15 July 1389). Richard also added individuals to commissions 'by association', the last time being in March 1386 (*C.P.R.*, *1385-9*, p. 168). This practice of 'association' was unpopular with the parliamentary commons and it was eventually forbidden by the Cambridge statute about J.P.s (*Proceedings*, ed. Putnam, p. lxxvii).

[22] Devon, Dorset, Holland (Lincs.), Notts., Surrey and Warwicks.

[23] Only Middlesex seems to have been omitted from the issue of July 1389; it was given a commission of eight members in December following, of whom three were 'professionals'.

two or three of the members were judges or serjeants-at-law, who would have been occasional visitors to the counties as justices of assize and gaol delivery. There had been the same number of professional justices in commissions before 1389, but by taking them into account it emerges that the number of J.P.s drawn from the ranks of 'the most sufficient and able' men in their shires had been halved.

The second contrast in these new commissions is yet more striking. This was the entire absence from them of all lords. In the past, peers with a territorial stake in a county, even if they rarely resided, headed its commission of the peace; thus the duke of Lancaster and the earl of Northumberland had been the premier J.P.s in Cumberland, Northumberland and the three Yorkshire ridings. Richard was not discriminating between friends and enemies in the peerage: all were removed. Nor did their dismissal fully account for the smaller commissions of 1389. The knights and squires were also purged. If we exclude the professional justices from the reckoning, in six shires none of the justices of 1389 had been on the previous commission,[24] in five there was a solitary survivor,[25] and in only five counties were as many as four J.P.s reappointed,[26] while Kent was unique in retaining five local members. Many of the dismissed J.P.s were still alive; a number were subsequently reappointed. On what grounds they had been dismissed is not clear. The reason for discrimination does not appear to have been political. The shires where the three leading Appellants had been dominant fared no differently from the rest, and in any case, as has already been observed, the Appellants had shown little interest in the commissions of the peace when they had been in power and had obviously not taken the opportunity to pack local benches with their nominees. Seventeen of the J.P.s appointed by Richard in July 1389 had been members of the Merciless Parliament.[27] It is more probable that competence for office was the yardstick applied. This reconstruction of the county commissions, however, was probably inspired by a general political consideration.

[24] Dorset, 1382; Glos., 1383; Somerset, 1385; Wilts. and Yorks. W.R., 1386; Salop, 1388. (The dates are of the previous commissions.)

[25] Devon, 1382; Cambridges, 1383; Essex and Worcs., 1386; Beds., 1388.

[26] Kesteven and Sussex, 1384; Staffs. and Hunts., 1386; Northants., July 1388.

[27] Cf. *Return of the names of every member*, part i; Parliaments of England, 1213-1702 (Parliamentary Papers, 1879), pp. 231-3.

The commons at Cambridge had shown great interest in the commission of the peace. The most important legislation of that parliament was the statute of Cambridge designed to regulate the wages of labourers and the J.P.s were charged with its execution. Another statute required that the ministers of state, judges and any others who might be asked to nominate J.P.s, sheriffs and other officers should be sworn to support the appointments only of men whom they knew and believed to be conscientious and well qualified; bribery and favouritism were to be foresworn. The commons had also petitioned that there should be only six J.P.s in every county in addition to the justices of assize. They were to hold sessions at least four times a year; if any J.P.s were negligent in this respect, any subject thus aggrieved might petition the king's council, which could punish such offending justices. On the other hand, statutory provision was now made, for the first time, to pay the justices a certain daily wage (4s) for attendance at quarter sessions. The reduced membership of the 1389 commissions reflected this statute. It had not prescribed the exclusion of peers, but the commons might have petitioned for this; certainly the debate on liveries had revealed their entire lack of confidence in the lords as champions of law and order, and at least the statute stipulated that no steward of a lord was to be a J.P. In their petition for this statute, the commons had asked that justices should be empowered to deal with cases of maintenance, which they defined as the use of his influence by a lord or any other in a lawsuit in return for a share in the profits, and as the assembly of large numbers of men with the objects of committing offences and preventing the execution of the law.[28]

The Cambridge statutes were published on 20 November 1388, but nothing was done to put this statute on justices into effect until Richard resumed power. This inaction by the Appellant regime indicated that the distrust shown by the shire-knights was reciprocated. The chancellor had a major responsibility for the issue of commissions of the peace, and Thomas Arundel was naturally more sympathetic to baronial sentiments. In contrast, his successor from May 1389, William of Wykeham, owed his rise from humble origins to his outstanding administrative

[28] *Proceedings*, ed. Putnam, p. xc; *Statutes*, ii, pp. 55–60; Monk of Westminster, pp. 191–2.

capacity, and his preference of true worth to blue blood is well known: '*Manners* makyth man'. The decision to remodel the shire commissions and take the unprecedented step of excluding the baronage would, however, have been the king's. Richard had discovered in the Cambridge parliament that the interests of lords and commons were apparently incompatible on the issue of public order. The lords tenaciously defended their privilege to keep liveried companies, while the commons considered these companies a menace to the security of English society and put their trust in the commission of the peace as the best instrument for upholding order in the shires. Richard had in May 1389 declared his intent to give the realm better justice than it had enjoyed for many a day. This was his customary royal duty, enjoined by his coronation oath, but in his circumstances in 1389 such a programme was sound policy. The Merciless Parliament had left him without an organized body of adherents, and he was now striving to enlist the loyalty of a wider range of his subjects and particularly of the class which filled the lower house of parliament. That it was the Cambridge parliament which had inspired this programme is confirmed by the high proportion of its shire-knights appointed to commissions of the peace in 1389-90.[29] By adopting a policy which resembles that which we more usually associate with the Tudors, Richard showed his awareness that an appeal to the defence of law and order might win a political dividend.

New commissions of the peace were issued on 10 November 1389. The major amendment made to the July commissions was the restoration to the justices of power to determine the cases of felony, maintenance and the other matters which they had been empowered only to hear since 1382.[30] This change also can be associated with the Cambridge parliament. The statute on J.P.s enacted there had only in part met the wishes of the commons; they had asked that J.P.s be empowered both to hear and determine, but the statute had omitted this provision.[31] The requirement of this statute about numbers was now more widely observed. It had ordered the appointment of six J.P.s in addition to the justices of assize, which

[29] Cf. *Return of every member*, i, pp. 234-6.

[30] *Proceedings*, ed. Putnam, p. xxiv; *C.P.R., 1388-92*, pp. 137-9 (for all shires except Staffs.).

[31] Monk of Westminster, p. 191; *Statutes*, ii, pp. 58-9.

in effect fixed the total at eight. In November eleven of the sixteen county benches which had less than eight members in July were raised to this number by the addition of one or two members, and only the five smallest counties now had less than eight J.P.s. The membership of the commissions was left unchanged in only nine of thirty-nine shires,[32] and additions alone were made in six others. Three of the J.P.s of July 1389 were removed from the commissions for both Gloucestershire and Norfolk, two from six others, while sixteen more each lost one member, a total of thirty-four dismissals. This is convincing evidence of the care being taken by the king's council in keeping itself informed about the availability or suitability of justices; it is noticeable that the unchanged commissions include those for all the most remote northern counties, whence information would be slow in reaching Westminster, while the high proportion of Gloucestershire dismissals may well be linked with illegalities reported from there.[33] The majority of J.P.s appointed in November 1389 who had not been in the July commissions had served before 1389.

This fresh review of the commissions was presumably made in November because this was the customary season for the crown's annual appointments to the offices of sheriff and escheator. The former was, of course, a key figure in the local administration of justice and Richard's nominees in 1389 would have attracted particular interest for evidence of the sincerity of his professed concern about this. The subject of sheriffs had regularly exercised the parliamentary commons; in 1377 they obtained a statute that no sheriff would be reappointed within three years, but further petitions in 1378, 1383 and 1384 that none should be continued after one year indicate that the statute was being disregarded; while article 36 of the appeal of the Merciless Parliament alleged that the king had ordered the appointment of sheriffs who would influence the election of shire-knights.[34] The Monk of Westminster stated that there was an innovation in the making of sheriffs in 1389: instead of their being appointed by the chancellor, treasurer, keeper of the privy seal and barons of the exchequer, they were

[32] Cambridges., Cumb., Holland, Lindsey, Northumb., Salop, Sussex, Westm. and Yorks. W.R.
[33] *C.P.R., 1385-9*, p. 323; *1388-92*, p. 61; and see note 40 below.
[34] *Statutes*, ii, p. 4; *R.P.*, iii, pp. 44, 159, 201, 235.

chosen by the king in his privy council and made to swear that they would well and faithfully perform their duties.[35] Of the twenty-four sheriffs appointed on 15 November, no more than six had previously held the office in their counties, only one within the previous three years, and two more had been sheriffs in other counties.[36] One of the six and two others were the 'king's knights'.[37] Sir Edmund de la Pole was the brother of the disgraced earl of Suffolk, but he had retired from royal service and was establishing himself as a substantial tenant-in-chief in Cambridgeshire, a county obviously requiring firm control. Sir James Pickering had served in Ireland under William of Windsor, but he subsequently involved himself in the county business of Westmorland and later in that of Yorkshire, where he became sheriff in 1389.[38] What can be discovered about the recent careers of most of the sheriffs of this year indicates that they had been resident in their counties and occasionally engaged on local affairs by royal commissions.[39] Four had been in the Cambridge parliament,[40] but one of these and two others were members of the Merciless Parliament.[41]

There is no evidence here that the king was attempting to pack the shrievalties with instruments of an authoritarian royal policy. The Monk of Westminster made no such allegation, and if his statement can be credited the principal departure from normal practice in 1389 was that the sheriffs were sworn before the king

[35] Monk of Westminster, p. 217.

[36] *C.F.R., 1383–1391*, pp. 306–7; *List of Sheriffs for England and Wales* (P.R.O. Lists and Indexes, ix, 1898, repr. 1963).

[37] Walter atte Lee (Essex and Herts.), see *C.P.R., 1385-9*, p. 424; John Paveley (Northants.), see ibid., p. 352; and Richard Redman (Cumb.), see J. S. Roskell, 'Two Medieval Westmorland Speakers, Part ii', *Transactions of the Cumberland and Westmorland Antiquarian and Archaeological Society*, n.s. lxii (1962), p. 119.

[38] A. Steel, 'The Sheriffs of Cambridgeshire and Huntingdonshire in the reign of Richard II', *Cambridge Antiquarian Society Proceedings*, xxxvi (1936), pp. 19–22; J. S. Roskell, 'Two Medieval Westmorland Speakers, Part i', *Trans. Cumb. and Westm. Soc.*, n.s. lxi (1961), pp. 85–100.

[39] Several had been J.P.s: Robert Fraunceys (Notts. and Derbys.), Hugh Fastolf (Norf. and Suff.) and Thomas Sakevyll (Beds. and Bucks.) were and remained J.P.s while they were sheriffs. Thomas Broke (Som. and Dorset), Edward Acton (Salop) and John Calverley (Rutland) were J.P.s in 1389 but were removed from the commissions of June 1390, while they were still sheriffs. Of the J.P.s dismissed in July 1389, only Robert atte Mille became a sheriff (Surrey and Sussex) in 1389.

[40] Acton and Sakevyll (note 39), Pickering (note 38) and atte Lee (note 37).

[41] Atte Lee, William Bonevyle (Devon) and Broke (note 39). See *Return of every member*, i, p. 232.

and council instead of in the exchequer. The point of this innovation, presumably, was to impress on the sheriffs in particular, but also on his subjects generally, that Richard was personally concerned about how these sheriffs would conduct themselves in office. The next parliament made no complaint about sheriffs; on the contrary, it regretted the loss of amenities suffered by those in shires where the king had granted away the custodies of royal castles which had served as shrieval offices and prisons.

The Westminster parliament of 17 January 1390 was the first called since Richard's resumption of power. On the 20th, his ministers and council resigned and were reappointed on the next day when first the commons, and then the lords, declared their satisfaction with their services. This curious, and doubtless contrived, episode must be seen as part of Richard's public relations programme. When opening parliament, Bishop Wykeham had invited the commons to report how the law was being kept and name those who had disturbed the peace and maintained quarrels, and he asked for proposals for the reform of these matters.[42] The commons, who included thirty-four shire members of the Cambridge parliament,[43] vigorously resumed their campaign against liveries, demanding their total abolition. They reminded the king of his promise to provide a remedy, and complained that no remedy had yet been submitted to the judgement of parliament. The debate was long and bitter, for the lords refused to give up their badges. Finally they agreed that their badges might only be worn by men whom they had retained for life by indenture, and that no yeomen or archers might do so unless they were regularly domiciled with their lords.[44] The commons were not satisfied and threatened to reopen the issue at the next parliament if this remedy was not effective. In another petition they sought that liveries should be given by lords only to their household servants, kinsmen and officials. The king concluded the debate by again promising that he and his council would provide a remedy. The commons were more successful with another petition which also arose from their fear that the law was being undermined. The king accepted their

[42] *R.P.*, iii, pp. 275 258, 257.

[43] Lewis, op. cit., pp. 366, 369. The total number of shire-knights who had sat in previous parliaments (60) was the record for the reign.

[44] Walsingham (ii, pp. 195–6) starts his account of the parliament with a report of this debate. The Monk of Westminster does not mention it.

argument that pardons were too easily granted to murderers. A statute was enacted regulating the procedure for the grant of pardons which was intended to make it more difficult for deliberate homicides to escape justice. In future, letters of pardon for such crimes had to state that they had been committed deliberately. It was presumed that these pardons would be obtained by the suit of other persons to the king, and these petitioners were now required to pay for the royal clemency. The statute adopted the scale of fines proposed by the commons, running down from £1000 by an archbishop or duke and 1000 marks by a bishop or earl.[45] Obviously this scale was designed to discriminate against the clients of lords: the earl of Derby would have faced a bill for £4666 13s 4d in 1388 had this statute then been in existence.[46]

This parliament was dismissed on 2 March 1390. Its statutes were published in May. There was nothing particularly unusual about this interval.[47] They were published by proclamation and chancery recorded them as copies of the writs of proclamation on the statute roll. This was normal practice. What is unusual is that there were three writs of proclamation. The first to be enrolled, following the writ proclaiming the Cambridge statutes, was dated 16 May; it gave the text of twenty statutes. Then came a second writ, dated 15 May, containing the statutes of (i) pardons and (ii) provisors. Third was a proclamation concerning liveries which was dated 12 May. The first proclamation begins with a variant on the customary formula, a reference to the recent parliament in which the king had ordained the following (statutes) with the assent of lords and commons there present. The second likewise refers to the late parliament and then to the commons' complaint about charters of pardon, and the preamble to the statute of provisors also makes a reference to the commons. The proclamation of 12 May is quite different. It opens by declaring the king's obligation to provide justice to all and then alludes to complaints made in the recent parliaments at Cambridge and Westminster, by lords as well as commons, that oppression and maintenance were flourishing, those guilty being encouraged because they were retained

---

[45] R.P., iii, pp. 265, 266, 268; Statutes, ii, pp. 68–9.   [46] Above, p. 135.

[47] E.g. these dates of publication, with dates of ending of parliaments in brackets: 1 Feb. 1378 (c. 1 Dec. 1377); 17 May 1381 (25 Feb. 1381); 18 May 1383 (10 Mar. 1383); 14 June 1385 (14 Dec. 1384). See Statutes, ii, pp. 5, 23, 31, 37.

by lords and others and had fees and 'liveries of company'. Then comes the enacting clause: 'We have ordained and strictly forbidden, with the advice of our great council'. The two other writs end with identically expressed orders that their contents should be proclaimed and kept 'according to the form of the said statutes'. The third orders the proclamation and observation of 'this our ordinance'. In the two first, the statutes are in French but the opening and final clauses are in Latin, as was usual; the third proclamation is in French throughout. It was not chancery's usual practice to record notes of warranty after its enrolments of writs proclaiming statutes. There are none for those of 16 and 15 May, but one follows that of 12 May: *per ipsum regem et consilium*.[48]

These substantial differences between the text of the proclamation of 12 May and the form normally employed in writs proclaiming statutes point to one conclusion: the order restricting to secular peers the right to grant liveries was not a statute of the parliament of January 1390. It was a by-product of that parliament, for it was the remedy Richard had promised the commons in response to their petitions against liveries. It cannot, however, be regarded as a statute which was made in parliament 'at the request' or 'with the assent' of the commons. Its nature is declared. This is an ordinance made in 'the great council'. No evidence has been found to show that an assembly of all the lords spiritual and temporal was held in the interval between parliament's dismissal and 12 May. At this time, however, the term 'great' was also applied to meetings of the king's council which were attended by a number of great lords; indeed it was used in parliament with reference to the king's council on 20 January 1390.[49] Such a council was held in London on 25 April 1390, its principal purpose being the instruction of an embassy to France, and it was attended by the archbishop of Canterbury, three dukes, seven bishops, three earls, two barons and one banneret.[50] A council with this composition and agenda

[48] P.R.O., Chancery, Statute Rolls (C. 74), no. 3, mm. 11–10; printed in *Statutes*, ii, pp. 61–75, and see note 1 above.

[49] J. F. Baldwin, *The King's Council in England during the Middle Ages* (Oxford, 1913), pp. 109–10; *R.P.*, iii, p. 258.

[50] *P.P.C.*, i, pp. 22–4. Privy seals to attend were sent to the archbishop, the dukes of Gloucester and York, the earls of Kent and Salisbury, Lord Lovell and Richard Lescrop, banneret (P.R.O., Exchequer, Issue Rolls (E. 403), no. 530, m. 1). Two of the ambassadors (the bishop of Durham and the earl of Northumberland) are included in the above total of councillors.

might well be called 'great'. Presumably, then, it was on this occasion that the ordinance restricting liveries was finally determined. Its actual terms, however, had apparently been made by the king and lords during the parliamentary session, when the commons expressed their misgivings about its efficacy.[51] The council had thus decided to ratify the agreement made with the lords and consequently ordered its publication. In addition to the regulation of what persons might give and receive liveries, the ordinance ordered lords to dismiss retainers who committed maintenance and kindred offences. This requirement was, in fact, only making compulsory a concession offered by the lords themselves during the debate in the Cambridge parliament.[52] That the council should prefer to endorse the views of the lords on livery and disregard the opinion of the commons would be easily understandable if it had been at the heavily aristocratic meeting of 25–28 April that the ordinance was approved for promulgation. Among those present then was John of Gaunt, who had returned to England in the previous November after an absence of three and a half years. In 1384 he had silenced the commons' complaint against liveries by declaring that every lord was well able to control and punish his followers.[53] No doubt he was of the same mind in 1390, and he doubtless tried to convert the king to his view.

The ordinance arguably provided the most realistic solution for the problem of liveries, granted the social conditions of the time. If the king was neither able nor willing to deny the lords freedom to keep liveried retinues, it was certain that no one could discipline retainers but the lords themselves. Legislation was useless, for the machinery available was too exposed to manipulation by the lords. Significantly, the ordinance made no specific provision for its enforcement. Penalties of fine and imprisonment were threatened for its violation, but it was not decreed what procedures or courts were to be employed. The petitioners in parliament would hardly have been satisfied with this remedy. The ordinance was unsatisfactory in another respect. It did not touch the issue of retaining; it only regulated the grant of liveries. Secular lords indeed were to

[51] *R.P.*, iii, p. 265. A commons' petition in 1393 refers to the measure as 'ordeine par vostre tres sage conseill et de l'assent de les grantz seignurs de vostre roialme' (ibid., p. 307).
[52] Above, p. 135.   [53] Monk of Westminster, p. 41.

have the sole right to attire their followers in 'liveries of company', but the ordinance did not deny any other person the liberty to retain whomsoever he pleased. Prelates might not give liveries, but they naturally still required and presumably still continued to engage servants of various social categories to attend and minister to their needs, and this was equally true of other men of substance, be they lords or not. Moreover another person not specifically licensed to grant liveries was the king himself; Richard surely did not understand, when assenting to this decree, that he was denying himself the right either to retain or to give liveries.

The lack of provision for the ordinance's enforcement makes it less remarkable that evidence of prosecutions for its violation still await discovery.[54] Apparently its regulation of liveries was disregarded, for so the commons complained in 1393, and they sought a remedy by seeking that justices of assize and of the peace should be empowered to enquire and punish men wearing liveries who were not domestic servants of lords, or knights and squires retained for life. The king assented to this petition but no corresponding statute was published. That such a statute was made is indicated by Haxey's petition in 1397, which complained that it was not being kept. In 1399, however, Henry IV's first parliament enacted a statute forbidding all liveries save those of the king. When new statutes were made about matters already the subjects of previous legislation, it was usual to refer to earlier measures; neither the statute of 1399 nor the petition for it made any reference to the ordinance of 1390 or any other acts against liveries.[55] It would appear, therefore, that Richard's ordinance does not merit the significance which it has been given in the study of bastard feudalism. It no more created a 'baronial monopoly on retaining' than it was a statute, and as an instrument against 'livery and maintenance' it appears to have had little if any effect. In the immediate context of Richard's current policy, however, the ordinance was important, for it marks the end of his efforts to woo the commons.

The commons of January 1390 had apparently endorsed Richard's policy of excluding lords from commissions of the

---

[54] None were found in an examination of the *Rex* sections of *Coram Rege* rolls for 1390–3 (K.B. 27/515–30). Offenders might have been called before the council but few of its judicial records survive.

[55] *R.P.*, iii, pp. 307, 339, 428; cf. *Statutes*, ii, pp. 82–7, 113.

peace. They asked that there should be fresh appointments of justices of the peace, to be chosen from the 'most sufficient' knights, squires and men of law. The reason why the commons wanted new commissions presumably was the novel requirement that the justices should be sworn before the chancellor and council that they would execute all ordinances and statutes without favour. The king granted the petition and new commissions were issued on 28 June.[56] Only the Westmorland commission was markedly changed in its composition; of the seven members of the commission of November 1389, the two justices of assize alone remained and six new local men were appointed. This purge must obviously be related to the recent disorders in the county.[57] Elsewhere the membership suffered little change and remained at the previous size. In seventeen counties all the J.P.s of 1389 were retained, but evidence of the council's continuing supervision appeared in the commissions for the other twenty-two: in half, one member was replaced, and in the rest there were two changes of personnel. On this occasion, however, the choice of men to replace the dismissed J.P.s was governed by a special consideration. As it was published on 16 May, the statute enacted the commons' petition with regard to making new commissions and having the justices sworn, but it also waived the exclusion of lords' stewards ordered by the Cambridge statute on J.P.s.[58] It may be presumed that this statute was reviewed before publication at the same council which had approved of the ordinance about liveries, and that the same magnates who had affirmed baronial privilege in the latter had succeeded in pressing claims, contrary to the preference of the commons, to recover influence in the commissions of the peace through the agency of their stewards. That Richard's reconstruction of the commissions in 1389 had encountered opposition is indicated by the issue on 20 November of orders to former baronial J.P.s and their colleagues to surrender the records relating to their offices to the newly appointed justices;[59] the recipients of these orders had in fact already been displaced by the commissions appointed in the previous July. The commissions of 28 June 1390 therefore included stewards. Five of these new J.P.s can be identified

[56] *R.P.*, iii, p. 269; *C.P.R., 1388-92*, pp. 341-3.   [57] See note 8 above.

[58] Cf. *R.P.*, iii, p. 269, and *Statutes*, ii, pp. 62-3.

[59] *C.Cl.R., 1389-92*, pp. 38-40.

as officers of John of Gaunt, another indication that his views were persuading Richard to modify his programme.[60]

This policy met its demise in the next parliament. The commons of 12 November 1390 asked once more for the creation of fresh commissions of the peace. This time they urged that justices should be chosen in the present parliament and not removed until the next; they should be the most substantial and loyal men of their shires, 'who best know and have the power' to execute statutes. What was meant by the second qualification was expressed in the ensuing statute: there were to be eight justices in every shire, according to the Cambridge statute, 'beside the lords assigned in this parliament'. Consequently when commissions were appointed on 24 December, lords headed all but four.[61] Gaunt was the first-named justice in eighteen commissions. This is further evidence of his outstanding influence: in contrast, the earl of Northumberland, who came second in frequency of appointment, became a J.P. in five shires, the duke of Gloucester in three, and five other earls in three or two counties each. With the restitution of their baronial members, the composition of commissions reverted to that observed before July 1389, although the total number of members remained lower.

The initiative in causing this return to the *status quo ante* 1389 thus seemingly came from the commons themselves. There is, moreover, no record that they had expressed any views on the subject of liveries. This departure from the demands of the two previous houses of commons on the crucial issues in a campaign to restore public order suggests that the commons of November 1390 was of a very different composition from its immediate predecessors. This was not the case: this commons contained no less experienced members than most of Richard's parliaments; twenty of the shire-knights had been in the January parliament, seventeen had been at Cambridge.[62] Moreover, thirty-one of the seventy-

---

[60] Both chief stewards of the duchy of Lancaster: Thomas Hungerford (Som. and Wilts.) and Philip Tilney (Lindsey); and Thomas Walsh (Leics.), John Woderove (Yorks. W.R.) and John Rochford (Lindsey); see R. Somerville, *The Duchy of Lancaster 1265–1603*, i (London, 1953), pp. 367, 375, 472, 575. For Gaunt's friendly relations with Richard in the summer of 1390, see Monk of Westminster, pp. 238–9.

[61] *R.P.*, iii, p. 279; *Statutes*, ii, p. 77; *C.P.R.*, *1388–92*, pp. 344–6 (all shires except Yorks. W.R.).

[62] Lewis, op. cit., p. 366.

four shire-knights had been J.P.s since 1389.[63] Despite this, they sought the restoration of responsibility for keeping order in the shires to the lords, even though they had placed the blame for deteriorating conditions on the liveried retainers of lords. This might seem proof that the ordinance on liveries had instantaneously succeeded in its object. If so, it must have been unique in all medieval legislation. It is a more credible explanation that those shire-knights who were justices had found from experience that it was an impossible task to carry out their duties without the moral and practical support of the most influential men in their shires, of those 'who had the power' to have the law enforced. Such would have been as realistic an appraisal as was Richard's when he decided to countenance baronial liveries. This decision of the king's, however, cannot have failed to influence the shire-knights. The ordinance of 12 May ended the hopes of those commoners who had so vigorously pressed for the abolition of all liveries. It must have seemed to them that Richard had surrendered to baronial pressure, and in so doing his promise of May 1389 to champion justice had been forgotten. Knights and squires could not act independently of the baronage without the support of royal authority. Now there could be no confidence that Richard would take their part. That there was disillusion is revealed by the poet John Gower, himself a connection of the knightly class and a small landowner. The original version of his *Confessio Amantis*, completed in 1390, had expressed devotion to Richard because of his princely virtues,

> In whom hath evere yit be founde
> Justice medled with pite.

Within a few months Gower was recasting the poem in order to castigate Richard for abandoning the ideals of virtuous kingship. The country had lost its unity. The 'knyghthode', instead of defending 'the comun right',

> . . . of here large retenue,
> The lond is ful of maintenue,
> Which causith that the comune right
> In fewe contrees stant upright.[64]

---

[63] Cf. *Return of every member*, ii, pp. 239–40, and commissions cited above.

[64] *The Complete Works of John Gower*, ed. G. C. Macaulay (Oxford, 1899–1902), ii, pp. xxi–v, iii, pp. 469–71. See also G. Mathew, *The Court of Richard II* (London,

Royal writs of 16 May 1391 suggest that people other than Gower had been dismayed by Richard's apparent *volte-face* in 1390. The king had received numerous complaints that J.P.s were failing to hold sessions and perform their duties, and every commission was now ordered to act with proper diligence.[65] These writs suggest that the morale of the justices had been undermined.

Richard, in fact, had taken a new course between issuing the ordinance on liveries and the parliament of November 1390. The month before it met he made his first distribution of badges of the white hart. Although he might not be able to forbid baronial retinues, he could not only emulate but even aim to surpass the lords by recruiting the greatest number of retainers in the country. His success in this is shown by the accounts of the royal household: its expenditure rose by one-third in the year starting from Michaelmas 1390, and by the end of the reign it was double what it had been in 1389–90.[66] This new programme was likewise more in keeping with the social structure of the time than the attempt to enlist the commons by a crusade in defence of public order. It is unlikely that Richard took up this cause as anything but an expedient demanded by the isolation of his position in 1389. After 1390, his interest in commissions of the peace soon waned, and with the replacement of Wykeham by Arundel in May 1391 he no longer had a chancellor sympathetic to the 'gentry' class. Four almost complete sets of commissions had been issued in 1389 and 1390, and in the course of this unprecedented process of constant review the judicial authority of the justices had been raised to its highest point and the terms of the commission itself had been developed to the form it was to retain throughout the following century.[67] The next general review was made in June 1394, when twenty-one of the shires were still under J.P.s appointed in December 1390.[68] A similar interval followed before the whole country

1968), pp. 74–7; R. H. Jones, *The Royal Policy of Richard II* (Oxford, 1968), pp. 147–8.

[65] *C.Cl.R., 1389–92*, pp. 252–3.

[66] M. V. Clarke, *Fourteenth Century Studies* (Oxford, 1937), p. 277; A. Steel, *Richard II* (Cambridge, 1941), pp. 168–9; Tout, *Chapters*, vi, pp. 97–101. The accounts of the great wardrobe, which was responsible for the supply of royal liveries, show a parallel rise (ibid., p. 108).

[67] *Proceedings*, ed. Putnam, pp. xx–xxix.

[68] *C.P.R., 1392–6*, pp. 435–41. For the exceptions, see *C.P.R., 1388–92*, pp. 516, 524–7; *1392–6*, pp. 292, 434.

was given new commissions on 12 November 1397.[69] Their purpose was patently political: after the destruction of the old appellants, the influence of Richard's noble partisans was spread throughout the land. Most counties were given three or more baronial members; there were seven in the North Riding, five dukes were appointed to the Norfolk bench. Gaunt still held primacy in the number of his commissions, but the 'duketti' were given far flung authority.[70] In the previous week Richard make his first systematic effort to bring the shrievalties under his control; a third of his nominees were members of the royal household, and he was to retain them and a further ten for a second year in office.[71] Richard's acts from this time fully demonstrate that the commons at Cambridge had made no permanent contribution to his concept of the royal office.

[69] *C.P.R., 1396–9*, pp. 230–6.
[70] Dukes were appointed to these total numbers of commissions: Lancaster (23), Albemarle (16), Surrey (13), Exeter (9), Norfolk (8), York (7), Hereford (4).
[71] Tout, *Chapters*, iv, pp. 43–4.

VIII

Henry of Derby's Expeditions to Prussia 1390-1 and 1392

F. R. H. DU BOULAY

LATE IN his life King Henry IV had occasion to interview a German envoy called Arndt von Dassel at Gloucester. In that autumn of 1407 he recalled how in his 'gadling days' he had gone with three hundred men to join the marshal of the Teutonic order in a '*Reyse*' against the Lithuanians and spent four weeks with him in an attempt to take the sacred city of Vilna, till their powder had been all shot off and approaching winter had driven them back to Königsberg. Yet, Henry is reported to have said, he had been ready the next summer to undertake another *Reyse*, and he was indeed a 'child of Spruce', for there was no land beyond the sea he would rather serve.[1]

Henry was an accomplished diplomatic liar, and at the moment of speaking had been playing off Germans and Poles against each other, evading the demands of the one side for compensation in respect of English piracies, and of the other for help against the Teutonic predators. For all that, his recollections of Prussia seem accurate. They accord with the tone, even the words, of Prussian and English chroniclers, and they attest that Henry had enjoyed the Prussian expeditions of his early manhood.

Nor was the quite detailed attention given by English chroniclers to such episodes the result of mere curiosity over adventures in a far-off country of which they knew nothing. The fortunes of Prussia in the late fourteenth century were linked with those of all Europe. Even in Henry's brief excursions several threads of history

Grateful acknowledgement is made to Mr Andrew Parrett for drawing the maps.
[1] J. H. Wylie, *History of England under Henry IV*, iv (1898), pp. 8–9. Vilna was referred to as the 'sacred city' presumably because the cathedral had been founded there in 1387, in a barely Christian land.

are caught up and intertwined: English, German, Lithuanian, Polish, French, Scottish and papal.

It does not seem necessary to look for subtle reasons why Henry, earl of Derby, should have set out for Prussia in the summers of 1390 and 1392. In the Merciless Parliament of 1388 he had been only 22, and probably more embarrassed than involved by the bitterness between the king on the one hand and the principal Appellants, Gloucester, Arundel and Warwick, on the other. Henry was a young man of action, not a *politique*. He had been the first to prepare himself for battle against Robert de Vere, and had held the field against him on 20 December 1387 at Radcot Bridge. But if he had felt political emotion in the miserable succeeding weeks, a sense of rivalry with his uncle of Gloucester is more likely than anger with his royal cousin. As a boy Henry had been with King Richard in the Tower during the Great Revolt and had been able to observe his courage.[2] In 1388 Henry opposed the execution of Sir Simon Burley with all his force, and this meant dissension with Gloucester, though it was soon resolved, according to Walsingham.[3] But when the king had (almost certainly) been deposed for three days in December 1387 by the Appellants, he was reinstated because of Henry's protest that he and not Gloucester should be the rightful successor.[4] Rivalry with Gloucester was in fact a long-term *motif* of his early life, from their contention for the Bohun inheritance up to their expeditions to Prussia in the early 1390s, when Gloucester's unlucky failure even to arrive was matched by Henry of Derby's well-advertised success. There is no evidence that Henry left England out of fear of the king. Indeed, the king wrote several times to foreign princes on Derby's behalf.

Soon after the Merciless Parliament Richard II reasserted his right to rule and the Appellants could not withstand him. Henry of Derby was quickly restored to favour. In giving himself up to foreign tournaments and expeditions he was simply doing things he enjoyed, and what members of his family had been doing for a long time. The Henry, duke of Lancaster, who died in 1361 had, for example, made the crusade to Prussia before going on to

[2] Knighton, ii, p. 132.　　[3] Walsingham, ii, p. 174.
[4] M. V. Clarke, *Fourteenth-century Studies*, ed. L. S. Sutherland and M. McKisack (Oxford, 1937), pp. 91–5.

Rhodes, Cyprus and other eastern places.[5] Other English nobles were doing the same. Henry of Derby was like so many of them a natural adventurer, encouraged further by his own father's example. Perhaps he went to Calais with John of Gaunt in 1384. Certainly in 1386 he saw his father off to Spain from Plymouth, went on board before the moment of sailing, and looked at the ships drawn from many ports of England for this long-prepared summer departure.[6] In March and April 1390 his own chance of independent travel overseas came, when he took part in the great tournament at St Inglevert near Calais. Here he won a chivalric reputation and met young men like his challenger, Jean de Boucicaut, who had already been to Prussia and the near East and was to have further astonishing adventures.[7] In January 1390 the king of England was asking Jagiello of Poland to allow Derby safe-conduct; and on 4 May 1390 Derby got licence from the king and from his father to make his own expedition against the 'Saracens'.[8]

In short, Henry of Derby was brought up amongst rich and restless travellers and acquired their tastes at an early age. To these men foreign countries were not places to be understood but enjoyed and used. They were at home almost anywhere. Even if they married foreign wives they did not learn new languages but left the women behind and took interpreters with them. Experts could deal with currency problems and negotiations with the natives. It was a man's world in which slight discomforts and occasional dangers were as nothing against the comradeship and startling luxuries of the officers' mess.

But why was Prussia a suitable destination? Kings of England had been granting the German knights an annual subsidy since 1235, and the English chroniclers of Richard II's day were interested and well informed about the supposedly romantic conflicts in those distant parts, but they do not explain the political situation for us. Nor does Chaucer, though he gives literary colour to the knightly

[5] John Capgrave, *Liber de Illustribus Henricis*, ed. F. C. Hingeston (Rolls Series, 1858), p. 161.

[6] Knighton, ii, p. 207. Lists of Gaunt's ships and their places of origin are given in P.R.O. Exchequer Accounts (E.101), 40/19–21. I owe this reference to Mr P. N. Guthrie.

[7] 'Le Livre des faicts du Mareschal de Boucicault', printed in *Scriptores Rerum Prussicarum*, ed. T. Hirsch, M. Toppen and E. Strehlke (Leipzig, 1861–74), (hereafter referred to as *S.R.P.*), ii, pp. 785–7.

[8] *Correspondence*, no. 116, cf. nos. 166, 199; Monk of Westminster, p. 235.

tradition of Prussian warfare:

> Ful ofte tyme he hadde the bord bigonne
> Aboven alle nacions in Pruce.
> In Lettow hadde he reysed and in Ruce . . .[9]

The fourteenth century saw the rise of a united Lithuania against the pressure of the Teutonic Knights. This state comprised Lithuania itself, Samogitia and part of western Russia, and was pushing further eastward into a Russia where Tartar power was in decline. Lithuania's capital was the new city of Vilna where the Catholic cathedral was founded in 1387 by Jagiello. A contemporary describes the town as built of wooden houses and brick churches protected by bulwarks of wood. The main castle stood on a sandhill surrounded with a wall of stones and earth. The men had long hair streaming over their shoulders; the women were plainly dressed like Picard peasants, and the country was full of lakes and vast forests filled with bears, wild dogs, wolves, hogs and stags. No stranger, if properly introduced, was allowed to pay anything for his keep.[10] The power of these people lay in the warlike spirit of the inhabitants and a rough discipline learned from the Germans themselves but given force by despair and a thirst for vengeance.

Poland too was suffering from Teutonic attack. Casimir the Great (1333–70) found it necessary to unite the Polish provinces more closely, and began the annexation of a Russian province which brought Poland eastwards into contact with Tartars, Romanians, Lithuanians and ultimately Muscovites.

To the Lithuanians, allies of Poland, fell the difficult task of defending the north of their country against the grand master of the Teutonic order, Winrich von Kniprode (1351–82). By this time the Germans had pushed almost to the River Memel or Niemen in the south-east, had occupied Estonia in the north, and in the middle were occupying Samland and Samogitia. Samland was the forested territory just north of Königsberg, between the

---

[9] *The Canterbury Tales: Prologue*, l. 52–4. When Chaucer says the knight had 'The bord bigonne' ('taken the head of the table') he refers to the *Ehrentisch*, for which see below, p. 160.

[10] Guillebert de Lannoy (1386–1462), *Voyages et Ambassades*, ed. C. P. Serrure (Société des Bibliophiles, Mons, 1840), p. 24. See also Petras Klimas, *Ghillebert de Lannoy in Medieval Lithuania* (New York, 1945).

huge bays known in contemporary sources as the *Königsberger Haff*
and the *Kurisches Haff* (the Curonian Bay). Here there was a mixed
settlement of Germans and Prussians whose villages were distinct
but who lived untroubled by racial tension, as Henry of Derby's
financial accounts of his expeditions show well enough. The older
Prussian place-names endured.[11] Those in *-au* were common and
indicated administrative centres or fortifications taken over by the
Order. Those in *-itten* were ancient field-settlements of Lithuanian
origin. It was a colonizing area open to rich traffic and no stranger
to foreign men and foreign goods. Samogitia, north of the River
Memel, was yet unconquered and unconverted: the 'Wilderness'
of the accounts, the Graudenwald of modern times, and the arena
of the fighting under discussion.

Shortly before Derby's journeys a complex dispute arose within
the Lithuanian ruling house itself. King Olgird (1345–77) was
succeeded by his son Jagiello, who wanted to become a Christian.
To this course Olgird's younger brother Kinstut was bitterly
opposed. Kinstut and Olgird had in fact shared the rule of Lithuania, the younger man concerned more with defence against the
Germans, the older attracted to eastern policies. Civil war followed,
and Kinstut died as a prisoner in the hands of his nephew Jagiello,
leaving a son who now enters the story. This was Vitold, one of
history's great turncoats, but praised by a German writer as 'a
soldier and a statesman of genius'.[12] In the war (1382–1401) between
the cousins Jagiello and Vitold, each allied himself in turn with the
Teutonic Knights, who for their part made use of their ally of the
moment, but trusted neither. After Kinstut's death in 1382,
Jagiello got help from the Order in return for the surrender of
Samogitia and a promise to receive baptism. For the Order to gain
Samogitia would mean the bridging of a territorial gap between
their existing conquests, and the conversion to Catholic Christianity
of the last heathen country on the eastern borders of Europe.

[11] Hans Mortensen, *Siedlungsgeographie des Samlandes* ([Forschungen zur
deutschen Landes- und Volkskunde, hrsg. R. Gradmann, Bd. 22,] Stuttgart, 1923),
pp. 279-358.

[12] C. Krollmann, *The Teutonic Order in Prussia*, transl. Ernst Horstmann (Elbing,
1938). The Lithuanian name Vytautas is variously spelled, but the common wes-
ternized form Vitold is used here. For the detailed history of his relationships with
the Teutonic Order, see Karl Heinl, *Fürst Witold von Litauen* (Historische Studien,
165, Berlin, 1923).

The alliances between the Order and Vitold were broken and remade several times during the late fourteenth century. When Derby was undertaking his expeditions, Vitold was on the side of the Germans, invading his own country after having suffered desperate reverses at the hands of Polish forces and Skirgiello, brother to Jagiello. In the warfare between Germans and Poles, Lithuanians were in fact to be found on either side, divided against each other by family rivalry.

To Vitold's cousin Jagiello, king of Lithuania, the course was clear: to ally himself with the Poles, to convert his own people to Christianity, and to fight the German Order. Some Polish princes were already interested in plans to convert Lithuania to Catholicism independently of the efforts of the Teutonic Knights. They invited Jagiello to make a gratifying dynastic alliance. In 1386 he entered Cracow in state, received Catholic baptism, married the Polish princess Jadviga (Hedwig), and was crowned with her as co-monarch of Poland under the name of Vladyslav II (1386–1434). Within the briefest time the Polish magnates who had supported this action had thus secured their own political predominance and brought about the union under one ruler of Poland, Lithuania and part of Russia. On this basis Jagiello began the conversion of Lithuania. Samogitia, though theoretically part of Poland-Lithuania under its Christian kingship, remained for the time pagan. The description of warfare from Prussia against the Lithuanians as a 'crusade' has been branded as hypocrisy in view of Jagiello's conversion. But it was not yet wholly a misnomer.

Jagiello made his brother Skirgiello who was devoted to him regent in Lithuania. The enmity between the cousins Vitold and Jagiello was not unnaturally extended into harsh rivalry between Vitold and Skirgiello. To Vitold, the dream was of a large eastern dominion in which the Lithuanians not the Poles would enjoy the rule of north-eastern Europe. In the present context, the important matter is that Vitold, conceiving himself the great Lithuanian leader, was making use of the Teutonic Knights to drive out his cousin Skirgiello and acquire the regency for himself. Only then could he discard the help of the Germans, and at the price of granting them Samogitia.

Hence Samogitia was in the 1390s a centre of political interest, its territory desired by each side for the strongest political reasons, its conversion to Catholicism ironically contested by German and Pole. It is scarcely surprising that the sincerity of manacled converts should on occasion be suspected. 'Nominal Christians' a German contemporary called such men: '*Cristen mit dem Mundt*'.[13] From the Samogitians a cry of complaint to the Order went up in 1399:[14]

> Oppressed and exhausted by torments, we ask you to hear us, you princes, spiritual and secular! The Order desires not our souls for God but our fields for itself. It has brought us to the point that we must become either beggars or robbers in order to maintain our existence. And how dare they after all this call themselves our brothers and baptize us? He who wants to wash others should himself be clean. It is true that the Prussians are already baptized, but they are as ignorant of the Faith as before. Whenever they invade a foreign land in company with the knights of the Order, they conduct themselves more evilly than the Turks; and the worse they rage the greater the praise bestowed upon them by the Order. The knights have taken from us all the fruits of our country and all the bees. They permit us neither to hunt nor to fish nor to carry on trade with our neighbours. Every year they lead away our children as hostages. Our eldest they have carried off to Prussia, others together with their families they have exterminated with fire; and they have forcibly abducted our sisters and daughters. And there they go, wearing the Holy Cross on their coats! Have pity on us. We ask therefore to be baptized. But give a thought to the fact that we are human beings, created in the image of God, and not some kind of animals . . . We wish with all our hearts to become Christians, but to be baptized with water and not with blood.

This sketch of events explains why regular expeditions, or *Reysen*, against the Lithuanians of the Wilderness were so prominent a feature of the Order's activity in the late fourteenth century. Advertised with the attributes of a crusade, they provided a training-ground for the Order's armies and a vast field of campaign for foreign knights whose support was welcome to the Germans and encouraged by the promise of secular adventure and ecclesiastical indulgence.

There were two forms of tactic.[15] One was the large-scale,

---

[13] J. Twinger or Königshoven (1349–1420), in *Chroniken der Deutschen Städte*, i (Leipzig, 1870–1), p. 913. Cf. K. Heinl, op. cit., p. 80.
[14] *Geschichte in Quellen*, ii (Mittelalter), ed. Wolfgang Lautemann (München, 1970), no. 607, citing Valentin Gitermann, *Geschichte Russlands*, i (1965), pp. 396 ff.
[15] For what follows, see Hans Prutz (ed.), *Rechnungen über Heinrich von Derbys*

long-prepared campaign, announced and heralded in Germany and abroad. Its object was not harassment but the permanent conquest of some Lithuanian castle or territory. Distinguished knights from abroad were induced to take part by a splendid banquet of honour (*Ehrentisch*), usually held at Königsberg before the departure of the combatants for battle or home. Prutz wrote that about a dozen knights who had performed the most notable deeds were entertained, but the numbers could be much greater.[16] They too spent money on display, to the profit of goldsmiths, silversmiths and luxury merchants of Königsberg. The *Reyse* was virtually a term of art: the *Reise*, the Journey, the 'blessed viage' of English texts which refer to late medieval crusade. When Derby turned away in 1392 without completing his campaign he was said by John of Posilge to have departed *ungereyset*.[17]

The armies of the *Reyse* launched into the Wilderness often set off from Ragnit, divided into the three columns of Prussian battle-order; but the results of such an array were rarely impressive.

The other tactic consisted of frequent small raids striking into the northern Wilderness from bases at Ragnit, Insterburg, Nordenburg or Angersburg. The object of these was harassment, their method terror, their significance the clash of two cultures no less than on the Anglo-Welsh or Anglo-Scottish borders. The German Order had its intelligence experts who worked on natives or refugees to become spies and guides. The terrain was appalling and could in general be traversed only under drought or ice. Route-reports were made on obstructions, suitable camping-grounds and available forage. The raiders hoped to burst in upon villages, plunder and burn them, massacre the men and lead off women and children tied together as suitable 'converts'. The habit of destruction so fostered makes men insensitive to cruelty, and writers who celebrated chivalric excursions described, without inner repugnance, the contrast between the knightly encampment with its

Preussenfahrten, 1390–1 und 1392. (Verein für die Geschichte der Provinzen Ost- und Westpreussen, Leipzig, 1893), Introduction.

[16] In 1385, 93 were at the *Ehrentisch* (*Codex Diplomaticus Prussicus*, ed. Johannes Voigt, Königsberg, 1853, iv, no. 31).

[17] *S.R.P.*, iii, p. 182. For the 'blessed viage', see *Registrum Thome Bourgchier* (Canterbury and York Society, liv, 1957,) p. 117. Cf. H. J. Cohn, *The Government of the Rhine Palatinate in the fifteenth century*, (Oxford, 1965), p. 80.

warm plenty and the horrors of the surrounding desolation. We have this in far-away England, where to the author of *Sir Gawayne and the Green Knight* the social joys of the armed court

> With alle the mete and the mirthe that men couthe avyse;
> Such glaum ande gle glorious to here

are set against the savagery of nature's winter and the enemy outside:

> With mony bryddes unblythe upon bare twyges,
> That pitosly ther piped for pyne of the colde.[18]

The Prussian scene had its own poetic observer in Peter Suchen-wirt, a sort of Austrian Froissart, through whose verse we may hear the beat of hoofs and see the River Memel, an arrow's flight across and thick with craft to ferry over an army in an afternoon. All hurry forward against the pagans, he says, amidst difficulties of terrain unknown to those who have merely fought in Hungary. The horses go hither and thither, up and down, jumping, slithering and rearing, and clambering wearily over huge trees which storms have thrown across the path till it is all but impassable. Even on the return there is danger: horses sink into the morass till the spurs can no longer urge them forward, and at the end of the ride the flooded river may easily sweep the boats past Königsberg and out to destruction in the waters of the *Haff*:

> Der herzog dâ ze schiffe saz
> mit manigem hern, wizzet daz;
> zu Chunigesperch traib in der wint.
> Die dâ nâch im gevarn sint
> des wazzers chaum ein ganze meil,
> di slûg der wint in sneller eil
> weit hin auf daz Cheurisch hab:
> maniger wônt, ez solt sein grab
> in der sê gewesen sein;
> doch tet in got genâde schein.[19]

[18] *Sir Gawayne and the Green Knight*, ed. J. R. R. Tolkien and E. V. Gordon (Oxford, 1936, rev. edn. 1968), l. 45–6, 746–7.

[19] *S.R.P.*, ii (1863), p. 167. 'The duke, you should know that, sat with many a lord on board ship; the wind drove him to Königsberg. Those who came sailing barely a whole sea-mile behind him were tossed by the wind in tearing haste far up the *Kurisches Haff*. Many a one thought his grave was to be in the sea, but God made manifest his mercy towards them.'

This was the scene of Derby's crusade. Henry was preparing to go abroad in the spring of 1390. He took part in the jousts at St Inglevert near Calais between 20 March and 24 April, and at that time seemed likely to join the French crusade to Tunisia. The reason why he changed his mind at the last moment and went to Prussia has caused puzzlement.[20] The commission to Richard Kingston to act as Derby's special treasurer for war, dated 6 May 1390, says that he was undertaking voyages both to Barbary and Prussia. Derby certainly was at Calais during May, in command of men who were expecting to go to Africa. But he returned to England on 5 June after he had called off the Barbary venture. Previous writers have supposed that Prussia offered a stronger inducement. It may be so. But not only had he made two attempts to secure a safe-conduct through France from the French king, but the Monk of Westminster, not hitherto quoted, says explicitly that the earl went to Prussia after his vow to cross into Barbary had been frustrated.[21] A reasonable inference is that the king of France had for some reason refused Henry a licence to pass through his dominions.

Derby sailed from Boston soon after 20 July 1390. The two ships sighted the Pomeranian coast at Leba, where three men were sent ashore; Derby with an advance party landed at Rixhöft on 8 August, spent the night in a mill near Putzig, and reached Danzig where they joined up with the main party which had disembarked there. From this point the route may be followed on the accompanying map, though the later stages, in the vicinity of Vilna, must remain conjectural since the unsettled nature of the country gave the writer of the wardrobe account no clearly identifiable landmarks. When towns or villages are mentioned here they were places off the main line of advance where small parties of men were seeking supplies.

The object of the *Reyse* was to join up with the German knights

[20] The following narrative of the expeditions is of course based on *Expeditions to Prussia and the Holy Land made by Henry earl of Derby*, ed. Lucy Toulmin Smith (Camden Society, new series lii, 1894). Much information is given in the text and introduction for which there can be no place here. See also Grace Stretton, 'Some aspects of medieval travel', *T.R.H.S.* 4th series, vii (1924), pp. 77–97; and J. L. Kirby, *Henry IV of England* (London, 1970), ch. 3, which appeared after the present paper had been written.

[21] Item xxii° Julii dominus Henricus comes Derbeye frustratus voto transeundi in Barbariam obtenta licentia transivit in Prussyam (p. 238).

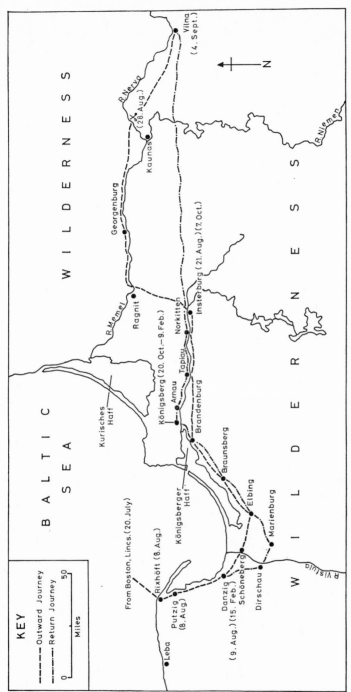

Henry of Derby's expedition 1390–1

under Marshal Engelhardt Rabe near Ragnit and move into the Wilderness against Skirgiello, who lay with his army near the confluence of the Rivers Memel (Niemen) and Wilia (Nerva or Neris). The supply lines were formed by hired barges (*Prahme*) moving up-river from Königsberg, and by baggage-carts going overland from Königsberg to Insterburg castle, where the forward supply base was set up. Two German knights were detailed to act as liaison officers with the English, handled the native labour and employed a German notary from Königsberg to keep the accounts. Junction was made with Marshal Rabe on 22 August. On 25 August at Georgenburg an Anglo-German striking-force left the main body, marched towards Kaunas and on Sunday, 28 August, achieved an opposed crossing of the River Wilia. This was the main engagement of the *Reyse*, and indeed of Henry's whole time in Prussia. The chroniclers describe an allied victory with 300 enemy dead and three Russian dukes and eleven boyars among the prisoners. It was in the main an archer victory but, amongst others, the English knight, Sir John Lowdham, was killed there at the age of 25, and his body taken back to Königsberg under German escort. Alone of the English knights he had been serving not for wages but for a loan of £50, for which he had mortgaged his services. Skirgiello, who had watched the battle from a fort, then fell back on Vilna. After a night's rest by the river the Anglo-Germans were re-supplied by barge and reinforced by a crack army from Livonia.

There were then evidently three armies: the Anglo-Germans under Marshal Rabe, the Livonian detachment, and Vitold himself with a force of Samogitians and Lithuanians.[22] According to the Monk of Westminster they moved on Vilna under unified command. The hill-city consisted of a civilian settlement protected by at least two fortifications. The upper one, constructed of wood, was assaulted and taken on 4 September, pillaged of merchandise and burned. Karigal, another brother of Jagiello, was killed. German though he was, Posilge was saddened by the destruction: 'das unczelich was, dy dorynne vortorbin und vorbranten.'[23] According to both English and German chroniclers the success was largely due to the English, and it was an English squire who first carried the standard to the ramparts.

[22] *S.R.P.*, iii, pp. 164–7.   [23] Ibid.

The main castle was well defended by archers against whom neither English archers, nor a 'gunner archer' who was present, nor sappers working against the walls in a 'sow' could do anything. The besiegers' supply was adequate, for Vitold's column had brought food and fodder with it, while according to Posilge it was possible to ride safely within six miles of the army to bring in provisions. But their sufferings were otherwise great. 'They stood five weeks in continual agony day and night', wrote Wigand of Marburg;[24] tormented by disease and with 'the powder all shot away', the invading armies at last dispersed about 7 October.

Derby returned to Königsberg by way of Kulwa Castle near the entrance of the Wilia into the Memel. His casualties had been light, though two of his knights had been captured. Unfortunately we do not know who they were or whether Jagiello let them go as a result of Derby's negotiations.

In Königsberg Derby stayed from 20 October till 9 February 1391, when he began to move homeward via Danzig. In Danzig the English party gathered in February, billeted partly in a town house belonging to Klaus Gottesknecht and partly in a mansion outside the city belonging to the bishop of Cujavia.

The homeward voyage was made from about 31 March to 30 April 1391 in two chartered ships, again with Prussian masters and English pilots from Boston. Henry disembarked at Hull and the baggage was taken to Bolingbroke. Not until January 1392 were the accounts of the *Reyse* made up from the detailed documents. This was done at Peterborough, where Henry himself was then present.

★   ★   ★

Derby's second journey turned into a tour of Europe and the Near East in the grand style, but its Prussian stage, which alone is the present concern, was an anticlimax.

On 27 June 1392 the king granted letters of protection to Derby and his companions, Hugh and Robert Waterton. Kingston's renewed appointment as treasurer for war for Derby's 'voyage towards the parts of Prussia' suggests that the original objective was the same as in 1390. On 24 July the party sailed in three ships

[24] *S.R.P.*, ii, pp. 642–3.

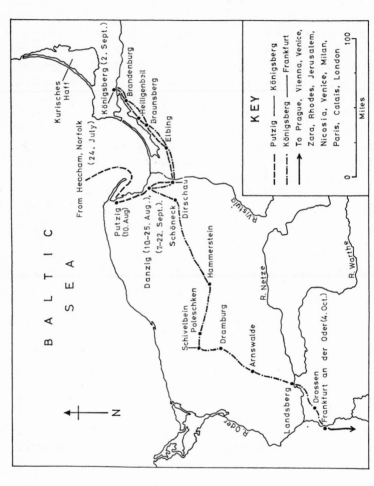

Henry of Derby's expedition 1392

from Heacham near King's Lynn and arrived at Putzig on 10 August. The expedition went at once to Danzig and was billeted in three houses, one of which belonged to Klaus Gottesknecht, their host of the previous occasion. After two weeks the journey was continued to Königsberg, but from this point no further progress was made on the *Reyse*. Derby's departure was explained differently by different chroniclers. In general, the Germans took the view that Derby had misconducted himself in some way, either by allowing his retinue to kill an unfortunate local man called Hans Terganwisch or by refusing to put away the banner of St George under which both he and the Knights claimed to fight. Capgrave, the English chronicler of 'the illustrious Henries', wrote on the other hand that the lords of the province were unfriendly and Derby left them. The truth is that Vitold did in fact send all the foreign volunteers away with the correct excuse that he did not want them, for he was then in the act of deserting the Teutonic order once more and returning to the allegiance of Jagiello.[25] King Sigismund of Hungary was negotiating with the Order to buy Dobriszin and Cujavia. This move was not in the interests of either Jagiello or Vitold, but the Order had no time for Vitold's objections. In return for his resumption of loyalty, Jagiello gave Vitold back all his inheritance in Lithuania and set him in the place of the less efficient Skirgiello. From now on Vitold and Jagiello worked mostly in harmony. Derby's termination of his second *Reyse* is therefore to be explained in terms of local politics. He was certainly not on hostile terms with the Teutonic Knights: he had been met at Danzig by his old comrade-in-arms, Marshal Rabe, and before he left the country the Order granted him the impressive sum of £400 towards his expenses.

At Danzig the earl's household was streamlined, and on 22 September 1392 he left for the peaceful progress to Prague, Vienna, Venice, Rhodes and Jerusalem, and back again to Cyprus, Venice, Milan, Paris, Calais and England.

Behind these bare itineraries were a number of situations to which attention may now be called.

In the first place, it is very doubtful if Derby played any diplomatic role worth the name, as has been suggested by some writers. It is true that the *Reysen* happened to take place in a crucial phase

25 Karl Heinl, op. cit., pp. 88–9.

of Anglo-Prussian relations. Trade rivalry between English merchants and the Hanseatic towns of the Baltic had been getting
worse during the last quarter of the fourteenth century. Efforts
were made to improve them by Richard II's government and by
the Teutonic order which was at least formally a member and
protector of the Hanse.[26] The Grand Master often complained
about injuries done to Prussian merchants by Englishmen, and he
wrote to any notable person he thought might help, whether the
king of England, the queen, the duke of Lancaster or parliament.[27]
Embassies were exchanged during the whole of this period and
long afterwards, but the trade agreement which so pleased the
Monk of Westminster in 1388 was of little effect.[28] To the Germans
the English were still in 1406 (and despite Henry IV's rapid confirmation of their privileges) 'a perverse nation, lost to all honesty
and truth and steeped in trickery, treason and venomous lies',[29]
though English subjects could always present as their side of the
story the jeers and aggressions of the Germans. But the professional work of negotiation was done by English clerks and merchants from London and York, not by war-lords whose talents
lay elsewhere. Admittedly the duke of Gloucester was commis-
sioned in 1391 to treat with 'the Master of Prussia', but his main
purpose cannot have been diplomatic and his expedition was in any
case wrecked by bad weather or bad navigation.[30] There is no real
evidence that Derby was even an amateur negotiator. His business
with merchants was confined to his private advantage.

Henry of Derby's adventures were undertaken mainly at the
expense of a lavish father. The costs of the first *Reyse* were
£4438 8s 3½d, of which Henry found only £950 1s 3d. The
balance of £3488 7s 0½d was supplied by John of Gaunt, much of it
in gold florins of Aragon conveyed on mule-back to Kenilworth
as part of the indemnity paid by the king of Castile for Gaunt's

[26] See the excellent, annotated study 'The Economic and Political Relations of
England and the Hanse from 1400 to 1475' by M. M. Postan in *Studies in English
Trade in the Fifteenth Century* (London, 1933), pp. 91–153.

[27] *Codex Diplomaticus Prussicus*, ed. Johannes Voigt, iv (Königsberg, 1853), nos.
12, 89, 98, etc.

[28] Monk of Westminster, p. 198. For the text of the 1388 treaty, *C.Cl.R.*,
1385–9, p. 535.

[29] Wylie, op. cit., iv, p. 2.

[30] Rymer, *Foedera*, etc. (orig. edn. 1727–35), vii, p. 705. Walsingham, ii, p. 202;
Monk of Westminster, pp. 260–3.

renunciation of his claims in that country. The second voyage was financed by Gaunt in an even more overwhelming manner. Out of £4915 5s 0¾d he paid £4341 9s 6d, and of the balance of £573 15s 6¾d Derby received £400 from the marshal of Prussia and further small sums from other European notabilities. Derby's whole apparatus of financial accounting, borrowings and exchanges through merchants dwelling in Prussia ran mainly on money derived from Spain and the Lancastrian inheritance in England.

The man who later was to be so impoverished a king of England enjoyed during these months in Prussia a life of luxury. From East Anglia to the remote Wilderness there was no shortage of the most variegated food and drink bought from English, Germans, Slavs and Balts. Ginger, garlic, rice and almonds were used abundantly in addition to basic meats and cereals. Pears, apples and cherries were available in Prussia. A cow supplied the earl with milk. During the long sojourns in Königsberg shopping expeditions to nearby towns and villages brought in whatever was lacking on the doorstep: white bread, dates, sweetmeats and so forth. The very falcons were fed on fresh chicken, at sea and ashore. Beer, mead and the wines of France and Germany were on sale: the Rhine wine was hardly dearer than that of Gascony though in London it fetched double the price. The local spirits (*aqua ardens*) was bought in Königsberg. When the household officers wanted to know where to buy, local officials and merchants were there to tell them. Germans, English, Prussians and Lithuanians were engaged in the victualling trades, and transactions could be made even in the Wilderness. The financial accounts allow a view also of 'consumer durables' bought for the earl: the golden signet ring engraved with plume and collar; the beaver hat; the painting of banners, hangings and escutcheons to decorate apartments; the golden chain fancied by Derby and taken by him from Sir John Dalyngridge and for which he gave £6 13s 4d compensation. On the second journey a pet parrot escaped and the finder was rewarded with 6s and a keeper appointed to cage it more securely. Henry's chief indoor amusements were listening to minstrels and dicing to which he had been addicted since early youth. Gambling money was religiously accounted for, whether he won or lost. On one occasion he played with a certain John Rye for two nights and these sessions cost the earl £28. It is interesting to note that on the first journey the expenses of gaming amounted to about £69 in contrast with about £12 recorded as alms.[31]

Derby's voyages illustrate not merely his mode of life but the religious preoccupations of himself and of Latin Christendom, divided by schism. Prussia's loyalty to Pope Boniface IX of the Roman obedience appears in the disagreeable story of the Blessed Dorothy, patroness of Pomerania. This peasant woman (*mulier idiota*) was born in the swamps of the Vistula and became the wife of a bladesmith. In twenty-six years of married life, we are told with approval, she bore nine children 'without any pleasure'.[32] After experiences of a religio-erotic or hysterical kind, reminiscent of those of her contemporary Margery Kemp, she was bricked up in a cell at Marienwerder in 1393 and died there a year later. In 1404 a commission of enquiry into her sanctity sat at Marienwerder under an order from Boniface IX, concerning whom Dorothy had had a revelation that God loved him and called him a good man. The canonization, however, did not succeed.

Derby himself made offerings at churches in Danzig for the plenary indulgence granted by Boniface IX (*a papa nostro*), though the offerings were remarkably small. His many small conventional gifts of piety were varied by an unusual activity which must probably be regarded as religious, namely, in the purchase of a number of Lithuanian boys destined for Christian upbringing. Payments for clothing them and the hire of matrons to look after them are recorded in the accounts. The boys themselves seem not to have been seized by Derby in a raid but to have been sold him by one of their countrymen at 3s 4d each. The earl liked to name such protégés after himself: there was a 'Henry the Lithuanian',[33] just as the second voyage produced a 'Henry the Turk'. Their fate is unknown, but the grant of an annual stipend in London in 1393 to 'Peter the Prussian, a convert' suggest a destiny not unworthy of the pages of Ronald Firbank.[34]

Since knights from different countries were attracted to Prussia, it is not surprising to find alien quarrels imported. The Douglas-Clifford incident echoes both Anglo-Scottish rivalries and the

[31] Toulmin Smith, pp. 115–18.

[32] Wylie, op. cit., ii, p. 364, citing T. C. Lilienthal, *Historia Beatae Dorotheae* (Danzig, 1744).

[33] Toulmin Smith, pp. 52, 90, 91.   [34] *C.P.R., 1391–6*, p. 323.

strife between the two obediences of western Christendom. William Douglas was a bastard son of Archibald Douglas, lord of Galloway. Some time before 1390 he had been challenged to do wager of battle for some disputed lands by Lord Clifford.[35] When Douglas went to France to buy the best weapons possible, he was taunted with having fled through cowardice, and returned the insult. The Monk of Westminster took up the story at this point.[36] According to him, a priest was saying mass in Königsberg during the summer of 1391 when Sir William Douglas came into the church. The priest stopped abruptly and refused to continue in the presence of 'schismatics'. Douglas shouted angrily that this was the work of Lord Clifford, and stormed out uttering threats. Outside the church Douglas and his men attacked the English after mass but, in wounding a squire, he himself was run through and killed. A number of English lords in the town seized a standard and rallied a force against the Scots. Germans, Bohemians and men of Guelders joined them, and only the French came in on the Scottish side. 'At last', wrote the Monk, 'they quietened down at the instance of a great man of that country, although lasting enmities remained in their minds.' The tale is inconclusive but illustrates in miniature the loutish realities of Border warfare and religious politics, carried by participants to the ends of the world.

In sum, the Prussian expeditions are an occasion for assessing the character of Henry Bolingbroke. He appears throughout as a man of physical competence and small sensibility. In King Richard's earliest years on the throne, Henry had suffered ill health from the 'pokkes', but neither this nor the medicines administered by master John Middleton had deterred him from games, gambling and the tourney.[37] Nor, later on, did an illness in Königsberg deter him for long. His wardrobe accounts constantly betray in Henry a taste for

[35] S.R.P., ii, p. 644 n. 1899. Douglas, who had a suit in the military court against Clifford, received a safe-conduct on 6 June 1390 (Rymer, Foedera, etc., (orig. edn. 1727–35), vii, p. 678).

[36] Pp. 258–9. According to The Complete Peerage, iii (1913), p. 292, Thomas lord Clifford is 'said to have been killed in Prussia in 1391'; while the Dictionary of National Biography suggests Douglas was alive in 1392. But errors in both these accounts sap confidence in them.

[37] P.R.O. Duchy of Lancaster 28/1/1. I am grateful to the president and fellows of Magdalen College, Oxford, and especially to Mr Karl Leyser, for kind permission to see the transcripts of the late K. B. McFarlane concerning Henry of Derby which are in their keeping.

luxurious equipment and 'subtelties' no less than that for which Richard II is famous. In contrast with his personal spending his almsdeeds were derisory. Sea voyages, the transport of armed expeditions and the cameraderie of campaigns were his skills at this period of his life. Of his personal bravery there is no question and his enthusiasm for swordplay is shown again in 1402 when he gave £10 to Bartold van der Eme who fenced with him with the long-sword and was hurt in the neck.[38] His private apartments, richly furnished in the most unpromising circumstances, were the scene of gambling rather than of dalliance. In love he also gave perhaps more wounds than he received, for it was said of Lucia Visconti in 1398 that if she could be sure of having the widowed earl for husband she would wait for him to the end of her life even if she knew she would die three days after the marriage.[39] More positively, the future proved a mutual loyalty between Henry and his knightly followers, many of whom served him long after the days in Prussia. To that time may be traced the fortunes of various families: Staveley, Swinburne, Norbury, Erpingham, Waterton, Bucton and Rempston among others. The type of enterprise suited him, and the Monk of Westminster noted[40] that he returned in 1391 *sanus et hilaris*: 'healthy and jovial'.

[38] F. Devon, *Issues of the Exchequer from King Henry III to King Henry VI* (1837), p. 284.
[39] *Calendar of State Papers in the archives of Milan*, ed. A. B. Hinds (London, 1912), p. 2.
[40] P. 247.

IX

The Quarrel of Richard II with London 1392-7

CAROLINE M. BARRON

In 1392 Richard II declared that he had found 'notable and evident defaults in the government and rule of the city of London'.[1] In the several judgements against the Londoners during the summer of 1392, the reasons for the royal displeasure are never given more precisely. It is possible that no specific charges were made against the Londoners, but rather that Richard kept the reasons for his anger purposely clouded in mystery so that the citizens might be trapped into self-accusation.[2] The contemporary chroniclers, in their wild guesses and imaginative supply of fable where fact has failed, reflect the general air of mystery. Had there been any official statement of formal accusation, it is likely that the West-minster Chronicler, at least, would have known of it or seen it. Richard's reluctance to show his hand may, in this case, have been supported by the desire of the Londoners not to write down, or to preserve, any of the documents which could later be used against them. While the course, and consequences, of Richard's seizure of the liberties of the city of London may be traced with some cer-tainty, the causes of that quarrel can be only tentatively suggested.

William Venour, the grocer who was mayor of London in the years 1389–90, was accused and convicted in 1392, together with his fellow sheriffs and aldermen, of having allowed defaults and misprisions to arise in the city 'for lack of good ruling'.[3] It is true that Venour's election in October 1389 was the occasion of some

---

[1] C.F.R. 1391–9, p. 49; Calendar of Letter-Books of the City of London: Letter-Book H 1375–1399, ed. R. R. Sharpe (London, 1907), p. 379 (hereafter cited as L.B.H.).

[2] This suggestion may be reinforced by the fact that William Venour and his fellow aldermen of 1389–90 were found guilty on 22 July 1392, by their own acknowledgement, C.Cl.R., 1392–6, pp. 87–9.

[3] C.Cl.R., 1392–6, pp. 87–9.

contention, for the old 'non-victualling' party argued that the goldsmith, Adam Bamme had, in fact, gained the greater number of votes. But in the end the victualling party prevailed and Venour was declared elected, for the Londoners realized that it was disastrous for them to be divided as they had been since the time of John of Northampton.[4] There is no other evidence to suggest that there was lawlessness or trouble in London during Venour's mayoralty.[5] Moreover in October 1390 Adam Bamme, the rejected goldsmith of the previous year, was elected as mayor. It is true that during Bamme's year of office, the erstwhile leader of the non-victualling party, John of Northampton, was finally pardoned by the king, but this was specifically stated to have been done at the request of the late mayor William Venour and the other aldermen.[6] It would seem, therefore, that the factions and troubles which beset London in the 1380s had been finally laid to rest and that, whatever defects there were in the government of the city, they did not arise from a recrudescence of this 'good old cause'.

There were, it is true, other cases which might conceivably have justified some royal intervention in the affairs of the city, but none of them could compare with the rioting and disorder of the struggles of the 1380s. John Walpole, a tailor, had complained in November 1388 about the malpractices and inhumanities of the keeper of Ludgate prison, John Bottesham. Walpole was not alone in his complaints, but he was most persistent, and when his bill and the verdict against Bottesham were later quashed, incorrectly, by the city's recorder, Walpole turned his venom against the mayors

[4] Monk of Westminster, p. 217; *L.B.H.*, p. 348. For the details of the original struggle between John of Northampton and Nicholas Brembre see Ruth Bird, *The Turbulent London of Richard II* (London, 1949), chs. 5 and 6.

[5] The mayor's court plea and memoranda rolls are missing for Venour's year of office, but this may indicate only that they were examined in 1392 and not returned. In any case these rolls do not all survive.

[6] Northampton's full pardon dated 2 December 1390, *L.B.H.*, p. 359; *C.P.R.*, *1388-92*, p. 335; *R.P.*, iii, p. 282. Adam Bamme ordered the men of the city to be of one accord in this matter and the citizens were forbidden to wear any badge or sign which would indicate to which of the two parties they belonged, *L.B.H.*, p. 364. The letters patent revoking the judgements against John of Northampton, and his associates John More and Richard Norbury, followed on 1 December 1391 as a result of a commons' petition in parliament, *R.P.*, iii, pp. 291-2; *L.B.H.*, pp. 370, 371. A royal signet letter referring to a petition from the mayor and citizens about John of Northampton and what may be the petition in question are to be found in the P.R.O. Chancery Warrants (C.81) no. 1355/32 and Ancient Petitions (S.C.8) File 341, no. 16100.

and other civic officers. In 1390 he brought his case on petition to the duke of Lancaster, before the King's Council and, although his cause had some justice, he pursued it in such an immoderate way that a jury summoned to hear the case in February 1395 concluded that 'a great part of the uproar and rancour in the city from the time of Nicholas Twyford [Mayor 1388-9] to the present day was made and spread by the ill-will of John Walpole, who was a great disseminator of discord'.[7] It is clear that Walpole had some reason for complaint and that the city's law officers were incorrect in quashing a verdict in his favour, but this decision was reversed on appeal in the usual way to the justices-in-error sitting at St Martin's-le-Grand. By itself this case can hardly have justified so drastic a punishment for the city as a whole as the seizure of the corporate liberties.[8]

The city further attracted the disapproving attention of the king and his council in these years, over the problem of the disposal of butchers' offal in the Thames. The statute of 1361 had confined the slaughter of beasts to the west of Knightsbridge or to the east of Stratford. But this limitation had been ignored by the London butchers who were slaughtering beasts as near to the city as Holborn Bridge. The king instructed the mayor and sheriffs to see that the statute was enforced before 27 February 1392.[9] In February, and again in May 1392, the Londoners were allowed some respite in executing this writ.[10] This can, however, hardly be the cause of

---

[7] *Calendar of Select Pleas and Memoranda of the City of London, 1381-1412,* ed. A. H. Thomas (Cambridge, 1932), p. 230 (hereafter cited as *Cal. P. and M., 1381-1412*). The details of this case, which began in 1388 and continued at least until 1397, can be traced in *Cal. P. and M., 1381-1412,* pp. 158-61, 170, 187-8, 228-30, 236, 242; *L.B.H.,* pp. 368-9, 374, 392, 395-6; *C.P.R., 1391-6,* pp. 76, 290. Walpole's petition to the duke of Lancaster and the consequent council proceedings in March 1390 are to be found in P.R.O. Parliamentary and Council Proceedings (C.49) File 67, no. 17. For a similar case of a London petition to the duke of Lancaster see *Cal. P. and M., 1381-1412,* pp. 109-13 and Ruth Bird, op. cit., pp. 108-9.

[8] The case may, however, explain the London petition to the parliament of 1394 asking for a modification of the statute of 1354, see below p. 196, n. 96, and also the obscure passage in Monk of Westminster, pp. 276-7, see below p. 177, n. 14.

[9] 6 December 1391, *C.Cl.R., 1389-92,* pp. 409-10; *L.B.H.,* p. 372. See E. L. Sabine, 'Butchering in Mediaeval London', *Speculum,* viii (1933), pp. 335-53, esp. pp. 348-9.

[10] The Londoners' request for a respite in this matter was discussed by the council at its meeting on 27 February 1392, see John Prophet's journal printed as Appendix II in J. F. Baldwin, *The King's Council in England during the Middle Ages* (Oxford, 1913), pp. 489-504, esp. pp. 491-2. Other writs 22 February 1392, *C.Cl.R., 1389-92,*

the king's displeasure for, as a result of a petition from the Londoners to the Winchester parliament of 1393, the king relaxed the stringency of the 1361 statute. Since the slaughtering of beasts so far out of London raised their price, the king agreed that a special house should be built on Thames-side for the butchers' use and that they should only dispose of their offal there. All other slaughter houses were to be destroyed.[11]

Neither the wrongs done to John Walpole, nor the nuisance of butchers' offal, sufficiently explain the drastic royal action in 1392. There remain three spheres of contention. The seemingly impregnable, and highly irritating, realm of city custom; the ever-present problem of the financial relations between London and the crown, and the frequent lawlessness in the city which provided a watchful king with his most obvious pretext for interference.

There is some evidence to show that at least two city customs (which usually took the form of financial or legal privileges) were called into question in the months immediately preceding the king's seizure of the London liberties. One of these disputes arose between November 1391 and January 1392 and concerned vessels or goods in the Thames water at London which the king claimed as deodand. The London sheriffs, however, argued before the king's council that such deodands, like escheats, belonged to them since the waters of the Thames lay within their franchise. Such goods, therefore, they claimed, could not be granted by the king to his servants (as Richard had done), although the chancellor argued on the king's behalf that the Londoners had such forfeitures only by trespass and not as deodands.[12] Another civic custom upon

---

pp. 409–10, L.B.H., p. 372; 23 May 1392, L.B.H., p. 375; 28 May 1392, C.Cl.R., 1389–92, p. 567, L.B.H., p. 376.

[11] R.P., iii, p. 306; C.Cl.R., 1392–96, p. 133; L.B.H., pp. 392, 394.

[12] A deodand was a personal chattel which was considered to be the immediate cause of death of its owner. As such it was forfeited to the king to be applied by him to pious uses, i.e. prayers for the soul of the deceased. In fresh water both the vessel and its cargo, which were considered to be the cause of the owner's death, were treated as deodand. 17 November 1391 a writ was sent to the London sheriffs about a boat called a 'shout' which had been abandoned in the Thames and was currently in the possession of John Trygg, fishmonger. The king claimed the boat as deodand, but there is no recorded reply to the writ, P.R.O. Exchequer King's Remembrancer Memoranda Roll (E.159) 168. The case was argued in the council on 24 and 26 January 1392, Baldwin, op. cit., pp. 490, 491. There is no evidence which supports the claims made by the London sheriffs, although the city was granted deodands in Southwark by charter in 1550, Walter de Gray Birch, ed.,

which the mayor, John Hende, appears to have stood firmly in January 1392 was the Londoners' right to be informed if the chancellor wished to summon a citizen to appear before him. The mayor argued that it was one of the London privileges that no one might be arrested in the city, without the assent of the mayor or his officers. The council was, however, clearly dissatisfied with Hende's reply on 20 January 1392, for he was required, together with three other Londoners, to attend the council daily for the next eight days, and each of them was bound in a recognizance of £1000.[13] The outcome of this dispute is not recorded. If it (or the question of deodands) was responsible for the king's anger against the city in 1392, there is no indication that the negotiations which led up to the final settlement, dealt with these problems. Indeed there is no evidence of a detailed compromise following the seizure of the city's liberties, but only of their comprehensive removal and, ultimately, comprehensive restoration. The Westminster chronicler, it is true, mentions that three of the city's liberties were not restored, but none of these three corresponds to any custom which is known to have caused friction in the period immediately before the breach between the king and the city.[14]

The Historical Charters and Constitutional Documents of the City of London (rev. edn. London, 1887), p. 117 (hereafter cited as Birch, Charters). See also L.B.H., p. 125 and n.

[13] Baldwin, op. cit., p. 489. This London privilege had been confirmed by Edward III in 1327, Birch, Charters, p. 56.

[14] Monk of Westminster, pp. 276-7. The three liberties which the chronicler says were not restored were: (i) The privilege claimed by the London freemen of being able to bequeath rents or goods for founding chantries or fraternities, without buying a special licence from the king. In fact the means whereby the city fraternities, by the use of feoffees, had been evading the provisions of the statute of 1279, had been revealed by the enquiry of 1388-9. A new statute had, therefore, been made in 1391 making land acquired on behalf of guilds and fraternities, subject to the same restraints as other lands covered by the statute, see L.B.H., p. 371 and n. 4; Statutes of the Realm ii (London, 1816), pp. 79-80; H. M. Chew, 'Mortmain in Medieval London', E.H.R., ccxxxvi (1945), pp. 1-15. This privilege had therefore been withdrawn before the seizure of the city's liberties in 1392. (ii) The exact meaning of this second privilege is obscure. The chronicler appears to state that the right of appeal from decisions given in secular London courts was now to be as effective as in any other part of the realm. But, in fact, appeals on writs of error from decisions given in civic courts had always gone to special royal justices sitting at St Martin's-le-Grand, and continued to do so after 1392. There is no observable change in procedure. In effect, the decisions of city courts were subject to revision, but by a process different from that in operation in the rest of the realm. London continued to occupy a unique place in the kingdom. There may be some

What, then, of the financial relations between London and the crown in the years 1388–92? The last corporate loan advanced by the mayor and commonalty of London to the crown was in March 1388.[15] Since then, not only had the city failed to lend money in its corporate capacity, but there was also a marked decline in loans from individual Londoners,[16] although the city contributed as usual to parliamentary taxation. The explanation may be, as Professor McKisack suggests, that 'the fate of Brembre may well have made the citizens chary of financial dealings with the Crown, and the cessation of fighting in the Channel had removed the main inducement to generosity'.[17] According to the author of the *Eulogium*, after the parliament of 1389 the Londoners excused themselves from providing the king with money on the grounds that they were not *potentiores aliis mercatoribus*.[18] In an attempt to extract money from the Londoners the king, in February 1392, sent a writ to the sheriffs to make a return of suitably qualified persons who had not yet taken up knighthood. Similar writs had been sent to the London sheriffs in 1344, 1356, and 1366, and the reply on those occasions, as in 1392, was that there was no one in the city who certainly enjoyed £40 a year in land or rents since tenements often stood empty and could easily be destroyed by

oblique reference here to the case of John Walpole, see p. 175, n. 8, above, and Birch, *Charters*, pp. 3–4, 53, 58; A. H. Thomas, ed., *Calendar of Early Mayor's Court Rolls, 1298–1307*, (Cambridge, 1924), pp. ix–xi; G. Norton, *Commentaries upon the History, Constitution and Chartered Franchises of the City of London* (3rd edn., London, 1869), pp. 361–3. (iii) The privilege claimed by the Londoners that any villein should be able, in London, to defend himself as a free man against charges brought against him by his lord. The chronicler states that the king now required that lords should be able to exercise their rights as fully in London as elsewhere. Again there is no observable change in London custom or practice in this matter after 1392, and villeins continued to gain their free status by living in the city, see *Cal. P. and M., 1364–81*, pp. xxiv–xxvi.

[15] The sum lent was £5000, 6 March 1388, P.R.O. Exchequer Receipt Roll (E.401) 570. Tallies were issued 10 April 1388, P.R.O. Exchequer Receipt Roll (E.401) 571.

[16] Six Londoners between them lent Richard £1533 6s 8d in 1388; eight Londoners lent £501 18s 7½d in 1389; four Londoners lent £239 13s 4d in 1390. There were no London loans in 1391. 23 February 1392, William Venour, who had been a regular royal creditor, lent Richard £333 6s 8d (to avert disaster?), but there are no other London loans in 1392. Other regular London royal creditors had been the goldsmith, Nicholas Exton and the vintner, William More. This information all derived from P.R.O. Exchequer Receipt Rolls (E.401).

[17] M. McKisack, *The Fourteenth Century* (Oxford, 1959), p. 468.

[18] *Eulogium*, iii, p. 367.

fire.[19] Such a bland return from the London sheriffs must have been particularly vexing to the king for, while it may have been true in 1344 that no Londoner certainly was worth £40 p.a., by 1412 there were at least seventeen London citizens who were worth this amount, or more.[20] It seems clear that Richard was irritated and annoyed by the Londoners' refusal to provide him with money during these years. Thomas Walsingham and the Monk of Westminster both record that the citizens declined to lend Richard a sum of money for which he asked. Their accounts of this incident differ somewhat, and the details seem improbable, but their general conclusion that money lay at the root of the quarrel, is likely to be correct.[21] Richard had extravagant tastes and grandiose schemes, and even his peaceful foreign policy required money for subsidies to foreign allies.[22] The king knew that Londoners could, even if they would not, lend him the money which he required, and in these circumstances he could only transform requests for cash into inescapable demands by a judicious use of the royal power and prerogative.

But such high-handed action by the king would not have been tolerated by the king's councillors if there had not been reasonable pretexts for the seizure of the city's liberties. The privileged customs of London could provide some justification for royal interference: so too, could the ever-present, but usually submerged, lawlessness in the city. Here, there are signs that the situation in London was approaching a point where royal action might be justified. In December 1391, William Mildenhall of London appeared in chancery accused of having concealed the fact that his father, Peter, had spoken disrespectfully of Richard II saying that he was

[19] *L.B.F.*, p. 105; *L.B.G.*, pp. 68, 205–6; *L.B.H.*, p. 378. The sheriffs' return in 1366 is to be found in P.R.O. Chancery Miscellanea (C.47) 1/16 nos. 16 and 17, and the 1392 return in Sheriffs' Accounts (E.199) Bundle 26 no. 5.

[20] J. C. L. Stahlschmidt, ed., 'Lay Subsidy temp. Henry IV', *Archaeological Journal*, xliv (1887), pp. 56–82.

[21] Walsingham, ii, pp. 207–8 mentions a sum of £1000. He says that the Londoners followed their refusal by assaulting a Lombard merchant who was prepared to lend the king the money. He concludes his account with some general invective against the character of the Londoners. Monk of Westminster, p. 270, mentions a sum of 5000 marks or pounds to be advanced upon the security of a jewel worth considerably more. He says that the citizens, having refused the king, were then prepared to lend such an amount to a Lombard who subsequently lent it to Richard, who was understandably annoyed when he discovered the origin of the money.

[22] J. J. N. Palmer, above, pp. 75–107.

unfit to govern and should stay in his latrine. The king kindly agreed to allow William to go free on condition that in future he would 'so far as reasonably he may speak respectfully of the king's person' and that if he heard other unfavourable sentiments in the city he was to report them.[23] Again in November and December 1391 the mayor and aldermen imposed an 8 p.m. curfew in the city, prevented transport by boat across the Thames at night, and enjoined an armed watch nightly in the wards, committing all those who broke the curfew to the counters.[24] On 23 December the king sent a writ to the mayor and sheriffs instructing them to prevent unlawful assemblies, since he had heard that the city was infested with armed peace-breakers, who committed assaults and felonies and hindered the civic officers in the exercise of their duties 'which the king will not, and ought not, to endure'.[25] This writ was followed by a further one in January instructing the mayor and sheriffs to prevent unlawful secret assemblies in which Londoners disputed heretically and subverted the Catholic faith, and which gave rise to tribulations and tumults. 'It is the king's will that within the bounds of his power shall bud forth no heresies or errors to infect the people.'[26]

These writs suggest that the situation in London in the months of November 1391 to January 1392 was tense and restless. The authors of Continuation C of the Brut Chronicle and the Harley 565 London Chronicle, describe an incident of mob violence to which they attribute the seizure of the city's liberties. A baker's servant, carrying a basket of horse loaves along Fleet Street to a hostelry, was accosted by a member of the household of John Waltham, bishop of Salisbury and, at that time, treasurer of England. The bishop's servant, who was called Romayne, not only stole a horse-loaf but, when the baker's man protested, hit him over the head. A brawl ensued instantly, Romayne fled to his master's inn in Fleet Street, and the following crowd, finding the gates shut against them, threatened to fire the house. Just in time John Hende, the mayor, arrived with the sheriffs and persuaded the crowd to disperse. As a result of this display of mob violence Waltham complained to Thomas Arundel, archbishop of York and chancellor,

---

[23] *C.Cl.R., 1389–92*, p. 527.   [24] *L.B.H.*, pp. 371–2, 373.
[25] *C.Cl.R., 1389–92*, p. 530; *L.B.H.*, p. 373.
[26] 21 January 1392, *C.Cl.R., 1389–92*, pp. 530–1.

and together the two men took their grievance to Richard himself.[27] The Brut continuator's account is a highly partisan one, laying the blame fully upon the bishop and his household servants, and emphasizing the legitimate desire of the citizens to see 'justice' (as they called it) done to the bullying Romayne.[28] This story cannot be substantiated from any record source, but some such incident is likely to have provided Richard with the pretext which he needed to set his campaign against the city in motion. Further, such an incident could well have gained the king a certain measure of support amongst the lords of the council who, having great houses in or near London, were particularly susceptible to such acts of lawlessness on the part of the Londoners.

It is clear that the mayor and aldermen miscalculated the strength of Richard's determination, or they would have taken steps both to placate him and to protect their liberties, long before a crisis was reached. It was Richard's skill that he concealed from the Londoners for so long the parlous nature of their situation. When the king decided to move against the citizens he had much which he could throw into the scales against them: the injustices done to John Walpole; the butchers' nuisances; the detaining of royal deodands; the intransigence of civic custom; the lack of financial support and the general lawlessness. In the face of a campaign which had been devised over a period of months, if not years, and which was sprung upon them by surprise attack, the Londoners were helpless. For their recent stubbornness and financial stringency, Richard made them pay remorselessly with their pride and their pockets. In desperation John Hende instructed his aldermen to see that all the inhabitants of their wards took fresh oaths of allegiance for the better preservation of the peace.[29] Conciliation and reform had come too late, for Richard had opened his campaign.

The first salvo in Richard's attack upon the city came with the writ of 13 May 1392, sent to the London sheriffs and informing

[27] *The Brut or the Chronicle of England*, ed. F. W. D. Brie (Early English Text Society, 1908) part ii, Continuation C, p. 345 (hereafter cited as Brut C). *A Chronicle of London 1089–1483* (Harley 565), ed. H. Nicolas, (London, 1827), pp. 79–80.

[28] Tout, *Chapters*, iv, p. 479, suggests that the southern chroniclers believed that the two north country ministers had prejudiced their master against the southern city. It is possible, also, that it was Arundel who persuaded Richard to move the courts to York, in order to favour the chief city of his diocese. See John H. Harvey; below pp. 202–15.

[29] 17 May 1392, *L.B.H.*, p. 375.

them that the Court of common pleas had been removed to York.[30] The continuator of the Croyland chronicle explains that this action of Richard's came as a result of 'the ill-will shown by the citizens of London',[31] and it was a move certain to be detrimental to the interests of the city. Not only would London litigants be compelled to travel a great distance, but the Londoners would be deprived of the trade which the concourse of people to Westminster inevitably produced. Moreover it was not only the common pleas which were moved to York, but also the chancery, exchequer and inmates of the Fleet prison.[32] It is possible that Richard hoped to set up a new capital in the north of England, away from the antagonistic counties of the south-east, and he may have wished especially to favour and encourage the city of York,[33] but the only explanation to be found in the writs removing the various institutions of government was 'urgent causes affecting the king and the estate of the realm'.[34] If the king's motive was indeed to damage the interests of the Londoners, such an exodus was also of great inconvenience and expense to many other subjects, as the Monk of Westminster pointed out.[35] The efficiency of the courts must have been greatly impaired and there was general relief when they returned again to Westminster in the autumn.

Having thus suggested his displeasure to the citizens of London,

[30] *L.B.H.*, p. 378. Later in the month the king made provision for the transport of the chancery rolls and the writs and memoranda of the common bench to York, 18, 31 May 1392, *C.P.R.*, *1391-6*, p. 65.

[31] *Ingulph's Chronicle of the Abbey of Croyland with the Continuations by Peter of Blois and anonymous writers*, ed. and trans. H. T. Riley, (London, 1854), p. 352.

[32] 30 May 1392, *C.Cl.R.*, *1389-92*, pp. 466, 467, 565-6. 7 June 1392, *C.P.R.*, *1391-6*, p. 67. Special chests had to be bought for keeping the exchequer rolls and memoranda in St Peter's York at a cost of 47s, and for keeping the king's treasure in York castle at a cost of 29s 2d, payments made 11 July 1392 and 30 October 1392, P.R.O. Issue Rolls of the Exchequer (E.403) 538 and 541. For a general survey see Dorothy M. Broome, 'Exchequer migrations to York in the thirteenth and fourteenth centuries', in *Essays in Medieval History presented to T. F. Tout*, ed. A. G. Little and F. M. Powicke (Manchester, 1925), pp. 291-300. The suggestion (pp. 292-3) that Richard moved the courts away from Westminster in order to be able to hold the enquiry into London iniquities on ground less favourable to the citizens, can hardly be supported since the trial of the Londoners was held before the council, which could meet anywhere; in the Londoners' case at Nottingham and at Windsor.

[33] See John Harvey, below, p. 205; Walsingham, ii, p. 213; Victoria County History, *The City of York* (Oxford, 1961), p. 57.

[34] 30 May 1392, *C.Cl.R.*, *1389-92*, p. 466.

[35] Monk of Westminster, pp. 267-8.

by the removal of the chief organs of government to the distant city of York, Richard then openly declared his dissatisfaction. By a writ sent from Stamford on 29 May, and addressed to the mayor, sheriffs and all the aldermen of London, which was couched in terms described by the Westminster chronicler as *satis terribile et valde horribile sic quod aures audientis faceret pertinnire*,[36] all the recipients were instructed to appear before the king and his council at Nottingham on 25 June, under pain of forfeiture of life and limb. Together with the mayor, sheriffs and aldermen, the Londoners were to send a further twenty-four citizens *in secundo gradu potentioribus civitatis*.[37] The whole deputation was to be endowed with *plena potestas* to answer whatever should be laid before it, notwithstanding any of the city's privileges and customs. Moreover before leaving, the delegates were to make provision for the safekeeping of the city as they should later have to answer for it at their peril.[38] The Londoners made a return to the writ stating that the mayor, two sheriffs and remaining aldermen, together with twenty-four other named citizens would be present at Nottingham on the appointed day.[39] The deputation was furnished with a commission under the common seal whereby its members were given full and sufficient power by the commonalty of the city to reply on its behalf to what the king should lay before them, and further to receive whatever the king and his council should ordain in accordance with the royal writ of 29 May.[40] This written commission however did not, it should be noticed, empower the deputation to act 'notwithstanding the customs and privileges of the city' as had been specifically requested in the royal writ.

Events on 25 June did not go well for the Londoners. The mayor, John Hende, and John Shadworth and Henry Vanner, the sheriffs, were all removed from their offices by the king and his council, and sent to prison.[41] The ostensible reasons given for this action were twofold. Firstly the commission which the London deputation

---

[36] Ibid., p. 268.   [37] Knighton, ii, p. 319.
[38] 29 May 1392, *C.Cl.R., 1389–92*, p. 466; *L.B.H.*, p. 377; Monk of Westminster, pp. 268–9. It may be that William Staundon, grocer, who was not currently an alderman (he had been alderman of Aldgate 1383–90 and sheriff in 1386–7), was appointed as the mayor's locumtenens during the absence of the city governors at Nottingham, ibid., pp. 272–3.
[39] *L.B.H.*, pp. 377–8; Monk of Westminster, pp. 269–70.
[40] *L.B.H.*, fo. cclxxᵛ.   [41] *C.Cl.R., 1392–6*, p. 2.

had brought under the common seal was considered by the king to have 'divers defects'.[42] This may be explained by the refusal of the Londoners to override their customs and privileges. Secondly the king declared that he must pay heed to the 'notable and evident defaults which he had notoriously and openly found in the governance and rule of the city during the time of John Hende, John Shadworth and Henry Vanner'. These 'intolerable damages and perils' required that the king should lend a 'helping hand'.[43] The royal helping hand now took the form of appointing the royal councillor and 'king's knight', Sir Edward Dalyngridge, as warden of the city, and replacing the elected sheriffs by two other Londoners, Gilbert Maghfeld and Thomas Newenton who were selected by the king. These changes, the king believed, would provide a 'better and sounder governance and rule of the city . . . especially in the administration of justice'. The choice of Dalyngridge for the office of warden of London is easy to understand since he was an assiduous member of the king's council and also of what has been called 'the king's party'.[44] Both the ironmonger Maghfeld and the mercer Newenton were comparatively inexperienced aldermen. Maghfeld was known to the king as a London customs collector, but the selection of Newenton is less easy to explain.[45]

After depriving the city of its elected officers, the king continued

[42] *L.B.H.*, p. 379.

[43] *C.F.R., 1391-9*, p. 49; *C.P.R., 1391-6*, p. 100; *L.B.H.*, p. 379; cf. Monk of Westminster, p. 272.

[44] Tout, *Chapters*, iii, pp. 352, 411 n. 1, 413 n. 3, 470. The career of Dalyngridge, as Tout admitted, showed signs of vacillation and his adherence to Richard's cause was not unqualified.

[45] Maghfeld's career is exceptionally well documented because of the chance survival of one of his ledger books among the exchequer records, P.R.O. Various Exchequer Accounts (E.101) 509/19. This volume has been analysed and Maghfeld's career investigated by M. K. James, 'A London merchant of the fourteenth century', *Economic History Review*, viii (1955–6), pp. 364–76. See also Martin M. Crow and Clair C. Olson, *Chaucer Life Records* (Oxford, 1966), ch. 25. Maghfeld had been an alderman in 1382–3 and had been re-elected in March 1392. Newenton was elected for the first time in March 1392, A. B. Beaven, *The Aldermen of the City of London*, (London, 1908), i, p. 401. Maghfeld had been a collector of tunnage and poundage in London from March 1388 to December 1391, and was still a collector there of the cloth and alien petty custom to which he had been appointed in May 1389, see Olive Coleman, 'Collectors of Customs in London under Richard II' in *Studies in London History presented to Philip Edmund Jones*, ed. A. E. J. Hollaender and W. Kellaway (London, 1969), pp. 179–94. Thomas Newenton had been a collector of the wool subsidy in Southampton in 1386–7, *C.F.R., 1383–91*, pp. 129, 164.

the process of 'taking over' London. On the day after the judgement against Hende and the others, Sir Edward Dalyngridge was appointed royal escheator in the city, an office customarily held by the mayor.[46] On the same day the king instructed the new keeper of the city to see to the election of a new alderman for the ward of Lime Street since the grocer John Hadle had been transferred by the king to the office of mayor of the Calais staple.[47] Two days later, still at Nottingham, the king issued a commission of oyer and terminer to the dukes of York and Gloucester, John, earl of Huntingdon, Thomas, earl marshal, John Devereux, the steward of the household, Robert Charleton and Walter Clopton, the two chief justices, William Thirning, a justice of the common bench, and Sir Lewis Clifford and Sir Richard Stury two members of the council, to enquire into the notorious defaults in the government of the city of London. Their enquiry was to be carried out in accordance with the statute provided for such cases,[48] i.e., the statute made in the 1354 parliament which laid down the procedure to be followed in correcting faults in the government of London. It stipulated that if the mayor, sheriffs and aldermen, upon whom lay the burden of civic government, should fail in their duty, they should be tried by royal judges and should answer for themselves. For the first offence the fine was to be 1000 marks; for the second offence 2000 marks, and for the third offence the liberties of the city were to be seized into the king's hand. Moreover the statute was to be put into operation regardless of any civic franchise, privilege or custom, although its provisions were to apply not

[46] *C.F.R., 1391-9*, p. 49; *L.B.H.*, p. 379. Dalyngridge's accounts as escheator in London for the period 26 June-22 July 1392 are enrolled, P.R.O. Escheators' Accounts (E.357) 11 fo. 33.

[47] 26 June 1392, *C.Cl.R., 1392-6*, p. 1. Hadle had been an alderman intermittently since 1375, sheriff in 1375-6 and mayor 1379-80. Whether Hadle was immediately replaced by Adam Bamme as alderman of Lime Street ward is not clear, see Beaven, op. cit., p. 174 and n. Hadle's appointment as mayor of the Calais staple coincides with the final return of the staple to Calais in the summer of 1392. See Tout, *Chapters*, iii, pp. 478-9.

[48] *C.P.R., 1391-6*, p. 166. 10 September 1392, Charleton was paid £10 for his costs and labours in the sessions at Nottingham, Windsor and elsewhere, enquiring into the various articles objected against the citizens and commonalty of London. Alexander Domenik, a clerk, William Hornby, a king's attorney in the common bench, and Edmund Brudynell, a king's attorney in the king's bench, were each paid 66s 8d for the same reason, P.R.O. Issue Roll of the Exchequer (E.403) 538. Huntingdon, together with the duke of Lancaster, was considered by one chronicler to have been the instigator of the quarrel, Monk of Westminster, p. 268.

only to London, but to all the cities and boroughs of the realm.[49] Richard had studied the provisions of this statute and in his attack upon the city he was most careful to observe its letter, if not its spirit.

On 29 June 1392 Sir Edward Dalyngridge left Nottingham to take up his new duties as warden of London.[50] At 9 a.m. on Monday, 1 July, he came to Guildhall with those aldermen who had not been imprisoned and was well received there by a crowd of Londoners. His commission of appointment was read out and he was sworn to office in the same form as the London mayors. Then the new sheriffs' commission was read and they also were sworn.[51] On the same day Dalyngridge borrowed £20 from Gilbert Maghfeld to provide, perhaps, for the immediate expenses of his new office.[52] The business of the city appears to have returned to normal quite rapidly. The mayor's court was functioning under the new warden by 6 July, and it would seem that he appointed William Venour as his deputy for some cases.[53]

Meanwhile the duke of York and his fellow commissioners began their work. John Hende, John Shadworth and Henry Vanner were brought by their several custodians to a preliminary hearing held at Aylesbury on 10 July.[54] As a result of this hearing, there appears to have been a slight change of direction in the royal policy. Three days later the duke of York sent a writ from Aylesbury to the constable of the Tower of London instructing him to summon William Venour, John Walcote and John Loveye, the

[49] R.P., ii, pp. 258-9; Statutes of the Realm, i (London, 1810), pp. 346-7. The immediate cause of this statute was the lax observance of the Statute of Labourers in London, where the royal justices could not operate. In effect, therefore, the city had been in the position of acting as judge in its own cause.

[50] For the particulars of Dalyngridge's movements see his account as a member of the king's council from Christmas 1391 to February 1393, P.R.O. Exchequer Accounts Various (E.101) 96/1. Dalyngridge had been constantly attending the council at Stamford and at Nottingham since 18 May 1392.

[51] L.B.H., p. 379.

[52] Maghfeld account book, fo. 30v. Dalyngridge also bought three pipes of red wine from Maghfeld for £10, ibid., fo. 30v. 28 July 1392, Dalyngridge borrowed a further £10 and the same sum again on 10 August. These debts, as well as an old one of £3 13s 4d are all recorded as paid, ibid., fo. 38. Thomas Newenton, Maghfeld's fellow sheriff, bought a tun of wine from him on 12 July, costing 6 marks, ibid., fo. 31.

[53] Cal. P. and M., 1381-1412, pp. 182-3.

[54] C.Cl.R., 1392-6, p. 9. Hende had been imprisoned at Windsor, Vanner at Wallingford and Shadworth at Odiham.

mayor and sheriffs for the years 1389–90, together with twenty-two other aldermen serving in those years, to Eton on Thursday, 18 July. With these men, the constable was further to summon the deposed Hende, Shadworth and Vanner and the aldermen for the current year who had already appeared at Nottingham.[55] Clearly the commissioners had decided that the defaults in the government of London sprang from errors of the past, as well as the present governors.

The gloomy mood in which the fifty or so Londoners arrived at Eton on 18 July is not hard to imagine. Although John Shadworth made some show of resistance, in the end they all submitted to the king's judgement.[56] On the feast of St Mary Magdalen, 22 July, the commissioners announced their verdict. There had been faults in the government of the city due to the negligence, not only of the present mayor, aldermen and sheriffs, but also of William Venour the mayor in 1389–90 and his fellow sheriffs and aldermen who were convicted by their own acknowledgement. Consequently they were fined a total of 3000 marks, that is, for the first and second offences, as stipulated by the statute of 1354.[57] Then, for the third offence, and still in accordance with the statute, the liberties of the city were forfeited to the king. Upon hearing the verdict, with the advice of his councillors, the king decided to use his direct authority to 'cherish the good rule and wholesome government of the city' by himself appointing a warden, two sheriffs and twenty-four aldermen. Accordingly Thomas Arundel, as chancellor, selected a place within Windsor Castle where William Venour and the other Londoners could appear before the whole council and hear the king's will. The large gathering of councillors included the archbishop of Canterbury, the bishops of London, Winchester, Salisbury and Coventry; the duke of Lancaster and his two brothers the dukes of York and

[55] 13 July 1392, *L.B.H.*, p. 386.

[56] Monk of Westminster, pp. 273–4. Some evidence of Shadworth's resistance is, perhaps, also to be found in the obligation of £3000 entered into by three London mercers, John Loveye, William Shiringham and Thomas Vynent, to Sir Bernard Brocas (a king's knight) to ensure that Shadworth, their fellow-mercer, would not escape or absent himself, 9 July 1392. This was cancelled 18 October 1392, *Cal. P. and M., 1381–1412*, pp. 182–3.

[57] The close roll entry recording the verdict against the Londoners does not mention these fines, but the subsequent pardon makes it clear that they were imposed at this time, *C.P.R., 1391–6*, pp. 171, 173.

Gloucester and the earls of Huntingdon and Rutland. In the presence of this august company, the chancellor announced the king's appointment of Sir Baldwin Radyngton as warden, and Gilbert Maghfeld and Thomas Newenton were chosen again as sheriffs. The king, on this occasion, selected fifteen other men to serve as aldermen and three more were chosen on the following day. Since the french oaths of the warden, sheriffs and aldermen are recorded in the Close Roll it seems clear that all these men were sworn to office before the king and his councillors.[58] On the same day, 22 July, John Hende and the two sheriffs who had been in prison since 25 June were now released on a bail totalling £3000. They were to be ready to appear before the king and his council to make reparation for the offences of which they had been convicted earlier at Nottingham.[59]

The reasons which lay behind Richard's replacement of Dalyngridge by Radyngton may only be guessed. Radyngton was, perhaps, a more convinced 'royalist' than Dalyngridge, and he had been responsible as controller for building up the military side of the king's household.[60] The author of the Brut continuation wrote that Richard had found Dalyngridge to be 'too gentle and tender unto the Londoners' and Walsingham, not necessarily better informed but perhaps more imaginative, explained that the king had removed Dalyngridge because he discovered that he had taken an oath to the Londoners to protect their liberties, and to work for their secret restoration as far as he could.[61] Moreover the Westminster chronicler agrees that Radyngton executed his new office 'satis rigide'.[62] But Richard may have intended, in replacing the diplomatic Dalyngridge with the more rigid Radyngton, both to frighten the Londoners and also to release Dalyngridge to act as a 'free agent' in the complicated negotiations between the crown and the city which were to follow.

Radyngton was duly appointed warden and escheator of London, and the citizens were to pay all reasonable expenses incurred

[58] 22 July 1392, C.Cl.R., 1392-6, pp. 87-9. All the men chosen by the king to serve as aldermen had already held this office, and their number included the deposed sheriffs, Shadworth and Vanner.

[59] 22 July 1392, C.Cl.R., 1392-6, p. 12; 23 July 1392, ibid., pp. 78-9; L.B.H., p. 383.

[60] For Radyngton's career see Tout, Chapters, iii, pp. 196-9.

[61] Brut C, p. 346; Walsingham, ii, p. 209.   [62] Monk of Westminster, p. 274.

by him and Dalyngridge while they acted as wardens of the city.[63] The king further instructed Radyngton to charge another five named Londoners to act as aldermen during the royal pleasure, thus bringing the total number of aldermen up to the usual twenty-five.[64] Then, by two drastic moves the king placed at his own disposal the entire income of the city of London. On 22 July 1392 the new sheriffs were instructed to account at the exchequer for their whole income and not merely for the customary city farm of £300.[65] Seven days later Richard re-appointed the current city chamberlain, Stephen Speleman, during his pleasure, to receive all the monies, issues and profits of that office. But out of this income Speleman was to be allowed only his expenses and necessary charges, and for the remainder of the city's income he was to answer at the exchequer.[66] Taken together these royal acts of policy leave no doubt that Richard's motive in quarrelling with the city of London was primarily financial.

It is clear, moreover, that at some point, probably along with the judgements of 22 July, a corporate fine of £100,000 had been laid upon the city.[67] And, while the income of the city was mortgaged to pay this enormous sum, many individual Londoners laboured under further financial obligations to the king. To add to the financial troubles, the city's cherished privilege of electing its own mayor and sheriffs lay in abeyance as Radyngton presided over meetings of the court of aldermen and mayor's court.[68] Further, in August the king appointed John Spencer as keeper of the great beam and two royal valets as collectors of scavage in the city. Both the choice of these officers, and the profits of their offices, had been controlled and enjoyed by the citizens by chartered right or immemorial custom.[69]

[63] 22 July 1392, *C.P.R., 1391–6*, p. 125; *L.B.H.*, pp. 382, 383; *C.F.R., 1391–9*, p. 51. Radyngton's account as escheator is enrolled, P.R.O. Escheators' Accounts (E.357) 12 fo. 1 v. 24 July 1392, *L.B.H.*, p. 384.

[64] 24 July 1392, *C.Cl.R., 1392–6*, p. 12. One of the five aldermen selected by the king on this occasion, William Cresswyk, had not previously occupied the office.

[65] Maghfeld and Newenton were formally appointed as sheriffs, *C.F.R., 1391–9*, pp. 53–4; *L.B.H.*, p. 383.

[66] 29 July 1392, *C.P.R., 1391–9*, p. 53.

[67] Pardon of 19 September 1392, *C.P.R., 1391–6*, p. 130.

[68] *Cal. P. and M., 1381–1412*, p. 184; 13 September 1392, *C.P.R., 1391–6*, p. 150. Recognizances for debt were also made before Radyngton, see Guildhall Record Office, Roll of Recognizances, no. 12.

[69] 27 August 1392, *C.P.R., 1391–6*, pp. 144, 147; *L.B.H.*, p. 385. The choice of

But behind the scenes peace negotiations were being carried on and, as a preliminary to the thorny questions of cash and custom, the city gave Richard and his queen a magnificent reception on 21 and 22 August. Detailed accounts of these festivities survive in several sources, and the reception itself seems to have followed a pattern which was to become increasingly familiar throughout the fifteenth century.[70] The king, accompanied by Queen Anne, was met on the south side of London Bridge by Radyngton, the warden, and aldermen and the men of the various crafts arrayed in distinguishing liveries.[71] After a ceremony of welcome the procession moved across London Bridge and along Cheapside, past houses decked with cloths of gold and bunting, to St Paul's. The conduits flowed temporarily with the proverbial red and white wine and the journey was enlivened by various tableaux, including a scene representing St John the Baptist in the wilderness; a saint who was known to be especially revered by Richard II.[72] Finally, after a brief visit to the tomb of St Erkonwald in St Paul's cathedral, the king, queen, lords and Londoners moved on to feast in Westminster Hall. On the second day of the festivities the king and queen dined in the city as guests of the warden and were presented with further gifts. After this the whole party made its way back to Westminster with the now-gracious king inviting the Londoners in for a drink before they finally left for home.

The writers vary somewhat in the details of this pantomime but the general course of events is clear. There are one or two unusual

the keeper of the great beam, and the profits of his office, had been granted to the commonalty of London by Edward II in 1319, Birch, *Charters*, p. 48. For the city's claim to scavage see *Munimenta Gildhallae Londoniensis*, ed. H. T. Riley, i, *Liber Albus*, (Rolls Series, 1859), pp. 223-6, 230.

[70] See Knighton, ii, pp. 319-21; Brut C, p. 347; Walsingham, ii, pp. 210-11; Monk of Westminster, pp. 274-6. The Carmelite friar, Richard of Maidstone, wrote a long Latin poem to celebrate the occasion, *Political Poems and Songs*, ed. T. Wright, 2 vols. (Rolls Series, 1859-61), i, pp. 282-300. An unknown member of Richard's entourage wrote a letter describing the events of these days in French, see Helen Suggett, 'A letter describing Richard II's reconciliation with the City of London 1392', *E.H.R.*, lxii (1947), pp. 209-13.

[71] Walter Strete, a mercer, owed 13s 8d to the company wardens for his livery of baldekyn which had been ordained 'for the coming of the king', Mercer's Hall, Account Book 1347-1464, fo. 12v.

[72] Maidstone, op. cit., pp. 294, 296. John the Baptist is also represented on the Wilton Diptych.

features. The anonymous letter-writer, the Westminster chronicler and Richard of Maidstone all agree that at the beginning of the ceremonies the king was symbolically given both the sword and the keys of the city which he returned again to the citizens at the end of the first day to demonstrate his pardon.[73] In all the accounts, the gifts to the royal guests feature prominently. Amongst these were two golden crowns; two gold cups or basins; two golden images of the Trinity and St Anne; two horses; an exotic 'tabula' for the king, large enough to be a reredos or altar and worth 500 marks and a crystal chest and ewer inlaid with gold for the queen.

This magnificent, but somewhat forced, merry-making was followed by tangible signs that Richard's anger was abating. On 17 September a royal writ informed the warden, aldermen and good folk of London that the city might elect two sheriffs on the feast of St Matthew (21 September) according to ancient custom.[74] Then, two days later, Richard issued from Woodstock the crucial pardons for which the Londoners had been waiting. In effect, there were four separate pardons, all granted, it was stated, at the queen's request. Firstly, William Venour and his fellow aldermen of 1389–90 who had been convicted at Windsor on 22 July were pardoned their two fines of 1000 and 2000 marks. Secondly, John Hende the deposed mayor, and the two sheriffs Henry Vanner and John Shadworth who had been sent to prison at Nottingham on 25 June and had only been released on bail on 22 July, were now pardoned their faults and contempts and their fines were remitted.[75] Thirdly, by other letters patent the king forgave the citizens their corporate fine of £100,000 and all their offences and trespasses except treasons and felonies.[76] Finally, again by letters patent, the liberties of the city of London were restored to the citizens but with the vital proviso 'until the king shall otherwise ordain'. That is, the citizens did not receive back their liberties in perpetuity but only during good behaviour and at the pleasure of an

[73] Maidstone, op. cit., pp. 286, 299; Monk of Westminster, p. 275.

[74] 17 September 1392, *L.B.H.*, p. 384.

[75] 19 September 1392, *C.P.R., 1391–6*, p. 171; *L.B.H.*, pp. 380–1. The obligations into which their friends had entered to secure their freedom on 23 and 24 July were now cancelled on the grounds that the king had pardoned the three men their fines and ransoms, *C.Cl.R., 1392–6*, pp. 78–9; *L.B.H.*, p. 383.

[76] 19 September 1392, *C.P.R., 1391–6*, p. 130; *L.B.H.*, p. 381. The original of these letters patent is preserved in the Guildhall Record Office, Charter no. 47 (274 A).

unpredictable king.[77] This conditional restoration of the city's liberties explains much in the uneasy relations between the crown and the Londoners in the last years of Richard's reign.

So the reconciliation was achieved, at least upon the surface of events. The official documents, followed by many of the chroniclers, attribute the Londoners' return to favour to the gentle supplications of Richard's consort, Queen Anne. Walsingham suggests that it was the duke of Lancaster and his brother the duke of Gloucester who especially pleaded for the Londoners, while the anonymous letter writer acknowledges the labours of the archbishop and of Robert Braybrook the bishop of London.[78] Professor Tout believed that the reconciliation was the work of Baldwin Radyngton, but the signs are that it was, in fact, the judicious labours of his predecessor as warden, Sir Edward Dalyngridge, which achieved the final result.[79] When he was replaced by Radyngton as warden of London on 22 July, there is no evidence that Dalyngridge was in any way in disgrace. He was in London at the king's request from 23 to 29 July negotiating with Radyngton, and from 17 to 26 August Dalyngridge was again in the city at the king's request *pro concordia facienda versus Regem pro civibus London'*.[80] Dalyngridge had been present at Nottingham on 25 June, he had been warden of London from then until 22 July, he had negotiated with Radyngton and had been present in London before, during and after the royal reception in the city on 21 and 22 August. He was also present at Woodstock in September, and it seems that this assiduous, but moderate, royal councillor who enjoyed the confidence of both the Londoners and the king is likely to have been the real architect of the practical terms of the settlement.

[77] 19 September 1392, *C.P.R., 1391-6*, p. 173; *L.B.H.*, p. 381. The letters patent contain no exceptions to the liberties which were restored to the Londoners, but the Monk of Westminster (see pp. 177-8, n. 14 above) and the anonymous letter writer (Suggett, op. cit., p. 212) both state that some of the city's privileges were not restored at this time.

[78] Walsingham, ii, pp. 209, 210. For Lancaster's financial dealings with certain Londoners see Ruth Bird, op. cit., pp. 108-9.

[79] Tout, *Chapters*, iii, p. 199. It would appear that Radyngton lacked the flexibility needed by such a negotiator and, although he was praised by Walsingham (ii, p. 209), his reputation must suffer somewhat from the account of the attack made by him, and members of his household, upon the abbey and city of Chester in July 1394, see A. R. Myers, ed., *English Historical Documents 1327-1485* (London, 1969), pp. 1222-3.

[80] Dalyngridge's account, P.R.O. Exchequer Accounts Various (E.101) 96/1.

In the city the situation began to return to normal. On St Matthew's day the new sheriffs were elected in accordance with civic custom. With prudence the Londoners selected the royal nominees, Thomas Newenton and Gilbert Maghfeld.[81] Four days later the royal grants of the profits and offices of scavenger and keeper of the king's beam in London, were revoked.[82] Finally on 13 October, the feast of the translation of St Edward and the traditional day for the election of the mayor, William Staundon was chosen in the customary way by the aldermen and a gathering of the commonalty at Guildhall.[83] There remained merely some clearing up of the financial aspects of the royal tenure of the city's liberties, before Radyngton handed over the government of the city to Staundon on 28 October.[84] Moreover now the dispute with the Londoners was settled, on 25 October the king issued the first writ for the return of the common bench from York to Westminster.[85] So this costly and inconvenient experiment was brought to an end.

[81] 21 September 1392, *L.B.H.*, p. 385. There is no record of their being sworn to office in P.R.O. Lord Treasurer's Remembrancer Roll (E.368) 165. This may be because the sheriffs were sworn, not before the barons of the exchequer, but before the constable's lieutenant at the Tower of London, *L.B.H.*, p. 386.

[82] See p. 189, n. 69, above. 25 September 1392, writ of *supersedeas, L.B.H.*, p. 385. The letter of privy seal authorizing this writ survives and shows that the Londoners had petitioned against the grant of these offices to the royal valets, and that the king, wishing right to be done to the citizens, granted their request and acknowledged that these offices belonged to the Londoners, P.R.O. Chancery Warrants (C.81) 8317B.

[83] *L.B.H.*, pp. 386–7. Staundon was sworn before the constable's lieutenant at the Tower of London, as the sheriffs had been (see n. 81, above) and this is specifically mentioned in Brut C, p. 346. More unusually, Staundon was also sworn before the king in person at Westminster, *L.B.H.*, p. 387.

[84] The four sheriffs for the year 1391–2, Henry Vanner, John Shadworth, Gilbert Maghfeld and Thomas Newenton had to account at the exchequer, writ 7 October 1392, *L.B.H.*, p. 390 and P.R.O. Lord Treasurer's Remembrancer Roll (E.368) 165, *praecepta* Hilary fo. 1 v. 18 October 1392, eleven aldermen undertook, in Radyngton's presence, to pay Stephen Speleman, the chamberlain, £5 on 30 November 1392. Four days later nine of the same aldermen, together with six others, similarly agreed to pay Speleman £11 6s 8d on the same day, *L.B.H.*, p. 391. The purpose of these undertakings is obscure. 1 November 1392, Speleman, who had had a difficult task in accounting to two masters in the year 1391–2, was acquitted on his accounts by the mayor, aldermen and citizens, *L.B.H.*, p. 390.

[85] 25 October 1392, *C.Cl.R., 1392–6*, p. 21. Further instructions for the return of the exchequer, king's bench and Fleet prisoners followed, ibid., p. 76. Writs of aid were issued for the various clerks appointed to transport the rolls and memoranda southwards, *C.P.R., 1391–6*, pp. 189, 191, 196. It is clear that this was not achieved without considerable difficulty, ibid., p. 218. Robert Rodyngton and

But in spite of the magnificent reception and expensive gifts which the citizens offered to the king at the end of August, and in spite of the manifest expression of royal pardon and grace which was accorded to the citizens by the charters emanating from Woodstock on 19 September, the matter did not rest there. The financial pressure upon the Londoners was only just beginning. On 22 October the warden, accompanied by the sheriffs and other Londoners, rode to the duke of Lancaster's house in Holborn where he was staying with his two brothers, the dukes of York and Gloucester. Each of the brothers was presented with two silver gilt basins together with an unspecified sum of money which the writer of an anonymous letter, from which this incident is known, places at £400 for Lancaster and £200 each for York and Gloucester.[86] But apart from the costs of these receptions and gifts, it is clear that the king demanded £10,000 as the cost of his pardon. Here again, the chronicle accounts vary considerably but John Stow, Walsingham and the author of Harley Ms 565, agree that the sum was £10,000 and this, moreover, is the amount for which the king acknowledged receipt on 28 February 1393.[87] It is clear that the collection of this sum, and possible further sums for the king in the city, caused considerable hardship. One chronicler says that the collection of such a large sum in the city caused many citizens to

Thomas Sywardleby each received 13s 4d for their special labours in bringing south the exchequer records and a special escort of archers was paid £4, P.R.O. Issue Rolls of Exchequer (E.403) 541, 6 and 26 November 1392. The sheriff of York received a reward of £40 and a grant of £15 towards the repair of the new bridge at York, C.Cl.R., 1392–6, p. 31. John de Ravensar, the keeper of the hanaper, received £105 16s 6d on 19 April 1393 for his expenses in transporting the chancery rolls to and from York, ibid., p. 55.

[86] M. D. Legge, ed., *Anglo-Norman Letters and Petitions* (Anglo Norman Text Society, Oxford, 1941), pp. 185–6.

[87] *C.P.R., 1391–6*, p. 226. The official receipt states that the Londoners paid the sum 'with good heart' which is at variance with Walsingham's account (ii, p. 211) of the great bitterness with which the sum was collected. See also John Stow, *Annales or a General Chronicle of England* (London, 1631), p. 307; *A Chronicle of London*, p. 80. Brut C, p. 347 states that the Londoners gave Richard £20,000; *Eulogium*, p. 368 says that the sum was £40,000; the Monk of Westminster, pp. 274, 278, says that the original demand for £40,000 was reduced at the queen's request to £20,000. As this sum was, according to the chronicler, to be composed either of cash or jewels it may be that the gifts were estimated as worth £10,000, which left the Londoners with a further £10,000 to be paid in cash. The anonymous letter, Suggett, op. cit., p. 213, states that the amount was £10,000 plus 2000 marks annually.

flee from London in order to avoid contributing,[88] and in the Westminster parliament in January 1394 both the clergy and the widows of London petitioned the king to be free of a novel tax imposed by the city's governors. In this case the mayor, aldermen and common council put a counter-petition to the king in parliament stating that it was only just that all those who had benefited from the return of the king's courts to London, and the restoration of the city to royal favour, should contribute towards the cost of the royal fine.[89] From scattered evidence it is clear that various sources in the city were tapped. There was a civic tax collected in the wards assessed on lands and rents; the London companies contributed, the chamberlain raised money by loans and the bridge estates were called upon to provide cash.[90]

Moreover, this direct royal fine of £10,000 was not the only financial demand made by Richard during these years. The king and queen spent the Christmas of 1392 at Eltham and the Londoners contributed to his festivities there by providing seasonal mummers and presents of two unusual jewels for the royal couple, a dromedary with a boy seated on its back for the king and a great bird with a wide throat for the queen.[91] In the following summer of 1393, at Richard's express command, the wardens of London Bridge paid Thomas Wreuk, a mason, to carve two stone statues of the king and queen to be placed above the stone gate on the

[88] *Eulogium*, p. 368.

[89] *R.P.*, iii, p. 325; P.R.O., Ancient Petitions (S.C.8) nos. 6036, 7343, 1052. No royal response to these petitions is recorded.

[90] Ordinance for levying 5000 marks in the wards, undated but circa 1393, *L.B.H.*, fo. cclxxx. This ordinance makes it clear that there had already been one levy for tallage in the city, and those who were then assessed were to pay according to that assessment. Parish churches, chantries, mysteries and fraternities were to contribute at a lower rate of 40d in the pound, see *L.B.H.* fo. cclxxx and *R.P.*, iii, p. 325. 5 June 1394, the mercers paid £10 'for certain businesses touching the franchise of the City', Mercers' Hall, Account Book 1347-1464, fo. 13v. 4 June 1394, Gilbert Maghfeld lent £5 to the chamberlain 'pour notre franchises', Maghfeld Account Book, fos. 35, 47v. In the year ending Michaelmas 1392 the Bridge House Estates contributed £60 'pro diversis negotiis' touching the city, and in the year ending Michaelmas 1393 a further £4 11s, Guildhall Record Office, Bridge House Accounts Roll 11 m. 1, Roll 12 m. 1, 1v.

[91] Monk of Westminster, p. 278. The mercers provided five men as mummers at a cost of £3, Mercers' Hall, Account Book 1347-1464, fo. 12. Gilbert Maghfeld lent the city chamberlain 40s for the mumming at Eltham at Christmas, Maghfeld Account Book fo. 35. Again Sir Edward Dalyngridge may have arranged these festivities for he spent ten days in London in December 1392, P.R.O. Exchequer Accounts Various (E.101) 96/1.

bridge. The canopies above the statues bore the arms of the king and queen and of St Edward the Confessor, and all the stonework was to be painted, while the surround was to be whitened with plaster to show off the statues and shields to better effect. In their hands the statues bore gilded latten sceptres. The total cost to the bridgewardens of this piece of required royal propaganda was £37 os 10d.[92] Further in December 1394 the citizens provided the king with a loan of 10,000 marks, although this appears to have been repaid in March and April the following year in the usual way.[93]

But these financial demands should be considered in the light of the concessions which the king made to the Londoners in the Westminster parliament of 1394, and the exceptionally large spending revealed by the royal wardrobe account roll for the years 1392-4. In the 1394 parliament the king allowed the London aldermen to remain in office from year to year, instead of the annual turn-over which had been in operation since 1377. This concession would clearly contribute a great deal to the permanence and efficiency of civic government.[94] Secondly, the king acceded to the Londoners' request that the ward of Farringdon might be divided into two with an alderman for the area outside the walls and another for the area inside the walls.[95] Thirdly, and most importantly, the statute of 1354 which dealt with the punishment of the city's transgressions and which had so recently been brought into operation against the Londoners, was now modified. The king conceded that the general words 'errors defaults and misprisions' should not include an erroneous judgement given in a city court of law. Such errors could, in any case, always be corrected, upon a writ of error, by the judges sitting at St Martin-le-Grand.[96] All

[92] Guildhall Record Office, Bridge House Accounts Roll 12 m.8, 9, 10. Cf. John H. Harvey, 'The Wilton Diptych—a Re-examination', *Archaeologia*, xcviii (1959), pp. 1-28, esp. p. 52 n. 7.

[93] 5 December 1394, P.R.O. Receipt Roll of Exchequer (E.401) 596; repayments 1 March, 3 April 1395, Issue Roll of the Exchequer (E.403) 549. This money was probably raised specifically for the king's journey to Ireland. Gilbert Maghfeld on 4 December 1394 lent £50 towards the city's 10,000 marks, for which he was promised, and received, repayment by 15 March 1395, Maghfeld Account Book fo. 52v.

[94] R.P., iii, p. 317. Beaven, op. cit., i, p. 402, notes that the last annual election of aldermen took place in March 1394.

[95] R.P., iii, pp. 317-18, P.R.O. Ancient Petitions (S.C.8) no. 1050.

[96] R.P., iii, p. 317. There is an undated and unendorsed petition from the mayor,

these were useful and important concessions to the Londoners.

The wardrobe account for the years 1392-4 reveals that the king purchased over £13,000-worth of saddlery, mercery, skins and drapery in these two years. Only when the wardrobe was equipping Richard's two expeditions to Ireland did its expenditure exceed this amount.[97] Of this £13,000 about 90 per cent went into the pockets of London merchant suppliers of whom the two most prominent were the draper, John Hende, the imprisoned mayor of 1392, and the young and rising mercer, Richard Whittington.[98] It may be, therefore, that much of the money which Richard extorted from the citizens found its way back into their pockets in the form of purchases for the royal wardrobe and household. Of course, far more Londoners contributed to the £10,000 fine than acted as royal suppliers.

But in spite of these concessions, and the unusual profits enjoyed by certain London merchants as a result of Richard's 'spending spree' in the city in 1393-4, a cloud hung over London. For Richard's restoration of the city's liberties on 19 September 1392 had not yet been made permanent. Unlike the personal pardons, it was only to be effective until the king should ordain otherwise.[99] Hence, in spite of the magnificent reception of August 1392, the multitudinous and expensive presents, the corporate fine of £10,000 paid to Richard in February 1393, the mumming at

aldermen and sheriffs of London addressed to the king and lords of the 'present parliament' which also asks for a modification of the 1354 statute whereby the crimes of individual London governors should not be able to bring corporate punishments upon the city. It may be that this more sweeping petition was refused by the king in the parliament of 1394, P.R.O. Ancient Petitions (S.C.8) File 121/no. 6040.

[97] Account Roll of Richard Clifford for the years 1392-4, P.R.O. Exchequer Accounts Various (E.101) 402/13. This is the only such particularized account to survive for Richard's reign, although the enrolled accounts give the totals of expenditure, see Tout, *Chapters*, iv, pp. 423-4; vi, p. 108.

[98] The actual total of the roll was £13,242 9s 11¼d made up of £387 10s 2d (saddlery); £6203 15s 7½d (mercery); £2219 4s 11d (furs); £4431 19s 2¾d (drapery). For the career of Richard Whittington see Caroline M. Barron, 'Richard Whittington: the man behind the myth', in *Studies in London History presented to Philip Edmund Jones*, ed. A. E. Hollaender and W. Kellaway (London, 1969), pp. 197-248.

[99] *C.P.R., 1391-6*, p. 173. The calendar of the patent rolls does not, however, give the crucial wording at the end of the document, 'quousque aliter ordinandum que eisdem in cuius etc.', P.R.O. Patent Rolls (C.66) 336 m. 31.

Christmas 1392 and the new and flattering statues which now dominated London Bridge, the city liberties remained still in jeopardy. In parliament in 1394 the Londoners petitioned the king for a 'plein et perpetuel restitucion' of their liberties as they used to enjoy them, to have and to hold for themselves and 'lour heirs et lour successours a tous jours'. There is no recorded royal reply to this petition in the parliament rolls and it is clear that Richard did not accede to the London request.[100]

From September 1392, therefore, the Londoners held their liberties not in perpetuity but only during good behaviour. Their position was weak. Then, on 6 June 1397, the mayor of London, Adam Bamme died in office. Two days later Richard took the unprecedented step of appointing a mayor for the city. His choice fell on Richard Whittington.[101] Twice in Edward III's reign the mayor had been deposed by the king but his successor had been chosen by the citizens. The right of the Londoners to choose their own mayor had been established in 1215.[102] The king had appointed wardens before but never a mayor. The unusual nature of Richard's action can be barely ascertained from the contemporary evidence, but Arnold in his chronicle has preserved a unique reference 'This yere, in Junii, decessid the Mayre, and for him chosen Richard Whittington, who the Lords wold not admytt till on the morowe was admitted be the king and occupied tyl Saint Edward's day'.[103] It would seem, therefore, that although the king chose Whittington, the barons of the exchequer, before whom a new mayor was normally sworn, refused to swear him and so the king himself

[100] R.P., iii, pp. 324–5; P.R.O. Ancient Petitions (S.C.8) no. 6041. There is also in the P.R.O. another undated and unendorsed petition from the mayor, aldermen and citizens of London to the king, in which they recite the judgments of 1392 and ask for a restoration of the city's liberties 'en cest present parlement', which is probably to be dated to 1394. In this petition the Londoners ask also for a modification of the statute made at York in the ninth year of Edward III's reign, to the effect that merchant strangers might not sell goods retail between themselves within the franchises of the city of London, P.R.O. Ancient Petitions (S.C.8) file 190 no. 9456. Knighton (ii, p. 321) records that in September 1392 the king deferred any final decision about the liberties of London until the next parliament. He then goes on to state, incorrectly, that in the parliament of 1394, the Londoners were restored 'ad sua pristina privilegia'.

[101] L.B.H., p. 436; H. T. Riley, ed., Memorials of London and London Life in XIII, XIV and XV Centuries 1276–1419 (London, 1868), p. 544.

[102] Birch, Charters, p. 19.

[103] The Customs of London, otherwise called Arnold's Chronicle (London, 1811), p. xxx.

performed the task. Two pieces of evidence substantiate this supposition. In the Lord Treasurer's Remembrancer rolls, where the swearing of the London mayors is normally recorded, there is no record of Whittington being sworn in June 1397 although he duly appears in October when he was re-elected by the citizens.[104] Secondly, there is recorded on the close roll for this year a full copy of the mayor of London's oath. This is the normal oath taken by the mayors and although the entry is undated it was probably enrolled there for the king's own reference.[105] This episode throws an interesting light on the attitude of the judiciary to Richard II and suggests that the barons of the exchequer, at least, were prepared to make a stand in defence of legality and the liberties of London.

There are many reasons for believing that Whittington was a close friend of Richard II.[106] In 1397 he served his sovereign well and, in so doing, served also the interests of the city. As mayor, he negotiated the 'loan' of ten thousand marks ($£6666$ 13s 4d) whereby the Londoners bought a full and perpetual confirmation of their liberties from Richard II, and Whittington managed also to keep London peaceful during the contentious autumn parliament of 1397.

The London 'loan' of 10,000 marks was one of a number of loans, totalling in all over $£20,000$, which Richard raised from his subjects in the summer of 1397. It was not repaid.[107] But in return Richard, on 12 June 1397, four days after Whittington's appointment as mayor, granted a full charter of liberties to the Londoners in which their rights were confirmed *in perpetuum*.[108] The problem of raising so large a sum in the city was again acute. The bridge revenues and resources of the city companies were called upon as in 1392.[109] Moreover, individuals paid contributions

[104] P.R.O. Lord Treasurer's Remembrancer Roll (E. 368) 169 and 170.

[105] *C.Cl.R., 1396-99*, p. 135; P.R.O. Close Rolls (C. 54) 239 m.1ᵛ. Cf. p. 188, n. 58, above.

[106] Caroline M. Barron, 'Richard Whittington', pp. 205, 229-30.

[107] Caroline M. Barron, 'The Tyranny of Richard II', *B.I.H.R.*, xli (1968), pp. 1-18, esp. pp. 1-6.

[108] *C.P.R., 1396-99*, p. 136; P.R.O. Patent Rolls (C. 66), 345; Guildhall Record Office, Charter no. 49 (297A).

[109] 'Paid $£50$ to the Chamber (of London) by order of Richard Whittington, Mayor and the Aldermen', Guildhall Record Office, Bridge House Accounts roll 15 m.1ᵛ. The Grocers' Company on 23 July 1397 paid $£13$ 6s 8d to Whittington and the aldermen, 'Pur le frawnchises de Londres', *Facsimile of the First Volume of*

to the chamber at Guildhall and received receipts for their money under the chamber seal.[110] In just over two months Whittington appears to have collected the necessary amount and on 22 August 1397 the exchequer acknowledged the receipt of 10,000 marks from the Londoners.[111] The king wrote to thank the Londoners for their 'pecuniary assistance' and referred to the need for good government in the city during the forthcoming meeting of parliament.[112]

So the quarrel of 1392 was finally resolved. The manner of its solution strongly suggests that Richard's motive for seizing the London liberties in 1392 was financial, although he concealed his objectives with general complaints about lawlessness and bad governance. But Walsingham observed that the Londoners were not ignorant of the fact that the end of the business would be silver and gold.[113] The citizens' aloof refusals in the years 1388-92, cost them in the succeeding five years £16,666 13s 4d in straight exactions, £10,000 or so in jewels and gifts, the costs of a magnificent reception and Christmas entertainment, and the new statuary on London Bridge; in all, perhaps, a total of £30,000.[114] Clearly the poorer citizens, such as the widows and clergy who petitioned parliament in 1394, found these exactions hard to pay, but the signs are that the city as a whole could afford the demands which Richard made. If London were prosperous, this could

the Ms. Archives of the Worshipful Company of Grocers of the City of London 1345–1463, ed. J. A. Kingdon (London, 1886), i, p. 78.

[110] John Woodcock, a mercer and associate of Whittington, contributed £50 which he was fortunate enough to have repaid by Henry IV. 7 April 1400, Woodcock was paid by assignment a total sum of £1300 6s 6½d. This was mainly to cover money owed to him by Richard II and Isabella for purchases of mercery. These debts amounted to £1250 6s 6½d which left £50. The entry in the issue roll states that this sum was Woodcock's contribution to the loan of 10,000 marks lately made by the mayor and citizens of London to King Richard, P.R.O. Issue Rolls of Exchequer (E.403) 565. The grocer and ex-mayor William Venour contributed £100, which he was repaid during Richard's reign, 4 November 1397, P.R.O. Issue Rolls of Exchequer (E.403) 556.

[111] P.R.O. Receipt Rolls of Exchequer (E.401) 606.

[112] 21 August 1397, L.B.H., p. 438.

[113] Walsingham, ii, p. 210.

[114] There can be added to this sum the cost, estimated at 12,000 francs, of a circlet of gold set with precious stones and pearls, which the Londoners presented to Queen Isabella when she arrived in the city as Richard's bride in November 1396, Choix de pièces inédites relatives au regne de Charles VI, ed. L. Drouet-D'Arcq (Paris, 1863–4), ii, p. 277.

explain the king's original biting irritation. Moreover while some Londoners such as Gilbert Maghfeld may have sunk into debt as a result of Richard's interference, others like Richard Whittington rose to prominence and wealth in the sunshine of royal favour. If Richard could be a harsh tax officer, he could also be a generous patron. Hence it is clear that, notwithstanding the friction between the crown and the city in these years, there was a group of Londoners, small but powerful, which supported Richard II. In spite of the events of 1392-7 Richard does not appear to have alienated the city as a whole, and the reluctance of the Londoners to commit themselves openly to the cause of Henry Bolingbroke in 1399 is striking. Henry had been in England at least a month, and had taken Richard prisoner, before the Londoners sent a deputation of submission and fealty to him at Chester. Moreover if Bolingbroke had considered that the Londoners were ripe for revolt against Richard he would have landed in the south, rather than in the Lancastrian strongholds of the north.

Where the city of London was concerned Richard had walked the tightrope of royal absolutism with some success. His action against the Londoners in 1392 had been well planned and was carefully legal; he had acted constantly with the advice of his council and had involved his powerful uncles in the unpopular decisions; he had observed the statute of 1354 to the letter: he had balanced fierce anger with gentle pardon; he had imposed great penalties in order to gain favour by reducing them; and when the storm was abated he cultivated a few powerful and sympathetic Londoners. By these judicious methods he gained the money which he wanted without seriously forfeiting the goodwill of the citizens. If Richard's policy in other spheres of royal activity had been as successfully planned and consistently carried through, the Lancastrians might never have entered upon their greater inheritance.

X

Richard II and York

JOHN H. HARVEY

THROUGHOUT the history of urban civilization the role of the capital city as a seat of government has been prominent, and changes of capital have been used as instruments of the power wielded by a monarch or a dictator. Rivalry between old cities contending for pre-eminence, or the overweening arrogance of an old capital, led to the creation of new cities: Tell el-Amarna, Byzantium, Madrid, Washington, Brasilia; or to the deliberate removal of political pre-eminence from one city to another: from Burgos to Toledo, Seville and Valladolid, from Moscow to St Petersburg and back from Petrograd to Moscow, from Peking to Nanking and back, from Istanbul to Ankara. At first sight it may seem that England has been immune from this tendency, for it is little more than a romantic notion that Winchester was ever the real capital of England—as distinct from that of Wessex. Since long before the Norman Conquest London has held an immense lead over all its rivals, and there has never been any long-term transfer of power away from London. But has such a transfer of power never been seriously contemplated? There is some evidence suggesting that Richard II, seeking for a means to defeat the economic stranglehold of the citizens of London, did consider the transference of the capital to York.

The temporary transfer of the courts of justice to York was no new thing.[1] By reason of the Scottish wars, Edward I had virtually made York his capital from 1298 to 1304, when all the three royal courts—of king's bench, common pleas and exchequer—

Besides the persons mentioned in note 38 below I am indebted to the staff of the York City Library and particularly Mr Maurice Smith; to successive City Archivists, Mrs Percy, Miss Tanner and Mrs Green; and to Miss K. M. Longley, archivist to the dean and chapter.

[1] Victoria County History, *The City of York* (Oxford, 1961), pp. 29, 522.

sat there. Nor was this an isolated phenomenon: it was repeated under Edward II and Edward III on many occasions, sufficient to prove that York was regarded as their second city in importance, as it then certainly was in population.[2] If there were to be any question of a transfer of the capital in the fourteenth century, York was the only conceivable choice. There is at any rate contemporary evidence that transfer of the courts to York was sometimes intended as a deliberate punishment to London for its unwilling response to royal demands for loans, and to lessen the dominance of its citizens by forcing them to plead at a distance.[3]

The period of adult government by Richard II is notable as a self-conscious and highly sophisticated attempt by a medieval king of outstanding intellect and sensibility to achieve real power—not only for himself, but for his legitimate successors. Richard was alarmed at the threats which, from several different quarters, menaced the institution of kingship in England.[4] That kings were directly appointed by God, and that he himself had a burden of duty laid upon him by the Almighty, were cardinal points of his personal religious belief.[5] He was free from any philosophical doubts on the subject and knew precisely where his duty lay. In this he was undoubtedly encouraged by the strongly legitimist theology preached by his Dominican confessors.[6] Richard set himself formally to traverse all former actions—notably the deposition of Edward II—which in any way assailed the theory of royal

[2] For the populations of cities in 1377 and 1381, from the poll tax returns, see C. Oman, *The Great Revolt of 1381* (1906), pp. 162–6. York in 1377 still far outstripped any rival in the provinces with 7248 persons enumerated, against 6345 for Bristol—London had 23,314. In 1381, with notoriously 'cooked' returns, York appeared to have dropped to 4015, while Bristol had almost held its own at 5652.

[3] Ruth Bird, *The Turbulent London of Richard II* (London, 1949), p. 104; Caroline M. Barron, above, pp. 173–201.

[4] For a detailed study see R. H. Jones, *The Royal Policy of Richard II: Absolutism in the Later Middle Ages* (Oxford, 1968).

[5] The clearest evidence for Richard's beliefs is to be found in his will, dated 16 April 1399, and printed in Latin in J. Nichols, *Wills of the Kings and Queens of England, etc.* (1780), pp. 191–200. An English translation, based upon collation of this text with the sealed original in the Public Record Office (E.23/1), is printed in John Harvey, *The Plantagenets* (2nd edn. 1959, pp. 222–7; Fontana paperback edn. 1967, pp. 219–24).

[6] See, for example, the exordium of Roger Dymmok, *Contra errores Lollardorum*, written in 1396 and edited by H. S. Cronin (Wyclif Society, 1922). Richard read the hours daily after the Dominican use (*Cal. Papal Registers 1396–1404* p. 67). See also R. H. Jones, op. cit. especially pp. 147–63.

supremacy under God, and had begun this campaign as far back as 1387.[7] This was in the period of his first personal rule, at the age of 20, and before the insolent rebellion of the Lords Appellant.

It is the affair of the Appellants that gives the clue to Richard's later policy, just as their wanton humiliation of Queen Anne and cruel murder of his loyal friends and supporters form the root of his personal tragedy. Here it is necessary only to remark that the rule of the Appellants came to an end on 3 May 1389 when they were unable to challenge the king's right, now that he was of full age, to choose his own advisers and conduct his own affairs.[8] From this time onward it is not merely possible, but imperative, to see royal policy as following a deliberate and coherent plan, doomed to failure as matters fell out, but at the time rational enough. This serious policy involved the punishment of guilty men, but to describe it as 'revenge' is to interject gratuitously an atmosphere of personal and subjective ethics.[9]

It is of fundamental significance for the present study that London had defected from the king in the crisis of 1387-8.[10] Suspect on this account, the city was given an opportunity to rehabilitate itself in 1392, yet not merely declined to grant a civic loan but even attacked a Lombard who had found the money. The city 'was taken into the king's hand'—its mayor and sheriffs imprisoned and a royal warden appointed—as the appropriate and traditional punishment.[11] It is reasonable to think that in this episode there may have lain the germ of a later intention to move the seat of government to York. What is certain is that, from his

[7] By attempting to secure the canonization of Edward II. See E. Perroy, *L'Angleterre et le grand schisme d'Occident* (Paris, 1933), pp. 301, 330, 341-2; F. Devon, *Issues of the Exchequer,* p. 259.

[8] For the Appellants, see H. Wallon, *Richard II* (Paris, 1864), i, pp. 336-82; ii, 1-14; A. Steel, *Richard II* (1941), pp. 141-79; H. F. Hutchison, *The Hollow Crown* (1961), pp. 103-28; V. H. H. Green, *The Later Plantagenets* (London, 1966), pp. 226-33; R. H. Jones, *The Royal Policy of Richard II* (1968), pp. 47-63.

[9] Hutchison, op. cit., pp. 167-87. For some aspects of Richard's policy see John H. Harvey, 'The Wilton Diptych—A Re-examination', *Archaeologia,* xcviii (1961), pp. 1-28, especially pp. 17-19, 27-8.

[10] Bird, op. cit., pp. 91-2; Steel, op. cit., p. 141; Hutchison, op. cit., p. 114; Jones, op. cit., p. 44; Green, op. cit., pp. 228-9.

[11] Wallon, op. cit., ii, pp. 59-62, 416-18; Bird, op. cit., pp. 102-13; Steel, op. cit., p. 198; Hutchison, op. cit., pp. 138-40. Hutchison makes the important point that 'by the feudal standards of his own day, and in the judgement of his peers, Richard was wholly in the right' in his quarrel with London. Caroline M. Barron, above, p. 189, regards the motive of the quarrel as primarily financial.

assumption of real power in the spring of 1389 onwards, Richard went out of his way to do signal honour to the city of York. It is probably of considerable significance that the new keeper of the privy seal, appointed the very day after the king's bloodless victory in council, was Edmund Stafford who had been dean of York since 1385, and held the office until his promotion to the bishopric of Exeter in 1395. Stafford was a conspicuously loyal and intelligent servant of the crown, and a man of notable integrity.[12] Nor must it be overlooked that the chancellor who lost his office on 3 May 1389, Thomas Arundel, was archbishop of York from 1388 to 1396 when he was advanced to Canterbury, and was reinstated as chancellor by Richard for the period 27 September 1391-14 November 1396, when he was succeeded by Stafford, the former privy seal. In the last years of Richard's reign another dean of York, Richard Clifford, was privy seal from 14 November 1397; and the keeper of the wardrobe from 27 July 1390 to the abdication was John Carp, a canon of York as well as of St Paul's. Richard's closest advisers and leading administrators were, therefore, men who during the relevant period were closely involved with the affairs of the church of York in all its aspects.

How far did this association with York churchmen imply any special regard for the city? On account of the notoriety of disputes between the citizens and the clerical authorities it might be thought that the king could hardly be in favour of both. Yet it is recorded that Richard had visited York in 1387 for the express purpose of settling differences that had arisen between Archbishop Alexander Neville, the dean and chapter, and the mayor and citizens, and that his decision was favourable to the citizens.[13] It may be that it was on this occasion, as is commonly stated,[14] that the king gave to York its first sword of state, though the tradition that with it he conferred the title of 'lord mayor' upon William Selby and his

[12] See Steel, p. 183; Hutchison, p. 131. For the life of Stafford see *Dictionary of National Biography* and Emden, *Oxford*, iii, pp. 1749–50.

[13] Knighton, ii, p. 233: 'reddidit rex civibus quasi in omnibus votum suum'; cf. Monk of Westminster, p. 90.

[14] V.C.H. *York*, p. 546, but giving the year as 1389, following F. Drake, *Eboracum* (1736), p. 106. The earliest reference to a civic sword seems to be in the record of election of mayors and city officers in the York register of freemen (York Corporation Archives D.1—Reg. C/Y, f. 9): on Monday 8 February 1388/9 Thomas de Barneby was sworn 'ad portand. gladium pro feodo consueto'. The mention of an accustomed fee suggests, however, that this may have been an earlier sword.

successors in the office of first citizen, does not seem to be confirmed by any contemporary record.[15] What is certain is that Richard had indeed given a sword to the city by 1396,[16] and also the right for the serjeants-at-mace of the mayor and sheriffs to bear maces adorned with the king's arms. Traditionally, again, he presented the city with a cap-of-maintenance which is shown as surmounting the civic shield-of-arms. Even making some allowance for the accretions of legend, it must be accepted that the two charters to York, granted on 11 February 1393,[17] and on 18 May 1396,[18] contained distinguished and increasing marks of royal favour. At the same time, London was under a menacing cloud of royal displeasure, and this too was increasing. Whether the king actually intended that the two cities should exchange roles, or simply meant to frighten the Londoners into a more amenable frame of mind, his benevolence towards the northern city was real and of lasting value.

It was the second charter, of 1396, that contained really significant changes. The city was in future to have, instead of three bailiffs, two sheriffs as did London, and they were to have complete freedom of jurisdiction within the city. York and its suburbs were to form a county, with the mayor as escheator, and the sword which the king had given, or another sword, was to be carried point erect unless the king were present in person. What is perhaps more significant still is that this charter was not a mere exercise of government by remote control but, like its predecessor of 1393, the outcome of substantial periods of residence in York by the king and his court. Although Richard had stayed in York on occasions in 1383,[19] 1385,[20] 1387,[21] and 1391,[22] it was at the time of the transference of the courts to York in 1392 that he first stayed in the city for many weeks on end—from early June to late

---

[15] Sir Thomas Widdrington, *Analecta Eboracensia*, ed. C. Caine (1897), p. 84; Maud Sellers in *City of York Supplemental Yearbook* (1928), pp. 45–6; T. P. Cooper, *York—the Titles 'Lord Mayor' and 'Right Honourable'* (York Corporation, 1935). There is some evidence that from early in the fifteenth century there was a growing tendency to accord to the mayor the title of 'lord mayor' and/or the epithet 'right honourable', but this does not seem to have had royal sanction until the visit of Henry VII.

[16] Charter of 18 May 1396 (*C.Ch.R.*, v, p. 360).   [17] *C.Ch.R.*, v, pp. 336–7.

[18] Ibid., pp. 358–60.   [19] Monk of Westminster, p. 21.

[20] In July and August (*C.P.R.* and *C.Cl.R.*, passim).   [21] Knighton, loc. cit.

[22] In June (see note 20 above).

1. See overleaf for caption.

1. York Minster: head of an Emperor carved at springing of south-east pier of main crossing, after cleaning, 1970; for condition in 1967 see Plate 2a. For appearance in 1795 see Joseph Halfpenny, *Gothic Ornaments of the Cathedral Church of York*, Plate 30. Here dated to *c.* 1397–8 and identified as Richard II as Emperor-designate. See p. 214.

2a (at left). York Minster: head of an Emperor (see also Plate 1); view before cleaning, 1967.

2b. York Minster: Richard II's badge on capital at springing of main arcade, south-east crossing pier, towards south choir aisle. Here dated to *c.* 1395 as acknowledging the royal gift to the works.

November, with only occasional absence.[23] This long stay seems to have produced the charter issued early in the following year. The king revisited York for part of August 1393, and was there again in December 1395, when he kept Christmas at York. During that year he had shown his interest in the works of York Minster by a gift of 100 marks ($£66$ 13s 4d),[24] and this gift was duly acknowledged by the carving of his badge of a chained hart upon a capital above the entry to the south choir aisle, beside the great south-east pier of the central crossing (Plate 2b).

In the history of York Minster this visible sign of a dated gift is of importance, for it shows the stage reached by the major works in progress in the eastern arm of the cathedral. The twelfth-century choir of Archbishop Roger had been demolished, and new bays in Perpendicular style were linking the earlier crossing to the new eastern Lady Chapel built in 1361–73 for Archbishop Thoresby. Structural evidence indicates that the eastern arch of the crossing was a work of underpinning, carried out while the old thirteenth-century central tower still stood.[25] Stylistically, as judged by the

[23] C.P.R. and C.Cl.R., passim. For the removal of the courts to York see Monk of Westminster, pp. 267–8; Wallon, ii, p. 417; payments were allowed for repairs and making of houses in York Castle against the coming of the king's courts between 23 June 1392 and 10 January 1392/3 (P.R.O. Issue Rolls E.403/554, m. 13, 14), and see H. M. Colvin (ed.), History of the King's Works (London, 1963), ii, p. 892.

[24] Issue Roll, under 12 July 1395 (P.R.O. E.403/551, m. 14): 'in subsidionem perficiend. et sustentand. operaciones infra ecclesiam beati Petri Ebor'. To obtain a roughly corresponding value in terms of building works of 1969 it is necessary to multiply by 120 or more, so that the king's gift was worth say $£8000$ (see, for building costs, John Harvey, The Gothic World, (London, 1950), pp. 42–5; cf. E. V. Morgan, The Study of Prices and the Value of Money, Historical Association, Helps for Students of History, no. 53, 1950; and articles in The Amateur Historian, ii (1954–6), nos. 8, 9, 10, pp. 238–44, 271–3, 304–8). The king had earlier appropriated St Sampson's church, York, to the vicars choral of the minster on condition that they should celebrate the obits of himself and his queen. The grant to the vicars is dated 1 March 1393/4 (C.P.R., 1391–6, p. 386; cf. C.Cl.R., 1392–6, p. 420) and on Saturday 14 March the vicars, according to the king's ordinance, began to sing the anthem inter natos at the altar of St Mary and St John Baptist after vespers in the minster ('vicarii chorales inceperunt primo cantare antiphonam inter natos coram altari beatae Mariae et sancti Johannis Baptistae immediate post vesperas secundum ordinationem domini regis Richardi Secundi, qui eis appropriavit ecclesiam sancti Sampsonis in Eboraco', Historians of the Church of York, ed. J. Raine (Rolls Series, 1886), ii, p. 425 (hereafter referred to as Church of York).

[25] It did not fall until 1407, when petitions for help were sent to the pope and to King Henry IV (Cal. Papal Letters 1404–15, pp. 137–8; C.P.R., 1405–8, p. 383). The petition to the king claimed that the collapse of the famous old tower was due

profiles of its mouldings, the crossing arch (and the other three added within the next few years) come from the same designer as the next five bays to the east, which differ markedly in detail from the earlier work of the Lady Chapel, and later work done after 1407, when Henry IV sent the Westminster mason William Colchester to York to take charge. The master of the choir and crossing was Hugh de Hedon, evidenced as chief mason at the Minster by 1399, and who died in 1408.[26] There is strong presumptive evidence that the building of the new choir had begun about 1385, when the chapter leased a stone quarry at Huddleston for eighty years, but in 1390 complaint was made at the slow progress of the work.[27]

York Minster is the largest of the surviving medieval churches of Britain and it was, at the Reformation, second only to Old St Paul's. This great scale implied very high building costs, and it is not surprising that funds should have run short, with consequent delays. In many cases such financial difficulties prevented the com-

---

to 'carelessness of the stonecutters' and it is all but certain that by this was meant the additional works of underpinning done to complete the crossing with three more arches—to north, south and west—equal in height to the new eastern arch already completed. The masonry of the north and south arches and of the shafts supporting them appears to be added against the new work (c. 1395–1400) of the eastern arch.

[26] See J. Harvey, *English Medieval Architects* (Boston, Mass., 1954), p. 124; for Colchester, and for the earlier masters William de Hoton and Robert Patrington, ibid., pp. 71, 139, 205–6. Identity of the profiles of mouldings in the five bays of the choir to east of the crossing, and of all four arches supporting the central lantern, indicates that the whole of this work must be due to Hugh de Hedon.
[27] *The Fabric Rolls of York Minster*, ed. J. Raine (Surtees Society, xxxv for 1858, 1859), p. 13n. The lease of the Huddleston quarry from the prebend of Fenton is evidenced by its renewal after 80 years in 1465 (J. Browne, *The History of the Metropolitan Church of St Peter, York*, 1847, i, p. 248). Oak trees for the works were to be delivered to the chapter in 1388 (*C.Cl.R., 1385–9*, p. 413). See also A. Hamilton Thompson in *Eighth Report* of the Friends of York Minster (1936), pp. 21–7; J. H. Harvey, 'The Tracing Floor in York Minster', *Fortieth Report* of the Friends (1968); and for the sequence of building works, John Harvey, *English Cathedrals* (paperback edn., London, 1961/63), p. 169. It was probably not intended to demolish the Early English central tower of c. 1235–50, for it was regarded as of outstanding beauty. The petition to the pope (above, note 25) referred to the old bell-tower as 'lofty and delectable to see', a valuable aesthetic comment which takes its place in the evidence for artistic sophistication in the middle ages. See J. Harvey, 'Mediaeval Design', *Transactions of the Ancient Monuments Society*, vi (1958), pp. 55–72; 'Architecture in Mediaeval Writings', *Sussex Archaeological Collections* xcvii (1959), pp. 21–34.

pletion of great works which have remained for ever unfinished. That this fate did not overtake three of the most notable English churches was due largely to Richard II who, by his benefactions, greatly furthered the rebuilding of Westminster Abbey,[28] Canterbury Cathedral,[29] and York Minster. At York the actual gift of 100 marks was but a first instalment, for the king was about to present the chapter with something of far greater potential value. He gave to the Minister the relics of one of the Holy Innocents, which the chapter then had enclosed in a silver and gilt shrine and borne into the church in full procession by four choristers on the feasts of Innocents, evidently 28 December 1395, while Richard was still in York.[30] The offerings of pilgrims at the shrine of such an outstanding relic must have been a substantial factor in enabling the work of the new choir to proceed rapidly towards completion within the next few years.

In the meantime the king was concerned with the business leading up to the grant of the new charter to the city. Richard returned to York on 24 March 1396 and stayed until 5 April.[31] He took up his residence in the archbishop's palace behind the Minster and there held the royal Maundy on 30 March, after hearing a sermon preached in the chapel by Brother William Bircheley (or Betheley), an Austin friar, master of theology. On the next day,

[28] R. B. Rackham, 'The Nave of Westminster Abbey', *Proceedings of the British Academy*, iv (1909–10), p. 40; cf. R. P. Howgrave-Graham, 'Westminster Abbey, the sequence and dates of the transepts and nave', *Journal of the British Archaeological Association*, 3rd series xi (1948), pp. 60–78; J. Harvey, 'The Masons of Westminster Abbey', *Archaeological Journal*, cxiii (1957), pp. 82–101.

[29] P.R.O., Memoranda Rolls (E.159/172), *Brevia directa,* Easter rot. 9; (/173), Michaelmas rot. 11, showing that the prior and chapter were discharged of £160 in taxes owed by them in the year 1396, in satisfaction of a sum promised to them by the king on account of their heavy expenditure on their works, in aid of the building of the (west) front of their church (*promys pur la feseur de la gable de leur eglise*). See J. H. Harvey, 'The Origin of the Perpendicular Style', in *Studies in Building History*, ed. E. M. Jope (1962), p. 156 n. 51.

[30] *Church of York*, ii, p. 426 'unum puerum de Sanctis Innocentibus Martyribus obtulit'. That the date must have been 1395, not 1396 as might be thought from the chronicle, is evidenced by an entry in the chamberlain's roll of York Minster for Martinmas (11 November) 1395 to Whitsun (21 May) 1396 (Minster Library, E 1(23): 'Et post compotum factum responsum est capitulo de Lvj.*s.* v.*d.* receptis de oblationibus factis Innocenti datis per Regem . . .').

[31] *Church of York*, loc. cit. The dates are confirmed by the surviving account book of the controller of the wardrobe (P.R.O., E.101/403/10), covering 30 September 1395 to 30 September 1396.

Good Friday, he again attended services in the palace chapel (now the Minster Library), before noon and again after dinner, the sermons being preached by the Dominican brother John Richard. With his own hands, the account tells us, the king distributed 4d each to the enormous number of 12,040 poor people. On Easter Day, 2 April 1396, he went to mass in the Minster and heard a sermon by Brother John Parys, another Dominican who had been vicar-general of the English province.[32]

The number of persons receiving alms on Good Friday 1396 is so large as to deserve comment. Since the record is contained in an official account-book which duly, and correctly, puts the total spent at £200 13s 4d, the number is beyond question. The problem is how this number of 'poor people' is related to the total population of a given area; and how far that area may be regarded as equivalent to York and its suburbs. In round figures the 'poor' of 1396 were twice the total adult population of York as given by the poll taxes of 1377–81, but against this must be set the certainty that the figures of 1381 were a gross understatement, while those of 1377 too may already have omitted very large numbers of the untaxable real poor. It seems most unlikely that any very large influx of individuals from remote parts of Yorkshire could have turned up to receive the king's alms, and there must have been a great many of the citizens of York who would not have applied for the dole or who would have been officially debarred from it as not falling within an acceptable definition of poverty. Tentatively it must be supposed that the real population of the city and its neighbourhood was a good deal larger than is commonly accepted. In turn this must modify the scepticism felt at the statement that in 1390 a contagious disease had caused 1100 deaths in York.[33] In

[32] P.R.O., E. 101/403/10, ff. 35v, 36. For William Bircheley and John Richard see Emden, *Oxford*, iii, pp. 2152, 2210; for John Paris, see Emden, *Cambridge*, p. 441, and *Oxford*, iii, p. 1425. Precisely what is meant by the phrase that the alms were distributed by the lord king's own hands (*distribut' manibus propriis domini Regis*) may be doubtful, but is irrelevant to the number of persons relieved.

[33] F. Drake, *Eboracum*, p. 106, quoting Stow and Holinshed; cf. V.C.H., *York*, pp. 84–5. Stow's *Annales*, criticized as a source for medieval events, have recently been vindicated and shown to depend upon contemporary authorities (J. H. Harvey, 'The Fire of York in 1137', *Yorkshire Archaeological Journal*, xli (1965), pp. 365–7). The statement that a second outbreak carried off eleven *thousand* victims from York alone must indeed be regarded as improbable, and perhaps a clerical error produced in repetition of the figure first given.

any case this substantial almsgiving shows that York was a very large centre of population at the time, and that it thus formed a by no means contemptible rival of London.

When the new charter of privileges was granted, on 18 May, the king was no longer in York, but he returned to a civic reception on the feast of Corpus Christi (1 June 1396). The chamberlains' roll of accounts for the city includes a large expenditure in connection with the charter and also refers to items of work 'done at the bars [? barriers erected for the performance of the pageant plays] in the presence of the king' and payments to the minstrels of the king and other lords present at Corpus Christi. It appears that a special performance of the Corpus Christi plays was enacted by the York guilds in the royal presence. Another meeting is evidenced by the expenditure of 2s 5d (say £15 now) 'for a long bench for the use of the Mayor and city elders (*proborum*) in the chapter house of the greater church of St Peter of York'.[34] It must be remembered that before the building of the new Guildhall, in 1448–53,[35] York had no large civic hall. The use of the Minster chapter house would have been normal for any great public meeting that could not be held in the open air, and parallels the use of the Westminster chapter house for the sittings of the commons in the reign of Edward III.[36]

The reference to a 'long' bench rather suggests the use of the arm of the vestibule leading to the doors of the chapter, as well as the great octagon itself, to cope with the multitude of courtiers and clerics, as well as leading citizens, present on the occasion. Be this as it may, the vestibule seems to have had an extensive scheme of redecoration at about this time.[37] Much of the painting consisted of heraldry obviously concerned with the history of the

[34] York Corporation Archives, C.1:1, mistakenly dated by some former custodian to '1398', accepted as the year of this civic reception in V.C.H., *York*, p. 57. The references to journeys in regard to the charter make it certain that the roll belongs to 1396 (i.e. the mayoral year 3 Feb. 1396–1397). The year of the king's visit to the York plays is put at 1397 by O. E. Saunders, *A History of English Art in the Middle Ages* (1932), p. 128; but again some confusion seems likely. For text of the relevant entries from the roll see Appendix.

[35] A. Raine, *Mediaeval York* (1955), pp. 136–8; cf. J. H. Harvey, 'Some Notes from the York Guildhall', *The Builder*, 31 Aug. 1945, pp. 165–6.

[36] G. G. Scott, *Gleanings from Westminster Abbey* (2nd edn. 1863), p. 39; H. St. G. Saunders, *Westminster Hall* (1951), p. 64.

[37] J. Browne, *Arms on the Glass in the Windows of York Minster*, 1859, ed. A. P. Purey-Cust (1917), pp. 31–2.

minster and its benefactors, but on the south end wall of the first arm of the vestibule, beyond the doorways leading out of the north transept, was an arrangement of shields and inscriptions (now largely defaced) of more particular purport. At the top of the wall, beneath the vault, was *England* (standing for the original royal foundation of York Minster) flanked by *Ros* and (*Old*) *Percy*, for the two regional families regarded as the chief benefactors of the works. Lower down are roses, presumably as a royal and national badge, and several shields of which most have long been completely blank and seem never to have been recorded. Above the doorways remains of three rows can be made out, comprising four shields in each row. By putting together the evidence, still visible in 1968 during cleaning,[38] with what could be read by John Browne in the middle of the nineteenth century, we get some indications both of date and purpose.

In the lowest range the four panels from left to right (i.e. east to west) contain: (1) the arms 'Eight osier twigs interlaced in cross' with the inscription 'Walterus Skyrla(w)'; (2) 'Seven mascles' and 'Scs. Willms. eborac(ensis) archiepis(copus)'; (3) 'A cross flory between five martlets' and 'Sanctus (Edwardus)'; (4) 'Two bendlets' or possibly 'A bend cotised'. In the second row up only the first shield of 'Three bars overall an inescutcheon on a chief three palets between two esquires' gyrons' and the inscription 'Comes Marchie' yields identifiable sense. The third row starts with a blank shield but continues with three which allude to the Three Kings of the Epiphany, viz. (2) 'An estoile enclosed by a crescent' (for Jasper); (3) 'Six estoiles, three two and one' with '(M)elchior rex arabu. et Saba'; (4) 'A man holding a staff' with 'Baltazar rex aetioppe . . .'

This programme yields sense in connection with the royal visit of 1396, for the arms assigned to the Three Kings would be a direct compliment to Richard's own birth on the feast of the Epiphany (6 January 1367), and would indirectly be linked to the narrative of the Holy Innocents in the nativity story. Roger Mortimer (1374–98), fourth earl of March, had been recognized in 1385 as heir-

---

[38] I am indebted to the dean and chapter for kindly permitting me to inspect the remains of this decoration when scaffolding was erected in the vestibule in 1968; to Mr Christopher Richmond; and to Dr E. A. Gee, Mr T. W. French and Mr C. B. L. Barr for much help in the interpretation of the paintings.

presumptive to the crown and certainly bulked largely in the king's plans between the death of Queen Anne in 1394 and Mortimer's death in an Irish ambush in August 1398. Walter Skyrlaw, though bishop of Durham from 1388 until his death in 1406, was throughout his career a friend of York Minster, to which he made outstanding benefactions, and had been archdeacon of the East Riding and prebendary of Fenton in the period 1359–85. He had also been Richard's keeper of the privy seal from 1382 to 1386. The two central shields of the bottom row are St William of York, the major local saint, and St Edward the Confessor, the king's special royal patron. The fourth shield, which bears arms probably of Scrope, may be that of the archbishop, though he was not provided to York until 15 March 1398. It seems more likely that it referred to some considerable benefactor of his family, perhaps Stephen Scrope, the king's close friend, who had recently been one of his ambassadors to Rome to press for the canonization of Edward II.[39] Several members of the family were great benefactors of the Minster.[40]

Although a direct connection with the king's visits in 1395–6, his own noteworthy gifts to the minster, and the meeting in the chapter house to celebrate the grant of York's new charter, seems the most probable explanation of this series of allusions, there is another possible, not necessarily incompatible, reason for the surprising appearance of the 'heraldry' of the Three Kings. Richard had for some years been trying to obtain election as Holy Roman emperor in the place of his ineffective brother-in-law Wenzel, who was indeed ultimately deposed in 1400. Richard's main hopes lay with the Rhenish electors and particularly with the archbishop of Cologne, who in fact became vassal and liegeman of Richard, in return for a pension, in 1397.[41] Negotiations were conducted through the dean of Cologne, who visited England, and in view of Cologne's position as the cult centre of the Three Kings it is not

[39] J. H. Harvey in *Archaeologia*, xcviii (1961), p. 16.

[40] See for example *The Fabric Rolls of York Minster*, ed. J. Raine (Surtees Society, xxxv, 1859), as indexed.

[41] D. M. Bueno de Mesquita, 'The Foreign Policy of Richard II in 1397', *E.H.R.*, lvi (1941), pp. 628–37; E. Perroy, *L'Angleterre et le grand schisme d'Occident* (Paris, 1933), pp. 342–3. Richard's activities were so far successful by December 1397 that he then had four of the electors as his pensioners: the archbishop of Cologne, the count palatine, the archbishop of Trier and the duke of Saxony; four German knights had taken an oath of homage to him at Windsor in October.

unlikely that a double-barrelled diplomatic compliment was intended, linking the king's own birthday with his imperial ambitions and the great German city which was coming to owe allegiance to him.

Within York Minster itself is a more definite allusion to King Richard as emperor. Above the internal caps of the south-east pier of the crossing is a carved stone head, bearded and moustached, with flowing locks beneath a tiered triple crown or tiara, bearing a sword in the right hand and possibly the remains of a sceptre in the left (Plates 1, 2a). The triple crown can mean only a pope or an emperor, but the civilian hairdressing and equipment proves conclusively that an emperor was intended. Furthermore, the features are by no means unlike those shown in known portraits of Richard II, the prominent nose being particularly characteristic. The date too should fit very well, for we have seen that the king's gift of 1395 had been indicated lower down, on the other side of the same pier. If this head was carved in anticipation of Richard's expected election as emperor, when the news of the adhesion of several electors became public in 1397, it would agree precisely with the date when the underpinning of the eastern part of the crossing might be expected, on technical grounds, to have reached the high springing level. Here then is a news-scoop of 1397–8, unfulfilled, but perhaps authorized by the new dean, Richard Clifford, who was also keeper of the privy seal, and carried out by Master Hugh de Hedon or one of his chief carvers.

The king became increasingly preoccupied with other matters after the summer of 1396. On 1 November he married Isabella of France and believed that his policy of peace had put an end to the long epoch of chronic warfare. Through the next year he was deeply involved in the negotiations for the empire and other foreign affairs; in 1398 the home stage was overshadowed by the quarrel between Henry Bolingbroke and the duke of Norfolk, then by the death of Mortimer in Ireland. The tragedy moved on inexorably to its climax, and any intention to transfer the capital to York must have been brushed aside. Yet one may wonder whether the close association built up between the city and Richard II did not have a good deal to do with the attachment of its martyr-archbishop, Richard Scrope, and of the citizens through the ensuing century to the cause of Richard's rightful heirs who, fortuitously enough, were known as the house of York.[42]

[42] The publication, after this essay had been completed, of J. L. Grassi's important paper 'Royal Clerks from the Archdiocese of York in the Fourteenth Century', *Northern History*, v (1970), pp. 12–33 makes it possible to penetrate further into the background of the royal association with York. The fact that there were not merely sporadic associations but a continuous tradition throughout the whole of the fourteenth century, when most of the important posts in the chancery and many of those in the wardrobe and exchequer were held by members of a closely knit group of clerks from York and Yorkshire, greatly increases the likelihood that Richard's policy would have been influenced. What might have seemed a completely unrealistic programme became, in the light of Richard's grave difficulties with the city of London, a serious policy capable of fulfilment.

Appendix

York City Archives. Chamberlains' Roll, C.1:1 (A.D. 1396)

Expens' in festo de Corpore Christi cum donis ministrall

Item comp. pro steynyng de iiij.^{or} pannorum ad opus paginor. iiij.*s.* Et in portacione et reparacione meremij ad barr' coram Rege ij.*s.*j.*d.* Et pro factura barr' Et viij. portitoribus ducent. et mouent. paginam v.*s.* iiij.*d.* Et pro vexillo nouo cum apparatu xij.*s.* ij.*d.* Et ludentibus xv.*s.* iiij.*d.* Et in pane ceruisia vino et carnibus et focal. pro maiore et probis hominibus in die ad ludam xviij.*s.* viij.*d.* Et Janitori Sancte Trinitatis pro pagina hospitanda iiij.*d.* Et ministrallis in festo de Corpore Christi xiij.*s.* iiij.*d.* Et pro clauis ferri ad emendacionem pagine v.*d.* Et pro xx. fursperres ad barras predictas coram Rege v.*s.* x.*d.* Et Roberto Paton pro factura pagine in opere carpentar' per duos dies xij.*d.* Et pro pictura pagine ij.*s.* Et pro xix. sapplynges emptis de Johanne de Crauen pro barris predictis vj.*s.* viij.*d.* Et Willelmo de Barneby carpentario pro opere suo ibidem iiij.*s.* iiij.*d.*

Summa iiij.*li.* xj.*s.* vj.*d.*

Et ministrallis domini Regis ac aliorum dominorum superuenient'

vij.*li.* vij.*s.* iiij.*d.*

Exennie et expens' ministr' domini Regis et pro aduentu eius

Item comp. in remuneracione facta capitali prouisori pro ospicio domini Regis xl.*s.* Et pro vno equo conducto ad opus ministri Ostelar' et Johannis Gode per v. dies xx.*d.* Et in presentacione facta domino Rege in duabus peluibus argenti deaurat' CC.*li.* Et in eisdem peluibus prec' x.*li.* Et Senescallo hospicij domini Regis C.*s.* Et Coreby clerico mercati hospicij domini Regis et locum suum tenenti xlvj.*s.* viij.*d.* Et Seneschallo mareschalcie xl.*s.* et eius locum tenenti xiij.*s.* iiij.*d.* Et clerico mareschalcie xiij.*s.* iiij.*d.* Et clerico subseneschall. xl.*d.* Et Preston Mareschall. xiij.*s.* iiij.*d.* Et alio ministro mareschalcie xl.*d.* Et clerico coronator' mareschalcie xl.*d.* Et vni bedello xx.*d.* Et cuidam Grene de camera domini Regis vj.*s.* viij.*d.* Et pro vna longa formula ad opus maioris et proborum in domo capitulari ecclesie maioris beati Petri Ebor. ij.*s.* v.*d.*

(Thomas Gra and William de Selby—expenses to London to Parliament Monday on St. Hillary in r.r. 20 [13 January 1396/97] 'qui iter suum arripuerunt xvj. die Januarij'—for part of their wages?)

(Fees of servants of the [City] Chamber etc. Et ministris camere in albo panno et rubio pro adventu Regis lviij.*s.* x.*d.*)

Expense Maioris, Willelmi de Selby, Johannis de Hewyk Camerarij [John de Hewyk was Chamberlain in the year 3 Feb. 1396–2 Feb. 1397] cum xj. hominibus et xv. equis versus Notyngham apud Regem per v. dies eundo et redeundo cum conduccione equorum mareschalcia equorum . . . (£4 18*s.*; also the same to London on City business for 5 weeks and 4 days—details include references to the cost of the King's new charter:— 'in feodo Carte domini Regis cum duobus breuibus viij.*li.* xj.*s.* viij.*d.* Expens' fact' circa allocacionem noue carte [the Charter of 18 May 1396] . . . pro irrotulacione dicte Carte et pro feodo super allocacionem eiusdem in Communi banco et in Scaccario domini Regis liij.*s.* x.*d.*'—total of expenses 'circa perquisicionem Carte' £60 11*s.* 0½*d.*)

Note: In 1396 Corpus Christi fell on Thursday, 1 June; the Mayor of York from 3 February 1396 to 2 February 1397 (1396/7) was William Frost.

XI

The Crown and Local Government: East Anglia under Richard II

ROGER VIRGOE

THE METHODS used by Richard II to establish his control over government and the country at large have been much studied. The constitutional and political crises of the reign have been minutely scrutinized and Tout and others have examined the machinery of patronage and bureaucratic innovation by which the crown attempted to take control of the central financial and administrative machinery.[1] Yet such control at the centre was of limited practical value if not accompanied by a tight hold on local government: without this neither the king's peace nor the king's finances could flourish. It is a commonplace that the loss of this essential control over local institutions and officials was one of the chief problems of late medieval government. The methods used by the king to deal with the problems of bureaucratic inflexibility which hindered the effective supervision of local officials have been analysed in detail by Tout, and more recently Dr Tuck has shown how the king tried to weaken the local dominance of the magnates by establishing countervailing areas of influence controlled by his own friends: the crisis of 1386–8 and 1399 arguably derive largely from this policy.[2] But magnates' influence and a third source of weakness—the development of local communities of shire and borough impatient of the supervision of central government— could best be dealt with by the tightening of the crown's control

---

[1] Tout, *Chapters*, iii–v; R. H. Jones, *The Royal Policy of Richard II* (Oxford, 1968); J. A. Tuck, 'The Baronial Opposition to Richard II, 1377–1389', unpublished Cambridge Ph.D. thesis, 1965.

[2] Tuck, 'Baronial Opposition', pp. 319 ff.; 'Richard II and the Border Magnates', *Northern History*, iii (1968), pp. 27–52.

of its local officials. It has been suggested by Tout and more recently by Professor Jones that Richard undertook a deliberate policy to strengthen this control and that this policy was crucial in arousing opposition to him among the gentry of the shires and thus among the commons in parliament.[3]

There is, indeed, no doubt that local government was an important source of conflict during the reign, but it is not so clear that the king took the initiative in this conflict or pursued the deliberate policy suggested by Tout and Professor Jones, and the evidence for the implementation of this policy seems worth testing. Many years ago Dr. A. B. Steel attempted by a study of the sheriffs of Cambridgeshire and Huntingdonshire under Richard II to test the validity of contemporary accusations that the king arbitrarily interfered with appointments to that office in order to increase his personal control over local government and over elections to parliament.[4] The purpose of this essay is to attempt a rather broader survey of the attitude of the crown and commons to the problems of local government, mainly within the context of two counties— Norfolk and Suffolk. It is proposed first to examine briefly the evidence provided for such attitudes by parliamentary petitions and statutes, then to outline the political structure of East Anglia during this period, and finally to analyse the changes in the personnel of commissions and the holders of the main offices in the two shires in relation both to this political structure and to the policies of crown and parliament.

Certain reservations must be made about the scope of this study and the validity of its conclusions. Although there is no reason to suppose that these two counties are not typical of many others, other local studies are needed before any conclusions reached here could be regarded as proved. Secondly, considerations of space have made it necessary to omit any investigation into the government of towns or feudal liberties. Thirdly, the large number of individuals involved would make full biographical treatment impossible, even if the sources permitted it. Networks of interests, patronage, kinship and rivalries connected the governing class of

---

[3] Tout, *Chapters*, iv, pp. 42 ff.; Jones, *Royal Policy*, pp. 25–6, 164–6.
[4] A. B. Steel, 'The Sheriffs of Cambridgeshire and Huntingdonshire in the Reign of Richard II', *Proceedings of the Cambridge Antiquarian Society*, xxxvi (1934–5), pp. 1–34.

the shires and their force is not adequately represented by the few examples given below.

The activities of the sheriff and the nature of his office had long been a source of friction between the crown and the commons and in the fourteenth century such friction also occurred, if to a lesser extent, over the office of escheator. Earlier hostility to the sheriff as a rapacious and corrupt agent of the king had changed into a general opposition by the local aristocracy to any crown-directed bureaucratic form of local government on the French model which might threaten the jurisdiction and finances of the governing class of the shire. Thus came demands by the commons in parliament for limitation in the authority of the sheriff, his nomination by the great officers and judges, the necessity of his being a resident gentleman of the shire and his annual replacement in office.[5] Inevitably such demands clashed with the desire of the crown and its agents to provide efficient local government which would maintain law and order and extend the legal and financial rights of the king. Under Richard II such clashes may have been intensified because of suspicion that the king wished to use his control of local government in the service of a faction or for the construction of a personal despotism. Yet even if such suspicions were justified these royal policies were only incidental to the perennial conflict between central authority and local interest.

It was, indeed, in the early parliaments of the reign before Richard had any personal power, that petitions from the commons about the sheriff's office were most numerous. In 1377, for instance, they asked that no sheriff or escheator should be reappointed within three years of the expiry of his term while there were other 'sufficient' men available.[6] The council agreed, so far as the sheriffs were concerned, and the petition was enacted, but the commons remained suspicious. In 1378, 1380, 1383 and 1384 petitions were presented asking for the observance of statutes requiring the annual replacement of sheriffs, escheators and undersheriffs and seeking their extension to include under-escheators.[7] In 1378 the council agreed that sheriffs and their deputies should

[5] See, for example, *R.P.*, iii, pp. 44, 159, 279; *Statutes of the Realm* (Record Commission 1810–28), i, pp. 160, 174–5, 258, 264, 283, 346, 388–9; S. T. Gibson, 'The Escheatries, 1327–1341', *E.H.R.*, xxxvi (1921), pp. 218–25.

[6] *R.P.*, iii, p. 24; *Statutes of the Realm*, ii, p. 4.

[7] *R.P.*, iii, pp. 44, 96, 159, 173, 201.

serve for only one year if suitable replacement could be found, and escheators and their deputies for three years at the most but, although these rules were generally followed down to 1397, the government in the 1380s grew increasingly impatient with the commons' pressure for the full observance of the statutes. In 1384, when the court was firmly in control, the chancellor replied to this almost annual petition that such limitations were against the king's prerogative and would deprive him of good service. The commons repeated their demands in the new political climate of the 1386 parliament, significantly combining them with a request for the confirmation of the Charters, but, perhaps because their grievances were largely met, this was the last such petition for ten years, although in October 1390 they were successful in seeking a property and residence qualification for the sheriffs.[8] The last years of the reign brought the subject to the fore again. In the parliament of January 1397 Haxey's petition included a request for the observance of all statutes concerning the qualifications and term of office of sheriffs and escheators. It received the reasoned reply that officials took a year to learn their job and that a short term of office made them too cautious of offending their lords and neighbours.[9]

The strong feeling which lay behind these persistent demands had more than one origin. The office of sheriff could involve heavy burdens and expenses and the petition of 1380 argued against re-appointment explicitly on the grounds of financial hardship.[10] There were frequent complaints, too, that the sheriffs' allowances, particularly in some shires, were unrealistic.[11] But the attempt to extend the ban on re-appointment to escheators and deputies makes it clear that the main purpose of such petitions was to prevent the establishment of a local bureaucracy and thus to avoid excessive crown interference in local affairs.

At each of the major crises of the reign it was alleged in parliament and by chroniclers that appointments to local offices had been made by the crown for personal and political reasons.[12] The names of the sheriffs in the eastern counties provide no support for these

---

[8] *R.P.*, iii, pp. 221, 279–80.   [9] *R.P.*, iii, p. 339.   [10] *R.P.*, iii, p. 96.

[11] For examples of such complaints see *R.P.*, iii, pp. 20, 45, 62, 116, 211–12 etc.; and see below note 39.

[12] Walsingham, ii, p. 161; Monk of Westminster, pp. 138–9, 217; *R.P.*, iii, pp. 418–20.

charges for the period before 1388, but there is strong circumstantial evidence to support the allegations made in 1399 that the king had arbitrarily appointed sheriffs and illegally retained them in office for two or three years.[13] Such a wholesale breach of statute law involving twenty-one counties was clearly not due to inability to find suitable replacements. It represented the implementation of the policy asserted in the reply to the petition of 1397, but more particularly it was connected with the king's need for subservient local officials to fulfil the distasteful tasks of extortion, punishment and security which he imposed upon them in these years.[14] Although the sheriffs appointed in 1397 could not, as implied in the charges, have influenced the returns made to the autumn parliament of that year, the names of the knights returned do suggest that court pressure had been exerted and it would be unwise to reject out of hand the allegations, made on several occasions, that the king's government did use the sheriffs to influence the election of knights of the shire.[15]

Although the local officials remained an essential element in the crown's control and exploitation of the shires, the fourteenth century saw many of their duties taken over by commissions appointed by the crown but composed largely of resident knights and squires who were, as Tout says, 'more likely to voice the views of their class or district than to be the executors of orders from above'.[16] There ensued the same sort of conflicts of interest that occurred in connection with the sheriffs. The crown sought, through the appointment of trailbaston commissions and general commissions of oyer and terminer, to continue the supervision of local justice that had been provided by the general eyres. The local gentry, on the other hand, resented the descent upon their shire of magnates, judges and officials who weakened the authority of the natural rulers of the county and might mulct it of large sums of money, whilst they were naturally suspicious of judicial authority given to magnates who were themselves often responsible for crime and disorder. They preferred semi-permanent commissions to keep the peace issued to resident gentlemen. Such commissions

[13] Steel, art. cit., pp. 5–7, 32–4; Caroline M. Barron, 'The Tyranny of Richard II', B.I.H.R., xli (1968), pp. 1–18, esp. p. 14.
[14] Barron, art. cit.
[15] Walsingham, ii, p. 161; Monk of Westminster, pp. 138–9; R.P., iii, p. 419.
[16] Tout, Chapters, iv, p. 42.

of the peace had become by 1377 an established feature of local government but their role and nature remained a subject for controversy.[17]

In fact general commissions of oyer and terminer were not very frequently issued during the reign of Richard II, but protests were made in the early years of the reign about the use of such commissions.[18] Although the Peasants' Revolt perhaps produced a temporary change in attitude, the issue of a small number of commissions of oyer and terminer from 1389 brought a hostile response from the commons in the parliaments of 1391 and 1393, and few such commissions are enrolled thereafter.[19] Indeed, there appears to have been a marked falling-off in the total number of *ad hoc* commissions enrolled during the later years of the reign partly, perhaps, owing to the renewed emphasis placed upon the sheriff as the main crown agent in local affairs, and partly owing to the increased activity and status of the commissions of the peace.[20]

In the early parliaments of Richard's reign the commons continued the interest in the composition and powers of the peace commission that they had shown under Edward III. A series of petitions was presented in which they asked for the exclusion of magnates and 'insufficient men' from the commission which should be composed of six or seven resident knights and squires nominated in parliament and should not be expanded by later 'associations'. They also asked that J.P.s should be paid and that they should hold regular sessions.[21] A number of these petitions were accepted by the government and in February 1380 the determining powers of the commission were considerably extended,[22] but in general the petitions had little effect: numbers

[17] B. H. Putnam, *Proceedings before the Justices of the Peace in the Fourteenth and Fifteenth Centuries* (London, 1938), pp. xxxvi–lvii; 'The Transformation of the Keepers of the Peace into the Justices of the Peace, 1327–1380', *T.R.H.S.*, 4th series xii (1929), pp. 19–48.

[18] *R.P.*, iii, pp. 24, 65.

[19] *R.P.*, iii, pp. 286, 302; cf. *C.Cl.R., 1389–92*, p. 515. In 1393 the king promised to issue no further such commissions before the next parliament, but specifically excepted two commissions already issued, one of them to investigate the murder of Edmund Clippesby in Norfolk—see n. 31 below.

[20] In Norfolk, for instance, 65 commissions (excluding peace and subsidy commissions) were enrolled between 1377 and 1387; only 32 between 1388 and 1399.

[21] *R.P.*, iii, pp. 44, 65–6, 83–5.

[22] *R.P.*, iii, pp. 83–5; Putnam, *Proceedings*, pp. cxlvii–viii.

223

continued to rise and associations to be made, while there is no evidence that the J.P.s were paid.

The shock of the Peasants' Revolt and the growing authority of the court weakened pressure for change, but the parliaments of the years after 1387 show that the attitude of the commons had not altered. During and immediately after the rule of the Appellants petitions were enacted which greatly modified the peace commissions in ways sought by the commons since the beginning of the reign. New powers were granted, payment of wages was begun, and the demand for small commissions composed of 'sufficient knights, squires and men of law in the country' was agreed to and, in fact, implemented in all commissions issued from 1389.[23] Only in their attempt to exclude magnates and their stewards from the commissions were the commons unsuccessful. Although they were omitted from the 1389 commissions the statute of 1388 excluding stewards was repealed in 1390, while in November 1390 a commons petition requesting the nomination of J.P.s in parliament was enacted only with the proviso that to each commission so named there were to be added 'the lords assigned in this parliament'.[24] Consequently one or two lords were added to each of the commissions issued in December 1390.

The peace commission does not figure largely in the records of Richard's later parliaments. The crown made no attempt to add to the commission by association or to extend the number of justices. The addition of large numbers of court magnates to the commissions issued in November 1397 suggests that the king was alive to the potential political significance of the J.P.s but it was apparently the sheriffs whom he saw as the main agents for the implementation of royal policy, and the accusations against him in 1399 include no reference to the treatment of the peace commissions.

★   ★   ★

An examination of the personnel of local government in East

---

[23] Monk of Westminster, p. 191; *Statutes of the Realm*, ii, pp. 58–9, 62, 77; J. A. Tuck, 'The Cambridge Parliament of 1388', *E.H.R.*, lxxxiv (1969), pp. 225–43; Putnam, *Proceedings*, pp. xxiv–v; R. L. Storey, above, pp. 131–52.

[24] *R.P.*, iii, pp. 269, 279–80; *Statutes of the Realm*, ii, pp. 62, 77.

Anglia during the reign of Richard II should illuminate the disputes between king, magnates and gentry over the administration of the shires and show in some detail how decisions of the crown and parliament were put into effect. Any account of changes in the personnel of local offices and commissions, however, needs to be prefaced by some comments on the structure of private authority in the region—the local sources of power and patronage—and this is peculiarly difficult to define for East Anglia in this period. After 1381 the region was not, as in some other periods, dominated by one or two great magnates.[25] The great estates of the Bigods, which had been granted by Edward I to Thomas of Brotherton, were divided until 1382 and then united in the hands of an elderly widow, Margaret Marshal, countess of Norfolk, who appears to have been a woman of spirit and energy but could not wield the same direct authority as her Bigod predecessors or Mowbray successors.[26] Her grandson and heir, Thomas Mowbray, succeeding his brother as earl of Nottingham in 1383, held little land in East Anglia and there is no evidence that he was active there before 1397. He never had seisin of the lands of his grandmother, who died in 1399 while he was in exile. The vacuum was filled in the early years of the reign by William Ufford, earl of Suffolk, who by marriage added to his own substantial estates a large part of the Brotherton inheritance, including the castles of Bungay and Framlingham. From the 1370s he settled at Framlingham and his active role in commissions and widespread connections among the East Anglian nobility and gentry suggest that he played a major part in the politics and government of the two counties.[27] When he died without heirs in January 1382 his wife's estates reverted to her aunt, Margaret Marshal, whilst the earldom and the lands appurtenant

[25] Biographical information on the magnates is drawn, unless otherwise noted, mainly from the *Dictionary of National Biography* and G.E.C., *The Complete Peerage* (2nd edn. 1910–58).

[26] Margaret was active in the pursuit of her rights, as is clear from the number of petitions presented by her and the special commissions issued to deal with her complaints—e.g. P.R.O., Ancient Petitions (S.C.8), files 19/938–48, 125/6209–11, 129/6440; *R.P.*, iii, pp. 30, 127; *C.P.R., 1377–81*, pp. 95, 303; *1381–5*, pp. 79, 260, 352, *1385–1389*, p. 85.

[27] Among his feoffees, executors and legatees were Sir Robert Ufford, Sir William Wingfield, Sir John White, Reynold Eccles, Robert Ashfield, Roger Wolferston and Ralph Walsham, each of whom played an important part in the administration of Norfolk and Suffolk, (Lambeth Palace, Register of Archbishop Courtenay, fos. 191–4).

to it escheated to the crown. His position in the region was only partly filled by Michael de la Pole, whose estates in the area, acquired through marriage, were a less important factor in his authority than was his position as chancellor and royal favourite. He secured grants of a number of the escheated Ufford estates or their reversion and finally, in 1385, the earldom of Suffolk, but his period of dominance seems to have left few traces in East Anglian affairs, though his attack on Bishop Despenser of Norwich in the 1383 parliament may well have been partly inspired by local rivalry.[28] De la Pole's fall from power in 1386–7 again left East Anglia leaderless; his son only received livery of his full inheritance in 1397 and, though active in local affairs from the 1390s, never had the authority of the previous two earls.

Other magnates, of course, had power in the region. The duke of Lancaster held extensive lands and liberties in north Norfolk: his estate officials were men of substance and both he and they sat on many commissions in the shire. He had close ties with a number of the leading gentlemen of Norfolk and Suffolk, a network of alliances which appears to have played a substantial part, for instance, in elections of knights of the shire.[29] The earls of Arundel, March and Oxford, too, all held considerable estates in the region but there is no evidence that they had much political authority there during this period. More important, judging from his appearance on commissions in the 1390s, was Edward, earl of Rutland.[30] Of the spiritual lords the abbot of Bury St Edmunds had extensive jurisdiction over a large part of the population of Suffolk and his lay officials were men of authority in the region. But it is likely that the most important figure in the region after 1388 was Bishop Despenser, who, besides his ecclesiastical position and

[28] *R.P.*, iii, pp. 152–8,
[29] His East Anglian officials included Sir John White, Thomas Pinchbek, Edmund Gournay, Edmund Clippesby, John Heth and Robert Cayley, all active in East Anglian administration (R. Somerville, *The History of the Duchy of Lancaster* (London, 1953) i, pp. 367, 377–8). For local Lancastrian influence, particularly in parliamentary elections, see E. L. John, 'The Parliamentary Representation of Norfolk and Suffolk, 1377–1422', unpublished Nottingham M.A. thesis 1959, 2 vols., i, pp. 24–6, 64–7, and 'Sir Thomas Erpingham', *Norfolk Archaeology*, xxxv (1) (1970), pp. 96–108.
[30] There is no evidence that Rutland held any lands in the region or any local office before 1397, though he was admiral of the north from March 1391. He may have held an important wardship or stewardship.

the wealth and patronage it brought, had great influence at court, where his brother, Thomas, was one of the leading intimates and councillors of the king. Although his clerical status kept him off most commissions, he must have played a central role in East Anglian politics. The episodes of his quarrel with Lynn and with his own cathedral priory are well-known, but it is only occasionally that the records make clear his involvement in local faction.[31]

Local politics were not, however, wholly concerned with the enmities and alliances of the great lords. The government of the shire was for the most part in the hands of lesser men and it was, in the absence of a dominant magnate, their individual and communal interests that formed the stuff of local politics and of the relations between the local community and the crown. This governing group can be partly reconstructed from appointments to offices and commissions. If we take as a criterion appointment to the offices of sheriff and escheator, election as knight of the shire, appointment to the commission of the peace or membership of other commissions, some one hundred and seventy men helped to govern Norfolk during the reign of Richard II.[32] Excluding the assize judges, of whom eight held office during the reign, they can be divided into five broad categories. At the top were the great magnates already mentioned whose local role was a basis for and a reflection of their role in national affairs. Secondly, there were a number of barons—the successive Lords Bardolf, Morley and Scales, and Lord Willoughby—and their near equals, men like Sir

[31] F. Blomefield, *An Essay towards a Topographical History of the County of Norfolk*, 2nd edn. (London, 1805–10), iii, pp. 515–25. It is clear from the indictments on the case that Despenser was involved in the murder of Edmund Clippesby in 1392 and that this incident was connected with faction in the shire but its implications are not altogether clear (*R.P.*, iii, p. 302; *C.P.R., 1391–6*, p. 234; P.R.O., King's Bench, Ancient Indictments (K.B.9) file 173 (1)/14–28; Plea Rolls (K.B.27) roll 531, rex, rot.1).

[32] Only the government of Norfolk has been analysed in detail: the situation in Suffolk was not dissimilar, though fewer men were involved. All the commissions enrolled on the patent rolls have been analysed, together with the subsidy commissions enrolled on the fine rolls. See *C.P.R., C.F.R.* and the typescript list in the Public Record Office of the uncalendared assize and gaol delivery commissions on the patent rolls. Information on the sheriffs is taken from *P.R.O. Lists and Indexes*, ix: *List of Sheriffs of England and Wales* (1898) and the names of escheators from the typescript 'List of Escheators' in the Public Record Office. Only a few under-sheriffs and coroners are known from this period and these are omitted from the statistics save when they also performed other duties; the many men who sat on only one commission during the reign are also omitted from the calculations.

Thomas Morieux, Sir William Elmham and Sir Robert Knolles, who were much involved in war, diplomacy and national politics and who, though often appointed to important commissions, took little active part in their work. There were, perhaps, fifteen of these. Thirdly, and most important, there were the 'buzones' of the shire, of whom there were some fifty during the reign as a whole but only about fifteen active at any one time. Three-quarters of these men were still at this time belted knights—men like Sir Stephen Hales, Sir Robert Berney and Sir Ralph Shelton, the heads of a comparatively small group of families who filled the most important shire offices, were appointed to the more important commissions, attended the shire court and no doubt saw themselves as representing the community of the shire.[33] The fourth group, mainly lawyers and administrators, often acting as counsel, executors and feoffees, were the main working members of the commission of the peace and of most other commissions; sometimes knights of the shire or sheriffs, more often J.P.s and escheators. There were some thirty of these men often moving into the class above them but rarely knighted: men like Edmund Gournay, local steward of the duchy of Lancaster, counsel to Norwich and Lynn, a working J.P. in the county and on numerous commissions until his death in 1387.[34] The fifth group consists of the sixty or so men of varying status but mostly lesser gentlemen, who sat on occasional commissions and sometimes filled minor offices but played only a small part in local affairs.

It was these men then, particularly those of the third and fourth groups, numbering, even in one of the most populous counties of England, no more than about forty or fifty men at any one time, who carried out the work of local government and whose interests and attitudes were, when not distorted by undue influence of crown or magnates, represented by the knights of the shire in parliament.

Nineteen men served as sheriff of Norfolk and Suffolk during

[33] By far the most active of this group was Sir Stephen Hales, who besides acting as sheriff, J.P. and knight of the shire was appointed to twenty-four commissions during the reign.

[34] D. Gurney, *Records of the House of Gurney* (London, 1848), pp. 279, 286, 357–58. Others of this group who were particularly active in local affairs were Robert Cayley, Simon Baret, Robert Martham and Nicholas Massingham: all of them seem to have been lawyers.

the period.[35] All except Geoffrey Michell, who served from March to December 1387, appear to have been resident knights or squires with adequate 'lyvelode' in one of the counties, most of them among the leading figures of the region.[36] Eleven were elected as knight of the shire during the reign, ten were J.P.s and all but three were on local commissions, some on very many. In these counties at least there is no evidence of the appointment by the king of unqualified outsiders, save perhaps in 1387. The same is true of the escheators of whom there were fourteen during the reign.[37] Apart from John Knyvett (sheriff 1391–2, escheator 1394–5) no man filled both offices and the escheators were usually men of lower status. All, however, seem to have been resident members of the governing class of the two shires: six were J.P.s and virtually all sat on commissions.

The commons' petitions of the reign complained particularly against the non-observance of statutes limiting these officials' term of office. In Norfolk and Suffolk during the first ten years of the reign no sheriff served a second term, but three escheators held office for two or more years. Thus the government's promise made in the 1378 parliament was kept, at least for these officials. It is, unfortunately, impossible to say whether the same was true for their deputies. The events of 1386–7 produced a practice as regards the escheator, more in accordance with the commons' demands: between 1386 and 1392 there was an annual change in this office. Curiously enough, however, in Norfolk and Suffolk, though in no other counties, the sheriff appointed in November 1387, Thomas Curson, was continued in office for another year by the Appellants. It is unlikely that this reversal of recent practice had any political significance. Curson was not a man of the first rank but he may have been an able administrator for he filled the office again from November 1395 to Easter 1397.[38] It is clear that

[35] Those who did not account and did not die during their term of office are presumed not to have taken up their duties and are not included among the nineteen.

[36] Michel was domiciled in Essex, where he was sheriff from 1390 to 1391, but he had a certain amount of property in Suffolk (*C.Cl.R., 1377–81*, pp. 350, 354 etc.; *C.P.R., 1381–5*, p. 582).

[37] Again, those not accounting have been excluded from this number.

[38] Thomas Curson of Foulsham, Norfolk, was the brother of William Curson, escheator 1383–6, and in 1397 returned his nephew, Sir John Curson, as knight of the shire for Norfolk, John, 'Parliamentary Representation', i, p. 233; W. P. Baildon, ed., *Select Cases in Chancery* (Selden Society vol. x, 1896), p. 20 ff.

the crown had been finding it difficult to appoint suitable men as sheriffs in these counties: the allowances made on the sheriffs' farm were apparently insufficient and there were several complaints in and out of parliament that a sheriff might be impoverished by his term of office.[39] In the autumn of 1385 the original nominee, Sir Edmund Reynham, had to be replaced by Sir Ralph Bygot, and in the following year two nominees, Sir Edmund Thorpe and Sir Thomas Berney, refused to serve and the office was not filled until half-way through the financial year when Geoffrey Michell was appointed.[40] The situation recurred in 1388 when Curson was only re-appointed after the unsuccessful nomination of Sir John Tuddenham.[41] Berney and Tuddenham had earlier received letters patent exempting them from the obligation to perform such duties.[42] Curson's re-appointment was an exception, although the tendency to appoint men of lower status (only three of the eight sheriffs from 1388 to 1399 were knights compared with nine out of eleven up to 1387) suggests continuing difficulty in filling the office. Until 1397 sheriffs continued to be changed annually but there was a tendency for the escheators to revert to longer terms: Simon Baret served between 1392 and 1394 and Roger Cavendish (in Suffolk alone) between 1395 and 1397. So East Anglian practice only partly justifies the terms of the petition of 1397. The last years of the reign, however, show, as in many other shires, a quite different pattern. On 1 December 1396 Robert Ashfield, a Suffolk gentleman, probably a lawyer, was appointed to succeed Thomas Curson as sheriff. In fact, he never accounted and it is unlikely that he served, for in May 1397 the office was given to William Rees, who had been knight of the shire for Norfolk in the parliament that had just been dissolved.[43] Rees was a retainer of the earl marshal, by now deeply committed to the king's party.[44] In July the

[39] Petitions concerning the Norfolk and Suffolk allowances were presented via the commons in the parliaments of 1385 and 1398—R.P., iii, pp. 221, 321. Individual sheriffs also petitioned the council for relief, among them Sir John Ulveston (sheriff 1382–3) and Sir Robert Carbonell (sheriff 1390–1), P.R.O., Ancient Petitions (S.C.8), file 29, no. 6421; Exchequer: Council and Privy Seal (E.28), file 3, no. 43.

[40] C.F.R., 1383–91, pp. 107, 151–2.   [41] C.F.R., 1383–91, p. 249

[42] C.P.R., 1381–5, p. 537; 1385–9, p. 63.

[43] C.F.R., 1391–9, p. 197. Ashfield was certainly still alive in 1398—Norfolk and Norwich Record Office, Consistory Court of Norwich will registers, 246 Harsyk.

[44] Cal. Inquis. Misc., 1392–9, nos. 387, 391.

earl marshal was added to the Norfolk commission of the peace for the first time and in the autumn he was rewarded for his part in the attack on the Appellants by the title of duke of Norfolk, while Rees was re-appointed sheriff for the following year. In spite of the duke of Norfolk's later disgrace Rees was again appointed sheriff in November 1398, having clearly shown himself subservient to the king's demands over the previous two years.

It is possible that such subservience included the return of knights of the shire favourable to the king in the parliament of November 1397. It is not possible to bring much evidence to support the allegations made in 1388 that the king appointed sheriffs to return knights favoured by him. The names of the knights returned for Norfolk and Suffolk to parliaments in the 1380s do not show any sure signs of court pressure, though it is true that some, particularly Sir Stephen Hales (seven times knight for Norfolk between 1380 and 1386), had been retainers of the Black Prince, and Sir William Wingfield (seven times knight for Suffolk between 1378 and 1386) was closely connected with Michael de la Pole.[45] The most radical change in representation took place at the elections to the Merciless Parliament when the two previous knights for Norfolk, Hales and Sir Thomas Gerberge, steward to the duke of York, were succeeded by two Lancastrian retainers, Sir John White and Sir John Strange: Wingfield was also replaced. The returns of September 1397, however, are more suggestive of court influence. Rees returned two courtiers, Nicholas Dagworth and Edmund Thorpe, for Norfolk and Robert Bukton, steward of Thomas Percy, soon to be earl of Worcester, for Suffolk: Sir William Elmham, who would have been the natural court choice for Suffolk, was not available and Rees returned Sir William Berdwell. Berdwell was probably a retainer of Michael de la Pole who in the ensuing parliament was to regain most of his inheritance.

Thus it is possible that the appointment of Rees as sheriff in May 1397 was useful in securing knights of the shire amenable to the king's purposes. There is no evidence, however, that this was an important factor in the appointment of sheriffs either in the early or the last years of the reign, though the king was certainly alive

[45] Information on these and other knights of the shire is mainly derived from John, 'Parliamentary Representation', op. cit.

to the political as well as the administrative advantage of appointing malleable, dependent sheriffs in both periods.

The evidence for appointments of justices of the peace comes from the commissions on the dorse of the patent rolls. For Norfolk and Suffolk, as for other counties, such commissions are not enrolled at regular intervals. Between 1377 and 1399 seventeen commissions were enrolled for Norfolk, nineteen for Suffolk. Four commissions were enrolled between 1377 and 1382 for each shire, with a number of associations. A few associations followed but no full commission was enrolled for Norfolk until 1386, for Suffolk until 1387. In each county there were eight commissions enrolled between 1388 and 1394, but no more until a new period of frequent commissions begins in 1397.[46] In spite of the irregular gaps it is probably safe to conclude that the enrolments give an accurate picture of the membership of the commissions. In the Tudor period and perhaps in the fifteenth century also, it was common for commissions to be issued but not enrolled,[47] but it is clear from the associations that this did not happen in the first part of the reign, and surviving records of the activities of the J.P.s provide no evidence that such a practice existed in the later years.[48]

Neither in Norfolk nor in Suffolk did the composition of the commissions issued on 2 July 1377 show much change from the previous commissions, though the men since associated, who included Gaunt's steward, Sir Thomas Hungerford, were all omitted. The petitions of the commons in the parliaments of 1378 and 1379 appear to have had little effect, as Hungerford and five other men were added to the Norfolk commission by association early in 1378 and no full commission was issued until May 1380. It is true that in that year there was a substantial change of personnel, particularly in Norfolk, where ten members of the old commission (including all five associated since 1377) were omitted and the total numbers of J.P.s fell from eighteen to twelve, but numbers remained well above the six or seven that the commons had

---

[46] References to particular commissions may be found in the indexes to the Calendars of Patent Rolls: there is no index reference to the 1394 commission for Norfolk, (*C.P.R., 1391–6*, p. 43).

[47] A. H. Smith and T. G. Barnes, 'Justices of the Peace from 1558 to 1688: a Revised List of Sources', *B.I.H.R.*, xxxii (1959), pp. 221–42: Putnam, *Proceedings*, pp. 3–7.

[48] See below, note 66.

demanded and there is little evidence of a change in the type of
J.P. appointed. Indeed, the addition of the duke of Lancaster to
the Norfolk commission flouted the commons' request for the exclusion of magnates, though it is true that it was accompanied by
the omission of Lord Bardolf.[49] The Peasants' Rising in East
Anglia saw attacks made on many of the J.P.s, particularly those who
were active. Apart from Chief Justice Cavendish, Reynold Eccles
was killed by the rebels, Edmund Gournay and John Holkam
had to flee for their lives, and a number of others, particularly the
lawyers, had their property pillaged.[50] It is not surprising that there
was a large turnover when the commissions of 20 December 1382
were issued. Numbers rose in each county to fifteen and fourteen
respectively, but there does seem to have been an attempt to
appoint men of higher status: with the exception of Edmund
Clippesby, steward of the duchy of Lancaster in Norfolk, and
Hemmyng Leget, a royal clerk, together with a new assize judge,
all those added to the two commissions were knights or resident
barons.[51] Many of them also served on the commission of oyer and
terminer which was issued the following day.[52]

It was three and a half years before the next Norfolk commission
was issued, though there had been three associations in the interval,
two of them clearly intended to act for Lynn.[53] The new commission of 24 April 1386 contained no fewer than eighteen names:
it omitted four members of the 1382 commission (two of whom
had died) together with the three men who had been associated
with it, but added the chancellor, the earl of Suffolk, together with
Thomas, Lord Morley, and five men of lower status of whom
three at least were lawyers.[54] The 1382 commission had been short
of such men and the new commission was well balanced, including

[49] R.P., iii, pp. 275. Bardolf was apparently not an active J.P. (C.Cl.R., 1389–92,
p. 91).
[50] A. Réville, Le Soulèvement des Travailleurs d'Angleterre en 1381 (Paris, 1898),
pp. 69, 78, 81, 93, 97–98, 105–6 etc.
[51] For Leget see Tout, Chapters, iv, p. 332; Blomefield, v, p. 308.
[52] C.P.R., 1381–5, p. 247.
[53] John Burnham and John Waryn of Lynn, together with John Pagrave, were
associated to the commission in July 1383 and John Methwold, a lawyer, in March
1386 (C.P.R., 1381–5, p. 349, 1385–9, p. 168).
[54] James Billingford, clerk of the crown in chancery, William Snettisham and
Geoffrey Somerton were certainly lawyers; the other two were John Curson who
probably was not, and John Spark of whom little has been discovered.

two great magnates, Lancaster and Suffolk, two local barons, Morley and Scales, the two assize judges, five of the most powerful knights of the county and seven men of lesser rank, most of whom were lawyers.

Suffolk had to wait until April 1387 for a new commission to be issued, perhaps because the chancellor was already a J.P. there. Fifteen men were appointed: as with Norfolk this was the largest commission of the reign, though associations had in fact raised the original fourteen of the 1382 commission to eighteen. All the four associated members were omitted from the new commission and there was one additional menber, Edmund Lakingheath, a lawyer and an official of the abbey of Bury St Edmunds.[55] There is no indication in the personnel or in that of the few other commissions issued during the year of any effects of the impeachment of De la Pole and of his replacement as chancellor by Bishop Arundel. Nor does there seem to be any political motive behind the decision to issue another new commission on 24 July 1387. This does show many changes but it still includes De la Pole and its main purpose seems to have been to reduce the size of the commission and to add more lawyers: seven men were omitted, including five knights, and were replaced by Sir John Ulveston, William atte Lee, a servant of Margaret Marshal, and two lawyers, John Staverton and John Glemham.[56]

The political role of the J.P.s was not sufficiently important for the Appellants to find it necessary to issue a new commission for Suffolk—or most other counties—in 1388. But one of only five new commissions issued in July 1388 was for Norfolk and this, as might be expected, saw the biggest turnover of personnel during the reign. Only four of the 1386 commission survived: Lord Morley, Sir Stephen Hales and Sir Ralph Shelton, two of the most active knights, and the chancery clerk, James Billingford. Of the others two of the lawyers had already been dismissed from the commission—Somerton in July 1386 and Snettisham in April 1387—for reasons unknown;[57] Lord Scales, Sir Robert Howard,

[55] The associated J.P.s were John (probably Robert) Carbonnel and William Berard (1383), Sir Andrew Cavendish (1384) and John Methwold (1386)—*C.P.R., 1381–5*, p. 244, *1385–9*, p. 168. Cavendish was dismissed in May 1385, having been appointed sheriff in the previous November—*C.Cl.R., 1381–5*, p. 635.

[56] For atte Lee's connection with Margaret Marshal, see *C.P.R., 1381–5*, p. 456.

[57] *C.P.R., 1381–9*, pp. 167, 223.

Sir John Clifton and Edmund Gournay were dead; the duke of Lancaster was abroad and the earl of Suffolk and the judges, Holt and Thirning, in exile, whilst William Elmham had been imprisoned by the Merciless Parliament: there is no obvious reason for the omission of John Spark, John Curson and Nicholas Massingham. The new J.P.s were the two assize judges, and four, possibly five lawyers, all of whom were active in local administration. They included Edmund Clippesby, former steward of the duchy of Lancaster in Norfolk, and John Gournay, son of a Lancastrian servant, and himself steward of the Norfolk estates of the earl of Arundel. These are the only signs of political implications in the new appointments.[58]

The next commissions for both shires, as for most others, were issued in July 1389 as a result of the legislation of the Cambridge parliament and the formal assumption of royal authority by the king in May 1389. In both Norfolk and Suffolk substantial changes in personnel took place, mainly as a result of the reduction in the number of J.P.s in each county to eight and the exclusion of all lords and their stewards. At last the aims of the commons since the beginning of the reign were embodied in statute: as a consequence both the size and the composition of the commissions remained fairly stable in each county until the last years of the reign. Seven members of the Norfolk commission of 1388 were dropped—Lord Morley, Sir Ralph Shelton and five of the lesser men, including Gournay and Clippesby. Although Morley's connections with the duke of Gloucester and those of Shelton, John Gournay and Edmund Clippesby with Lancaster might suggest a political motive for some of these changes, other reasons were more significant.[59] Morley was omitted in accordance with the general policy of excluding lords from the commission and John Gournay, and possibly Edmund Clippesby, were debarred by the statute excluding lords' stewards: possibly some of the others—Shelton, James Billingford, Richard Gegge and Robert Martham—were omitted for the same reason. Nor do the names of the new J.P.s, Sir Miles Stapleton, Sir Reginal Hakebeche, and the assize judge,

[58] For Gournay see John, 'Parliamentary Representation', i, pp. 356–64. The other new men were Simon Baret, Robert Martham and Richard Gegge.
[59] For Morley see *Complete Peerage*, ix, p. 216; for Shelton see John, 'Parliamentary Representation', ii, pp. 561–70.

John Cassy, appear to have any political significance.[60] In Suffolk where there had been no new commission since 1387 there was naturally an even greater change. Only the two lawyers, Glemham and Staverton, of the previous commission remained and the omission of the two powerful knights, Sir Richard Waldegrave and Sir William Wingfield, is particularly surprising. Wingfield may have been in bad odour through his connections with the disgraced earl of Suffolk and it is possible that Waldegrave was considered ineligible as steward of the queen's estates. Robert Hotot, steward of the queen's East Anglian estates, William atte Lee and Edmund Lakingheath, were no doubt also omitted as stewards.[61] Six new J.P.s were appointed to take the number to the statutory eight—the two assize judges, two knights, Sir George Felbrigge and Sir John Tuddenham, Hugh Fastolf, the London and Yarmouth merchant, now keeper of Lowestoft, and Robert Ashfield.

Waldegrave and Wingfield were not off the commission for long. In November 1389 both were added to the new commissions which restored to the J.P.s determining power over felonies; they replaced John Glemham and Sir John Tuddenham. In Norfolk there were similar changes. Sir Miles Stapleton had already in September been ordered not to carry out the duties of the office—it would be interesting to know why—and he was omitted from the November commission, together with Hakebeche and Thomas Pinchbek.[62] In their places Shelton and Martham were restored to the bench, together with Sir Robert Berney, another Lancastrian retainer, who had apparently recently returned from France.[63] The reason for these changes is not altogether clear but the inclusion of the two Lancastrian retainers, Shelton and Berney, suggests that they might in part have been due to the imminent return of John of Gaunt. Waldegrave and Wingfield were such dominant figures in Suffolk that it may have been found impos-

[60] Thomas Pinchbek remained a J.P. though he had ceased to be an assize judge on the eastern circuit in May 1389.

[61] For Waldegrave see J. S. Roskell, 'Sir Richard Waldegrave of Bures St Mary', *Proceedings of the Suffolk Institute of Archaeology*, xxvii (1957), pp. 154–75; for Wingfield see John, 'Parliamentary Representation', ii, pp. 682–700; for Hotot's position see P.R.O. Ministers' Accounts (S.C.6), no. 996/15.

[62] *C.Cl.R., 1389–92*, p. 32. Pinchbek was restored to the commission from December 1390 to June 1394, perhaps owing to his duchy of Lancaster offices (Somerville, *Duchy of Lancaster*, i, pp. 367, 373).

[63] For Berney, see John, 'Parliamentary Representation', i, pp. 158–72.

sible to provide effective government without their participation. They were returned together to the ensuing parliament of January 1390.

The legislation of this parliament, including the repeal of the clause of 1388 debarring lords' stewards from the commission of the peace, necessitated new commissions which were issued in June. These showed few changes in personnel: the Suffolk commission was unchanged, even though one of the J.P.s, Hugh Fastolf, was now sheriff, and in Norfolk there was only one—the replacement of the assize judge, Cassy, by John Methwold, who by 1391 was steward of the Norfolk lands of the duchy of Lancaster.[64] Numbers remained the same—eight in each shire. The commissions issued on 24 December 1390 in response to the commons' demand for their nomination in parliament again showed very few changes: Pinchbek and Hotot returned to the Norfolk and Suffolk commissions respectively in place of Shelton and Ashfield, whilst, as in most other counties, a magnate—the duke of Lancaster—was added to each commission.

Apart from the addition of a further magnate, the earl of Rutland, to both commissions in December 1391, the commission in both Norfolk and Suffolk remained very stable, both in numbers and general composition during the next five years. Individuals came and went, sometimes for no very obvious reasons, but the balance remained the same. During the whole period from 1389 the statutory requirements of the parliaments of 1388 and 1390 were observed: in each shire there were, apart from the magnates and assize judges, only six J.P.s—three knights and three lawyers at the beginning of the period, two knights and four lawyers from December 1390 in Norfolk, from February 1392 in Suffolk. The evidence suggests that most of these men took an active part in the work of quarter sessions.[65]

The working commission of six, together with the assize

---

[64] Norfolk and Norwich Record Office: Gressenhall Mss 241 × 3. Cassy returned to the commission in December 1391.

[65] The Pipe Rolls have not been searched for payments made to J.P.s but some indentures for payments made in the 1390s survive (P.R.O., Various Accounts (E.101), no. 575/29). Indictments taken before named J.P.s survive in King's Bench, Plea Rolls (K.B.27), rolls 516, *rex*, rot. 17, 515, *rex*, rot. 3d, 520, *rex*, rot. 1d, 4 etc., and Ancient Indictments (K.B.9), file 168/79, 180/24 etc. Simon Baret was the most active in Norfolk and was probably *custos rotulorum* (K.B. 9/168/1, 78).

judges, remained stable during the last years of the reign, but from December 1396 there were more changes in the composition of the commission, an aspect of the growing political unease. Between December 1396 and July 1397 Norfolk and Suffolk each received two new commissions. The first of these saw several changes, some of them due to the deaths of former J.P.s, and the return of the earl of Rutland to the Suffolk commission from which he had been omitted in 1394.[66] According to Dr Steel the commissions appointed in July 1397 just after the beginning of the king's action against the Appellants, were particularly royalist,[67] but there is little evidence of this in East Anglia where the only notable change was the addition of the earl marshal to the Norfolk commission for the first time, a sign of his increasing favour with the king. The events of the late summer, however, brought a new look to the commissions issued for virtually all counties in November 1397. In Norfolk, as in many other counties, the most striking change is an increase in the size of the commission. The number of 'working' J.P.s remained at eight, but they were supplemented by no fewer that five dukes, for to Lancaster and the earl marshal, now promoted duke of Norfolk, were added the duke of York and two more of the 'duketti', Albemarle and Exeter. The number of these men, who can have played little part in the ordinary work of the J.P.s, is indicative of a temporary change in the character of the peace commission which was now clearly intended to help to establish the authority of the court. The Suffolk commission had fewer dukes: Norfolk was made a J.P. there with Albemarle, but Lancaster, who had little Suffolk land, was omitted. The significant additions were those of the powerful councillor and speaker of the commons, Sir John Bushy, chief steward of the duchy of Lancaster north of the Trent, and of Gilbert Debenham, probably, like most of his family, a client of the Mowbrays.[68] Among the three omitted was Sir Richard Waldegrave, presumably for reasons of age.

[66] Rutland's omission in 1394 may have been due to his imminent departure for Ireland. His restoration to both commissions in 1396–7 may be explained by his custody of Queen Anne's lands in East Anglia and by his marriage to Lady Fitzwalter.

[67] A. B. Steel, *Richard II* (Cambridge, 1941), p. 234.

[68] W. I. Haward, 'Gilbert Debenham: a Medieval Rascal in Real Life', *History*, xiii (1928–9), pp. 300–14.

The November commissions lasted for a year. The disgrace of the duke of Norfolk produced the need for a revision of the peace commission and in November 1398 Lancaster replaced him on the Suffolk commission, while Debenham was replaced by another courtier, John Russell, who had married a Suffolk heiress.[69] Norfolk did not receive a new commission until February 1399, by which time Lancaster was dead: he and the duke of Norfolk were replaced by the young Lord Bardolf. In the following month a new commission for Suffolk added the earl of Suffolk, recently restored to most of his inheritance, in place of Lancaster.

Even in these last years the changes were mainly among the 'political' members of the commission: the working members were replaced only occasionally after 1390. The form of local government established in the parliaments of 1388–90 lasted the reign, and the change of dynasty, apart from removing the dukes from the commission, changed it little.

It is unnecessary to deal in such detail with other commissions and offices, which were by their nature less affected by national political controversies. Undoubtedly local faction played a part in appointments to some of them but it is rarely possible to show what effect this might have had. Apart from the general commissions of oyer and terminer of 1382, which contained a large number of the leading knights and gentlemen of the two shires, as did certain array, subsidy and sewers commissions, most were issued to some four to eight men of varying rank, only two or three of whom, usually those of the lawyer-administrator class, carried out the work. As has previously been shown, the number and activity of such commissions were greatest in the 1380s; they became fewer and more restricted in scope with the establishment of the powerful peace commissions between 1388 and 1390.

The study of the peace commission and officials in Norfolk and Suffolk suggests no simple connection between what was decided in parliament and council and what was local practice. The commons' demands for annual change in the office of sheriff would not have been of passionate concern to the East Anglian gentry: in both counties it was normal for a new, qualified resident sheriff

[69] Russell's wife was the widow of Sir John Wingfield and he appears to have continued to hold much of her land after her death in 1397 (Norfolk and Norwich Record Office, Consistory Court of Norwich: Register 243–44 Harsyk).

to be appointed each year. When this did not occur, as in 1
1388, the reason was probably the inability of the crown to
suitable and willing candidate. On the other hand the
practice regarding the appointment of escheators clearly
political change. From 1377 to 1386 and again from 1392 to
two or three years were common: in the period of royal
ness that intervened the escheator was changed annually. The
if not the membership of the commission of the peace wa
larly affected by political change. The early years of the reig
few of the commons' demands adequately implemented
though the 1381 crisis eventually produced a list of J.P.s
save in numbers, was much closer to that demanded by the
mons, they were deprived of important jurisdiction. The immediate results of the crisis of 1386–8 were small and there is no sign
of the Appellants using local government appointments for political purposes, but the new strength of the commons in parliament
produced the eventual triumph during 1389–90 of their concept of
the commission, even though certain concessions had to be made
to the interests of the magnates.

If there was a royal 'policy' towards local government between
1377 and January 1397, whether that of the king or of his advisers,
it was a continuation of the policies of the crown since the thirteenth century or before and not inspired by a new trend towards
an absolute monarchy. Indeed, for most of the period it was
neither king nor magnates who took the initiative in demanding
changes in local government, but the commons in parliament,
representing the knights and gentlemen of the shires. At times of
open conflict between crown and parliament, as in 1386 and 1388,
it is possible—though by no means certain—that the commons
were acting largely under the influence of magnate faction. But at
other times their petitions reflected the attitudes of those groups of
county society which have previously been described, together, of
course, with the views of the leading burgesses. These views on
local government were often at variance with the policy of crown
and magnates: the consequent tension was not, then, just the result
of occasional arbitrary appointments, as the chronicles seem to suggest, but derived from fundamental and enduring differences of
outlook.

The last years of the reign seem to show a different quality in the policies pursued by the crown, and it is difficult not to associate this with the increasingly arbitrary interference in politics of the king himself. There appears a determination to use control of appointments to local offices and commissions, not, as was implied in the answer to Haxey's petition, for the more effective royal supervision of local government, but for the establishment of the king's political security by direct personal involvement of the king and court with the local communities and the aggrandizement of the court magnates at the expense not only of their rivals, but also of the gentlemen of the shires. The Lancastrian revolution ended both this attempt at arbitrary rule and the more persistent royal pressure for control of local justice and administration. The commons' policies were not entirely successful: the number of J.P.s appointed in each county rose steadily during the fifteenth century and included a substantial number of magnates.[70] Indeed, the commons' victory over the crown had inevitably weakened the resistance of local government against the ambitions of the lords. It was more than a century before the re-establishment of royal authority restored effective direct relations between the crown and the local communities, and this in its turn was to produce in the sixteenth and seventeenth centuries a new tension between them.

[70] In Norfolk the average size of the commission rose from just under ten between 1389 and 1399 to 15.6 under Henry VI. Under Edward IV the average jumped to 24.

XII

'A Chaunterie for Soules': London Chantries in the Reign of Richard II

ROSALIND HILL

IN THE HISTORY of the English church during the later middle ages, the position of a secular priest without a cure of souls has always been something of an enigma. It is clear that his services were needed and desired; the evidence of wills shows that it was a most unusual testator who failed to make some provision, whether temporary or permanent, for the saying of masses to speed his soul upon its journey through purgatory.[1] It was not at all uncommon to leave money for a thousand or even more masses to be said (presumably by mass-priests hired for the purpose) during the period immediately after one's death.[2] In addition to this, testators who could afford to do so frequently declared their intention to establish permanent chantries, although their executors often thought otherwise when it came to disbursing the funds.[3] Children regarded it as an act of filial piety to set up a chantry for their parents, guilds (which we may reasonably suppose to have been made up of men of business, unwilling to waste money) established chantries for their deceased brethren, bishops in their visitations laid down strict rules as to how chantries were to be maintained. Yet at the same time satirists were deriding the cantarists and unbeneficed clergy, especially in London, as a notorious source of scandal. Chaucer praised his virtuous Poor Parson as one who would not neglect the duties of his parish in order to seek a

[1] R. R. Sharpe, ed., *Calendar of Wills proved and enrolled in the Court of Husting, London*, ii, (London, 1890) (hereafter cited as C.W.), pp. 228–353.

[2] Guildhall Library, Register of Robert Braybrooke, (hereafter cited as R.B.) fos. 473–5.

[3] Below, p. 252.

chantry at St Paul's,[4] and Piers Plowman blamed the avarice of those priests who took themselves off to London

> to singe ther for Simonye, for selver is swete.[5]

An investigation of bishops' registers in the same period makes it clear that this twofold attitude was not confined to popular opinion, but that it permeated also the rulings of ecclesiastical authorities. As Miss Bertha Putnam showed many years ago, in an essay of remarkable interest,[6] the decree *Effrenata*, by which successive English archbishops attempted to regulate the wages of stipendiary priests, was published three times between 1350 and 1378. In the final edition of this decree, dated 16 November 1378, Archbishop Sudbury castigates these people for their love of expensive pleasures, a passion which showed itself in ornate dress, sophisticated hair-dressing, resort to taverns and gaming-houses and a generally luxurious style of living which was unbecoming to their station. In order to bring the unbeneficed and the cantarists without the cure of souls to a proper sense of the decencies of their calling, he fixed their maximum stipend at seven marks a year.[7] This sum, in deference to the rising cost of living, was two marks more than that which Archbishop Islip had allowed them in 1350,[8] although it was still one mark less than the allowance for a priest who carried the responsibility for a cure of souls.

In the reign of Richard II it would, however, have taken a good deal more than seven marks a year to allow a man to give himself up to even a moderate course of luxurious living, unless he had private means or was unusually and persistently lucky with his dice. Five marks a year had been fixed as the minimum annual stipend for a vicar in 1215, and it is clear that already by the end of the thirteenth century this was not really enough, even by a frugal standard. For example, Bishop Sutton of Lincoln, who died in 1299, never set up a vicarage of which the guaranteed income was not higher than five marks, and he was a man who believed strongly that his clergy should set an example of godly, righteous

---

[4] Chaucer, *Canterbury Tales*, Prologue, ll. 509–10.

[5] *Piers the Plowman*, A text, ed. W. W. Skeat, Prologue, l. 83.

[6] Bertha Putnam, 'Wage-laws for priests after the Black Death', *American Historical Review*, xxi, (1915–16), pp. 12–32.

[7] *Reg. Simonis de Sudbiria* (Canterbury and York Society 1927–38) i, pp. 190–93.

[8] Lambeth Palace Library, Reg. Islip, fo. 188.

and sober living. Prices continued to rise in the fourteenth century, and especially in the second half of it; Archbishop Islip himself complained of the exorbitant cost of living 'especially in the city of London'.[9] When in 1386 Robert Newton, rector of Chiswick, exchanged his church for the chantry of Ralph and Lucy le Fenere in the church of St Benedict Shorhog, the cantarist's stipend of five marks was described as being so 'notably thin' that another chantry had to be added to make it up to a living wage,[10] while in 1392 two chantries in the church of All Hallows, Barking, had to be united 'because of the shortage of suitable chaplains and the dearth of victuals and other things necessary to sustain man's life'.[11] Robert Braybrooke, bishop of London, decided (as is well known) in the course of his visitation of St Paul's that many of the chantries in that cathedral were too poor, and must be united if they were to be properly served. He therefore obtained the king's permission to amalgamate a number of them, putting two and sometimes three together as the responsibility of a single cantarist. By so doing he went far beyond the maximum stipend of seven marks authorized by the archbishop of his own province thirteen years earlier. The combined revenues of the chantries of Richard Gloucester and Richard Foliot, for example, would come to thirteen marks a year, those of Walter Thorp and John of St Olave to twelve, those of Geoffrey Eyton and Philip Fauconberges to fourteen. The dean and chapter of St Paul's signified their approval of these arrangements, which were given full publicity and clearly regarded as entirely right and proper.[12] Braybrooke's register is far from giving the impression that he was a lax or irresponsible bishop. On the contrary, it is clear that he took his duties seriously. In fact by his ruling that henceforward the cantarists of St Paul's 'should live a common and collegiate life in the hall of the chaplains' dwelling commonly known as Presteshous'[13] he was severely restricting any opportunities, which might earlier have come their way, of taking part in those expensive gaieties of the tavern and the gaming-house which Archbishop Subdury had deplored in such fluent invective.

[9] Ibid., fo. 189.   [10] R.B., fo. 109.   [11] R.B., fo. 163.
[12] W. Sparrow Simpson, *Registrum Statutorum et Consuetudinum Ecclesie Cathedralis Sancti Pauli Londonensis* (London, 1873) (hereafter cited as S.S.), pp. 142–48.
[13] S.S., p. 149.

It is clear, then, that while some serious-minded people in the late fourteenth century thought that London was full of irresponsible clerics who were paid too much for doing too little, others, who had at least as good an opportunity to know the facts, thought that it was becoming increasingly difficult to obtain cantarists of the right type because the pay was too low.[14] The problem is an odd one. As Dr Kathleen Wood-Legh has wisely suggested, it is likely that any trouble which arose was due rather to the freelance mass-priest, who hired himself out to say a required number of masses, than to the relatively stable and carefully regulated cantarist.[15] It is difficult to pin down the mass-priest, whose activities Dean Sykes regarded as a potent contributory cause of the Reformation.[16] The cantarists of London, however, have left some traces in the records of the time, and by studying the register of Bishop Braybrooke, who held the see of London from 1382 to 1404, it is possible to find out a little about the kind of men they were, the way in which they were appointed, their resources and their activities. Sometimes this information may be supplemented from the legal and administrative records of the period. If we cannot solve all the problems connected with the cantarists, we may at least be able to see whether there was widespread justification for the charges laid at their door by Sudbury and by Chaucer.

During the twenty-two years of his tenure of the see of London, Braybrooke collated or instituted to chantries on 133 occasions. Of these 107 referred to chantries established in churches which lay within the city of London or its immediate suburbs (as defined by John Stow in his *Survey of London*),[17] and these do not include a very large number of chantries in St Paul's, to which the dean and chapter had the right to appoint candidates of their own choice.[18] Of the 107 London vacancies which appear in the register, 34 were filled by exchange with the incumbents of other livings, of whom 17 were rectors, 16 vicars, and one the priest in charge of a chantry outside the city. Of these 34 men who entered

[14] R.B., fo. 163v.

[15] Kathleen L. Wood-Legh, *Perpetual Chantries in Britain* (Cambridge, 1965), p. 190.

[16] In conversation with the writer he once described mass-priests as 'caterpillars of the Commonwealth'.

[17] John Stow, '*A Survay of London*' (London, 1598).   [18] S.S., p. 146.

into possession of London chantries by way of exchange, 17 came from benefices in the diocese of London, two of them, in fact, from city churches (one was the rector of St Leonard's in Foster Lane and the other the rector of St Mary Mounthaw),[19] and others from churches such as those of Twickenham and Chiswick which lay within a short distance of the city.[20] Of the priests coming in from other dioceses, 5 came from Norwich, 4 from Salisbury, 3 from Ely and one each from Canterbury, Chichester, Lincoln, Rochester and Winchester. Eleven of them were rectors and the rest vicars. The exchanges with the dioceses of Rochester (Greenwich) and Winchester (Bermondsey) did in fact involve migrations over a very short distance.[21] During Braybrooke's episcopate there is no record of an exchange with a man beneficed in the west or north of England, although it is known that such exchanges did, from time to time, take place (in 1374 the vicar of Ampney Crucis in Gloucestershire had exchanged with a cantarist in the church of St Michael, Cornhill).[22]

Four of the priests whose collation or institution did not involve an exchange are known to have come from dioceses other than London. They were John Clerk from Hedon in the diocese of York, William Trendill from the diocese of Norwich, and William Danvers and Ralph Matteshale, both from the diocese of Lincoln.[23] Since no place of origin is assigned to any of the others they had presumably been ordained in the diocese of London. At the end of the fourteenth century a man's patronymic is no longer a reliable guide to the place of his birth; when the families of Felton and Cornwallis had struck deep roots into London soil it is impossible to be sure that men called Scot, Clee or Whitby were not in fact born within the sound of Bow bells. In any case, the majority of Braybrooke's cantarists had names such as Baker, Benet, Green, Slowe or Warde, which give no clue even to the place from which their families originally came. Whatever his birthplace, once he was in possession of his chantry, the London cantarist tended to settle down for some years. The register shows

[19] R.B., fo. 120 and fo. 65.   [20] R.B., fo. 109 and fo. 108v.
[21] R.B., fos. 153, 80.
[22] Reg. Wakefield, fo. 6. I am indebted to P. M. Doody, former research student of Westfield College, for this reference from the register which he is at present editing.
[23] R.B., fos. 110, 222v, 163, 210.

no example of a cantarist playing the 'choppechurche' in the city, although one such example does occur in the diocese, in a chantry at Colchester.[24]

Since no parallel list of men entering into possession of chantries in St Paul's has been found, a complete survey of all the London appointments cannot at this stage be made. From the evidence of the register it appears that a steady, if unremarkable, trickle of beneficed clergy from the dioceses of south-eastern England were coming into London, and that of these men a majority were rectors, who would not of necessity be bound to reside in their parishes. Against these, however, we must set a few London cantarists for whom the exchange meant removal to a vicarage, which would normally have demanded residence, sometimes in a remote country parish such as Harwell in Berkshire or Caldecote in Huntingdonshire.[25]

When a chantry was filled by institution and not by collation the names of the patrons normally appear in the register. In a city church these patrons were most commonly the incumbent (who would have to see a good deal of the cantarist once he was instituted) and a small committee of 'trustworthy men' from among his parishioners. The same group sometimes acted as patrons for more chantries than one. Thus in the church of St Nicholas Shambles the rector, Sir James Band, assisted by Elias Weston, John Dorset and Walter Bean (or Bene), presented candidates both to the chantry established for the souls of Adam and Emma Langley and John Middleton and to that founded on behalf of Cecily Bristol, although in each case they co-opted one extra member, Henry Asselyn for the Langley chantry and Richard Stonham for Cecily Bristol's.[26] Similarly in the church of St Peter Cornhill the rector, assisted by Richard Manhale, John Brickhill, Richard Gregory and John Godard, presented candidates both to the perpetual chantry of Holy Trinity and to the chantry founded by William Elyot of Kingston, citizen and fishmonger of London.[27] When the patronage of a chantry escheated to the king (an exceptional state of affairs in this register) he appears to have been ready to consult local opinion in accordance with the will of the original testator; thus Thomas Bromley was presented to the chantry in

[24] R.B., fos. 89v–90v. [25] R.B., fos. 168v, 171. [26] R.B., fos. 81, 85.
[27] R.B., fos. 118, 194.

the church of St Antony,[28] founded for the soul of Nicholas Bole, late citizen and skinner of London, by the king at the nomination of Thomas Knolles, Richard Odiham, Geoffrey Broke and Walter Newton *quatuor validiorum hominum eiusdem parochie sancti Anto-nini*.[29] Sometimes founders who were themselves members of city guilds stipulated that their guild-brethren should be represented among those entitled to present. Candidates for the chantry in the church of St Matthew, Friday Street, founded by Thomas Worlingworth, citizen and goldsmith, were to be presented by the rector of St Matthew's, Thomas Panton and Thomas Polle, goldsmiths, and two trustworthy parishioners;[30] and Solomon Lawfare, citizen and cutler, had a brother-cutler named Richard Goodchild among the patrons of the chantry which he founded in St Mildred's Poultry.[31] The chantries in Guildhall had been organized earlier into an endowed college of five priests,[32] and presentations to membership of this body were made in Bray-brooke's time by the mayor, assisted by the chamberlain or recorder.[33] The official-principal of the bishop of London acted *ex officio* as patron of a chantry in the church of St Mary at Hill, under the will of its founder John Nazeing.[34] In St Paul's, where the majority of the chantries were in the gift of the dean and chapter, other patrons included Braybrooke himself, the arch-deacon of Colchester, the mayor of London and members of various city guilds.[35] A chantry at the shrine of St Ethelburga in Barking Abbey was founded in 1397 by Sybil Felton, the abbess, on behalf of a rather mixed collection of people, Sybil herself and her successors in office, Margaret Saxham (who co-operated in the founding) and the rest of the nuns of Barking, Joan Felton and Joan Hermesthorpe, Sir Thomas Felton and his parents, and John and Agnes Say. Patronage was to rest with the abbess and her successors in office.[36]

A general consideration of the people who made the presentations

---

[28] Called in the register 'Sancti Antonini'. St Anthony's in Budge Row is meant.

[29] R.B., fo. 214. See also Wood-Legh, op. cit. p. 316.

[30] R.B., fo. 128.　　[31] R.B., fo. 189.

[32] H. T. Riley, ed., *Memorials of London and London Life in xiiith, xivth and xvth Centuries* (London, 1868), pp. 288-90.

[33] R.B., fos. 250, 253.　　[34] R.B., fo. 199v.　　[35] S.S., pp. 145-8.

[36] R.B., fo. 210.

to London chantries would not, therefore, suggest that they were likely to be impressed by the irresponsible place-hunter. Most of them were people of some distinction, at least in their own ward of the city, who had reputations to lose and who would be unlikely to tolerate, much less to put forward, cantarists whose scandalous lives might redound to the discredit of their patrons. Braybrooke's register shows him to have been a conscientious and efficient bishop, who took some pains to enforce good order in his cathedral and diocese, and showed care in the choice of his subordinates. We have no means of judging the quality of spiritual discernment shown by such people as the mayor and the members of the city guilds, but one thing is certain—they were successful men of business who had worked hard and intelligently to gain their own positions, and they expected to see a reasonable return, in the shape of religious duties properly performed and of respectable behaviour, for any money which they might choose to invest in chantries. Moreover, they lived on the spot.

How much, in fact, did it cost to found or to maintain a London chantry in the time of Richard II? As we have seen, it is clear both from Braybrooke's register and from the rulings which he made at St Paul's that Archbishop Sudbury's reissue of the decree *Effrenata* could not be upheld, even in the official *acta* of the suffragans of his own province. The register suggests that a salaried cantarist in the city could look for an annual income of about ten marks, rather less than he would obtain if he were lucky enough to be instituted to one of the newly-combined chantries in St Paul's. Thus Agnes Preston, widow of Richard Preston, citizen and grocer of London, endowed in 1396-7 a chantry for her husband and members of his family in which the priest was to receive an annual stipend of ten marks,[37] and Richard Hunter left ten marks for a chaplain to celebrate in the church of St Faith for his soul and for those of his benefactors, apparently for one year.[38] The rate for London churches does not seem to have been significantly higher than that for chantries founded in country churches of the diocese or province. For example, in 1381 Walter of Wootton left ten marks as the annual endowment of the priests celebrating a daily mass for the souls of himself, his wife and his parents, at Our Lady's altar in the church of Gestingthorpe in Essex,[39] and in 1411

[37] R.B., fo. 210v.   [38] R.B., fo. 450v.   [39] R.B., fo. 448.

the chantry which Henry Sampson had in 1293 founded at Easton-on-the-Hill in Northamptonshire was re-united with the parish church because the income of about six and a half marks, which it derived from Henry's endowment of lands, was no longer enough to make it economically viable.[40] Braybrooke, as we have seen, thought that many of the chantries in St Paul's were inadequately endowed and therefore sought and obtained royal licence to combine them in order to provide decent livings for the cantarists. He took similar action in the case of two chantries which had been established in the church of All Hallows Barking.[41] One of these had been founded in 1295 by Adam Blakeney, citizen of London, who had endowed it with lands and tenements bringing in five marks a year. The other, founded early in the reign of Edward III by another London citizen, named John Cambridge, had already once been rescued from poverty by the generosity of Godwin Turk, citizen, who had given sufficient endowments to bring up the annual income to six marks. Moved by a petition from four parishioners to whom the right of patronage belonged, Braybrooke ordered an inquiry to be made by a committee of local worthies, including the incumbents of St Mary Magdalen's, Milk Street, St Swithin's, London Stone, St Clement's, Eastcheap, St Benet's Gracechurch and St Margaret's-on-the-Hill, as well as the vicar of All Hallows himself and some of his parishioners. Since the findings of these people confirmed the plea of the parishioners that 'because of the scarcity of suitable chaplains and the dearth of victuals and other necessities in these present times, the fruits and profits pertaining to the said two chantries are barely sufficient nowadays to maintain one chaplain properly', Braybrooke agreed to amalgamate these two chantries, to which he instituted a priest from the diocese of Lincoln named William Danvers.

Since the city churches of London tended to benefit from the wills of rich citizens, London cantarists could sometimes pick up some lawful supplementary income from the bequests of the faithful. Most of them, who were bound to celebrate mass each day for their own foundation, would have been excluded from a

[40] V.C.H. Northants, ii, p. 567. See also Rosalind Hill, 'Two Northamptonshire Chantries', *E.H.R.*, lxii (1947), p. 206.
[41] R.B., fos. 163–4v.

share of such bequests as that of John Chertsey, citizen and draper, who in 1396 left forty marks to be spent by his executors 'for six thousand masses in divers places according to their discretion',[42] but they could quite properly have benefited from the generosity of other testators, such as John Vyne, also a draper, who in his will dated 1384 declared that he wished to be buried beside Margery his wife in the church of Holy Trinity the Less and that he bequeathed half a mark 'to each priest who usually celebrates in the same church'.[43] Cantarists celebrating in St Paul's could share in the endowments left for distribution between those who at specified times attended the requiem masses in other chantries.[44]

In order to produce a permanent annual stipend for the cantarist a chantry had to be endowed. Some of the chantries in St Paul's were directly based upon the revenues of the dean and chapter: those of Hamo Chigwell and Henry Idesworth, for example, are described as deriving their finances *de camera dicte ecclesie*.[45] Occasionally, in other churches besides cathedrals, the endowments were established wholly in money, although no London example of such an establishment occurs in Braybrooke's register. At Colchester, however, in 1383 John Bayn bequeathed the sum of £86 13s 4d to endow in the church of St Nicholas a chantry for himself, Catherine and Joan successively his wives, and Milcencia, John and Robert his children.[46] More commonly endowments consisted of property, for example Thomas Cosyn, dying in 1383, bequeathed all his 'tenements in Cosyns Lane' to found a chantry in the church of All Hallows the Great,[47] and Thomas Carleton, *broderer*, not only endowed a chantry in the chapel of St John the Baptist in St Paul's, but furnished it with what may have been examples of his skill, vestments of blue silk, curtains and cushions.[48] The chantry of Thomas Stowe, dean of St Paul's from 1400 to 1405, was endowed with tenements in the parishes of St Nicholas Shambles, St Bartholomew Smithfield and St Giles-in-the-Fields,[49] while that of John Romayn, also in St Paul's, drew its revenues from marshland, *quodam marisco estimato ad sex marcas per annum*.[50] A large number of

[42] R.B., fo. 473.   [43] R.B., fo. 448v.   [44] S.S., pp. 135–8.   [45] S.S., p. 143.
[46] R.B., fo. 453.   [47] R.B., fo. 448.   [48] C.W., ii, p. 272.
[49] St Paul's, Ms WD 11, fo. 37v, section B.VII. I am indebted to Jeanette Hitchings, research student at Westfield College, for this reference and for allowing me to see her interesting work on the inventories of St Paul's.
[50] S.S., p. 143.

chantries are described as being maintained out of the proceeds of unspecified rents, Roger Laley's, for example, *consistit in annuo redditu certorum tenementorum estimatorum ad sex marcas et octo solidos per annum*.[51]

If the records of chantries in Braybrooke's register are compared with the provisions made in wills which were granted probate in the court of husting over the same period, it becomes clear that not everyone who wanted to found a chantry was in fact able to do so. Probably in many cases testators were unduly hopeful about their estates and their executors found themselves in the position of an unfortunate Lancashire lady fifty years earlier, whose husband, having exacted from her a vow to maintain two priests to pray for his soul, died heavily in debt.[52] About seventy of the wills proved between 1382 and 1404 contain bequests for the founding or endowing of chantries (the precise number is difficult to assess because the term 'chantry' is sometimes used to describe a temporary arrangement lasting for one or two years, and also because a phrase such as 'in trust for the good of my soul and the souls of my wife and parents' may, but need not, imply a chantry foundation). In a good many of these wills the bequest seems to be an extra endowment for a chantry which had already been established by somebody else; thus in 1382 John Blanket, skinner, provided for the maintenance of two chantries in St Swithin's, London Stone;[53] in 1393 William King, draper, made provision for a chantry in the church of St James, Garlickhithe, to which he presented also a bible in French (*gallicis compositum*) and a book called the Liber Regalis, 'desiring them to be chained';[54] in 1397 John Fressh, mercer, left a quitrent from a tenement in the parish of St Mary Magdalen, Knightrider Street, to Sir John Newton, rector of the church of St Benedict Shorhog 'in aid of a chantry in the same'.[55] Some testators, however, clearly wanted to set up an independent chantry of their own and were by no means content to improve an existing foundation. In 1399 Andrew Smyth, 'pyebaker', made his bequests to St Clement's Eastcheap conditional on the setting-up of a chantry for himself and other speci-

---

[51] S.S., p. 144. This chantry and Romayn's were regarded by Braybrooke as being too poor to maintain a cantarist, and amalgamated with others.

[52] York Diocesan Registry, Reg. Melton, fo. 449.

[53] C.W., ii, p. 245.　　[54] C.W., ii, pp. 312–13.　　[55] C.W., ii, p. 338.

fied people.[56] John Northampton, who died in 1397, was still more firm with his legatees. He left lands and tenements in the parish of All Hallows Barking to the Hospital of St Mary Cripplegate for the establishment and maintenance of a chantry for himself, his parents, Joan and Petronilla successively his wives, and his friends James and Matilda Andrew, with the provision that if the hospital should fail to set up the chantry, the property was to revert to the chantry-college in the Guildhall.[57]

In fact, however, John Northampton's chantry, together with Andrew Smyth's and most of the others, remained a pious aspiration. Probably the funds he left were insufficient. Of the new chantries desired by the testators of the period, two only appear in the register as receiving cantarists, that of Richard Preston, whose will was admitted to probate in 1391[58] and whose devoted widow Agnes took part in the presentation of the first cantarist in 1397,[59] adding further endowments of her own in 1402,[60] and that of Simon Winchcomb, armourer, whose will was admitted to probate in 1399[61] and whose cantarist was instituted in 1402.[62]

Braybrooke's register contains no detailed description of the way in which the endowments of a city chantry were managed, but a few details have survived in other records of the period. Thus in 1383 William Brikles, pepperer, executor of the will of Sabina Yerdale, brought a bill of complaint before the mayor and aldermen against Robert Corn, who, he claimed, held £100 in trust under the terms of Sabina's will to pay ten marks a year to the chaplain celebrating in her chantry, the which payment was now £20 in arrears. To this, Robert responded that Sabina had quit-claimed him at the time of her death, so that he was now bound neither to pay the chaplain nor to appoint a successor. The court found that the will of the testatrix contained a clause which exonerated Robert if he should at any time fall into poverty, so a respite was granted for the purpose of making an inquiry.[63] In 1390 Adam of Foxley, rector of St Andrew's Holborn, appointed John Bygonet and Roger Hillom to let, to lease, and receive the rents from, houses and tenements left for the maintenance of a chantry

[56] C.W., ii, p. 345.   [57] C.W., ii, pp. 333–5.   [58] C.W., ii, p. 291.
[59] R.B., fo. 210v, and see p. 249 above.   [60] C.W., ii, p. 353.
[61] C.W., ii, pp. 340–2.   [62] R.B., fo. 255.
[63] A. H. Thomas ed., *Calendar of Plea and Memoranda Rolls* (Cambridge, 1932), pp. 43–5.

by Avice, widow of William Edyman, who had directed in her will that 'two of the better men of the parish' should be chosen by the rector for this purpose.[64]

A very interesting and detailed entry in Braybrooke's register concerns the foundation in the church of Witham[65] (between Chelmsford and Colchester in Essex) and this may be used to throw light upon the running of a chantry in the diocese at this time. In 1397 Robert Rykedon and Thomas Bircheleigh founded in the church of Witham a chantry for themselves, the countess of Essex, the vicar of Witham and eighteen other named persons, including members of the families of both founders and the man who was subsequently to become the first cantarist, a certain Richard Hende. The duties of the cantarist are laid down with great precision, and he is to be bound under oath to keep residence and to accept no other paid employment. In addition to himself saying a daily requiem mass (no variations are specified) with the *Placebo, Dirige* and seven penitential psalms, he is to assist the vicar of Witham at mass, matins and vespers every day and at other services on feast-days. As well as fulfilling his religious duties (which must have taken up a considerable part of each day) he is also burdened with the duty of acting as rent-collector for a considerable estate (except in so far as he farmed it himself) consisting of two specified messuages, 132 acres of arable land, 12 of meadow, 18 of pasture and 30 of woodland, together with rents in money to the annual value of 7s 11d. From the income thus obtained he must keep his chantry and its furnishings in repair, maintain a light before the altar of Our Lady in Witham church, discharge the obligations due to the overlord of the estate, and pay to Thomas Bircheleigh (who seems to have made himself responsible for the business side of the arrangements) £10 a year in quarterly instalments. In return, Thomas Bircheleigh promises him, for the term of his (Thomas's) life, suitable board and lodging in his own house together with a yearly salary of four marks. If during Thomas's lifetime the quarterly payments should fall into arrears, distraint may be used against the cantarist's goods in order to compel him to pay up. After Thomas's death the arrangements about board and lodging are to cease and Richard Hende and his successors are to enter into possession of the lands and the income

[64] ibid., p. 171.   [65] R.B., fos. 413v–4v.

254

derived from them—an income which, unless the outgoing expenses were abnormally heavy, should have secured to the cantarist a satisfactory livelihood. Subsequent arrangements for this particular chantry are very carefully safeguarded. The founders are to be patrons during their lifetime; after their deaths the right of presentation is to devolve upon 'six of the more honourable and trustworthy parishioners'. Should these fail to present, the right is to pass successively to twelve other parishioners, to the vicar of Witham and finally, should all else fail, to the bishop of the diocese. Any cantarist instituted to this chantry may be turned out for non-residence, failing to keep the chantry chapel and its furnishings in repair, alienating any part of the endowments, or indulging in acts of adultery or fornication from which he does not desist at the warnings of six senior and respectable parishioners. On entering into possession of this chantry the cantarist was, in the presence of a notary-public, to take an oath to observe all its statutes.

For Braybrooke and for the responsible people of his diocese a chantry was clearly not intended to be a sinecure. It involved a good deal of hard work, both in the religious and in the secular field. London chantries, naturally enough, would have a special attraction for priests who enjoyed the life of a large and prosperous city, but there is little real evidence to suggest that these institutions were a cause of serious depletion in the clerical ranks of other dioceses. As far as the evidence of Braybrooke's register goes, it appears that the London cantarists were doing the work for which they were employed, and doing it reasonably well, even if their patrons did not succeed in founding as many chantries as they would have wished to do.

XIII

Richard II and the Principality of Chester 1397-9

R. R. DAVIES

ON 25 September 1397, the county palatine of Chester was raised to the status of a principality by parliamentary statute;[1] and thereby it enjoyed—albeit for only two years—a unique position in the history of the counties of England. The preamble of the statute made explicit the reasons for this unique creation. On the one hand it referred to sentiments, past and present—to Richard II's great love and affection for the county of Chester and its men and to the fact that he and his father and their predecessors had been earls of the county. On the other hand it looked to the future—to the creation of a greater patrimony and a more noble title for the king's eldest son. Henceforth the heir to the throne would not only enjoy the titles of prince of Wales and duke of Cornwall; he would also be assured of a new title of prince, rather than earl, of Chester. Plans for the future patrimony and title of the king's eldest son were, however, premature in 1397; Richard II's reasons for creating a new principality lay more obviously and immediately in the political events of the year. The king celebrated his victory over his baronial opponents with a lavish distribution of titles and lands; and the elevation of Chester to the status of a principality was, from this viewpoint, but the culmination of the victory parade.

The title of principality was, of course, the highest honour that it was within Richard II's power to confer. It placed Chester clearly above the rank of the county palatines of Lancaster and Durham and of the duchies of Cornwall and Aquitaine; its princely status was shared only with the principality of Wales. Never before had such an honour been conferred on an English county. The

I wish to thank Sir Goronwy Edwards and Mr D. A. L. Morgan for their invaluable comments on this article.

[1] 21 Richard II c.9; *R.P.*, iii, pp. 353-4.

closest parallel was the elevation of the duchy of Aquitaine to the status of a principality for the Black Prince in July 1362; and this was a precedent which Richard II may well have had in mind in September 1397. The creation of the new principality was clearly meant as a fulsome compliment to the men of Chester, but it also served to satisfy Richard's 'taste for self-dramatization' (to borrow Professor McKisack's phrase).[2] For though the new principality was ostensibly created for the greater glory of the royal heir, Richard II himself quickly added the title of prince of Chester to his own royal style.[3] He thereby showed clearly the personal nature of the link between himself and his new principality. It was truly a principality founded on affection.

The significance of the new principality was not, however, exhausted by its special title. Its territorial composition was equally novel. The core of the new principality was, of course, the ancient county of Chester, which had long since enjoyed palatine status and which had been treated since 1254 as part of the endowment of the king's eldest son. Attached to the county of Chester was the county of Flint which throughout the later medieval period was under the administrative control of the palatine government in Chester. And there is no doubt that the county of Flint, though it was not formally annexed under the terms of the act of 1397, was regarded as part and parcel of the new principality of Chester.[4] Had Chester and Flint alone been elevated from county status to that of a principality, the change would merely have been one of name. But there was more to the new principality than that: in area as well as in status it was markedly superior to the old county palatine. Four days before the creation of the new principality, the earl of Arundel had been sentenced and executed; and now his vast estates in the northern marches of Wales and Shropshire— the lordships of Bromfield and Yale, Chirk and Shrawardine, the hundred of Oswestry and Ruyton-of-the-Eleven-Towns, the castle of Dawley and its dependent fees, and the reversion of the lord-ship of Clun—were forever 'annexed, united and incorporated'

[2] M. McKisack, *The Fourteenth Century 1307–1399* (Oxford, 1959), p. 463.
[3] For his assumption of the title see below p. 262.
[4] See, for example, a reference to 'the county of Flint within the principality of Chester', P.R.O. Chester Recognizance Rolls (Chester 2), no. 73 m.3v. (All references to unpublished records refer to collections at the Public Record Office, unless otherwise stated.)

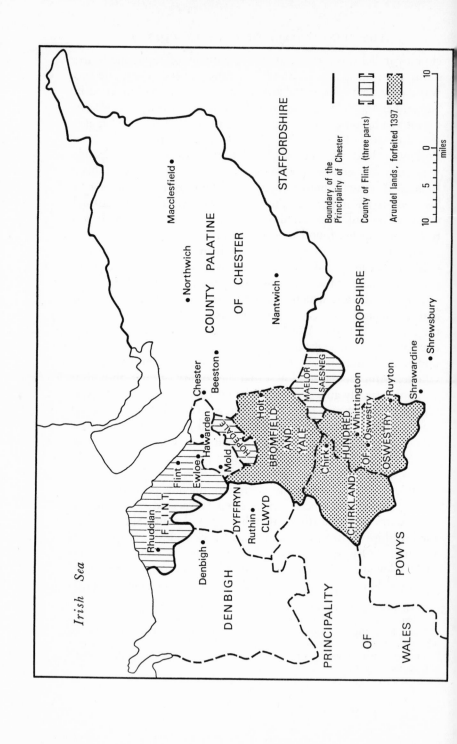

Irish Sea

STAFFORDSHIRE

Macclesfield •

COUNTY PALATINE

• Northwich

OF CHESTER

Nantwich •

SHROPSHIRE

• Shrewsbury

Beeston •

Chester •

• Shrawardine

• Ruyton

MAELOR SAESNEG

Holt •

Whittington •

Hawarden •

Flint •

Ewloe •

Mold •

HOPEDALE

BROMFIELD AND YALE

Chirk •

CHIRKLAND

HUNDRED OF OSWESTRY

• Oswestry

Rhuddlan •

F L I N T

DYFFRYN CLWYD

Ruthin •

Denbigh •

DENBIGH

PRINCIPALITY

OF

WALES

POWYS

Boundary of the
Principality of Chester

County of Flint (three parts)

Arundel lands, forfeited 1397

10   5   0   10
miles

to the new principality. Furthermore, the integrity of this greatly-augmented principality was guaranteed by a provision that no part of it was to be sold, granted or in any way alienated except to the eldest son of the king. Richard II had clearly not conceived his new principality as a temporary experiment; he meant it to be a permanent feature in the political structure of the kingdom.

The significance of the annexation of the Arundel lands within the new principality is immediately obvious in terms of political geography. Richard II might be recklessly generous in the way he disposed of the escheated estates of his political victims in 1397, but even he could not fail to see the vital importance of the Arundel marcher estates. The three lordships of Bromfield and Yale, Chirk and Oswestry formed a formidable territorial bloc astride the north-eastern borders of Wales; they lay next to each other and in several places they bordered on the counties of Chester and Flint. Control of these lordships was in large measure the key to the control of the northern marches and even of North Wales. The earl of Arundel had more than once demonstrated their strategic importance: during Richard II's earlier bid for power in 1387 the efforts of Robert de Vere and his Chester troops were largely neutralized by Arundel's formidable power in the marches;[5] and again in 1393 Arundel's studied neutrality in his castle at Holt during the Cheshire revolt infuriated Gaunt and once more focused attention on the strength of his marcher position.[6] Clearly for a king who was to base so much of his power on the west and especially on Cheshire, the annexation of the Arundel lordships was an obvious desideratum of his political strategy. Furthermore, from a military viewpoint the acquisition of the castles of Chirk, Oswestry, Shrawardine and above all Holt constituted a major accession of strength especially in providing at certain points an outer defence perimeter for the county of Chester.

The annexation of the Arundel estates was, therefore, dictated by obvious political and military reasons; and it is indeed significant that they alone of the great number of marcher lordships

[5] Holt castle was defended for six weeks 'tempore commocionis ducis Hibernie in marchia'; and the earl of Arundel celebrated his victory by nailing a copy of the appeal of de Vere on the door of St Peter's Church at Chester, Ministers' Accounts (S.C.6), no. 1234/5 (account of the receiver of Holt, 1387-8).

[6] See J. G. Bellamy, 'The Northern Rebellions in the Later Years of Richard II', Bulletin of the John Rylands Library, xlvii (1964-5), pp. 265-6.

which fell to the crown by way of escheat or custody in the crucial years 1397–9 were kept in the king's hand. Furthermore they could easily be controlled from Chester and amalgamated into the administrative structure of the palatinate. It is significant in this respect that the outlying Arundel marcher estates were sooner or later granted out and ceased to have any connexion other than a loose constitutional one with the new principality. The lordship of Clun had already been granted for life to the duke of Aumale in September 1397 and the scattered Arundel manors in central and eastern Shropshire were likewise given to the earl of Worcester.[7] This meant that the new principality formed a remarkably compact unit and had virtually continuous boundaries.[8] Furthermore, such major territorial enclaves as existed within the new principality were safely in the hands of the king's favourites: the lordships of Hawarden, Mold and Ewloe were under the control of the Montagu family and were specifically held of the new principality;[9] the custody of the Lestraunge lands was entrusted to Aumale;[10] and so anxious was Richard II to have as complete control as possible of his new principality that in January 1399 he arranged for the annexation of Hopedale, Northwich and Overmarsh from the duke of Exeter.[11] All in all the new principality formed the largest single territorial concentration on the political map of England in the years 1397–9; it is little wonder that Richard II considered it worthy of a special title.

It was not, however, the mere size of this new territorial complex which was the reason for the novel title bestowed upon it; that lay simply and avowedly in the affection which the king entertained for the county of Chester and its inhabitants. It was an affection in part filial. Richard II had certainly inherited a sense of indebtedness to the men of Cheshire for their services to his father. Several of the Black Prince's war captains—such as Sir Gerard Braybrook and Sir John Mascy of Tatton—were still on the payroll of Chester annuitants in the 1390s and as late as 1398 war veterans of the field of Poitiers were still trading on their services

---

[7] C.P.R., 1396–9, pp. 205, 213.

[8] The major exceptions are the lordship of Oswestry, which is divided into two halves by the lordship of Whittington, and the outlying Arundel lands in Shropshire.

[9] C.Cl.R., 1396–9, pp. 159–60; C.P.R., 1396–9, p. 265; Chester 2/71m.6, m.8v.
[10] Chester 2/71 m.4v.   [11] C.P.R., 1396–9, p. 467.

to the Black Prince as a sure way to an annuity from his son.[12] One of them was John Snelleston who could claim the dual distinction of having served both the Black Prince in France and Richard II at Radcot Bridge.[13] And Radcot Bridge, of course, was the seal on Richard's affection for Cheshire: it had converted filial affection into a personal sense of indebtedness, and an indebtedness which was all the deeper for being associated with a bitter failure. How much to the forefront of Richard's mind was the memory of Radcot Bridge was dramatically revealed in the autumn of 1398 when 4000 marks were deposited at Chester abbey for distribution to the men of the county who had suffered in the débâcle of December 1387. Petitions and claims were submitted by the victims and the full sum was scrupulously distributed throughout the county in December 1398.[14] This retrospective act of largesse was only the most measurable token of Richard's unbounded generosity to his beloved subjects of Chester. Favours of every kind were showered upon them: pardons, offices, lands, and confiscated goods were bestowed with careless liberality;[15] general pardons were granted to the counties of Flint and Chester;[16] and the charter of the city of Chester was exemplified and its judicial liberties extended.[17] Just as the seventeen counties were punished for failing to show 'constant good affection' to their king, so the men of Chester were continuously pampered for showing precisely that quality and showing it in good measure. And the crowning manifestation of Richard's 'immense friendship and affection'[18] for Cheshire was the elevation of the county to the status of a princi-

---

[12] S.C.6/774/6. In March 1398 Thomas de Baguley of Knutsford, who had been with the Black Prince at the siege of Calais and the battle of Poitiers and on all other expeditions overseas, was granted a pension of sixpence a day, Chester 2/71 m.32.

[13] S.C.6/774/6 m.lv (account of the chamberlain of Chester, 1396-7).

[14] The payment of the sum is entered on the Exchequer Issue Rolls (E.403), no. 561 m.3–m.4; its receipt at Chester and the details of its distribution are recorded in Chester 2/70 m.7v.; 2/73 m.6.

[15] See, for example, C.P.R., 1396-9, pp. 176, 197, 204, 205, 267, 282, 285, 328, 381, 385, 411, etc.

[16] Flint Plea Rolls (Chester 30) no. 16 m.2. (Flint, 14 Oct. 1397); Chester 2/71 m.10 (Chester, 15 Oct. 1397).

[17] Chester 2/71 m.9 (August–September 1398). For a summary see *The Thirty Sixth Report of the Deputy Keeper of the Public Records* (London, 1875), Appendix II (hereafter *D.K.R. xxxvi*) p. 99.

[18] The phrase appears as common form in the preamble of pardons to Chester men, e.g. Chester 2/71 m.6v.

pality. This affection was further demonstrated in the fact that the new title of *princeps Cestrie* was henceforth proudly incorporated in the royal style in letters issued by the Chester exchequer and was equally displayed on the new seal of the principality.[19] In terms of diplomatic practice, this usage was the more noteworthy because in his neighbouring principality of Wales, Richard II never deigned to use his local title of prince of Wales after his accession. No man can have made his political sentiments plainer: *ob amorem Cestrensium* could well have been the motto of the new principality.[20]

Nor was the sentiment of gratitude exhausted by the creation of a new title for the beloved palatinate, for it soon became evident that the whole administration of the new principality was to be geared to the greater glory of Cheshire. The annexed Arundel lordships were treated very much as political spoils whose wealth in offices and in revenue was to be deployed for the benefit of the men of Cheshire. Nothing could convey this atmosphere of political victory more graphically than the way the lordships were immediately placed under the control of Hugh of Knutsford, the escheator of the county of Chester.[21] All the leading Arundel officials in the marches were sacked and their place was taken by the key officers of the Chester palatinate. On the day after Arundel's execution William Bagot, one of the king's closest henchmen and a deputy-justiciar of Chester, was appointed steward and surveyor of the Arundel marcher lordships and constable of the key castle of Holt; and rather later the duke of Norfolk as justice of Chester since March 1394 had his commission extended to include the Arundel lordships for life.[22] This administrative control of the annexed lordships from Chester was taken a step farther in the spring months of 1398 when William Lescrope, the king's most trusted favourite, took over the justiceship of both Chester and the Arundel lands and when Robert Parys, the well-tried chamberlain of Chester, was entrusted with the financial control of the Arundel marcher estates.[23] The period of temporary custody was

[19] See below pp. 265-6.
[20] The phrase is that of Thomas Walsingham in *Annales*, p. 222.
[21] His account as receiver of the escheated lordships from 28 October 1397 to 20 April 1398 is in S.C.6/1234/6.
[22] Chester 2/71 m.23v. (18 Oct. 1397).
[23] *C.P.R., 1396-9*, p. 284 (Lescrope, 28 Jan. 1398); S.C.6/1234/6 (Parys, 20 April 1398).

at an end; in terms of personnel the administration of the Arundel lordships was now firmly under Cheshire control. So likewise the custody of the key Arundel castles was entrusted to loyal Cheshire men: Oswestry to Sir Robert de Legh, Chirk to Peter Dutton, Shrawardine to Thomas Beeston, and Holt to Richard Cholmondeley.[24] This Chester takeover of all major posts in the annexed lordships was completed by a lavish distribution of most of the minor offices and sinecures in them—parkerships, rangerships, keeperships and serjeanties—to other deserving Cheshire retainers.[25] The purge of Arundel officials was virtually complete.[26] The new principality of Chester was to be staffed by Cheshire men.

Not only was there a purge of personnel; there was also a clear attempt to reorganize the administration of the Arundel lordships for their new role within an augmented Cheshire. The first step in such a reorganization was to integrate the three lordships—Chirk, Bromfield and Yale, and Oswestry—into a single administrative unit. This presented no great problem, for the three lordships formed a coherent territorial bloc, and there had already been a good measure of administrative integration within them in the days of the earl of Arundel.[27] This process was now swiftly completed: a single steward was immediately appointed for all the lordships and he in turn appointed a single receiver. The next step in the process of reorganization was much more difficult, for it involved the integration of the annexed Arundel lands in a new unified administrative structure for the whole principality of Chester. In terms of personnel, as we have seen, this was quickly and easily achieved by a purge of Arundel officers and by the appointment of the justice and chamberlain of Chester to parallel posts in the Arundel lordships. At the secretariat level, likewise, the

[24] *C.P.R., 1396–9*, pp. 204 (Legh), 212 (Beeston); S.C.6/1234/7 (Dutton). Lescrope was titular constable of Holt; but Richard Cholmondeley was in actual charge there, E.403/562 m.10. Beeston and Cholmondeley were captains of the king's bodyguard; see below p. 269.

[25] For example Richard Doddington was appointed parker of Eyton, John Cholmondeley forester of Bromfield and Yale, and Thomas Beeston parker of Shrawardine, *C.P.R., 1396–9*, pp. 198, 205, 332.

[26] Among the few to retain office were David Holbache, deputy-justiciar of the Arundel lordships, and John ap Gwilym of Chirk who was retained as one of the yeomen of the crown, S.C.6/1234/7 m.2v, *C.P.R., 1396–9*, pp. 318, 323.

[27] Thus Oswestry and Chirk had shared a single receiver, Alan Thorp, in 1395–6 and at the same time Bromfield and Yale and Oswestry were subject to a single steward, John Whetales.

unity of the new principality was quickly established. Appointments to posts in the Arundel lands were punctiliously issued under the principality seal and carefully enrolled on the Chester 'recognizance rolls';[28] and when Richard II granted a charter of liberties to the burgesses of Oswestry 'within our principality of Chester' a registered copy of it was preserved in the Chester archives.[29]

Beyond the secretariat level, however, the reorganization of the new principality administration was no more than tentatively established. In the first place, the Arundel estates were still controlled by their own steward and supervisor. It is true that William Lescrope was the overall head of administration throughout the new principality; but he had two separate commissions, two salaries and two titles—justice of Chester and justice of Chirk, Bromfield and Oswestry.[30] Just as there was no single justiceship, so likewise financial control within the principality was less than unified. Robert Parys was chamberlain of both Chester and the Arundel lands; but he submitted two separate accounts annually, drew two salaries, and had two treasuries—at Chester and Holt. Even when a single officer was appointed with authority throughout the new principality as a whole—as was the case with Robert Fagan, the master mason, in April 1398—his commission was addressed to the faithful subjects and tenants of 'the counties of Chester and Flint and the lordships of Bromfield, Yale, Chirk, Oswestry and Shrawardine' rather than to the subjects of a single principality.[31] At the level of administrative structure the new principality clearly fell short of being a unity.

At the level of terminology likewise the identity of the new principality remained to be securely established. Chroniclers could be forgiven for thinking that it was a duchy rather than a principality that Richard II had created;[32] it is more surprising to find that royal clerks got themselves into hopeless tangles over the status and proper title of the new creation. Few of them managed

[28] For example, William Lescrope's appointment as justice of the Arundel lordships in January 1398 was issued under the seal of the principality of Chester, Chester 2/71 m.5.

[29] Chester 2/72.

[30] Furthermore the effective head of the administration of the Arundel lands was their steward, Sir William Bagot.

[31] Chester 2/71 m.3v.

[32] *Historia Vitae et Regni Ricardi Secundi*, ed. T. Hearne (London, 1729), p. 139; *Chronicon Adae de Usk*, ed. E. M. Thompson (London, 1904), p. 15.

to combine a diplomatic error with a geographical howler as did the exchequer clerk who referred to 'Holt castle in the county of Chester'; but even chancery clerks could refer to a duchy of Chester in an important legal context.[33] Slips of the pen were perhaps understandable at Westminster; they are certainly more surprising in the exchequer at Chester where professional pride in the new principality should have made for accuracy in this respect. Yet on one and the same membrane a clerk could refer to duchy and principality interchangeably and could even lapse into references to a county.[34] Likewise in the sealing department of the Chester exchequer, both the old seal of the county palatine and the new seal of the principality were available and were used interchangeably on official correspondence.[35]

The name of the new principality clearly had an unfamiliar ring about it even to the clerks of its own secretariat; and the looseness of its administrative structure likewise betokened a hasty federation rather than a successful amalgamation. That might be so; but Richard II was quite determined that his new principality should lack none of the trappings appropriate to its exalted status. The royal title was immediately changed on letters issued from the exchequer at Chester, in order to incorporate the two words 'princeps Cestrie' in the king's style.[36] With equal promptness a new great seal of the principality of Chester was engraved.[37] Furthermore, whereas the old exchequer seal at Chester had hitherto included only the title of the earl of Chester, the legend on the new principality seal was much more refulgent: *Sigillum Ricardi dei gracia regis anglie et francie et principis cestrie.*[38] The seal of

---

[33] E.403/562 m.10; *C.P.R., 1396-9*, p. 205 (lordship of Clun to be held of king as *duke* of Chester). Many other examples could be cited. Cf. Tout, *Chapters*, iv, p. 28 n.2.

[34] Chester 2/71 m.15; Chester 2/73 m.5v.

[35] Chester 2/71 m.34v registers two letters of the same date, one under the old exchequer seal and the other under the new principality seal. As a rule, it would seem that the exchequer seal was used fairly regularly until June 1398 but not thereafter.

[36] The earliest recorded use of the title in the royal style was on 25 October 1397 (Chester 2/71 m.4v); and it was generally, though not invariably, incorporated thereafter.

[37] The earliest recorded use of the new principality seal was on 15 October 1397, Chester 2/71 m.6v.

[38] Two examples of the principality seal of Chester are cited and illustrated in H. Jenkinson, 'The Great Seal of England: Deputed or Departmental Seals',

Chester was now worthy of comparison with the seal of England itself. A principality so richly endowed with honours clearly needed a herald of its own and so the king on one of his visits there appointed William Brugges as Chester Herald.[39]

Even more striking and significant than the appointment of a herald was the creation of three honorific posts within the principality: a stewardship, a constableship and a chamberlainship. These appointments convey more graphically than anything else how determined Richard II was to make a reality of his new principality. It was clearly his aim to reproduce in Chester the pattern of major offices within his court in England and to endow these offices with authority throughout the new principality. The duke of Aumale was appointed chamberlain of 'the whole and entire principality':[40] his honorific post was quite clearly to be distinguished from the more workaday chamberlainships of Chester and the Arundel lands exercised by Robert Parys. Another close confidant of the king, the earl of Salisbury, was likewise created steward of the principality of Chester.[41] The most interesting of these appointments—and the only one for which we have the original commission—was that of John of Gaunt as hereditary constable of the whole principality of Chester on 8 August 1398.[42] The appointment was made not only for Gaunt but also for his heirs male, and was specifically extended to the whole principality (*per totum integrum principatum*), both the old county and the lands newly annexed to it. Politically the interest of the appointment rests in the fact that it was one of the many favours whereby Richard II secured the friendship of Gaunt, so crucial to all his plans. Constitutionally the significance of the commission lies in the way a constableship was consciously established

---

Archaeologia, lxxxv (1935), p. 332 and plate xcvii. Dr M. Sharp has drawn attention to the difference between the legend on the old exchequer seal of Chester and that on the new principality seal in Tout, *Chapters*, v, p. 376 n.3.

[39] Chester 2/71 m.7v. It is interesting to observe that Richard II also appointed an officer of arms with the title Wales Herald, *Transactions of the Honourable Society of Cymmrodorion* (1969), part i, p. 32.

[40] He is referred to as such at least twice: once in the warranty of a letter of July 1398 and again in the financial account for 1398-9, Chester 2/71 m.2v.; S.C.6/774/10 m.5.

[41] He is addressed as such in a letter of July 1399, Chester 2/73 m.1.

[42] Chester 2/73 m.9.

for the principality with specifically the same authority as the constable of England had within the rest of the kingdom. Chester had long since enjoyed a palatine status which set it apart from the rest of England; but it was a status which it had shared with Durham and, latterly, with Lancaster. Now its constitutional position was truly unique; and it was this uniqueness which these honorific appointments expressed. Not even Richard II's other principality of Wales had a like pattern of honorific offices. Furthermore, the constitutional separateness of the new principality was accompanied by an extensive judicial immunity: 'the said principality' so the king vigorously asserted, 'has such a franchise that it has cognizance of all pleas arising within the same'.[43] The king was the greatest of franchise-holders; and he could be relied upon to defend the immunity of his new-born franchise with passion. Constitutionally the principality of Chester occupied a unique and unprecedented position within the body politic of England.

The new principality was to make an ample return for the honour conferred upon it in the contributions it made to the king's policies during the last two years of his reign, more especially of course by providing a permanent royal bodyguard. The role that the men of Chester were to play in the affairs of 1397-9 was dramatically heralded by an urgent summons of 13 July 1397—that is, immediately after the arrest of Warwick, Gloucester and Arundel —commanding the sheriff of the county to come immediately to the king with 2000 archers.[44] The summons, we may suspect, did not come altogether as a surprise; for if there was one area which the king could regard as a reliable training ground it was the palatinate of Chester. Its men were long since versed in the arts of war and in loyalty to their king. They had served his father on his continental campaigns; more recently they had formed the core of the royalist army at Radcot Bridge and it was the deputy-justice of Chester, Sir Thomas Molyneux, who was the sole distinguished victim of that ignominious débâcle. Again in 1394-5 the men of Chester had made a considerable contribution to the

[43] The statement was made in a letter ordering a case relating to the free chapels of Clun and Holt (in the former Arundel lordships) to be suspended in the royal chancery and to be heard instead in the court of the principality of Chester, Exchequer Council and Privy Seal Records (E.28) no. 4/68.

[44] Chester 2/70 m.7v. A like order to the sheriff of Warwickshire was dispatched a week later, C.Cl.R., 1396-9, p. 144.

impressive army that Richard II led to Ireland.[45] It was therefore to well-tried and well-trusted supporters that Richard turned in July 1397. Chester was converted into a virtually exclusive royal recruiting-ground by a proclamation that no archer from the county was to serve anyone until 2300 men had been chosen for the king's retinue.[46] Other counties contributed handsomely in men to the royal retinue; but in the number of its troops and in the trust placed in them by the king, Chester stood quite apart.

The role that the Cheshire archers played in the events of the last two years of the reign—especially in terrorizing the Michaelmas parliament of 1397—is too well known to need repetition. But the accounts of the chroniclers and of the articles of deposition with regard to them need to be and can be placed on a more secure footing. In the first place it is clear that the king's Chester retinue—like noble retinues generally—consisted both of a small regular body of men and a much larger but less permanent force. On great public occasions, such as the parliament of 1397 or the Irish expedition of 1399,[47] the king could count his Cheshire archers in thousands; but for most of the time he relied on a more select and regular body of men. This select bodyguard was placed on a permanent footing during 1397-8.[48] Each man was retained by an individual indenture of service and was granted an annuity either for life or during the king's pleasure. The process of retaining started in September 1397 and continued well into 1398. Its peak points came significantly immediately after the sessions of parliament in Michaelmas 1397 and January 1398.[49] By Michaelmas 1398 this permanently retained force numbered some 750 men, in-

[45] J. F. Lydon, 'Richard II's Expeditions to Ireland', *Journal of the Royal Society of Antiquaries of Ireland*, xciii (1963), pp. 135-49, esp. 141-2.

[46] Chester 2/70 m.7v.

[47] Evesham's number of 2000 Cheshire archers at the Michaelmas parliament (*Historia Vitae et Regni Ricardi Secundi*, p. 133) is confirmed by the records (Chester 2/70 m.7v.). For the Cheshire contribution to the expedition of 1399 see below, p. 278.

[48] The two main sources for the composition of the force of Cheshire archers are the long list of annuitants (495 in number) paid from the Holt treasury in Michaelmas 1398 (S.C.6/1234/7) and an exchequer account of the annuities drawn on the principality of Chester at the same date (Exchequer Various Accounts (E.101) no. 42/10). There is a good deal of overlap between the two accounts; but the latter is the more comprehensive and definitive.

[49] 157 men were retained 29 September–10 October 1397 and a further 79 were retained 30 January–2 February 1398.

cluding 10 knights and 97 esquires.[50] The core of the retinue consisted of 311 archers arranged into 7 squadrons of 44 to 46 men each, under the command of John Legh, Richard Cholmondeley, Ralph Davenport, Adam Bostock, John Donne, Thomas Beeston and Thomas Holford.[51] This force formed the king's personal bodyguard, his 'masters of watches' who accompanied him whereever he went by night and day.[52] It was they who boasted that the king could sleep safely under their care and who dared to address him in terms of unwonted familiarity.[53] Beyond this personal bodyguard lay a first reserve force of 101 archers of the livery of the crown for life. They were said to be *extra vigilias*; but they could clearly be summoned at short notice. A second reserve force of 195 archers of the crown were retained at the king's pleasure. Altogether in medieval terms the Cheshire archers of 1397-9 had the makings of a formidable standing army: the royal bodyguard of 311 men could be quickly doubled in size from the ranks of Cheshire retainers, and this force in turn could be augmented to well over 2000 men when the need arose. These Cheshire archers were not merely serving out of loyalty; in terms of wages and annuities (exclusive of all other perquisites) the crown was subsidizing them to the tune of £5140 a year.[54] It is little wonder that they flocked to Richard from as far as Berwick imploring to wear his livery and to join his bodyguard.[55] Royal service assured them of a steady income at the very least.

Richard II paid heavily for his security; but his trust was not misplaced. And it was absolute trust, as all the chroniclers were

[50] 769 men drew annuities in Michaelmas 1398, but 11 of them appear twice. The social and geographical composition of the force would repay further study.

[51] It is worth noting here the accuracy both of Walsingham's account of the size of the force in *Annales*, p. 218 and of the Dieulacres chronicler's list of the names of the leaders, *Bulletin of the John Rylands Library*, xiv (1930), p. 172.

[52] The phrase 'masters of watches of Cheshire' appears in a petition of 1399, *R.P.*, iii, p. 439. A description of the Cheshire guard accompanying Richard on a visit to Canterbury is given in *Eulogium*, p. 380. Cf. also *Adam of Usk*, p. 23.

[53] See the interesting passage from the unpublished Kenilworth Chronicle quoted in M. V. Clarke, *Fourteenth-Century Studies*, ed. L. S. Sutherland and M. McKisack (Oxford, 1937), p. 98. Cf. also *Annales*, p. 237.

[54] This figure is arrived at by doubling the payment in annuities made for Michaelmas term 1398. It probably errs on the low side. This sum is counterbalanced to a small extent by the fee paid by each annuitant for a letter patent of the grant of his annuity; and from April to September 1398 such fees yielded £436 to the Holt treasury.

[55] Chester 2/71 m.32, petition of John Hulgreve.

agreed. The events of the summer of 1399 were to prove that when all others lost heart and deserted, the *mastres del Wache de Chestreshire* stood by him to the end.[56] Their fate was bound up in his. And his fate in theirs, for the chroniclers—even those that were well disposed towards the king—are unanimous in declaring that the activities of the Cheshire archers were a leading cause of the king's unpopularity.[57] These men who (as one contemporary graphically puts it) pleaded their cases with pollaxes and points of swords were, in Adam of Usk's opinion, the chief cause of the king's ruin.[58] His infatuation with Chester and its men lost him his kingdom.

In the meantime, however, the new principality not only provided Richard II with an incomparable recruiting ground and a personal bodyguard; in terms of military strategy the control of its castles also certainly enhanced Richard's military power. Chester, Flint and Rhuddlan were already his; to them he now added the formidable Arundel fortresses of Chirk, Holt, Oswestry and Shrawardine. He took full care of them and was clearly aware of their military potential. Almost £200 was spent on the repair of the four Arundel castles in the financial year 1398; a further £210 was spent on improving the state of Chester castle; masons and carpenters were commandeered from England to attend to the needs of the new principality's fortresses.[59] Furthermore the castles were placed in a state of military preparedness: the Arundel castles were put in defence for a time from August 1397; arms were purchased for them; and in May 1398 a consignment of 300 bows and 600 sheaves of arrows as well as material for making gunpowder was dispatched to Chester castle.[60] With its military resources in men, munitions and castles the new principality certainly presented a formidable bastion of authority for its Prince.

Of these castles Holt was singled out for a special honour: it became the financial centre of the new principality and a veritable castle treasury of the Angevin variety. The role that it played under

[56] See below pp. 277-8.
[57] The Dieulacres chronicle op. cit., p. 172, concedes the point, albeit unwillingly. A specific and interesting example of the outrages of the Cheshire archers is cited in *C.P.R., 1396-9*, p. 427.
[58] *Richard the Redeles,* ed. W. W. Skeat (Early English Text Society, 1873), p. 497, ll. 327-8; *Adam of Usk*, p. 23.
[59] S.C.6/1234/7; S.C.6/774/6, 9, 10; *C.P.R., 1396-9*, pp. 402, 443, 503, 552.
[60] S.C.6/1234/7; S.C.6/774/9 m.4v.,; S.C.6/774/10 m.lv.

the command of its clerk-treasurer, John Ickleton, provides an interesting case study of how Richard II deployed his finances during his last two years. Walsingham refers only fleetingly to 'the castle of Holt in which a great part of the king's treasure lay';[61] but his statement is much elaborated by Jean Creton in an eye-witness account of the castle. Not only was it splendidly positioned and amply provisioned and garrisoned; it also 'contained a hundred thousand marks sterling in gold, and upwards, which king Richard caused to be treasured up there, besides a great quantity of other precious things'.[62] Indeed at a second attempt Creton doubles his estimate of the treasure. Creton, it is true, was given to exaggeration both in his descriptions and his estimates; but for once his guesswork may not have been wildly wrong. Holt had been an important treasury under the earls of Arundel;[63] and the existing Arundel treasure may have been the basis of the new royal establishment there. Be that as it may, vast sums of money were sent to it between 1397 and 1399. The few sums entered on the issue rolls represent only a fraction of this amount.[64] It was later calculated that £43,964 had been deposited along with goods and jewels of a high value; and this figure may well err on the low side.[65] For once Creton's figure of a hundred thousand marks may therefore have been more accurate than he realized. John Ickleton —'clerk of the king's treasure at Holt'—was a king's clerk and archdeacon of Wells.[66] He was clearly one of those clerks— Richard Maudeleyn was another—who occupied a crucial position in the last two years of the reign without holding a high official position. He was one of the king's *curiales*; and the king had in-structed him orally to dispose of the treasure and goods in his care at Holt not by written warrant but on the authority of certain

---

[61] *Annales*, p. 249.   [62] *Archaeologia*, xx (1824), pp. 123-5.

[63] There was a sum of £6649 in the Arundel coffers there in 1370, Shrewsbury Public Library, Craven Collection, 5923.

[64] Two sums of 2000 marks and 1000 marks respectively were dispatched there in December 1398 and February 1399; and 2 chests were made to carry money from London, Coventry and Lichfield to the king in Wales, E.403/561 m.6; m.14.

[65] The crucial letter is printed in T. Rymer, *Foedera*, etc. (Hague edn., 1739-45), iii, part iv, p. 191. Cf. also *C.P.R., 1401-5*, p. 167; *R.P.*, iii, pp. 487-8.

[66] The phrase 'clerk of the king's treasure at Holt' appears in E.403/561 m.6. Ickleton was arrested in January 1400, but later rose to high office under Henry IV as a chamberlain of the exchequer of receipt and treasurer of the household of Henry, prince of Wales *C.P.R., 1399-1401*, pp. 214, 501; *C.Cl.R., 1409-13*, pp. 131, 255.

codewords (*intersigna inter dictos nuper Regem et Johannem satis nota et limitata*). Some of this vast treasure was certainly used to pay the Cheshire archers,[67] some to meet the king's personal expenses;[68] but the greater part of it was either hoarded (to be avidly seized by Bolingbroke) or disposed of on various unidentifiable royal projects. For a king who spent so much of his time in the west and midlands and whose financial and political schemes were so secretive and irregular, a castle treasury had obvious advantages. And no safer location could have been found for it than the castle of Holt in the principality of Chester.

All in all, Cheshire was becoming 'the inner citadel . . . of Richard's kingdom';[69] his military strength and financial power were increasingly concentrated there. It is little wonder, therefore, that Richard eschewed the south and the east; and preferred to stay near his friends in the midlands and in his new principality. It is not always easy to determine his itinerary during his last two years; but it seems that he spent more of his time in the vicinity of his new principality than has been thought.[70] The January 1398 session of parliament was held within reach of it; and in February Richard spent a week at Chester before proceeding via Holt and Chirk to Shrawardine and thence to Oswestry to attend a meeting of the parliamentary commission on 23 February. He returned to Chester in March, April and June 1398 and spent most of August either there or at Macclesfield. He and his household paid a final visit to the capital of his principality for ten days in February 1399.

[67] 2000 marks of the Holt treasure was delivered to the chamberlain of the Arundel lands in October 1398 for the payment of the annuities of the Cheshire retainers, S.C.6/1234/7.

[68] 1000 marks was transferred by Ickleton to the king's cofferer in August 1398 to meet the expenses of the royal household, E.403/559 m.17.

[69] Tout, *Chapters*, iv, p. 59.

[70] Tout's attempt (*Chapters*, iv, p. 34 n.1) to establish Richard's itinerary during 1398 is self-confessedly uncertain. The details in the text are based on the warranties of letters from the Chester exchequer. The simple warranty *per ipsum regem* is, of course, of no real value for the purpose of establishing the royal itinerary; but when it is expanded, as it is on occasion, to *per ipsum regem apud X* we may assume the king's personal presence. Furthermore many of the dates given in the text are confirmed from independent sources. For example the account of the king's visits in February 1398 and February 1399 are confirmed both by memoranda in the recognizance rolls and by entries in the account rolls (Chester 2/72 m.1; Chester 2/73 m.lv; S.C.6/774/6; S.C.6/774/10) and likewise the central exchequer records refer to the king's visits to Flint, Shrawardine and Nantwich (E.403/559 m.14–m.16). For the February 1399 visit see *D.K.R., xxxvi*, p. 376.

It was on these visits that some of the most solemn business of the principality was transacted: as when in June 1398 William Brugges was appointed Chester Herald and on 8 August 1398 a proclamation issued from Holt castle by the king in person conferred the constableship on John of Gaunt and his heirs male.[71] In these circumstances we may assume that the repairs to the castles were designed to make them comfortable as well as defensible: it was on the king's own command that £68 was spent on a 'stew' in the inner royal chamber at Chester castle and in Leland's day a chamber within Oswestry castle was still known as the chamber of Richard II.[72] That Richard should have spent proportionately so much of his time in Cheshire is not of course surprising: for a man plagued as he was with his own problems of security there was no safer refuge than his newly-founded principality. It was the subjects of this principality, after all, who had assured him—'Dycun, slep sicury quile we wake'.[73]

The importance of Chester in the policies of Richard II from 1397 to 1399 is clearly to be explained in good measure in terms of the unwavering loyalty of its inhabitants; but its importance is also evident in terms of political geography. In itself, as has already been emphasized,[74] the new principality was a strong and compact territorial complex; but furthermore it formed part of a remarkable concentration of royal power in the west. It was here—in Wales and Chester—that it was easiest to build a secure territorial empire unshackled by the complexities of the English tenurial scene. It was here that ambitious politicians in the past—whether Hubert de Burgh, or the younger Despenser or Roger Mortimer —had tried to base their power; and it may well be that Richard II, after a fashion, now attempted to do likewise. Whether he had a deliberate design for a principality of the West we shall never know; the evidence is obviously wanting and two years is too short a time to unfold such a design.[75] It is undeniable, however,

71 Chester 2/71 m.7v; Chester 2/73 m.9.

72 S.C.6/774/10; John Leland, *The Itinerary in Wales*, ed. L. Toulmin Smith (London, 1906), p. 75. The normal contemporary meaning of the word 'stew' appears to be a heated room used for baths.

73 Quoted from the Kenilworth Chronicle in M. V. Clarke, op. cit., p. 98.

74 See above, p. 260.

75 One important clue, however, may be provided by Richard's active support for the attempt of his friend, the earl of Salisbury, to recover the key lordship of Denbigh from the earl of March in 1397. See *Adam of Usk*, pp. 15-17 and for a

that there were widespread rumours that Richard intended to rule from Wales and Ireland and that he would never return to England.[76] It is equally undeniable that between them the king and his close favourites—Lescrope, Despenser, Exeter and Aumale—controlled the greater part of Wales. More obviously and more relevantly is this true of North Wales. There the king's authority was virtually exclusive with the exception of the Grey lordship of Dyffryn Clwyd and the two small lordships of Mold and Hawarden secure in the hands of the earl of Salisbury.[77] From the point of view of Chester the importance of this control is obvious. The principality of Chester now had a common border with the principality of Wales and together they formed a remarkable unbroken territorial unit from the River Mersey to Cardigan Bay. Furthermore, they were meant to remain such an unbroken unit in the future, for they formed an inalienable part of the patrimony of the king's eldest son.[78]

Administratively the two principalities were entirely separate, the one organized from Caernarvon, the other from Chester; but logic would sooner or later dictate that there should be some amalgamation of personnel if not of administration. Indeed on occasion the two principalities were treated as if they were one;[79] and officers were appointed with authority within both.[80] This amalgamation of offices was naturally most evident—as indeed it had been in the past[81]—at the higher echelons, and nowhere more obviously so than in the remarkable concentration of authority in the hands of William Lescrope, earl of Wiltshire. That Richard II

discussion of the case G. A. Holmes, *The Estates of the Higher Nobility in fourteenth-century England* (Cambridge, 1957), p. 19 esp. n.3.

[76] *Annales*, pp. 239-40.

[77] The earl of Salisbury failed in his attempt to recover the lordship of Denbigh, but on the death of the earl of March, the Mortimer lands in North Wales were promptly transferred into the safe custody of William Lescrope, *C.P.R., 1396-9*, p. 408.

[78] For the inalienability of the principality of Wales see J. G. Edwards, *The Principality of Wales 1267-1967* (Caernarvon, 1969), pp. 9-10. The inalienability of the new principality of Chester was established at its creation, *R.P.*, iii, p. 354.

[79] See, for example, the phrase 'infra principatum nostrum Cestrie et Northwallie' Chester 2/73 m.5.

[80] Common auditors were appointed for the two principalities and so were other functionaries such as keepers of artillery, E.403/562 m.12; Chester 2/71 m.32.

[81] The earl of Nottingham had been both justice of North Wales and justice of Chester since 1394.

should have entrusted so much power in North Wales and Chester to one of his closest favourites is in itself a measure of the importance of the area in his political strategy. Lescrope held a life grant of the island of Anglesey and also secured the custody of the important Mortimer lordship of Denbigh in August 1398.[82] In themselves these two grants bestowed considerable power and wealth on him; but they were supported by an even more remarkable range of offices. His authority as justice—the head of the administration—embraced North Wales, Chester, Flint and the confiscated Arundel lordships; and to this vast commission he added the life constableships of Beaumaris, Caernarvon, Conway and Holt and some other minor offices to boot.[83] In the person of William Lescrope the administrative and military organizations of the two principalities were merged. That same unity of control likewise lay behind one of Richard II's last independent appointments, that of the earl of Salisbury to the unprecedented position of 'governor of the principality of Chester *and* of the parts of North Wales' on 19 July 1399.[84] Salisbury's commission demonstrated both the geographical extent of the king's lands in Chester and North Wales and the possibility of integrating them into a single power bloc under unitary control.

The appointment of Salisbury as governor was one of the measures which Richard II's supporters in Chester and North Wales took during July 1399 in an attempt to save the king's cause there. Chester castle was placed in a state of defence from as early as 3 July 1399;[85] the earl of Salisbury worked desperately hard to raise an army in his province of North Wales;[86] and on 30 July William Eggerton was appointed keeper of Harlech castle and was commanded to provision it immediately with supplies and to fill it with men.[87] As Bolingbroke's army swept all before it and as the king's supporters in England deserted his cause without a fight, it became increasingly obvious that Richard's final salvation could only lie with the men of Chester and North Wales. Adam of Usk realized this;[88] and so clearly did Bolingbroke. After the fall of

---

[82] *C.P.R., 1396–9*, pp. 82, 408.   [83] Ibid., pp. 10, 16, 284, 322, 347, 356, 402.

[84] Chester 2/73 m.1. His commission appointed him 'gubernator omnium et singulorum ligeorum nostrorum tam principatus [Cestrie] quam parcium North Wallie.'

[85] S.C.6/774/10.   [86] Creton, op. cit., p. 69.   [87] Chester 2/73 m.1.
[88] *Adam of Usk*, p. 27.

Bristol on 29 July Bolingbroke marched his army northwards for the final confrontation with Richard's forces.

That confrontation never took place; the principality of Chester fell without a fight. On 5 August Sir Robert Legh, the sheriff of Cheshire, and others travelled to Shrewsbury to negotiate with Henry Bolingbroke for the surrender of the city of Chester and its castle.[89] On that same day Robert Parys, the chamberlain of the principality lands, ordered that the new great seal of the principality of Chester should be brought from the exchequer to his house in Bridge Street, and from there—on the instructions of the duke of Surrey—he betook himself and the seal to Richard II in Wales.[90] Chester's resistance to the advance of the duke of Lancaster had collapsed. Four days later, on 9 August, Bolingbroke mustered his troops in a cornfield three miles outside the city and marched into the capital of Richard II's new principality triumphantly and without opposition.[91] Holt, Rhuddlan and Flint likewise fell without a struggle;[92] and the only measure of resistance that Bolingbroke's army met within the principality of Chester was occasional guerrilla harassment of its extensive pillaging and looting.[93] In the eyes of Creton, such a meek surrender by the men of Chester could only be explained either by art and cunning or more bluntly by cowardice.[94] By then, however, even Richard's most devoted supporters had to acknowledge that 'all the world seemed to support the duke';[95] and in those circumstances—what-

[89] The details of the submission of Chester are given in the monk of Evesham's chronicle, *Historia Vitae et Regni Ricardi Secundi*, p. 154. They are confirmed by the statement in the Chester chamberlain's account for 1398–9 that Chester castle surrendered on 5 August 'certa condicione', S.C.6/774/10 m.2v.

[90] Chester 2/73 m.1 calendared in *D.K.R. xxxvi*, appendix ii, p. 376. The chamberlain also took with him the 'old seal' of the king as earl of Chester. There is an example of this latter seal in B.M. Additional Charters 6103.

[91] *Adam of Usk*, p. 27; Dieulacres Chronicle, op. cit., p. 171.

[92] Creton, op. cit., pp. 125, 129–30.

[93] *Adam of Usk*, pp. 26–7; *Annales*, pp. 250–1; Dieulacres Chronicle, op. cit., 171–2. Chester castle was extensively rifled by Bolingbroke's troops, S.C.6/774/10.

[94] Creton, op. cit., pp. 123–5. A hint that support for Richard II in Cheshire was not complete may be contained in a recognizance of 5 May 1399 whereby Sir Ralph Radcliffe and Sir Robert Legh—two leading Chester men, the latter being sheriff of the county—swore loyalty to the king during his absence in Ireland and promised to inform him of any rising against him and to resist it. The recognizance could, however, be equally well interpreted as a further indication of Richard's utter lack of trust and his sense of insecurity, *C.Cl.R., 1396–9*, p. 505.

[95] Dieulacres Chronicle, op. cit., p. 172.

ever the proud boasts of happier days[96]—discretion was certainly the better part of valour.

The new principality had not saved the kingdom. The explanation of the collapse of Richard II's cause in July–August 1399 lies beyond the scope of this essay; but its suddenness and totality as far as the principality of Chester is concerned do call for comment. In the first place, it is clear that support for Richard within his new principality was too narrowly based and too exclusively confined to the old county of Chester. The bounds of the new principality certainly included Flintshire, but scarcely a Flintshire man was to be found in the guard of Richard II and indeed there had been a good deal of disaffection among the Welshmen of the county in the 1390s.[97] The new principality also embraced the Arundel lordships; but those lordships had been ruthlessly exploited as a source of patronage for the men of Cheshire and of profit for the king.[98] In such circumstances it was only the men of the county of Chester who felt a deep sense of loyalty and indebtedness to the king. The Welsh—both within the principality of Chester and in Wales generally—proved fickle allies in the hour of need. Aumale may have believed that they would stand firm by Richard and that they pitied his plight.[99] Armies cannot survive on pity; and neither Despenser in south Wales nor Salisbury in the north was able to recruit or at least to keep together an army of Welshmen.[100] Instead the Welsh took to plunder and did well out of it. Richard II, like Edward II before him, could find no final refuge in Wales.

The Welsh may have proved fickle; the men of Chester did not. They had too much to lose in the defeat of their prince; and when the rest of the army deserted Richard II in south Wales, his Cheshire

[96] Ironically the very boast of the Cheshire archers, according to Walsingham (*Annales*, 237) was that they would protect Richard 'contra totam Angliam . . ., immo, contra totum mundum'.

[97] There had been a major demonstration in the Flint county court in 1394 and in 1398 many of the leading men of Flintshire were bound over to keep the peace (*Transactions of the Honourable Society of Cymmrodorion* (1968), part ii, p. 157; Chester 2/71 m.11–m.11v.). The only notable Flintshire Welshman in Richard II's retinue was David Fychan.

[98] As late as June 1399 a commission was established to inquire into the debts owed to the earl of Arundel in Bromfield and Yale, Chester 2/73 m.5.

[99] Creton, op. cit., pp. 57, 105.

[100] For the failure of Salisbury and Despenser see respectively Creton, op. cit., p. 70 and *Adam of Usk*, p. 27.

bodyguard remained unshaken in their loyalty.[101] They were, however, given no opportunity to defend their principality, for Richard II had taken the cream of the military strength of Chester with him to Ireland. Indeed, if we are to believe Walsingham, he had deliberately kept other contingents to a minimum so that his own Chester troops could overawe the rest of the army in numbers.[102] The Chester contribution to the expedition was undoubtedly large, for it not only consisted of the royal bodyguard but also of at least a further 10 knights, 110 men at arms and 900 archers.[103] Tactically this demand on Chester's military resources proved to be a grave error, for it meant that Bolingbroke was never forced to face the reliable corps of Richard's army on its home ground. 'The inner citadel of Richard's kingdom' had been left virtually undefended; and it fell without a fight.

With the fall of Chester, Richard II's cause was all but lost. Bolingbroke immediately took over the reins of government within the new principality. Already by 14 August Hotspur had been appointed justice of Chester for his 'most dread lord, Henry duke of Lancaster and steward of England' and was issuing strict orders for the preservation of peace within Cheshire under his personal seal for want of the official seal (which Robert Parys had removed to Wales).[104] Two days later, the Chester administration was purged.[105] On that same day, 16 August, Richard II was brought to Chester as a prisoner.[106] One by one his faithful Cheshire followers—John Mascy, John Lee, John son of John Lee, John son of Robert Lee, Thomas Haslington and Robert Donne— came and submitted at Chester and found recognizances to be of good behaviour *erga ipsum ducem [Lancastrie] et statum regni et populi*.[107] Letters from the Chester exchequer still bore Richard's

[101] Dieulacres Chronicle, op. cit., p. 172. [102] *Annales*, pp. 238-9.
[103] E.403/562 m.10, m.16.

[104] Chester 2/74 m.3.—appointing keepers of the peace. Hotspur's appointment as justice of Chester by Bolingbroke is to be compared with the appointment of the earl of Northumberland as warden of the West March on 2 August, *English Historical Documents, iv, 1327-1485*, ed. A. R. Myers (London, 1969), p. 179. Though Hotspur was acting as justice of Chester on 14 August, his letters patent of office and his payment of salary were naturally dated from 13 October 1399, the day of Henry IV's coronation.

[105] John Trevor took over as chamberlain from Robert Parys on 16 August, but the constable of Chester had already been dismissed on 8 August. S.C.6/774/10.

[106] I follow here the chronology in M. V. Clarke, op. cit., p. 71.

[107] The terms of the surrenders are to be found in Chester 2/73 m.7.

title as prince of Chester as late as 23 September;[108] but by then the days of Richard II's reign were numbered. On 30 September the first—and last—prince of Chester was deposed; and with the revocation of the acts of the Michaelmas parliament of 1397 in Henry IV's first parliament, Chester reverted from the status of a principality to that of a county and the annexed marcher lordships were simultaneously restored to the earl of Arundel.

Thus ends the brief history of the principality of Chester. It had survived for just over two years; but during that period it had occupied a disproportionately important role in the political life of England. And in any analysis of Richard II's downfall, his overdependence on Cheshire and its men must occupy a prominent place. The principality of Chester had been created as a mark of affection in an hour of victory; as such it could have been regarded as no more than a temporary extravagance by a king who revelled in the distribution of new titles. But that affection was quickly transformed into an infatuation which profoundly affected the course of English politics. The events of 1397-9 showed that the creation of the principality of Chester was more than a fulsome gesture of gratitude for past services. It marked both the virtual separation of Cheshire from the body politic of England and, paradoxically, at the same time the king's increasing dependence on the men of Chester in his military and political calculations within his realm. Such dependence inevitably meant that while the basis of Richard's support within his new principality was steadily becoming more secure, his support within the rest of his kingdom was proportionately weakened. The events of July to August 1399 amply demonstrated the disastrous consequences of such political imbalance: Richard II was still acceptable as prince of Chester but no longer as king of England.

[108] Chester 2/74 m.3.

XIV

Richard II and the Wars of the Roses

MARGARET ASTON

'our eyes do hate the dire aspect
Of civil wounds plough'd up with neighbours' sword'
King Richard II, I. iii. 127–8.

'I am Richard II. know ye not that?' Queen Elizabeth's words amounted to a rhetorical question for their recipient, William Lambarde.[1] Now, they may act as a reminder of how the Tudors stand between us and Richard II. History being what it is every historian has some duties towards historiography, but for historians of the later middle ages in England, where the Tudor imprint is still powerful, the need is specially great. Such is the hold of poetry and accepted myth, the impact of oral and typographical repetition, that Shakespeare and the Reformation remain mediators of the past. Historical textbooks continue to repeat clichés about fifteenth-century bloodshed and the decimation of the nobility which stem from sixteenth-century interpretations.[2] The

I wish to thank Professor William Haller and Mrs Elizabeth Eisenstein for their helpful criticisms of this paper. To avoid misunderstanding I ought perhaps to stress the limitations of my argument. It does not attempt to discuss the 'Tudor myth' in its entirety—the important question of Tudor views of British history has been left altogether aside, not to mention other aspects. Nor have I explored the Yorkist case for Richard, which produced such favourable statements as a poem of the 1460s that looked back to his reign as a time of wealth and plenty.

[1] *The Progresses and Public Processions of Queen Elizabeth*, ed. John Nichols, iii (London, 1823), p. 552. This reported conversation of 1601 has received considerable attention in Shakespearean scholarship because of the queen's allusion to the playing of the tragedy of Richard II; cf. *King Richard II*, ed. Peter Ure (Arden Shakespeare, London, 1961), pp. lvii ff.

[2] For instance A. L. Rowse, *Bosworth Field and the Wars of the Roses* (London, 1966), p. 144 remarks 'we see the way in which families were being decimated'; or E. Harris Harbison, *The Age of Reformation* (Ithaca, N.Y., 1955), p. 15 speaks of how 'In Spain, France, and England the civil wars of the fifteenth century had decimated

Tudor myth has long been recognized, but it has not yet been banished. Nor has the full extent of this historical reconstruction ever been properly displayed. The idea of the Wars of the Roses, which was a framework for understanding the whole of the late medieval past, had a profound and pervasive influence, ecclesiastical as well as secular. Among the reigns and personalities whose interpretation it affected, Richard II was prominent. He held a critical position in the Tudor historical scheme, and it should help to clear the path to our own understanding to see more of the range and outcome of earlier misreadings.

★   ★   ★

It is a mistake to dismiss the term 'Wars of the Roses' as the invention of Sir Walter Scott. He may have been the first to use the phrase as such and to popularize its use, but very little credit, or discredit, need go to him for this.[3] The name, to all intents and pur-

---

the feudal nobility'. There have, of course, been warnings enough, both tentative and firm, against such statements and exaggerations of the casualties, destruction and dislocation caused by fighting in fifteenth-century England. Cf. K. B. McFarlane, 'The Wars of the Roses', *Proceedings of the British Academy*, l (1964), pp. 87–119, including the caveat (p. 115) 'if any generalization about the Wars of the Roses is sure of wide agreement it is that they resulted in the extermination of most of the "old nobility"; and none is more demonstrably false'; J. R. Lander, *The Wars of the Roses* (London, 1965), pp. 20–3; J. R. Lander, *Conflict and Stability in Fifteenth-Century England* (London, 1969), pp. 161–4; R. L. Storey, *The End of the House of Lancaster* (London, 1966), p. 7; V. H. H. Green, *The Later Plantagenets* (London, 1955), pp. 330, 351, 356, 381, 395–6; C. H. Williams, 'England: The Yorkist Kings, 1461–1485', *Cambridge Medieval History*, viii (Cambridge, 1936), pp. 421, 423–4; C. L. Kingsford, *Prejudice & Promise in XVth Century England* (Oxford, 1925), pp. 33, 48. Among earlier works credit for challenging the accepted view should be given to T. L. Kington Oliphant, 'Was the Old English Aristocracy destroyed by the Wars of the Roses?' *T.R.H.S.*, i (1872), pp. 351–6, which aimed to prove 'that the common notion of the old English aristocracy having been destroyed by the Wars of the Roses is a mistake'.

[3] S. B. Chrimes, *Lancastrians, Yorkists and Henry VII* (London, 1964), pp. xi-xiv; S. B. Chrimes, 'The Fifteenth Century', *History*, xlviii (1963), p. 24, where E. F. Jacob is praised for not using the term 'Wars of the Roses' in *The Fifteenth Century* (Oxford, 1961); Lander, *The Wars of the Roses*, p. 15. For the reference to Scott's *Anne of Geierstein* see n. 9 below. The most astringent objections to the use of the term are those of Professor Chrimes, who seems to weaken his case by saying 'The civil wars of that [the fifteenth] century were not about roses, badges, or other symbols'; moreover it is only literarily correct to state that Tudor writers 'stopped short of calling the series of battles "the wars of the roses"'; Chrimes, op. cit., pp.

poses, had been invented together with the idea, centuries earlier.
'The horrible murthers and bloody battels, that were of long time
between the factions of the red rose and the white, the houses of
York and Lancaster, for the crown of this realm, by the happy
marriage of king Henry VII. and Q. Elizabeth, were ended': so ran
a motion to parliament, on lines that were already conventional,
about the succession in 1571.[4] If Elizabeth I's subjects were kept
mindful of the inestimable benefits which had accrued to England
through the joyful union of her grandparents, they in turn made
sure that the queen remained conscious of the infinite perils which
threatened the land if she should fail it. Sir Thomas Smith, putting
the case in 1561 for Elizabeth to marry an English nobleman, chose
a dialogue form which enabled him with somewhat less than his
usual bluntness to appeal to her—in words spoken by the realm
itself—to perpetuate 'the race of the mixed rose, which brought
again the amiable peace long exiled from among my children by
the striving of the two roses'. His elaboration of the horrors of
such strife described it in terms which had already become standard.

I am afraid to speak, and I tremble to think, what murders and
slaughters, what robbing and rifling, what spoiling and burning, what
hanging and heading, what wasting and destroying, civil war should
bring in, if ever it should come. From the time that King Richard II.
was deposed, in whom all the issue of the Black Prince was extinct, unto
the death of King Richard III. the unkind and cruel brother of Edward
IV. whose daughter was married, as ye know, to King Henry VII. by
reason of titles this poor realm had never long rest. Noble men were
beheaded, poor men spoiled, both one and th'other slain in battle, or
murdered at home. Now this King prevailed, now th'other. No man
sure of his Prince, no man of his goods, no man of his life: a King to-day,
to-morrow a prisoner; now hold the sceptre, and shortly after fly
privily the realm. And when this fell upon the head, how sped the body,
think you? Those two blades of Lyonel and John of Gaunt never rested

xii, 177; cf. Storey, op. cit., Introduction, pp. 1–28 on 'The Wars of the Roses'
where the name is criticized for directing over-much attention to the dynastic
issue.

4 John Strype, *Annals of the Reformation* (Oxford, 1824), II, ii, p. 425, from 'A
motion in parliament, 13 Elizab. about the succession to the crown; according to
K. Henry VIII. his will'. Cf. J. E. Neale, *Elizabeth I and her Parliaments*, i (London,
1953), pp. 226–34.

pursuing th'one th'other, till the red rose was almost razed out, and the white made all bloody; and as it were Eteocles and Polynices, they ceased not till they had filled their country full of bloody streams. They set the father against the son, the brother against the brother, the uncle slew the nephew, and was slain himself. So blood pursued and ensued blood, till all the realm was brought to great confusion. It is no marvel though they lost France, when they could not keep England. And England in the latter end of King Henry VI. was almost a very chaos: parishes decayed, churches fell down, towns were desolate, ploughed fields waxed groves, pastures were made woods; almost half England by civil war slain, and they which remained not sure, but in moats and castles, or lying in routs and heaps together.[5]

It was a concept of civil discord—duly turned into a lesson for royal ears—which minimized no terrors in accounting for all England's calamities of the fifteenth century. The striving roses were the cause of all, from Richard II to Richard III.

To think of the red rose as a device of warring Lancastrians was certainly misleading and historically incorrect. Whereas the white rose was a recognized badge of York in the fifteenth century, evidence for the use of the red rose as a Lancastrian symbol is rare before 1485. The development of the red rose, like the whole idea of the factious roses, was the work of the Tudors, who had themselves been using the red rose in Wales long before Bosworth and who were as anxious to draw attention to their Lancastrian lineage as they were to harp upon the glorious theme of dynastic and civil union.[6] The warring roses, as much as the union rose which grafted them together, were successful Tudor plantings upon the Plantagenet past. There is no need to look far for results; it was an idea with luxuriant growth.

And for that the discendents of . . . the dukes of Lancaster and Yorke, came afterward to strive who had the best title to reigne, therof it came, that the controversie had his name of these two familes, which for more

[5] John Strype, *The Life of the Learned Sir Thomas Smith* (Oxford, 1820), pp. 216, 221–2; Mary Dewar, *Sir Thomas Smith: A Tudor Intellectual in Office* (London, 1964), pp. 84–6. It is to be noted that Strype, like Tyndale (see below p. 292), connected the civil wars with the effects of late medieval depopulation.

[6] Sydney Anglo, *Spectacle, Pageantry and Early Tudor Policy* (Oxford, 1969), pp. 36–7; C. L. Kingsford, *English History in Contemporary Poetry*, ii, *Lancaster and York, 1399 to 1485* (London, 1913), pp. 41, 45; Howell T. Evans, *Wales and the Wars of the Roses* (Cambridge, 1915), pp. 7–8; *Bishop Percy's Folio Manuscript. Ballads and Romances*, ed. John W. Hales and Frederick J. Furnivall, iii (London, 1868), p. 194.

distinction sake, & the better to be knowne, tooke uppon them for their ensignes a rose of two different colures, to wit, the white rose, and the redd, as al the world knoweth, wherof the white served for Yorke, and the redd for Lancaster.[7]

The world seems mistakenly to have been making this assumption long before Robert Parsons wrote these words in the 1590s. According to Polydore Vergil in the first Tudor reigns, seventy to eighty years earlier, 'the common people even at this day call the one [faction] the red rose, the other the white, for the white rose was the emblem of one family and the red rose of the other'.[8]

To refer, therefore, as Scott did in 1828–9, to 'the civil discords so dreadfully prosecuted in the wars of the White and Red Roses' was to do little more than capitalize and extend the currency of a long-established denomination.[9] The formula may itself have been mistaken, but if one wishes to contest its premises there is very little point in taking issue with the name which summarizes it. The 'Wars of the Roses', like the 'Renaissance', might as well be accepted as a term which has come to stay, given the proviso that it belongs more to historiography than to history. And though, like the 'Renaissance', it was not generally adopted by historians until the nineteenth century, it has its own long ancestry, and acts as a shorthand for the idea of civil discord which permeated Tudor views of the fifteenth century.[10]

---

[7] Robert Parsons [R. Doleman *pseud.*], *A Conference About the Next Succession to the Crowne of Ingland* ([Antwerp?], 1594), pt. ii, p. 38.

[8] Polydore Vergil, *Anglica Historia* (Basel, 1534), p. 315; Denys Hay, *Polydore Vergil, Renaissance Historian and Man of Letters* (Oxford, 1952), p. 143 quotes this passage from the later editions; for the composition of Vergil's work see pp. 79ff.

[9] Sir Walter Scott, *Anne of Geierstein or The Maiden of the Mist* (Boston, 1894), i, p. 111, a passage in Ch. vii in which the main emphasis is on Edward IV's intention of regaining 'those rich and valuable foreign possessions which had been lost during the administration of the feeble Henry VI'. The novel is set in the mid-fifteenth century and in Ch. iii (p. 66) appears a conventionally exaggerated sketch of the impact of the wars. '"Alas!" he said, "I deserve to feel the pain which your words inflict. What nation can know the woes of England that has not felt them—what eye can estimate them which has not seen a land torn and bleeding with the strife of two desperate factions, battles fought in every province, plains heaped with slain, and scaffolds drenched in blood! Even in your quiet valleys, methinks, you may have heard of the Civil Wars of England?"'

[10] Thus although the red and white roses were in the sixteenth century commonly associated with the Lancastrian and Yorkist factions, nineteenth-century writers must be held responsible for adopting and popularizing the name 'wars of the roses' as a title. The earliest book to be published with this name which I have

Now that we have so long become accustomed to the use and abuse of the idea of the warring roses, it is important to realize not only how it arose, but also how in its modern application it differs from its origin. The nineteenth-century writers who popularized the term narrowed its context—perhaps unconsciously, certainly unavowedly. In this we have followed them. Historians today who continue, somewhat defensively, to write about the wars of the roses, generally concern themselves with thirty years in the second half of the fifteenth century (1455 to 1485 or 1487) when Henry VI's incapacity and Yorkist claims brought the country to armed conflict and bloodshed. Writers of the sixteenth and seventeenth centuries, on the other hand, had in mind much more than this. They thought in terms of a whole century of dissension, brought to a happy conclusion when Henry VII married Elizabeth of York and, still more completely, when the last Yorkist pretenders had been snuffed out and Henry VIII, heir to both houses, succeeded. Not unnaturally the main focus of attention was upon the reign of Henry VI, but the beginning of the wars was placed long before this. They ran, as indicated by Sir Thomas Smith's rhetorical plea of 1561, from the reign of Richard II to the death of Richard III.[11]

discovered (but not seen) is J. G. Edgar, *The wars of the roses: or, stories of the struggle of York and Lancaster* (London, 1859).

[11] Modern historians who accept the limit of thirty years in the second half of the century include Lander, Storey, Green, Williams, Oliphant and Evans, in the works cited in notes 2 and 6 above. Plenty of other examples could be cited, including the classic over-statement of *The Encyclopaedia Britannica*, 11th edn. (Cambridge, 1911), s.v. Roses, Wars of the; 'a name given to a series of civil wars in England during the reigns of Henry VI., Edward. and Richard III . . . They were marked by a ferocity and brutality which are practically unknown in the history of English wars before and since'. R. B. Mowat's *The Wars of the Roses, 1377–1471* (London, 1914), despite its title, restricts the name to the years after 1455, while recognizing it as 'an invention of the sixteenth century'; p. 232, cf. pp. 10, 17, 34, 50–1, 95. A. L. Rowse, in *Bosworth Field and the Wars of the Roses*, though surveying the period 1377 until the Tudors, reserves the term 'Wars of the Roses' until ch. vii and events of the 1450s; pp. 127 ff., 281. Historians of the sixteenth and seventeenth centuries might differ over the exact period of the wars, but it is clear that where there is now a consensus on about thirty years there was once a consensus of a duration of about a hundred. In addition to the works cited in the following paragraph see n.18 below and pp. 282 and 299 for quotations from Thomas Smith and Robert Parsons; according to John Taylor, *A Briefe Remembrance of all the English Monarchs, From the Normans Conquest, until this present* (London, 1618), sig. C 2r, by the time of Edward IV 'These bloody broyles had lasted threescore yeares, . . . [and] wasted fourescore of the Royall Peeres'. Perhaps one might see evidence of this disjunction

Shakespeare might well have been surprised that a wars of the roses version of his historical cycle should limit itself to his plays about Henry VI and Richard III; for him the wars embraced the whole historical sequence. 'The blood of English shall manure the ground, . . . tumultuous wars Shall kin with kin, and kind with kind, confound.' The bishop of Carlisle's prophecy of 1399 was fulfilled by a continuous train of disorder until—in echoing words —it was closed up at the end of *King Richard III*. 'We will unite the white rose and the red: . . . England hath long been mad and scarr'd herself; The brother blindly shed the brother's blood.'[12] For Shakespeare and his contemporaries it was a commonplace that the roses had striven for a full century.

One important result of this viewing of the past was seriously to prejudice the history of Richard II. Placed in the context of the divided succession and civil disturbance, Richard's reign tended to be looked at for explanations of coming strife, focused upon the circumstances leading to the deposition, unnaturally detached from events of the fourteenth century to act as the explanatory prelude to those of the fifteenth. Changes in the succession, or fears of such changes, renewed civil war, or fears of civil war, caused the struggles of York and Lancaster and the fate of Richard II to be re-examined and re-written. During the last decade of Elizabeth's reign several disputants, joining issue with Robert Parsons on the succession question, combed through the rights and wrongs of Richard II's deposition and the rival claims to the throne thereafter.[13] In the mid-seventeenth century the Italian Giovanni

---

of opinion between modern and Tudor writers in the remark of Professor Hay, op. cit., p. 143 on Vergil's *Anglica Historia*; 'The actual outbreak of the "Wars of the Roses" is, of course, quite properly explained . . . when the rivalry of the Lancastrians and Richard duke of York finally provokes an open conflict; but there is no doubt that the main catastrophe for Vergil was Henry IV's seizure of the throne'. It should be noted that while accounting for the divisions of the factions of Lancaster and York in 1453, both then and in 1451 Vergil (op. cit., 1546, pp. 497, 502) speaks of the revival and renewal of domestic discord. Cf. Bernard André's slightly earlier description of the outbreak of civil war in the 1450s; *Historia Regis Henrici Septimi a Bernardo Andrea Tholosate Conscripta*, ed. James Gairdner (London, 1858), pp. 18–20. I owe this reference to the kindness of Professor Haller.

[12] *King Richard II*, p. 133, IV. i. 136–47; *Richard III*, ed. John Dover Wilson (Cambridge, 1954), p. 139, V. v. 19–31; Hay, op. cit., pp. 144–5; E. M. W. Tillyard, *Shakespeare's History Plays* (Harmondsworth, 1962), pp. 7, 59 ff, 304.

[13] Much of this controversy focused upon Robert Parson's *Conference About the*

3*b*. Biondi's *History of the Civill Warres* (1641) used as its title-page, with necessary adaptions, Reynold Elstrack's engraving for Henry Holland's *Bazilliologia*. See p. 289.

3*a*. The title-page of Stow's *Annales of England* (1592), which was also used in his *Chronicles* (1580). See p. 288.

4a. Richard II as delineated in Thomas Tymme's *Booke, containing the true portraiture . . . of the kings of England* (1597), which repeats the tradition that 'this king was comely of personage'. See p. 312.

4b. Reynold Elstrack's engraving of Richard II from Henry Holland's *Basiliωlogia* (1618). See p. 313.

Francesco Biondi produced *An History of the Civill Warres of England betweene the two houses of Lancaster and Yorke*, which carried lengthily into prose the topic of Samuel Daniel and Shakespeare and detailed the history of eight reigns, starting with Richard II and ending with Henry VII.[14] Later in the same century a new wars of the roses history appeared in a new succession context. *England's Happiness in a Lineal Succession; And the Deplorable Miseries Which ever attended Doubtful Titles to the Crown, Historically Demonstrated, By the Bloody Wars Between the Two Houses of York & Lancaster* aimed in 1685 to show England's fortune in the succession of James II by contrast with 'that Bloody, Unnatural and Fatal War, which had lasted about 106 Years' between York and Lancaster—traced here from Richard II's reign to the execution of the earl of Warwick by Henry VII.[15]

Next Succession, a work which was remarkable for its extremist arguments and which has been described as 'the chief storehouse of facts and arguments drawn upon by nearly all opponents of the royal claims for a century'; it was reissued in whole or in part in 1648, 1655 and 1681. In examining the titles of the various claimants to the English throne Parsons went fully into 'the great and generall controversie and contention' between Lancaster and York, and the justice of Richard II's deposition, showing reasons for supposing that the latter was 'iust and lawful'. He was assailed for this demonstration, combined with the assertion that 'the best of al their titles [to the crown] . . . depended of this authority of the common wealth', being 'ether allowed confirmed altered or disanulled by parlaments'. In this controversial literature on the succession Richard II remains attached to the Lancastrian–Yorkist dispute. Parsons, op. cit., pt. i, p. 195, pt. ii, pp. 56 ff., 72; *The Political Works of James I*, ed. C. H. McIlwain (Cambridge, Mass., 1918), pp. l–li, xcii–xciii; John E. Parish, *Robert Parsons and the English Counter-Reformation* (Rice University Studies, vol. 52, 1966), pp. 43–7.

[14] The rest of the title makes plain that Richard II's reign belonged to the wars; 'The originall whereof is set downe in the life of *Richard* the second; their proceedings, in the lives of *Henry* the fourth, the fifth, and sixth, *Edward* the fourth and fifth, *Richard* the third, and *Henry* the seventh, in whose dayes they had a happy period.' Giovanni Francesco Biondi (1572–1644) spent the years 1609–40 in England, where he enjoyed the patronage of James I, who knighted him in 1622, and Charles I, to whom the *Civill Warres* was dedicated. The first edition, in Italian, was published in Venice in three volumes in 1637–44, entitled *L'Istoria delle guerre civili d'Inghilterra, tra le due case di Lancastro, e di Iorc*. Henry Carey's translation, not completed until after the author's death, was begun 'out of [his] written Papers, whilst he was here in England': the preface to the second part, issued in 1646 after Biondi's death, expressed the hope that, appearing in a time of civil war, the book might offer persuasions of peace. Biondi, *History of the Civill Warres*, pt. ii, sig. A 2r–v; *D.N.B.*, s.v. Biondi, Sir Giovanni Francesco.

[15] Warwick's execution is dated 'about' 1504 (it was in fact 1499) so the 106 years run from 1398 to 1504. The wars were luridly described to add force to the

Title-pages—even of books which were not specifically concerned with the civil wars as a topic—represent graphically this
attachment of Richard II to the Tudor scheme. John Stow's
Annales of England dealt with English affairs from the first inhabitants and the legendary Brutus up to the author's own times, but
the segment of history which was singled out for illustration on
the title-page was that from Edward III to the reigning queen. It
was a depiction of the divided roses which illustrates the central
position of Richard II (Plate 3*a*). The descent—or ascent—of the
crown is shown as a rosework genealogical tree that springs from
the side of a recumbent warrior king Edward III.[16] The branches
of York and Lancaster rise to right and left, and the bust of Elizabeth placed centrally at the top appropriately occupies a position
exactly comparable to that of Richard II beneath: her stem was
terminating in the 1590s quite as clearly as had his in the 1390s. At
the front of Biondi's history is another version of the same theme.
Here the kings whose reigns bounded the wars are shown as full-
length figures. Between Richard II, erect and regal, clasping orb
and sceptre, and Henry VII, martially triumphant, his sword
resting negligently on his shoulder, lie strewn the corpses—royal
and otherwise—of the century that divided them. Below, linked
with this century of domestic strife, is a vignette of the battling
troops of that other, associated century of foreign warfare. Reynold Elstrack's engraving was no more new to Biondi than the

argument: 'it is almost incredible to believe, how many Bloody Battels were
fought, what Multitudes of Men were slaughtered, how many Treasons and horrid
Conspiracies were carried on and perpetrated, how much Noble Blood was spilt,
how many Families were ruined, how many Barbarous Executions, how many
unreasonable Fines, and perpetual Banishments hapned, during this unfortunate
War . . . the many miseries, which attended that Unfortunate Quarrel, may serve,
at once, to shew us their misery and our own happiness, under the Influence of the
most Auspicious and Promising Reign of our present Sovereign, James the Second,
who derives his Title from the happy Union of the two Houses, whereby that
War was ended'. *England's Happiness* (London, 1685), sigs. A 3r–v, A 6r, p. 228.
This book, like Biondi's, carries an illustration which shows how the Tudors'
union theme was adapted to the Stuarts; it also covers the same period as Biondi,
and of its 228 pages 63 are devoted to the reign of Richard II.

16 Stow's *The Annales of England* (London, 1592) was an enlarged version of his
The Chronicles of England (London, [1580]), which carried the same illustration as
its title-page. For the use of such genealogical trees in London pageants, including
a discussion of Richard Grafton's role in their planning and their possible relationship to the frontispiece of Hall's *Chronicle* (1550), see Anglo, op. cit., pp. 194–5,
334–5, 354.

idea which it depicted, but he followed it with a text more directly applied to its subject-matter than had Henry Holland's *Baziliωlogia*, whence it was borrowed.[17] (Plate 3 *b*.)

Richard II, sculpted thus as a figure annexed to the civil wars, was a monarch whose realities were no less (though less notoriously) blurred than those of Richard III. The two kings stood as the two poles of the Tudor historical sequence, and others besidet Biondi found their roles to be special and specially unfortunate. 'All the (Kings) *Richards*, and all the Dukes of *Gloucester* came to violent ends'.[18] Richard II as well as Richard III had been guilty of grave regnal injustices. Both were discrowned; both met untimely deaths; both gave way to new departures in history. The second Richard, unlike the third, was not regarded as a monster but he too, seen through the distorting glass of sixteenth-century interpreters, emerged—more convincingly but nevertheless markedly—as a constructed type. The facets of his reign and character which were selected and emphasized and known were those which best fitted the Tudor formula.

★   ★   ★

[17] H. Holland, *Baziliωlogia, A Booke of Kings* (London, 1618), title-page. In Biondi's work the portraits of Charles I and Henrietta Maria were substituted for those of James I and Anne, and the figures of Richard II and Henry VII are identified, but otherwise the engravings are the same. The upper part of Richard's figure, like the separate portrait of him in this volume, seems to be related to the Westminster painting; cf. below p. 313. The portraits of Holland's book, like its title-page, were used again elsewhere; H. C. Levis, *Baziliωlogia, A Booke of Kings. Notes on a Rare Series of Engraved English Royal Portraits from William the Conqueror to James I* (New York, 1913), pp. 1, 18–20, 28–9, 60–1; Freeman O'Donoghue, *Catalogue of Engraved British Portraits Preserved in the Department of Prints and Drawings in the British Museum*, iii (London, 1912), pp. 567–9.

[18] Biondi, op. cit., pt. ii, bk. viii, p. 115. Biondi was apologetic about devoting the final book of his history to Henry VII; 'The Civill wars whereof I write, ought to end with the death of *Richard* the 3. without any further progress', but could not because of the pretenders Simnel and Warbeck; ibid., pt. ii, bk. ix, p. 219. In 1651 Lambert van den Bos (or Bosch) published at Amsterdam his *Roode en Witte Roos. of Lankaster en Jork*, a play on Richard III which was possibly translated into Dutch from a lost English original. The action is focused on Richard III, but 'the feud begun of old by our ancestors' is discussed with explicit reference to the defects of Richard II, and his 'sly tricks'. In 1658 Bos published a prose account of the struggles of Lancaster and York which also took Richard II as its starting-point and allocated a hundred years to the subject. O. J. Campbell, 'The Position of the *Roode en Witte Roos* in the Saga of King Richard III', *University of Wisconsin Studies in Language and Literature*, No. 5 (Madison, 1919), pp. 1, 18, 103–7. The historical reputation of Richard III has been helpfully described by A. R. Myers, 'Richard III and Historical Tradition', *History*, liii (1968), pp. 181–202.

It is neither possible nor necessary here to trace the emergence of the wars of the roses myth in the political context in which it has received most salient recognition.[19] The pivotal place of Richard II was already recognized by sixteenth-century disputants, who pointed out that divergences of opinion about him belonged to the wars themselves.[20] Whereas for the Yorkists all wrongs stemmed from the criminal deeds of 1399–1400, Lancastrian supporters had every reason to go back behind the deposition to demonstrate the misdeeds which justified Richard's removal. Two major features of the Tudor thesis were already enunciated in the declaration of the Yorkist title in the first parliament of Edward IV; namely the idea that the deposition and death of Richard II had involved the land in untold tribulation, and secondly an elaborately exaggerated view of the scale of fifteenth-century troubles. The usurping Henry of Lancaster, it was asserted,

the same Kyng Richard, Kyng enoynted, coroned and consecrate, and his Liege and moost high Lord in the erth, ayenst Godds Lawe, Mannes Liegeaunce, and oth of fidelite, with uttermost punicion attormentyng, murdred and destroied, with moost vyle, heynous and lamentable deth; wherof . . . this Reame of Englond, . . . therfore hath suffred the charge of intollerable persecution, punicion and tribulation, wherof the lyke hath not been seen or herde in any other Cristen Reame, by any memorie or recorde ... unrest, inward werre and trouble, unrightwisnes, shedyng and effusion of innocent blode, abusion of the Lawes, partialte, riotte, extorcion, murdre, rape and viciouse lyvyng, have been the gyders and leders of the noble Reame of Englond.[21]

The next Yorkist reign, according to More's *History of King Richard III*, saw another link attached to the chain of supposition—the idea of the decimation of the nobility.

In which inward warre among our self, hath ben so gret effucion of the

[19] In addition to the works of Tillyard, Hay, and Lander already referred to, see Lily B. Campbell, *Shakespeare's "Histories": Mirrors of Elizabethan Policy* (San Marino, 1947), pp. 119–25, 168, ff.

[20] Both Robert Parsons and his opponent Sir Thomas Craig stressed this prejudice in Lancastrian and Yorkist disputants. Parsons, op. cit., pt. ii, pp. 62–3; Thomas Craig, *Concerning the Right of Succession to the Kingdom of England, Two Books; Against the Sophisms of one Parsons a Jesuite, Who assum'd the Counterfeit Name of Doleman* (London, 1703), p. 322. The 1703 translation was apparently the first edition of this work which the title-page states was originally written in Latin 'above 100 Years since'.

[21] *R.P.*, v, p. 464.

auncient noble blood of this realme, y^t scarcely the half remaineth, to the gret infebling of this noble land, beside many a good town ransakid & spoiled, by them that have ben going to ye field or cumming from thence. . . . So that no time was ther in which rich men for their mony, & gret men for their landes or some other for some fere or some displesure were not out of peryl.[22]

So, from the arguments of the disputants themselves Tudor writers were able to develop that conception of divine punishment and deliverance which Shakespeare inherited from Polydore Vergil through the chronicle of Edward Hall.

The idea of the wars of the roses arose therefore in the thick of political contest as a political moral which looked back to 1399 as a critical turning-point. Powerful moralizations are not, however, usually restricted in their application, and this one was no exception in that it grew in different contexts and was applied in different fields. The Tudor myth of history was not only a political myth relating to the secular order of the universe. Quite as evidently it was also a reshaping of the religious past, and here too the reign of Richard II was regarded as a point of departure which had profoundly affected the course of England's development. This tendentious patterning likewise magnified the disasters of the fifteenth century as the indicator of divine displeasure. But in this case it was the affairs of the church at the turn of the fourteenth century which Richard's reign and fate were seen to have so greatly affected. This part of the Tudor legend failed (for reasons which quickly become apparent) to establish itself so successfully,

[22] *The Complete Works of St Thomas More*, ed. Richard S. Sylvester, ii (New Haven, 1963), p. 71. Tales of mortality—royal and common as well as noble—grew in the telling and were used as warnings to both crown and subjects. Cf. Tyndale, 'and of their noble blood remaineth not the third, nor I believe the sixth, yea, and if I durst be so bold, I wene I might safely swear that there remaineth not the sixteenth part. Their own sword hath eaten them up'; a letter to Elizabeth on the subject of her marriage spoke of 'great ruines of great families, and great effusion of the bloud royal' in the time of Henry VI, and alleged that between the death of Richard II and the accession of Edward IV 'there was in the mean season slain fourscore of the bloud royal'; Thomas Craig said that as the result of Henry IV's usurpation 'Of all his most numerous Family *There was not one left to piss against the Wall*, to make use of a Scripture phrase; This gave beginning and rise to those Lamentable and deadly Factions between the Families of *York* and *Lancaster*; which was not expiated but with the slaughter and blood of a hundred thousand *Englishmen*'. William Tyndale, *Expositions and Notes on Sundry Portions of the Holy Scriptures*, ed. Henry Walter (Parker Society, Cambridge, 1849), p. 53; Strype, *Annals of the Reformation*, II, ii, p. 655; Craig, op. cit., p. 331, cf. p. 322.

and has therefore been less noticed by modern historians. Yet it was equally a part of contemporary theory, and is equally revealing of the ways in which interpretations of Richard's life and character were bent to shape Tudor preoccupations.[23]

In the Tudor Protestant myth Richard II is presented as the would-be defender of the Gospel, and the turmoils of the fifteenth century were attributed to the suppression of Wycliffe's admonitory voice. This view of things was propounded by William Tyndale when the Reformation in England was still very much in the making, and it was carried further by others who built on his suggestions.

> Wickliffe preached repentance unto our fathers not long since. They repented not; for their hearts were indurate, and their eyes blinded with their own pope-holy righteousness, wherewith they had made their souls gay against the receiving again of the wicked spirit . . . But what followed? They slew their true and right king, and set up three wrong kings a row, under which all the noble blood was slain up, and half the commons thereto, what in France, and what with their own sword, in fighting among themselves for the crown; and the cities and towns decayed, and the land brought half into a wilderness, in respect of what it was before.[24]

The land was devastated by dissension because it had failed to hear the contemporary call to repentance. Tyndale's exposition of the divine judgement manifested in fifteenth-century events was a variation of the theory which Polydore Vergil first published a few years later. But it was a theory with a difference, in that the fatal breach between Plantagenet and Lancaster was envisaged in strictly religious terms, and the deposition and death of Richard II were laid at the door of hypocritical prelates who were out to silence the prophetical voice of Wycliffe. It was they who 'to quench the truth of his preaching, slew the right king, and set up three false kings a row: by which mischievous sedition they caused half England to be slain up, and brought the realm into such ruin and desolation that M. More could say, in his Utopia,

---

[23] So far as I know the only person who has directed attention to this significant variant of the Tudor myth is William Haller, *Foxe's Book of Martyrs and the Elect Nation* (London, 1963), pp. 167–9.

[24] William Tyndale, *Doctrinal Treatises and Introductions to Different Portions of the Holy Scriptures*, ed. Henry Walter (Parker Society, Cambridge, 1848), p. 458, from the Prologue to the Prophet Jonas (1531).

that as Englishmen were wont to eat sheep, even so their sheep now eat up them by whole parishes at once'.[25] According to Tyndale's interpretation, the murderous leaders of the church were unable during Richard II's reign to carry out their wish to eradicate the true preachers of God's word, but they found their way out of the impasse in what proved to be both a political and religious crisis. While the king was in Ireland 'our prelates had another secret mystery a brewing. They could not at their own lust slay the poor wretches which at that time were converted unto repentance and to the true faith, to put their trust in Christ's death and blood-shedding for the remission of their sins, by the preaching of John Wicliffe'. So no sooner was Richard out of the realm on his way to subdue the Irish (who had been deliberately incited to rebellion by the scheming popish prelates) than Archbishop Arundel was up against him, and on his return took him prisoner and did him to death most cruelly. 'O merciful Christ!' Tyndale apostrophized, 'What blood hath that coronation cost England!'[26] This was the event that had turned England into a veritable sheep-walk, diminished towns, villages and people by a third, and eaten up the nobility so that only a fraction remained in the land. For Tyndale it was the bloodshed of religious martyrs more than of warring political factions. 'And then, when the earl of Derby, which was king Harry the fourth, was crowned, the prelates took his sword, and his son's Harry the fifth after him (as all the king's swords since), and abused them, to shed Christian blood at their pleasure.'[27] It was the spirituality, the pope and his abettors, who were criminally responsible, who had slain in England 'many a thousand, and slew the true king and set up a false, unto the effusion of all the noble blood and murdering up of the commonalty'.[28]

Improbable though this interpretation of events was, it did not end with Tyndale. Protestant propagandists saw to it that Anglican monarchs as well as Anglican martyrs should have good fore-

[25] Tyndale, *Expositions and Notes*, pp. 224–5, from the Exposition of the first Epistle of St John (1531). These views of Tyndale's were published before the first edition of the *Anglica Historia*, though Polydore Vergil was writing this work more than a decade earlier (see n. 8 above).

[26] Ibid., p. 296, from The Practyse of Prelates ([Antwerp], 1530).

[27] Ibid., p. 297.

[28] William Tyndale, *An Answer to Sir Thomas More's Dialogue*, ed. Henry Walter (Parker Society, Cambridge, 1850), p. 166.

bears, and though Richard II did not stay the course in this role there was a time when he was apparently being tailored for it. John Bale did nothing so striking for Richard II as he did for King John, who was well set by Thomas Cromwell's playwright upon a Protestant stage which he continued to occupy until seventeenth-century constitutionalists found better boards for him. Bale did, though, place both Edward II and Richard II alongside the supposedly poisoned hero of 1215, together with burned Lollard leaders and 'an infynite nombre of poore symple soules' who were victims of the persecution of Antichrist.[29] And John Foxe, taking up Tyndale's story, even his very words, made full use of the fact that no heretics were burnt in England during the first twenty years of the Lollard movement. If Henry IV seemed set as the staunch defender of cruel Catholic orthodoxy and inaugurator of persecution, could not a reverse case be made out for his predecessor?

In the *Acts and Monuments* Foxe considerably expanded and embellished the interpretation of the civil wars and Richard II's place in them which Tyndale had propounded. Near the beginning of his book, in his section on the primitive church, Foxe reproduced— without acknowledgement—almost verbatim a passage from Tyndale's *Prophete Jonas* (1531) with its examples of 'the terrible plagues of God against the churlish and unthankful refusing or abusing the benefit of his truth'.

Not many years past, God, seeing idolatry, superstition, hypocrisy, and

---

[29] John Bale, *The Image Of bothe Churches* (London, [1548?]), pt. i, sigs. P viiv–viiir; John Bale, *Select Works*, ed. H. Christmas (Parker Society, Cambridge, 1849), p. 351. Bale evidently wanted Richard to be included with the emperors and kings, some of whom 'were accursed, some deposed, some slaine, some poysoned', who suffered at the hands of the 'slayne sort'. Cf. F. J. Levy, *Tudor Historical Thought* (San Marino, 1967), pp. 89–92 for Bale as 'The first of the English church historians' and his suggestion that Arundel had arranged the deposition of Richard II in order to proceed against the Lollards with *De heretico comburendo*. The way in which Bale developed historical ideas in Tyndale's works (especially the presentation of King John) has been pointed out by Rainer Pineas, 'William Tyndale's Influence on John Bale's Polemical Use of History', *Archiv für Reformationsgeschichte*, 53 (1962), pp. 79–96. It should be noted that Bale, who apparently never completed the third and fourth parts of his *Actes of English votaryes*, planned that the final book should cover the years I Henry IV to the present (1550 or 1551). This would have fitted with both Tyndale's and Foxe's view of Richard II's deposition as a dividing-line in ecclesiastical history. *The first two partes of the Actes or unchaste examples of the Englyshe Votaryes*, (London, 1560), pt. ii, sigs. T viiv–viiir.

wicked living, used in this realm, raised up that godly-learned man John Wickliff, to preach unto our fathers repentance; and to exhort them to amend their lives, to forsake their papistry and idolatry, their hypocrisy and superstition, and to walk in the fear of God. His exhortations were not regarded, he, with his sermons, was despised, his books, and he himself after his death, were burnt. What followed? They slew their right king, and set up three wrong kings on a row, under whom all the noble blood was slain up, and half the commons thereto. What in France, with their own sword in fighting among themselves for the crown; while the cities and towns were decayed, and the land brought half to wilderness, in respect of what it was before. O extreme plagues of God's vengeance![30]

Although he did not elaborate on the civil wars as such, Foxe's interpretation of their significance was essentially an expansion of that already outlined by Tyndale. They were to be seen, that is, in the context of religious developments, in which the reign of Richard II held a key position. The martyrologist can here be watched struggling with certainly intractable material to make of Richard II a youthful hero who had attempted to maintain the true cause of the gospel in the face of bloodthirsty popish prelates. The king was exonerated from any direct responsibility in the proceedings against Wycliffe and his Oxford followers. Foxe stressed that he being 'but young and under years of ripe judgement' was not to be held personally answerable for the action of 1382, and his association with the statute of that year was explained by his having been 'partly induced, or rather seduced, by importunate suit' of the archbishop of Canterbury.[31] Foxe was trying to claim Richard as the would-be protagonist of Wycliffe and the Lollards. He opened his account of the reign with the statement that the youthful king, following in the steps of his grandfather Edward III, was 'no great disfavourer of the way and doctrine of Wickliff', though unfortunately, owing to circumstances, he could not accomplish all

[30] John Foxe, *The Acts and Monuments*, ed. Josiah Pratt (London, 1877), i, p. 93; cf. Tyndale, *Doctrinal Treatises*, p. 458, quoted above p. 292. Professor Haller, op. cit., p. 167, comments on this passage in Foxe, but does not note its debt to Tyndale.

[31] Foxe, op. cit., iii, p. 37; cf. p. 42 'The young king also, moved by the unquiet importunity of the archbishop' wrote to Oxford ordering the suppression of Wycliffite teaching there. Foxe agreed with his contemporaries in this emphasis on Richard's youth, but he used it as an argument to forgive, rather than blame the king.

that he would have liked. 'Notwithstanding, something he did in that behalf; more perhaps than in the end he had thank for of the papists . . .'[32] To bolster up his case the martyrologist inserted a fictitious admonitory letter from Richard to William Courtenay, in which the king, marvelling at the archbishop's desire for blood and recalling various telling historical precedents (in order to contrast royal lenity with ecclesiastical cruelty), cited Courtenay and the heretic Nicholas Hereford to be tried as equals before the king at the bar of scripture.[33] Richard was to be envisaged as the aspiring advocate of the gospel.

Foxe was, however, unable to sustain his attempted defence of Richard to the end. His praises could not extend beyond the fact that the followers of the gospel in this reign, though they were proceeded against, did not have to suffer the extreme penalty. Thus no great harm came to William Swinderby until after Richard's deposition. 'I find none who yet were put to death on that account during the reign of this king Richard; whereby,' Foxe concluded, 'it is to be thought of this king, that although he cannot utterly be excused for molesting the godly and innocent preachers of that time . . . yet neither was he so cruel against them, as others that came after him.'[34] Richard himself was not of a fierce disposition towards the heretics, and the actions which he took against them were to be explained by his fear of popes and prelates who egged him on to these 'strait and hard' dealings against the Wycliffites. 'Thus king Richard, by the setting on of William Courtenay, archbishop of Canterbury and his fellows, taking part with the pope and Romish prelates, waxed somewhat strait and hard to the poor Christians of the contrary side of Wickliff . . . albeit, during all the life of the said king I find none expressly by name that suffered burning'.[35] And of course there was Richard's end to be accounted for. Foxe did not go into details of the deposition but this event had its place in the course of his ecclesiastical history. Richard, to the martyrologist, was a man of virtues as well as vices,

---

[32] ibid., p. 1.

[33] Ibid., pp. 48–9. The letter, an imagined answer to the archbishop's formal signification of excommunication of Nicholas Hereford, is headed by Foxe; 'To this letter of the archbishop, might not the king, gentle reader, thus answer again, and answer well'. Its fictitious content is also stressed in the marginal 'Prosopopoeia. What the king might have answered again'.

[34] Ibid., p. 202; cf. p. 130.   [35] Ibid., p. 197.

who had shown signs of promise but ultimately failed. He was at fault above all in that 'he, starting out of the steps of his progenitors, ceased to take part with them who took part with the gospel'. The church historian drew a moral which bore very little relation to the articles of deposition. The judgement against Richard was a judgement of God and it was caused by the way in which the king had first supported and then abandoned the defence of the gospel. Richard II was forsaken by God because he had forsaken the Word, and 'considering the whole life and trade of this prince', nothing 'seemeth to be of more weight to us, or more hurtful to him, than this forsaking of the Lord and his word'.[36]

John Foxe, therefore, looked back upon the accession of the Lancastrians as a lamentable turning-point which marked the inception of bloodshed and disorder. For him, as for Tyndale before him, the blood was the blood of martyrs and the disorder the disorder of spiritual malaise. The death of Richard II brought the end of an era, the beginning of a melancholy new chapter of ecclesiastical history. He was the last king in whose time faithful followers of the gospel were not called upon to suffer death for witnessing to the Word. 'This is to be noted', wrote Foxe (again echoing Tyndale), 'that since the time of king Richard II, there is no reign of any king to be assigned hitherto, wherein some good man or other hath not suffered the pains of fire, for the religion, and true testimony of Christ Jesus.'[37] It was the Lancastrians who were responsible for this changed state of affairs. Henry IV, who was 'altogether bent to hold with the pope's prelacy' was 'the first of all English kings that began the unmerciful burning of Christ's saints for standing against the pope'. While the reign of the first Lancastrian was 'full of trouble, of blood and misery', the ruin of the last was also to be associated with the burning of good gospellers.[38] The troubles of the house of Lancaster, like the fate of

[36] Ibid., p. 216; cf. Haller, op. cit., pp. 168–9 where it is pointed out that for Foxe 'the deciding reason for the judgment which overtook Richard II was his yielding to the dictation of the Pope in the suppression of Wyclif and the gospel'. Foxe excuses himself for not going further into the deposition on the grounds that it was to be found in other works and 'for that it is not greatly pertinent to my argument'.

[37] Foxe, op. cit., iii, p. 755, referred to by Haller, op. cit., p. 169; cf. above p. 293 for Tyndale's similar statement.

[38] Foxe, op. cit., iii, pp. 229, 753; Haller, loc. cit.

Richard II, were to be explained on the same lines—persecution of the faithful.

Accepting and adapting to his own story the now hardy myth of fifteenth-century strife, with all its attendant slaughter and sacrifice, Foxe looked back, as the originators of the myth had looked back, to the reign of Richard II as a fatal cross-roads in English history. The advent of the house of Lancaster meant the arrival of a deplorable new distemper in the English church, from which there was no alleviation right up to his own day. Richard II had not persecuted to the death; Henry IV had started to burn the witnesses of Christ and thereafter the fires of persecution were never extinguished.

This feature of the *Acts and Monuments* did not escape the eye of Foxe's searching opponent, Robert Parsons. He took pains to point out the weakness of this visible seam lying between the fourteenth and fifteenth centuries, peculiarly differentiating the periods before and after. For, argued the Jesuit, it being Foxe's aim 'to exhibit unto us a reall visible Church on his part, that is to say, a succession or rather representation of divers professors of his religion', with continuous descent from early times onwards, it was to be remarked that it was not until he reached the time of Wycliffe and his followers that he succeeded in making this ecclesiastical lineage visible, despite the variety of 'sectaryes in former ages' whom he acclaimed. 'It is to be noted, that scarse ever throughout this whole volume of acts, and monuments from Christ downward (for the space of 1400. yeares) doth Fox talke of any visible Church on his side, but only now, when he commeth to these *Wickliffians* and other like sectaryes.'[39] But once Wycliffe arrived on the scene Foxe markedly began to change his tune, making martyrs of heretics, 'canonizinge them for Saints that were any way punished or called in question' from Richard II's time onwards.[40]

The argument might be attacked, but the moral and the myth remained. They were irresistibly accommodating and Parsons picked up the well-worn threads and wove them into his own

[39] Robert Parsons [N.D. *pseud.*], *A Treatise of Three Conversions of England from Paganisme to Christian Religion* ([S. Omer], 1603–4), i, pp. 484–5, 502.

[40] Ibid., p. 508. Of course Foxe's case did change with changes in the law; it was the cruelties of the persecutors, as well as the stand of the persecuted, which constituted the break between the reigns of Richard II and Henry IV.

polemic. The historical rift which had been made out of Richard II's reign served many causes, and what had reinforced Foxe's Protestant case was now made to support the Catholic position of his opponent. For Parsons too the sufferings of the fifteenth century had religious explanations, though in his case, of course, they were to be looked for not in the persecution of the Wycliffites but the precise opposite—the failure to take heresy firmly and speedily to task. It is amusing to see how, in turning the Protestant argument upside down, the Jesuit himself echoed its resounding emphases.

But what followed of this? I meane of this negligence in resistinge this sect of *Wickliffe* at the beginning? Truly there followed or rather flowed such seas of calamities, as were never seene in our countrey before, nor scarse heard of in others.

For wheras *K. Edward* the 3. had byn a most glorious king, his end was pittiful: his heyre *K. Richard* after infinite sedition, contention, and bloudshed of the nobility, and others was deposed, and made away. The bloudy division of the house of *Lancaster* and *Yorke* came in, & endured for almost an hundred years, with the ruine not only of the royall line of *Lancaster*, by whom specially *Wickliffe* was favoured at the beginning ... but with the overthrow also of many other noble princes, and familyes, and most pernicious warres & garboyles continued, both at home and abroad with the losses of all our goodly *States, Provinces & Countreyes* in France. Unto all which, the division of harts, mynds and iudgments brought in by *Wickliffes* doctrine did help not a little, and the calamityes so continued untill the tyme of the most wise, Christian, and Cath. *K. Henry* the 7. Who as he extinguished the reliques of this wicked *Wickliffian* seed ... so did he happily also extinguish all temporall division, about the succession of our Imperiall crowne.[41]

Richard II's role in the wars of the roses myth was therefore as various as it was inescapable. His reign being, by general consent, the seed-bed for the ensuing century of troubles, was accorded the moral which most suited the moralist. Whereas for Robert Parsons the misfortunes of the house of Lancaster might be traced back to the protection which John of Gaunt had afforded Wycliffe, for Tyndale and Foxe they were to be accounted for in exactly the opposite way: by Lancastrian failure to follow Richard II's tolerant example. It can scarcely be surprising that the *Acts and Monuments'*

[41] Ibid., pp. 544–5.

essayed portrayal of Richard as a proto-Protestant monarch never gained much currency. It was much too conspicuously at variance with known facts. If Richard flinched, as his successor did not, from making it legal to burn heretics, he certainly brought the law to bear against them in other ways, and there is not the slightest evidence of his wishing to encourage them. Everything rather pointed the other way, as proceedings against the Lollards were stepped up from 1382 onwards, and indeed the king seems to have prided himself for his efforts in this direction—witness his epitaph in Westminster Abbey. 'He protected the church . . . He overwhelmed heretics, and laid low their friends.' Though John Weever, who transcribed it, found the epitaph as a whole 'strange, if not ridiculous' in the qualities it attributed to Richard, given his ending, it was not easy to attack the substance of these phrases.[42] Even so, Foxe's story was not without some later echoes—even additions. John Lewis, in his *History of the Life and Sufferings of the Reverend and Learned John Wicliffe*, having written of how his subject was 'very happy' in the royal favour of Edward III and patronized by his 'very zealous Protector' the duke of Lancaster, added that 'K. *Richard* II was, at first, no Enemy to Dr. *Wicliffe*. He made him his Chaplain, and grac'd him with his Royal Favour. However afterwards he suffered himself to be made use of by the Ruling Clergy to be the Instrument of wreaking their Spight on him and his Followers'.[43]

★   ★   ★

In a variety of ways the Tudors' periodization influenced their assessment of Richard II. One particularly obvious result was the tendency to telescope events of the reign and to concentrate un-

[42] Royal Commission on Historical Monuments, *London*, i (London, 1924), p. 31; H. G. Richardson, 'Heresy and the Lay Power under Richard II', *E.H.R.*, li (1936), p. 23; John H. Harvey, 'The Wilton Diptych—A Re-examination', *Archaeologia*, xcviii (1961), p. 8, n. 6, p. 18; John Weever, *Ancient Funerall Monuments* (London, 1631), pp. 471–2. Weever, who found the epitaph too flattering to Richard (he quoted lines Fabian wrote 'to extenuate the force of such palpable grosse flattery') seems to have thought that the tomb and epitaph were the work of Henry V, when he moved Richard's body to Westminster. In fact the epitaph, together with the tomb, was presumably of Richard's own choosing in 1395–7 (a specially topical moment for the heresy question).

[43] (London, 1720), p. 198.

duly upon the critical happenings at its end, that were specially provocative of subsequent strife. This disposition began before and lasted long after Shakespeare, who was far from alone in focusing attention on the closing eighteen months of the reign, starting with the Hereford-Norfolk quarrel and ending with the display of Richard's corpse in March 1400.[44] The same, or similar perspectives were adopted by historians. John Hayward's history of the first year of Henry IV's reign devoted two-thirds of its space to the reign of Richard II but had little to say of the years before 1387.[45] To take the affairs of 1387-8 as a significant starting-point was natural for those, such as Hayward, who were concerned to trace the rising star of the future Henry IV, or who looked back, as did others, to the encounter at Radcot Bridge as the first battle of the wars of the roses. 'By reason of the contention of York and Lancaster were foughten sixtiene or seventiene pitched fieldes, in lesse then an hundreth yeares. That is, from the eleventh or twelfth yeare of K. Richard the second his reigne (when this controversie first began to bud up) unto the thirtienth yeare of K. Henrie the seventh.'[46] *Leicester's Commonwealth* (as this very outspoken book of 1584 later came to be called) regarded the activities of the Lords Appellant as the true beginning of England's prolonged troubles. Samuel Daniel likewise, spelling out the 'fatall causes of this civile Warre', returned to Richard II and the events of 1387-8.

> In this mans Raigne, began this fatal strife
> (The bloudie argument whereof we treate)

44 The action of the play runs from 29 April 1398 (when the king appointed the day for the Norfolk-Hereford combat) to March 1400 (when Richard's body was displayed in London). Shakespeare's starting-point was the same as Edward Hall's, though opinions differ as to the extent of this debt. *King Richard II*, ed. Ure, pp. xxxi, xlix–l; Tillyard, op. cit., pp. 40–9, 237 ff.

45 J. Hayward, *The First Part of the life and raigne of King Henrie the IIII. Extending to the end of the first yeare of his raigne* (London, 1599). On p. 12 Hayward reaches the year 1387, and of the total of 149 pages, 99 concern Richard II. Cf. *King Richard II*, ed. Ure, pp. lviii–lxii for the extensive literature on Hayward's book and the troubles he got into over its publication.

46 *The Copie of a leter, wryten by a master of arte of Cambrige, to his friend in London* ([Antwerp?], 1584), pp. 121–2. Cf. Hayward, op. cit., pp. 23–4 on the significance of the battle joined at Radcot Bridge at which though 'scarse ten ounces of bloud was lost on both sides', yet 'this was the firste acte whereby reputation did rise to the side, and the greatnes began, whereunto the Earle [of Derby] afterwards attained'—thanks to his magnanimity on this occasion.

That dearely cost so many a Prince his life;
And spoyld the weake, and even consum'd the great.[47]

The same posthumous prejudice continued in seventeenth-
century histories. John Trussell published in 1636 a history of England which was designed to fill the gap between Daniel's prose
history, which ended with Edward III, and Bacon's *Henry VII*. Of
his opening forty-nine pages devoted to Richard II only the first
twenty, however, are spent on the years 1377–96. The main concentration was upon 1397–9, when the catastrophic weakness of a
king 'so blinded and bewitched with continuall custome of flat-
teries' became fully apparent.[48] As long as Richard's life and reign
were overshadowed by Lancastrian-Yorkist struggles it was a dis-
tortion of balance which was with difficulty avoided. The imminent clash of the contending factions meant that the end was
already present in the beginning. 'It is not my purpose to write all
the acts of this king, a great part whereof I passe over; I will onely
treat of such things as caused his ruine', Biondi explained candidly
at the outset of his history, to make clear that he had no intention
of writing the entire story of Richard II. 'I take my rise from the
unfortunate reigne of *Richard* the second, who comming to the
Crowne at eleven yeares of age, doth prove the miserable condition of such States as are governed by an infant King.'[49] Richard,
like Oedipus, enters the stage to set in motion the unfolding of
foreknown disaster.[50]

But whatsoever mov'd him; this is sure,
Hereby he wrought his ruine in the end;
And was a fatall cause, that did procure
The swift approaching mischiefes that attend[51]

---

[47] Samuel Daniel, *The Civil Wars*, ed. Laurence Michel (New Haven, 1958), pp. 71, 77.

[48] John Trussel, *A Continuation of the Collection of the History of England* (London, 1636), p. 22.

[49] Biondi, op. cit., Introduction, sig. C 2v; p. 3.

[50] This parallel was pointed to in the sixteenth century by Sir Thomas Smith, with his allusion (above p. 283) to Eteocles and Polynices, warring sons of Oedipus and Jocasta.

[51] Daniel, op. cit., p. 82; M. M. Reese, *The Cease of Majesty; A Study of Shakespeare's History Plays* (London, 1961), pp. 227–9. In a similar vein of heralded disaster John Taylor opened his sonnet to Richard II, 'A Sunshine Morne, precedes a showry day, A Calme at Sea ofttimes foreruns a storme': Taylor, op. cit., sig. B 6r.

—and the foreknowledge was a historical commonplace before Daniel and Shakespeare.

It suited 'wars of the roses' portrayers of Richard to single out some incidents of the reign at the expense of others. The appointment of the parliamentary committee of 1398 had been highlighted among the doings of Richard's later years long before it received the attention of constitutional historians. It was pointed to as a signal of the unbridled abuse of power at the reign's most critical period; of all the thirty-three articles of deposition it seemed the most egregious example of royal perversion. It revealed the extremes to which the king was prepared to go in putting personal desires and sycophantic friends before public interests. 'And finaly', wrote Robert Parsons,

in the last parlament that ever he held, which was in the 21 yeare of his reigne, commonly called *the evel parlament*, he would needs have al authority absolute graunted to certaine favorits of his, which Thomas Walsingham saith, were not above 6. or 7. to determine of all matters with al ful authority, as if they only had bin the whole realme, which was nothing in deede but to take al authority to him selfe only.[52]

What cut across parliamentary rights on one hand seemed on the other to be a supreme illustration of Richard's lifelong propensity to rule through the favours of his friends. By the 1640s the example of the Shrewsbury commission had gained heightened interest in the context of the proceedings of the Long Parliament. William Prynne, who examined the precedent of Richard II's deposition in more than one context, in January 1649 utilized the 1398 committee as an instructive reprimand for that 'Unparliamentary Junto', the Rump. For, he argued, ingeniously—perhaps rather too ingeniously—turning Richard's precedent upside down, the reduced parliament of 1649 was just as unlawful in its form and quite as derogatory to the privileges and power of parliament as the committee of 1398, which had been prominent among the reasons for the king's deposition. The Rump, in fact, with its

---

[52] Parsons, *Conference*, pt. ii, pp. 65–6. Richard Grafton, in words which were still being echoed in the seventeenth century, said the commission was 'in derogation of the state of the house, and to the great disadvantage of the king, and perillous example in time to come'; *A chronicle at large* (London, 1569), p. 394. For modern historians' attention to the question see R. H. Jones, *The Royal Policy of Richard II: Absolutism in the Later Middle Ages* (Oxford, 1968), pp. 118–20.

designs of deposing Charles I, was guilty of one of the very usurpations of power for which Richard II had been deposed.[53]

Modern historians find the first important moment of Richard II's reign in the Peasants' Revolt, when the young king asserted himself to face the rebels at Smithfield.[54] This famous incident was recounted in full by Froissart and was therefore readily available to sixteenth-century readers in the various editions of his chronicles. Later on there was also the full account of the rising which was printed by Stow, drawn from various sources.[55] This glimpse of Richard as the royal saviour of the hour, worthy successor to his martial father and grandfather, had its Elizabethan stage version in *The Life and Death of Jack Straw*. The Richard of this play is the pattern of a youthful king whose justice, clemency and regality are the true counterpoise to the rebellious upsetters of the civil order. He shows himself in the height of crisis just as a monarch should show himself. And the earl of Salisbury observes to the queen mother,

> For though your sonne my Lord the King be young,
> Yet he will see so well unto him selfe,
> That he will make the prowdest Rebell know,
> What tis to moove or to displease a King,

[53] William Prynne, *A Breife [sic] Memento To the Present Unparliamentary Iunto Touching their present Intentions and Proceedings to Depose and Execute, Charles Steward, their lawfull King* (London, 1648), p. 9; (the pamphlet is dated 'From the Kings Head in the Strand Jan. 1. 1648'); cf. pp. 12–14 where Prynne denies that the depositions of Edward II or Richard II were precedents since they were not Protestant monarchs, 'And those Proceedings were only by Popish parliaments in time, of ignorance'. Unfortunately Prynne's position was not consistent (though he himself could claim the great alteration of circumstances), and he had earlier turned this argument from religion and the example of Richard II in the opposite direction, citing the Shrewsbury committee and Richard's 'judicial' dethronement in answer to 'the clamourous tongues of all ill Counsellours, Courtiers, Royalists, Malignants, Papists, and Cavaliers', to show that 'Popish Parliaments, Peeres, and Prelates', Lords and Commons, had previously exercised much greater powers and jurisdiction over kings than the contemporary parliament or any parliament in modern times. William Prynne, *The Soveraigne Power of Parliaments and Kingdomes* (London, 1643), pt. i, pp. 7–8, 28–30, 33, 78ff.; W. M. Lamont, *Marginal Prynne 1600–1669* (London and Toronto, 1963), p. 89.

[54] See, for instance the comments of Anthony Steel, *Richard II* (Cambridge, 1962), pp. 76–82, 123–4; Jones, op. cit., pp. 18–20, 22, 125–6; G. Mathew, *The Court of Richard II* (London, 1968), pp. 15–16, 18; M. McKisack, *The Fourteenth Century* (Oxford, 1959), pp. 411–14, 423, 425–6; V. H. Galbraith, 'A New Life of Richard II', *History*, xxvi (1942), p. 230; Harvey, art. cit., p. 17.

[55] The first English edition of Froissart's chronicles was published in 1523. Stow's long and detailed account of the rising in *The Annales* (1592) gave full recognition to the king's courage and initiative.

And though his looks bewray such lenitie,
Yet at advantage hee can use extremitie.[56]

But the view of Richard's maturity which was common in the sixteenth century was not related to this image of his early promise. Writers who were more concerned with fitting the reign into their general historical scheme than with welding together discrepant facets of the king's character, were inclined to omit or diminish the dramatic action of 1381. Smithfield was an occasion which displayed Richard's qualities probably at their best, and perpetuators of the wars of the roses mythology accordingly played it down. Daniel omitted the rising altogether. Polydore Vergil had already set the stage by describing the dangerous encounter at Smithfield with no reference to Richard's bravery, while William Warner attributed the laurels of that day not to the king who 'begun that civell warre', but to the mayor of London, William Walworth, 'because his courage chiefly gave an ende to that uprore'.[57] Later on neither Biondi, who launched his account of the reign straight into royal favouritism and Richard's impatience with the limitations of the law, nor the author of *England's Happiness in a Lineal Succession*, for all the fullness of his version of events, had any time for the daring deeds of 1381.[58] Obviously there were writers who made good such omissions, but it is surely noteworthy that the wars of the roses focus had this effect of blurring so outstanding an illustration of Richard's personality.

The most remarkable myth to be perpetuated about Richard II existed already during his own lifetime, thanks to his critics and political opponents, and was incorporated into the Tudor picture

[56] *The Life and Death of Jack Straw 1594*, ed. K. Muir and F. P. Wilson (Malone Society Reprints, 1957), sig. B 3v. This play was entered in the Stationers' Register on 23 October 1593 and printed at the turn of this year. Apparently nothing is known about its date of composition or authorship. For the picture it presents of Richard see David Bevington, *Tudor Drama and Politics* (Boston, 1968), pp. 236–8.

[57] Vergil, op. cit., (1546), p. 404; William Warner, *The First and Second parts of Albions England* (London, 1589), ii, p. 125.

[58] Others who—for their own prejudiced reasons—made little of the king's independent role at Mile End and Smithfield were John Trussell, op. cit., pp. 4–7, and Sir Robert Howard who, in his *Historical Observations Upon the Reigns of Edward I. II. III. And Richard II* (London, 1689), though he included a summary of the revolt, gave no stress to Richard's brave role and (p. 95) showed the city of London coming to his rescue. Cf. the same author's *The Life and Reign of King Richard the Second* (London, 1681), p. 22, where the king's exceptional courage is emphasized.

since it perfectly fitted that distorted landscape. This was the myth of the king's youth. Succeeding to the throne at the age of ten and dying in his thirty-fourth year, Richard seemed cut out to be the pattern of a feckless royal minor who demonstrated to the full the extreme insecurity of kingdoms ruled by infant kings. He was seen to exemplify these dangers not only during those early years when he was still technically a minor, but right up to the very end of the reign.

The effects of the minority were a feature of political argument during Richard's lifetime, as well as being insistently stressed thereafter. Richard II's minority was by no means the longest of medieval English sovereigns, but it was exceptional in that its political usage was unduly protracted. The king was over twenty-two when in that well-known scene of 3 May 1389 he declared that having passed the age at which ordinary subjects reached their majority, he intended to be full master of his own house. The circumstances were certainly peculiar. No doubt part of the peculiarity must be attributed to the king's own taste for theatrical scene-setting. Yet there are signs enough that contemporary politicians were making moral capital out of the situation, just as later writers were to do so. In January 1380 when Richard was thirteen, a year younger than Edward III had been at his accession, the commons (petitioning against government expenditure and for a reduction of the continual council) took the opportunity to suggest that the king 'being now of a good discretion and fine stature' and almost of the age at which his grandfather was crowned, might make do, as Edward had done, with only the five great officers.[59] It was clearly an argument of convenience, but those who chose to regard the king as politically immature continued to find his youth a useful platform for years to come. For as long as Richard could be treated as a minor he could be considered neither the only nor the best judge of his own and his country's interests; individuals whom he favoured unduly could be attacked for having abused the king's tender years and the innocence of the royal person. This approach, exploited to the full by the Appellants in 1388, has a conspicuous air of special pleading, given Richard's age.[60] Yet

[59] *R.P.*, iii, p. 73. The petition was made 'aiant regard, que notre Seigneur le Roi si est ore de bone discretion & de bele stature; aiant regard de son age . . .'

[60] Ibid., pp. 230, 241; McKisack, op. cit., p. 456.

eleven years after, at the end of the reign, it was still possible to make play with the same political fiction. The text chosen by Archbishop Arundel for his oration in support of Henry IV's claim to the throne on 30 September 1399 was from I Samuel ix: 'vir . . . dominabitur populo'—'Behold the man . . . this same shall reign over my people'. It was a theme which he artfully embroidered with reference to other texts, including I Corinthians xiii ('When I was a child, I spake as a child') to lay every possible emphasis on the advantages of having a *man*, not a child, as ruler. And England could now rejoice, for the perils of childish speech and behaviour were past, since a man not a boy was to govern.[61] The message cannot have been lost upon those of Richard's subjects who had so long been harping upon the errors of his youth. But it is an astonishing performance when one remembers that Henry, far from being Richard's senior was actually three months younger.

'Woe to thee, O land, when thy king is a child.' Richard had appeared in literature as a model for this proverbial lesson long before Polydore Vergil. The poet John Gower (who, unlike Henry of Lancaster, was old enough to have been Richard's father) criticized his monarch for damaging childish behaviour, and did not scruple to exaggerate the youthfulness of the king's favourites, or to rebuke the 26-year-old king as an 'undisciplined boy'.[62] Sixteenth-century writers, reading the reign backwards, as it were, from 1399, constantly harped upon this topic. Richard became the prototype of the wayward boy king, whose years of juvenility were prolonged by his circle of miscreant young friends. His image became frozen with the features of disastrously misspent youth.

Richard was firmly set into this scheme of things in the *Mirror for Magistrates* (1559), whose exemplary tragedies were largely chosen from periods of royal minority. It was intended to be 'a memorial of suche Princes, as since the tyme of King Richard the

[61] *R.P.*, iii, p. 423. Elaborating on the dangers of childish weakness and love of flattery, Arundel stressed the evils from which the realm was freed.

[62] In his revisions of Book vi of the *Vox Clamantis*, made about 1393, Gower changed 'puer immunis culpe' to 'rex, puer indoctus', *The Complete Works of John Gower*, ed. G. C. Macaulay, iv (Oxford, 1902), pp. 246, 399; *The Major Latin Works of John Gower*, trans. Eric. W. Stockton (Seattle, 1962), pp. 13, 21, 232–3, 445.

secunde, have been unfortunate in the Realme of England'.
Richard's own 'vicious story' was no exception.

> I am a Kyng that ruled all by lust,
> That forced not of vertue, ryght, or lawe,
> But alway put false Flatterers most in trust,
> Ensuing such as could my vices clawe:
> By faythful counsayle passing not a strawe.
> What pleasure pryckt, that thought I to be iust.[63]

And the fate of Robert Tresilian was an example of how the king
had turned everything topsy-turvy 'by synister advyse', ignoring
the limits of the law and 'not raygning but raging by youthfull
insolence'.[64] The implicit assumption was that Richard's misdeeds,
even those of his adult years, were in intention and effect the
actions of an errant minor. This interpretation, which gained
ground with the development of his allotted role in Tudor history, was clearly formulated by Polydore Vergil.

Is there anything more shameful than that one who ought to rule
should through his own idleness and ignorance by compelled to obey
others like a child under age—not of eight or ten years, but of twenty,
thirty or more—and be ruled instead of ruling? Such a king was Richard
II . . . a youth not of the worst disposition to begin with, inasmuch as he
was not everywhere of such deficiency of understanding, or weakness
of character, or poverty of judgement, that he could not take, receive,
and retain good advice, but profligate counsellors finally took control
of him.[65]

This concept of perennial political immaturity was the burden of
numerous other accounts, and it is remarkable how in literature, as
in his own lifetime, the fiction of Richard's youth was preserved
to the end of his days.

In Samuel Daniel's *Civil Wars* Richard, the 'unbridled King'

---

[63] *The Mirror for Magistrates*, ed. Lily B. Campbell (Cambridge, 1938), pp. 5–10,
70–1, 112–13.

[64] Ibid., pp. 78–9.

[65] Vergil, op. cit., (1546), p. 439; Hay, op. cit., p. 141 (where this passage is
quoted); Tillyard, op. cit., p. 33. Vergil stresses Richard's youthful failings
throughout his account of the reign; for instance pp. 400, 407 (quoting Ecclesiastes,
x. 16 'Vae tibi, terra, cujus rex puer est'), 418 (Richard's failure to revenge the
Scots in 1388), 425 (Edmund of York on the king's adolescent errors, 1399), 427–8
(Richard's confession of the offences of youth at his abdication).

who had been spoiled by youthful counsel, private gain and partial hate, was still the 'wanton young effeminate' at the time of Hereford's banishment near the end of the reign, as he was 'th' indiscreete young King' at its beginning. When finally challenged by Bolingbroke he excuses himself on the grounds of his youth and the argument that he is now moving towards a 'calmer state'.[66] John Hayward, like Edward Hall, put into Richard's mouth a speech of resignation in which, while admitting his faults, he offered the plea of youthful misjudgement. The unfortunate Richard who was deposed in Hall's account was a young king 'in whom if there were any offence it ought more to be imputed to the frailtee of his wanton youth then to the malice of his heart or cankerdnesse of his stomacke'. Richard is presented pleading to his deposers in the Tower that he was 'partely led by the frailtie of young waveryng and wanton youth', and had intended to correct his offences 'especially in my old age', the accustomed time for such improvements, in which he like other young men might, given riper years, have mended his ways and turned the proverbial ragged colt into a good horse.[67] The convention that Richard's defects were attributes of his youth became so well established that there was nothing unusual about attributing his undoing to his childishness.

> But, if this *King* had not so *childish* bin
> When *Mowbray* peacht th' *Usurper* of Treason,
> He might have bin secure from al his *Kin*:
> But blinded *Iudgment* is the *hire* of *Sinne*.[68]

John Davies of Hereford's summary assessment of 'Disastrous Richard' was based upon premises which left some marks on Shakespeare's play. Clearly the dramatist was not alone in glossing over the exact contemporaneity of Richard and his supplanter. 'Cousin, I am too young to be your father, Though you are old enough to be my heir'. Richard's words to Bolingbroke may be deftly ambiguous, but earlier remarks of the royal uncles leave no

[66] Daniel, op. cit., pp. 79, 85, 88.
[67] Edward Hall, *The Union of the two noble and illustrate famelies of Lancastre & Yorke* (London, 1548), ff, vir–v, viiiv–ixr; Hayward, op. cit., pp. 86–8. Cf. n. 69 below. Vergil (op. cit., 1546, pp. 427–8) had given Richard such a speech.
[68] *The Complete Works of John Davies of Hereford*, ed. Alexander B. Grosart (Privately Printed, 1878), i, p. 55 (from *Microcosmos*, 1603).

doubt that in their eyes, at least, the king was an 'unstaid youth'.

> The king is come, deal mildly with his youth,
> For young hot colts being rein'd do rage the more.[69]

This civil war type-casting of Richard II was reinforced, as was that of Richard III, by reference to the king's appearance. Just as the later Richard's unnatural cruelties were mirrored in his bodily deformity, so the earlier Richard's effeminate weakness was associated with his exceptional beauty. Richard II was generally acknowledged to have been of outstanding personal appearance, but this was itself regarded as a sign and cause of his deficiencies. He was the lover of minions instead of those feats of martial prowess appropriate to his estate; the very attractiveness of his features accentuated the unmanliness which determined his destiny. 'He was the goodliest personage of all the Kings that had been since the conquest; tall of stature, of streight and strong limbes, faire and amiable of countenance; and such a one as might well be the Son of a most beautifull mother', reported Richard Baker in 1643, embroidering some inherited facts.[70] But the other side of this desirable exterior had long been indicated, to the king's notorious disadvantage.

In beauty, bounty and liberality, he farre passed all his Progenitors; but was overmuch given to rest and quietnesse, little regarding matters of Armes: and being young, was most ruled by young Counsell, regarding little the Counsell of the sage and wise men of the Realm. Which thing, turned this Land to great trouble, & himselfe to extreme misery.

Ralph Brooke's brief biography of Richard II in his *Catalogue and Succession of the Kings, Princes, Dukes, Marquesses, Earles, and Viscounts of this Realme of England, since the Norman Conquest, to this present yeare 1619*, echoed the words of Grafton and Stow, fifty and

---

[69] *King Richard II*, ed. Ure, pp. 47, 54–5, 116; II. i. 2, 69–70; III. iii. 204–5; see p. 55 for a comment on Hall's use of the proverb 'Of a ragged [shaggy, untamed] colt comes a good horse'. Shakespeare's 'rein'd do rage' sounds like an echo of the *Mirror for Magistrates* 'not raygning but raging', quoted above.

[70] Richard Baker, *A Chronicle of the Kings of England From the Time of the Romans Goverment* [*sic*] *unto the Raigne of our Soveraigne Lord King Charles* (London, 1643), pt. ii, p. 27; cf. *England's Happiness*, p. 2; 'He was of such a comly and graceful Personage, that he is said to be the most Beautiful Prince, that ever wore the *English* Diadem.' The comment was so often repeated it became virtually a set piece.

thirty years earlier.[71] Richard's outstanding beauty had come, like so much else, to be appropriated to his defects: his youthful weakness, his preferment of young advisers, his dislike of military affairs. 'O flatt'ring glass, Like to my followers in prosperity, Thou dost beguile me.' Richard's face was part of his fate, and its failure to reflect his ultimate abasement might be taken as the final measure of the lifelong damages of his looks. Shakespeare's scene in which Richard calls for the looking-glass to read the book 'where all my sins are writ',[72] was not history, but was closely linked with Tudor versions of it.

As time went on pictorial evidence could be called upon to lend weight to statements about Richard's appearance. Thomas Hearne, who in 1729 published his edition of the chronicle attributed to a monk of Evesham, with its full description of the king, pointed out in his introduction that it was scarcely surprising—given his loveliness—that men as well as women loved Richard so much, and that his manners were affected by excessive praises. In support of the king's beauty Hearne referred to the Wilton Diptych and the engraving of it by Wenceslas Hollar, inscribed to Charles I, in 1639.[73] The diptych could certainly have reinforced stereotyped Tudor views of Richard's youth and beauty. Whether or not Richard had purposely had himself depicted in the guise of his past adolescence, as seems quite possible, the king of the painting is a youth, not a man.[74] But, since the whereabouts of the diptych is

[71] Ralph Brooke, *A Catalogue and Succession of the Kings, Princes, Dukes, Marquesses, Earles, and Viscounts* (London, 1619), sig. **. 6v. Cf. Grafton, op. cit., p. 324, and Stow, *Annales*, p. 434, for almost identical passages. Cf. also the modern view of Rowse, op. cit., p. 9; 'Richard's appearance was attractive, though of a distinctly feminine cast'.

[72] *King Richard II*, ed. Ure, pp. lxxxi–lxxxiii, 140–1; IV. i. 275, 279–81.

[73] *Historia Vitae et Regni Ricardi II. Angliae Regis*, ed. Thomas Hearne (Oxford, 1729), pp. vii–viii, xxvii–xxviii, 169, 402. On the Hollar engraving see Gustav Parthey, *Wenzel Hollar, Beschreibendes Verzeichniss seiner Kupferstiche* (Berlin, 1853), pp. 42–3, no. 229; George Vertue, *A Description of the Works of the Ingenious Delineator and Engraver Wenceslaus Hollar* (London, 1759), pp. 4, 139–40. According to Vertue the painting was in the Arundel collection when Hollar engraved it. The 1639 catalogue of Charles I's pictures, which contains the first certain mention of the diptych, records it as having come to the king from one Lady Jenings. Harvey, art. cit., pp. 2–4; Mrs Reginald Lane Poole, 'Notes on the History in the Seventeenth Century of the Portraits of Richard II', *The Antiquaries Journal*, xi (1931), pp. 145, 147–8.

[74] Richard's youthful appearance in the diptych has, of course, often been commented on. Harvey, art. cit., p. 13 n. 1 argues that there has been a tendency to

unknown during the sixteenth century—an obscurity which might well be connected with its iconography—nothing can be said of the influence of this image on the Tudors. The case is different with another well-known portrayal of Richard, the large panel in Westminster Abbey. If Tudor Protestant monarchs might have found unwelcome, or distasteful, a view of a royal ancestor 'kneeling in his golden robes to our Lady',[75] they could have no objection to this thoroughly regal portrait of Richard, crowned and enthroned with orb and sceptre. The Westminster painting, unlike the Wilton Diptych, was already known before the end of the sixteenth century and various copies of it existed by the time that Queen Elizabeth asked Lambarde whether he knew of 'any true picture, or lively representation' of Richard's countenance and person.[76] By this time interest in royal portraiture was becoming widespread, and though for many individuals imagined features might serve as truth, there were authentic sources for delineating Richard II and they were reproduced. The face of the king which appeared in Thomas Tymme's *Booke, Containing the true portraiture of the countenances and attires of the kings of England* in 1597, though

exaggerate this, and cites evidence which suggests that Richard did not start to grow a beard until 1394–5. Even if, however, he did preserve exceptionally youthful looks until he was 27–28, it is hard to accept this as his represented age in the painting, though the late 1390s seem on other grounds most probable for its composition. For suggestions that the king's appearance was deliberately idealized in a youthful form see Francis Wormald, 'The Wilton Diptych', *Journal of the Warburg and Courtauld Institutes*, xvii (1954), p. 202; Galbraith, art. cit., p. 238. Cf. also Mathew, op. cit., p. 41, for a miniature portrait of Richard 'still shown as a beardless adolescent although he was already twenty-four', and pp. 11, 114, 200 for several suggestive remarks about the adolescent qualities which were 'so prized in the international court culture'.

[75] As he was described in Charles I's catalogue; Mrs R. L. Poole, art. cit., p. 147. The objections of Protestants and the actions of iconoclasts against pictures, statues and idolatrous worship of the Virgin might well have provided reasons for concealing the diptych, especially at certain moments, in the sixteenth century.

[76] *Progresses and Public Processions of Queen Elizabeth*, p. 553; David Piper, 'The 1590 Lumley Inventory: Hilliard, Segar, and the Earl of Essex—I', *The Burlington Magazine*, xcix (1957), 227; Lionel Cust, 'The Lumley Inventories', *The Walpole Society*, vi (1917–18), pp. 21–2. Roy Strong, *Tudor and Jacobean Portraits* (London, 1969), i, p. 261, states that the painting which Elizabeth describes Lord Lumley as having discovered 'fastened on the backside of a door of a base room', and presented to her to 'put it in order with the Ancestors and Successors', was the Westminster painting—which Lumley certainly had copied. For an alternative suggestion that the gift was of the smaller of the two paintings of Richard II listed in the 1590 Lumley inventory, see Mrs R. L. Poole, art. cit., pp. 156–9.

not very lifelike was clearly based upon some known representation—witness the king's bushy hair and characteristic forked beard.[77] And in 1618 appeared Henry Holland's *Baziliωlogia: A Booke of Kings Beeing The true and lively Effigies of all our English Kings from the Conquest untill this present*, with an engraving by Reynold Elstrack which was reproduced in various seventeenth-century works. This 'true pourtraicture of Richard the 2' was certainly derived, though perhaps not directly, from the Westminster panel, a painting which in the original at least, helped to sustain belief in Richard's beauty: 'that beautifull picture . . . which witnesseth how goodly a creature he was in outward lineaments', wrote Weever.[78] (Plate 4*a*, *b*.)

Finally, appropriate in a consideration of this wars of the roses image, something may be said of Richard's own views of war. Military success being an established part of the conventional image of the successful monarch, Richard II was naturally blamed for his attitude to war, for being 'overmuch geven to rest and quietnesse' and for having 'loved litle dedes of armes and Martiall Prowes'.[79] Not surprisingly, a king who had not only failed to campaign in France but had also made peace and a marital alliance was contrasted unfavourably with those 'two thunderbolts of warre', Edward III and the Black Prince.[80] This aspect of Richard's shortcomings was linked with his domestic failure, for the hundred years' war with France and the hundred years' discord in England were seen to have an intrinsic see-saw relationship. Losses abroad meant faction at home; native turmoils were successfully buried

[77] T[homas] T[ymme], *A Booke, containing the true portraiture of the countenances and attires of the kings of England, from William Conqueror, unto our Soveraigne Lady Queene Elizabeth now raigning* (London, 1597), sig. D 1r. This reproduction may be compared, for instance, with the king's features in the Dymoke manuscript (see the frontispiece of Steel, op. cit.). An imaginary portrayal of Richard appears in the series of royal heads in the Pictorial Commonplace Book of Thomas Trevelyan (1608), Folger Shakespeare Library Ms. V.b.232, fo.111v (I owe this reference to the kindness of Professor John Hale). For Elizabethan portrait collections, and the fashion for sets of kings, both painted and, later, engraved, see Ellis Waterhouse, *Painting in Britain 1530 to 1790* (Harmondsworth, 1953), pp. 2–3, 25–6; Roy Strong, *The English Icon: Elizabethan and Jacobean Portraiture* (London, 1969), pp. 44–8.

[78] Weever, op. cit., p. 473; cf. Baker, op. cit., p. 28; Mrs R. L. Poole, art. cit., pp. 153, 156. I have not seen Henry Holland's *Baziliωlogia*; Levis, op. cit. reproduces the Richard II engraving on p. 60 and states (p. 2) that the portraits were originally issued as separate sheets. Cf. also Strong, *Tudor and Jacobean Portraits*, p. 261.

[79] Grafton, op. cit., p. 324.   [80] Daniel, op. cit., p. 76.

in foreign conquest. The idea of a century of duplicated inter-acting warfare existed long before Biondi made it a central feature of his narrative. His work, with its extensive interweaving of the troubles and fighting in France and England makes abundantly clear how foreign affairs reflected back upon English events, to make of the fifteenth century a double tale of war, resounding with the alternating clash of alien and domestic battles.[81]

Time, however, effected a change even upon such traditional judgements. Ultimately it became possible to see that England's continental ambitions were misguided, and Richard II, instead of being blamed for his pacifist endeavours, could be exonerated—or even praised for an innovatory policy.[82] Some steps in this direc-tion are discernable even in the sixteenth century, taken by those who judged the right and wrong of these affairs in the light of their own domestic history. Once England, thanks to Mary Tudor, had lost her last foothold in France, and Elizabeth's subjects had had time to come to terms with this, the long-acclaimed achieve-ments of Crécy and Agincourt could be regarded in a fresh light. '*Edward* the third was most victorious, . . . Yet were his *Con-quests* hurtfull to his *State*, For they the same did but debilitate.'[83] The idea that continental possessions were an unwarrantable drain upon domestic resources, and had themselves contributed to the disasters of Richard II's reign, had been propounded well before John Davies published these lines in the year of James I's accession. It seemed to Sir Thomas Smith, two years after Elizabeth came to

[81] Shakespeare was following Holinshed in using the argument at the beginning of *Henry V*, that the king's foreign exploits were intended to divert attacks on the church at home. Biondi saw Henry V as appeasing his kingdom and burying all its civil contentions through his foreign campaigning, while the renewal of the civil wars under Henry VI was chiefly to be ascribed to losses in France. That this inter-action of foreign and domestic faction was indicated does not mean, of course, that there was any clear idea of the 'Hundred Years' War' with France, which is another term with its own history. For its development see Kenneth Fowler, *The age of Plantagenet and Valois: The struggle for supremacy 1328–1498* (New York, 1967), pp. 13–14.

[82] For praise of Richard's negotiations as 'the most statesmanlike effort to mend the breach between England and France since the days of St Louis', see J. J. N. Palmer, 'The Anglo-French Peace Negotiations, 1390–1396', *T.R.H.S.*, 5th Series, xvi (1966), p. 94.

[83] *Complete Works of John Davies*, i, p. 55. Such views are in noteworthy con-trast with the more common untempered glorification of Edward III and Henry V, and show that the Elizabethan attitude was not as monolithic as has sometimes been supposed; cf. Jones, op. cit., p. 118.

the throne, that just as Henry VIII had undone his father's good work and beggared England by gaining Boulogne, so the misfortunes of Richard II and Henry VI were associated with the French acquisitions of their predecessors. 'But because we shall better and more near at hand see the advantage of heaping realms together, King Edward III and the Black Prince got almost all France. His next successor therefore must needs have his power marvellously increased. So it may appear. For though he were confessed the right heir, yet a nobleman of this realm of England bereaved him of both France and England.'[84] It was quite misleading to suppose that the territorial conquests of either Edward III or Henry V had been assets for their successors; in both cases the inheritors of such supposedly marvellous gains had been dispossessed of the crown. Although the argument (which was admittedly tendentious) was not pursued, Richard II was implicitly acquitted for his reluctance to prosecute the French war; his continental inheritance was seen to excuse, rather than magnify his failure. English lands in France were more expensive than glorious, more enervating than elevating. So, it seemed to Thomas Craig, Edward III's triumphs were misguided. Granted, this king had grievously plagued France, but he had 'exhausted *England* of its Men and Money for carrying on the War', and eventually Normandy, Maine, Aquitaine and Anjou were all lost. 'And all those toils and attempts with the vast Expences of Blood and Treasure which were made to the irreparable loss of *England*, vanish'd into Smoak. It had been much to the advantage of that Nation if it had never attempted any such thing.'[85] It was a chink, albeit a small one, in the armour of Richard II's traditional critics.

★   ★   ★

Historical interpretation had to change considerably before Richard II could be judged in modern times in a dispassionate light. Above all it was necessary for interpreters of the later middle ages to shift

[84] Strype, *Life of the Learned Sir Thomas Smith*, p. 256, cf. p. 249. This comes from the dialogue quoted above, and Smith was admittedly pleading a special case, though the speaker Axenius, or Homefriend, who argued so cogently against continental possessions (as among the disadvantages of a royal marriage with a foreigner) was clearly voicing the opinions of the author.

[85] Craig, op. cit., p. 180.

their attention away from the idea of the wars of the roses and the genesis of long and damaging conflict. The profound success of the Tudor thesis endowed the century preceding 1485 with the outstanding features of warfare, bloodshed and aristocratic mortality—all of which gained exaggerated scale in the retrospective view. The whole period, 1377–1485, was cast into a single distorting mould, a mould of disharmony and disturbance. Its lessons were equally instructive whether they were applied to church or state, directed at sovereigns or subjects. And the king whose reign lay at the beginning, whose times were regarded as the breeding-ground and starting-point for this century of disaster, was as damagingly affected as the royal tyrant whose death brought it to a close.

The portrait of Richard II which emerged was largely a literary construction. His was the stock image of the weak, over-influenced minor, who failed in counsel, in religion, and in war, whose inability to rise above the deficiencies of his youth was the overriding reason for his downfall. Those occasions when he was to be seen at his best, facing the rebels of 1381 or (as it is now possible to think) refusing to be pressed into conventional hostilities against France, tended to be discounted or isolated from the general view. Some parts of his character were emphasized at the expense of others. Reading even a part of the great amount of historical narration which, one way or another, was printed about Richard II during the first century or so of English renaissance historiography, one can see how little was lacking from the matter that we use today, but how much of it failed to be integrated. Divergent aspects of the king's character remained separated like individual icons, or different pictures by different artists of one sitter in varying moods.

Four hundred years should be enough time to gain some historical perspective, and the Tudors' history now seems very unlike our own. Yet for all our doubts about the wisdom of preferring 1485 before various other dates as terminal or seminal for England's well-being, or of ascribing unparalleled benefits to Henry VII, or to Henry VIII and his children, we have failed to free ourselves from some of the most outstanding platitudes of sixteenth-century historians. We quarrel with their terms—but we go on using them. We remark their exaggerations—but we continue to repeat them in attenuated forms. Dissatisfied with the whole concept of the wars of the roses we have half-consciously whittled it down to suit our own knowledge of events. As a result Richard II, fortunate in being prised away sooner than Richard III from this stultifying scheme, can now be recognized as a monarch who, more than an effete and misled minor, held bold and imaginative ideas of kingship, was courageous in his approach to the French war, and showed himself a discriminating patron of the arts.

Richard II held an exceptional and peculiarly unfortunate place in Tudor historical thought. It was important that he had been deposed—but he was not unique in that. More important was the fact that he had been deposed and replaced in a way which initiated England's most damaging century, the century of the wars of the roses. And by the time that Tudor rule and successful myth-making had themselves filled out a century, it was hard to take a fresh look back at that reconstructed past. Queen Elizabeth, in any case, was in no position to do so when, ageing, childless, and struggling to prevent the tarnishing of her own long-polished image, she conversed with Lambarde at Greenwich on 4 August 1601. The one thing which cannot have been absent from her mind that day, as she 'fell upon' the reign of Richard II with those accusing, self-accusatory words—'I am Richard II. know ye not that?'—was the notion of civil disturbance. Was not Richard II indelibly associated with a great, never to be forgotten lesson—the inauguration of the wars of the roses? For that offence he well deserved to find a last quietus.

Index

319